The Afrikaners

Also by Graham Leach

South Africa – No Easy Path To Peace

The Afrikaners

Their Last Great Trek

Graham Leach

MACMILLAN
LONDON

First published 1989 by
MACMILLAN LONDON LIMITED
4 Little Essex Street London WC2R 3LF
and Basingstoke

Associated companies in Auckland, Delhi, Dublin, Gaborone, Hamburg, Harare, Hong Kong, Johannesburg, Kuala Lumpur, Lagos, Manzini, Melbourne, Mexico City, Nairobi, New York, Singapore and Tokyo

A CIP catalogue record for this book is available from the British Library.

ISBN 0-333-48720-6

Typeset by Wyvern Typesetting Ltd, Bristol

Printed and bound in Great Britain by
WBC Ltd, Bristol and Maesteg

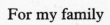

For my family

CONTENTS

ACKNOWLEDGEMENTS

Above all, I owe a debt of gratitude to the people of South Africa, especially those who amid the turmoil in their country gave me many hours of their time. The result was numerous rewarding insights which were invaluable to my work as BBC Southern Africa Correspondent and in the research for *The Afrikaners*.

Specific thanks are due to several people who read the entire manuscript and offered encouragement and advice. Tertius Myburgh, editor of the *Sunday Times* of Johannesburg, gave the book a clean bill of health from an Afrikaner standpoint. Michael Spicer, prominent commentator on South African and regional affairs, gave me the benefit of his extensive knowledge of recent events. Peter Hawthorne, correspondent in South Africa for *Time* magazine, offered advice based on his long experience as a foreign correspondent in Africa. Patricia Thomson devoted considerable time and editorial assistance which helped with the manuscript. The legal advice afforded by Peter Reynolds was essential.

Several people read individual chapters and suggested improvements. F. A. van Jaarsveld, Extraordinary Professor of History at the University of Pretoria, passed on much of his research and read the chapters on the Great Trek and Afrikaner history. Dr Franz Auerbach briefed me on Christian-National education and checked my draft notes. The chapters on the National Party and the Conservative Party were read by Willem de Klerk, former editor of *Rapport*, and Tim du Plessis, political correspondent of *Beeld*. Anne-Marie Mischke, political editor of *Rapport*, shared her wide knowledge of current political developments. South African journalist Hennie Serfontein read the chapter on the church, while W. A. de Klerk and Braam Viljoen enlightened me on the history of the Dutch Reformed Church. South African journalist Max du Preez read the chapter on the Dakar mission; he also allowed me access to his detailed transcripts of the *in camera* discussions between the liberal Afrikaners and the African National Congress. David Welsh, Professor of Political Science at Cape Town University and Guy Butler, Honorary Research Fellow at Rhodes University, offered guidance on the chapter about the Afrikaners and English-speakers.

Notwithstanding the advice and help from those already mentioned, I take full responsibility for the views expressed in the book.

I wish to thank all those who agreed to be interviewed for *The Afrikaners*. Unless otherwise sourced, their views contained here were all expressed in interviews with me. I do not have the space to mention all fifty or so whom I interviewed. But I would like to express special gratitude to Cape Town University professor Hermann Giliomee; the editor of the *Sowetan* Aggrey

Acknowledgements

Klaaste; Stellenbosch University professor Sampie Terreblanche; Minister of Information Dr Stoffel van der Merwe and his departmental colleagues; former liberal opposition leader Dr Frederik Van Zyl Slabbert, and Independent MP Denis Worrall for many informative sessions during my time in South Africa.

I am indebted to Helmut Bertelsmann for his translation work; to Deon du Plessis who kindly translated the poem *Amakeia*; and to the staff of the Carnegie Library in Standerton for information about the town. I am grateful for the right to reprint part of 'Seven Steps of Stone' from *District Six – The Musical* by David Kramer and Taliep Petersen.

I spent almost six years in South Africa from 1983 to 1989, a time when journalistic camaraderie was important. I owe a good deal to several distinguished colleagues who became good friends during those exhilarating times. As well as Peter Hawthorne, I wish to mention Michael Hornsby of *The Times* of London who was assigned to South Africa shortly before my arrival; also Alan Cowell of the *New York Times* who was expelled from South Africa, as was Peter Sharp of Independent Television News of London – all warm and generous colleagues. It was a privilege to work with BBC television correspondent James Robbins who arrived in 1987 to join the formidable TV team of François Marais, Andrew Thompson, Richard Atkinson and Glenda Spiro. A special word of appreciation goes to the journalists of Reuters News Agency in Johannesburg led by Tom Thomson, David Rogers and Jonathan Sharp, and to Michael Sposito and his staff at Visnews. I should like to pay tribute to the following members of the South African press corps who unfailingly gave their help and guidance as I reported events in their country: David Braun, André Brink, Anthony Johnson, Thami Mazwai, Brian Pottinger, Jon Qwelane, Tony Stirling, Barry Streek, Peter Sullivan, Lester Venter and the staff of the South African Press Association under Ed Linnington as well as Tim du Plessis and Anne-Marie Mischke who are mentioned above.

I should like to thank my BBC colleagues in London for their constant support during my assignment, in particular former Assistant Director General Alan Protheroe; Director, News and Current Affairs, Ron Neil; Managing Editor Ray Gowdridge; Radio Foreign Editor Christopher Wyld and his counterpart in television John Mahoney; producer Adam Raphael; and all those on the foreign desk, in the newsroom and the news traffic unit.

Finally, I extend my deepest appreciation to my wife Ruth as well as to Thomas, William and Oliver – always the first casualties when the story breaks.

PREFACE

Above all, it was a time of choices. At Africa's tip, the fault lines shifted and people faced decisions that determined lives: whose side are you on, black or white? Do you want war or peace? Are you for the past with its twin demons of supremacy and indignity, or for a future of which one can only say: it will be different?

– Alan Cowell, Johannesburg Bureau Chief of the *New York Times* 1983–7, in *Why Are They Weeping?*

One evening in 1987 I watched again *The White Tribe of Africa*, the outstanding television series produced in the late 1970s by David Harrison of the British Broadcasting Corporation. Seeing the programmes again, I was struck by how little some things had changed in South Africa while in other ways they had moved – either forwards or backwards. There now appeared to be far more serious division within Afrikanerdom. This provided the germ of the idea for *The Afrikaners*.

A further spur to write the book came in the wake of the black township revolt in the mid-1980s. During the violence many people in South Africa and abroad became convinced that the black protests marked the beginning of the end of the country's Afrikaner-led government and that white minority rule was about to crumble after forty years of apartheid. P. W. Botha, they believed, was destined to be toppled like the Shah of Iran and President Marcos of the Philippines. Yet the Afrikaners survived. They suppressed the black uprising and quickly regained the initiative. The Afrikaners had demonstrated that they were not about to surrender power.

Considering all these factors, it seemed an opportune moment to write a book about the current state of the Afrikaner people, more fluid and uncertain now than at any time in their recent history. Clearly what happens within Afrikanerdom will be a major factor in the country's future.

Opportune also because the year 1988 was one of politically charged anniversaries for the Afrikaners, commemorative events which starkly exposed both their divisions and their tortured relations with their fellow countrymen of other races. (Throughout the book the term 'coloured' to describe mixed-race people is used as convenient shorthand only, without bestowing legitimacy upon its use as a racial label by the authorities.) It was 500 years since the Portuguese explorer Bartholomeu Dias rounded the Cape and became the first European to set foot on the southern tip of Africa. Three hundred years had passed since the French

Preface

Huguenots, refugees from strife-torn Europe, made their first landfall at the Cape, boosting the white settler population started by earlier Dutch émigrés. The ruling National Party marked forty years in power, while President Botha celebrated ten years as South Africa's controversial leader.

Most important of all, though, was the hundred and fiftieth anniversary of the Great Trek, the heroic focal point in the history of the Afrikaners, South Africa's white rulers. Dragging their ox-wagons over mountains and through swirling rivers, Afrikaner fugitives from British rule at the Cape made their way north into the vast interior to establish their own republics, suffering death and hardship on the way. Some were massacred by the Zulu chief Dingane when they tried to negotiate land rights. In revenge the Boers killed 3000 Zulus at the Battle of Blood River. The commemoration of the Great Trek was therefore a tumultuous event for the Afrikaner people, albeit a divided people approaching the end of the century with its problems unresolved.

President Botha's cautious moves towards sharing power with black people led to Afrikanerdom's most fundamental schism to date. Hardliners seeking a return to rigid apartheid have defected to the right. Liberal Afrikaners have gone off in search of an accommodation with black nationalists. This leaves the National Party trying to hold a shifting centre ground. Every level of Afrikaner society has been shaken by the rifts.

Who are today's Afrikaners – these stubborn and often infuriating people who defy the world? One hundred and fifty years after they mounted their journey in search of liberation, the Afrikaners are still in many ways a homeless people – still seeking that elusive final and secure resting-place which prompted their exodus from Europe and their flight from British rule.

If the 1838 trek was their first great journey, their second came in the early part of this century when hundreds of thousands suffering abject poverty on the farms converged on the cities in search of work, coming face to face for the first time with millions of urban blacks who had made the same journey and whose political aspirations they have so far thwarted. The Afrikaners' search for an accommodation with their black compatriots is now their last great trek.

Graham Leach
Johannesburg
March 1989

CHAPTER ONE

The Battle of the Beards

After an overnight cloudburst, 16 December 1988 dawned bright and sunny over Pretoria. Thousands converged on a hillside on the outskirts of the city, in the shadow of a huge granite monolith – the Voortrekker Monument – which dominates the surrounding countryside.

The monument honours the *voortrekkers*, pioneers who 150 years before mounted a *Groot Trek* (Great Trek) across the vast interior of South Africa. They were *Afrikaners*, descendants of refugees and others from a strife-torn Europe who had arrived in the country in waves from the middle of the seventeenth century, having fled their homes in the Netherlands, France and Germany. The first immigrants had landed at the Cape, the southern tip of Africa, but slowly they had spread their wings, founding remote rural settlements further afield. Soon they had become known as *Boere* (Boers or farmers), but their new-found independence had been cut short with the arrival of the British at the end of the eighteenth century. The Boers mounted their trek north to escape their British rulers and to regain their freedom.

Every year Afrikaners gather at the monument on 16 December to celebrate *Geloftedag*, the Day of the Vow, commemorating the Boers' victory over the Zulus, South Africa's largest black tribe, at the Battle of Blood River in 1838, the historic centrepiece of the Great Trek. The commemoration in 1988 was therefore a double anniversary.

The overnight rainfall had turned the hillside into a mudbath. Afrikaners dressed in *voortrekker* costumes (women in bonnets and long dresses like those of the North American pioneers, men in German-style waistcoats and breeches) squelched through the mud which caked their shoes and splattered their frocks and trousers. Replicas of the Boers' ox-wagons became bogged down in the mud and their drivers had to haul them out, just as their ancestors must have done. The teams of oxen slithered around.

The wagons had made their way north from Cape Town in a re-enactment of the Boers' original journey. The gathering at the monument – a deeply religious occasion – was the climax of the anniversary. At noon exactly – as happens on every 16 December – a ray of sunlight pierced a hole in the dome-shaped roof and alighted on the cenotaph which honours the *voortrekkers*. The stone bears the words *Ons vir jou, Suid Afrika* (We for thee, South Africa). The shaft of sunlight represents the civilisation which the Afrikaners believe they brought to the country. A marble frieze depicts their arduous journey and graphically recounts the chain of

1

events leading to the historic encounter at Blood River, a story which is now part of Afrikaner folklore.

Having escaped the British in 1836 and made their way inland, the Boers decided to head for Natal on the eastern seaboard. That meant trekking over the Drakensberg mountains. When they reached the summit the Boers caught their first glimpse of the rolling hills of Natal, described as 'the most beautiful land I have ever seen in Africa' by the *voortrekker* leader Piet Retief.

British merchants and missionaries had earlier settled around the trading post of Port Natal. Some of them, including a legendary adventurer Henry Fynn, had earned a fragile place at the royal court of the Zulus in Natal. From the mighty Zulu chief Shaka, who had built a Zulu empire, Fynn had won land concessions in Natal. These were honoured by Dingane, who assassinated Shaka. But Fynn and his fellow Britons sensed the Zulus' anxieties about European settlement, uncertainties fuelled by fearsome *sangomas* (witchdoctors) who advised the Zulu chiefs that the arrival of the white man would mean the seizure of their lands.

When Retief and an advance party arrived at Port Natal the British traders told them the territory was open to them and that a courtesy call on Dingane would seal the arrangement. Retief visited Dingane on 27 November 1837 and reported back to his followers that all that was required of them was a demonstration of friendship by recovering livestock stolen by rival tribesmen. After doing this, Retief returned to the Zulu *kraal* (encampment) with seventy-nine of his men, and Dingane signed a document ceding to the Boers all the land between the Tugela and Mzimbuvu rivers. At celebrations two days later the Zulus reneged on the deal. As Dingane shouted the fateful words 'Kill the wizards!', the Boer party was massacred. Dingane's men then descended on the Boer families camped a few miles away and slaughtered forty-one men, fifty-six women and 185 children. In desperation the remaining Boers quickly tried to regroup, embarking on a punitive expedition against the Zulus which ended in further disaster.

Their spirits were revived with the arrival of Andries Pretorius, a large, charismatic figure who gave his name to South Africa's administrative capital. Hearing of the slaughter of Retief and his party, Pretorius, a successful farmer in the eastern Cape, immediately set off with sixty followers for the beleagured Boer *laager* (a camp formed by circled ox-wagons). He arrived on 22 November 1838 and within a week had reorganised the Boer ranks. The revenge at Ncome River (later renamed Blood River) quickly followed. Before the battle the Boers took a vow in which, according to the history books, they pledged to build a church and commemorate the day 'like a Sunday', if God would grant them victory. When the Zulu *impis* (war parties) attacked, 3000 warriors were killed. After the battle the Boers set off for the Zulu headquarters at Mgungundhlovo which they found five days later desolate and in flames with no sign of the *impis*. The trekkers buried the mutilated remains of Retief and his followers. In a leather shoulder-bag they found the worthless treaty which Retief had signed. Decades of subsequent mistrust between black and white South Africans can be traced directly to Dingane's treachery and the Boer reprisal at Blood River.

The Battle of the Beards

Yet at the 1988 commemoration President P. W. Botha, while honouring the early Boers, recalled that people of colour had joined the Great Trek and fought with the Afrikaners. They were mostly coloured (mixed racial descent) servants of the whites; more than 200 servants were killed by Dingane's war party. As Botha put it: 'On 16 December 1838, white, brown and black stood together in the laager at Blood River. . . . It was not only a trek of white Afrikaners.'

Why did Botha refer to blacks and coloureds on an anniversary which has traditionally been an annual reassertion of Afrikaner nationalism? The answer lay thirty miles away at a farm called *Donkerhoek* (Dark Glen) east of Johannesburg, where right-wing Afrikaners, committed to white supremacy over blacks, were holding a rival commemoration. They too had staged their own re-enactment, following a different route to that of the 'official' trek. Whereas Botha, realising whites had to change, was striving for a political accommodation with blacks, the right wing wanted to return to unequivocal racial segregation.

The hundred and fiftieth anniversary of the Greak Trek was therefore a vivid demonstration of the disunity which had descended upon the Afrikaner camp. The *volk* (people) were bitterly divided as they remembered their past and looked forward to an uncertain future.

Preparations for the anniversary had started a year or more before. Some prominent figures from the rival political camps began sporting beards and wearing *voortrekker* costumes – both powerful symbols of the trek – in a battle to win a kind of *voortrekker* look-alike competition and to stage the most convincing re-enactment of the original journey. Four months before the Day of the Vow a replica of a *voortrekker* wagon had trundled along the Grand Parade in Cape Town pulled by two oxen, its occupants wearing pioneer costumes, to begin the 1000-mile 'official' trek to Pretoria. A journalist from the *Sunday Star* newspaper caught up with it a few days out of Cape Town and reported that all was not going smoothly.

> When they arrived in Paarl [a town in the western Cape] in pouring Cape winter rains, the meagre beasts of burden with rather spindly legs were too tired and wet to pull the wagon to Wellington. That's a mere nine kilometres away, a distance the nineteenth century trekkers would laugh at. So the modern oxen, a far cry from the veld-fed [bush-fed] Afrikaner ancestors, were unceremoniously sardine-packed into a diesel truck and driven to Wellington in all mod cons. Another heavy-duty truck gently pulled the clattering ox-wagon, altogether a curious sight to crowds lining the sleek freeway, watching the party surrounded by police and traffic cars with flashing blue roof-lights.

The noisiest reaction came from motorists sounding their horns as they found themselves in long tail-backs behind the slow-moving oxen.

A public relations company employed by the trek organisers tried to ginger up the mood. As the wagon approached Port Elizabeth a handout to the news media

3

spoke of 'this trek ahead bringing about a whole new revival with regard to South African culture and morale. Dancing, lovely food, merrymaking and tomfoolery are the order of the day. . . . Novelties of the Port Elizabeth celebrations are a procession of children and holidaymakers – some on bicycles, others on roller skates – along the beach front, the lighting of a bronze torch more than one and a half metres high, a giant fun run and a gala dinner for more than six hundred guests.' As the trek progressed President P. W. Botha, hoping to rekindle the fire of Afrikaner nationalism, delivered a dewy-eyed appeal for Afrikaner unity to his arch-rival Andries Treurnicht, head of the right-wing Conservative Party, formed when hardline Nationalists defected from Botha when he started reforming apartheid. Treurnicht politely rejected the appeal, as his own commemorative trek rolled off a month later to the cheers of 300 people gathered on the Cape Town foreshore. The organisers denied that they were attempting to politicise the commemorations: the Afrikaner nation, they argued, simply wanted to retain its own identity.

In the same way that the original trek leaders could not agree on a single route and went their separate ways, so the 1988 Afrikaner leaders were divided in their celebration of the original exodus from the Cape. The right wing planned no less than thirteen trek routes across the country in a motorised column, with ox-wagons making their appearance from time to time. They thereby hoped to cover more ground and to visit more *dorps* (towns) where they would bring home the right-wing message. They had also secured the Blood River battle site for a special ceremony. By contrast, the National Party trek would follow one route only, though it would culminate at the Afrikaners' shrine at the Voortrekker Monument.

In small towns and hamlets across the country it was the time for showing the flag, for coming clean on whether one's loyalties lay with the Nationalists or with the right wing. Bank managers, schoolteachers, government officials were all caught up in the dispute over which political flag to raise as communities found themselves divided. It was all in marked contrast to the festivities of fifty years previously, celebrating the centenary of the original trek, which had witnessed a euphoric coming-together of the *volk* as a wave of nationalism swept the country. The 1938 trek had seen ox-wagons setting out on fourteen routes from Cape Town, winding their way across the vast interior on their way to Pretoria, visiting more than 500 remote towns and villages where special trek committees had been formed to make arrangements to receive the wagons and to organise the festivities. Five of the wagons were named after leaders of the trek, a sixth after Sarel Cilliers, who led the religious service when the Blood River vow was taken, the others after women and children who had died or suffered hardship while undertaking the long journey. One wagon, the 'Dirkie Uys', was named after a fourteen-year-old boy who was killed by the Zulus in a brave attempt to reach and defend the body of his dead father.

As the 1938 trek had progressed across the country, excitement reached fever pitch. At each town the trek passed through, streets were renamed after the *voortrekker* leaders. The closer they came to Pretoria, the more intense became the

4

call for Afrikaner unity and for a South African republic free from British suzerainty. A 'torch commando' carried a 'flame of white civilisation' across the country. By 16 December an estimated 100,000 people (nearly one tenth of the Afrikaner population) had gathered at the site designated for the Voortrekker Monument to be constructed in honour of the pioneers. The government of the day favoured white unity embracing Afrikaners and English-speaking South Africans. But that did not satisfy those gathered in Pretoria and the thousands of other Afrikaners who had participated in the commemoration. The elders of the growing National Party saw their opening and exploited the country's mood brilliantly, championing the cause of Afrikaner unity. Thus was the path prepared for the Nationalists' assumption of power ten years later followed by the gradual implementation of the policy of *apartheid* (apart-ness).

Five decades after those earlier trek celebrations the National Party, or at least sections of it, had finally woken up to the fact that apartheid had been the gravest mistake ever inflicted upon the country. But the party leaders were woefully short of ideas as to what to put in its place. Moreover, there remained a substantial number of Afrikaners still clinging to the ideals of the 1938 trek, and they provided a susceptible constituency for the party which during the 1980s emerged as the voice of those Afrikaners resisting the Nationalists' deviation from hardline racial segregation. The Conservative Party was hoping to turn the 1988 celebrations to its own political advantage just as the Nationalists had done fifty years previously.

The prime mover behind the right-wing trek festival was Carel Boshoff, formerly Professor of Theology at the University of Pretoria, who when he retired headed the Afrikaner Volkswag (People's Guard), founded in 1984 in the wake of the right-wing split from the National Party. Boshoff was previously chairman of the shadowy Afrikaner Broederbond (Afrikaner League of Brothers) formed in 1918 to revive the Afrikaners following their defeat by the British in the Boer War (1899–1902) and the loss of their two independent Boer republics in the Transvaal and the Orange Free State. Boshoff resigned from the Broederbond when, along with the ruling National Party, it started exploring ways of 'sharing power' with blacks. The organisation had supported P. W. Botha's new 1983 constitution which granted a limited say in power for coloured and Indian people. For Boshoff even this cautious reform amounted to a betrayal of Afrikanerdom. The formation of the Afrikaner Volkswag was the response by disillusioned Broederbonders and other figures previously regarded as pillars of the Nationalist establishment. The Volkswag was launched at a big open-air rally in Pretoria attended by the widow of Hendrik Verwoerd (Boshoff himself is married to Verwoerd's daughter), the architect of 'grand apartheid' under which the races were to be separated at virtually every level of their political, economic and social existence, with millions of blacks being hived off into *bantustans*, or black homelands. In the view of the right wing, Verwoerd's name and his place of honour within Afrikanerdom had been defiled by Botha and his National Party. The Volkswag's trek celebrations, the result of five years' planning since the break with the Nationalists, were aimed at winning back Afrikaners to orthodox apartheid untainted by infectious notions of sharing power with people who were not white.

Some months before the celebrations I had visited Dr Boshoff at his sprawling home on the outskirts of Pretoria. The driveway and courtyard were crammed with the cars of Volkswag organisers from around the country who had gathered to plan the December festivities. Boshoff received me in his drawing room, which had been converted into a temporary store for Boer memorabilia to be sold during the trek celebrations. There were rows of dolls dressed in Boer costumes; wooden models of the ox-wagons in which the *voortrekkers* braved mountain tops and swirling rivers as they pressed on into the interior of southern Africa; rows of books on the history of the Great Trek and on the suffering of Afrikaners over the centuries; beer mugs, salt and pepper shakers, wine goblets, brooches and chamber pots – a host of artefacts, mementos and curios bearing the 'Great Trek 150' logo: all to be sold to help finance the right-wing extravaganza, said to be costing over £100,000. Boshoff unveiled what can only be described as an Afrikaner version of the Swiss army knife, except that it is much larger: a pouch eighteen inches long in which the Boers' traditional tools – an axe, saw and knife – are neatly fitted into individual compartments. Also in the drawing room was a computer on which Volkswag membership records are stored. The Volkswag may be remembering the primitive life of its Afrikaner forefathers 150 years previously but, when it comes to the battle for the hearts and minds of today's Afrikaners, there is no shortage of 'high-tech' at its disposal.

After my tour of Boshoff's Afrikaner souvenir shop we withdrew to his study, which was equally congested. His filing cabinets were overflowing with correspondence about arrangements for the festivities. Away from the frenetic planning, Boshoff takes a quiet moment to explain the meaning of it all. The purpose of the thirteen separate treks touring every part of South Africa is not to re-stage the original trek, he says, but rather to take the right-wing message into every town and city in the country. 'The message of 1838 was of a people trekking towards liberty and self-determination. We feel the Afrikaner, under Botha, is losing his freedom and will in the end lose his future and identity.' Boshoff's argument is that if the country starts on a path towards power-sharing with people of colour it has to go the whole route. 'Our survival lies in the Afrikaner having his own land, his own government and his own community. Under the National Party the land, the government and citizenship is being handed out to everybody.'

The Volkswag message to the Afrikaners of today is that they face the same dangers as the *voortrekkers* who left their homes a century and a half ago to liberate themselves from 'oppression'. The 1988 festival is therefore an historic moment for Afrikaners to reject the government's diluted policies by throwing in their lot with those seeking to uphold a white nation, with the blacks leading their own lives in separate black homelands. 'This is the new Great Trek facing the Afrikaner,' says Boshoff. 'Let's call it the final struggle for his own survival.'

*　　*　　*

The Battle of the Beards

The Volkswag's attempted hijacking of one of Afrikanerdom's most hallowed anniversaries had clearly been of deep annoyance to the government, particularly as the right wing had no qualms whatsoever about exploiting the symbolism of the Great Trek to depict the government as having sold out Afrikaner interests. Addressing the all-white House of Assembly in Cape Town the Minister of Education, Piet Clase, announced that the government had bestowed the right to organise the 'official' Great Trek festival upon an Afrikaner body, the Federasie van Afrikaanse Kultuurvereninge (the Federation of Afrikaans Cultural Organisations), an umbrella association for scores of Afrikaner cultural groups and a front organisation for the Broederbond. The minister said the government would make a financial contribution towards the FAK celebrations. He went on: 'It is therefore expected that schools will cooperate and participate fully in this festival.' A Conservative Party MP asked if pupils were compelled to attend, while the CP leader Andries Treurnicht said his party was 'astonished' over the government's financial support of the FAK and its refusal to back the Volkswag festival as well. The government was using taxpayers' money to 'subsidise one sectional festival in competition with another.'

At FAK headquarters in Johannesburg (lying close to the head office of the South African Broadcasting Corporation – another body closely linked to the Broederbond) the organisation's festival director Rudi Prinsloo disclaims any concern about divided Afrikanerdom organising rival treks. For Mr Prinsloo the actual celebration of the anniversary overrides any political divisions. 'It is more important to have the festival and have divisions, than to have nothing at all,' he insists.

As if to forestall the occasion turning into a trial of strength between the National and Conservative parties, with the attendant danger that the National-ists might come off second-best, the government appears to play down or at least to redefine the significance of the event. Since the beginning of Afrikaner defections to the right, the National Party has had to pitch its appeal to English-speakers as well, to make up the shortfall of white supporters. The occasion is still important but, unlike 1938 when the Afrikaner was desperately striving for his independent nation, the hundred-and-fiftieth anniversary finds him politically secure, though troubled about how to dispense freedom and political rights to his black fellow-countrymen.

Mr Prinsloo explains it like this:

'The Afrikaners were divided even when the Great Trek got underway back in 1838. They were always at odds with each other in the selection of their leaders and so on. They left the eastern Cape, crossed the Orange River and held a *volksvegadering* [people's gathering] at Thabu Nchu [in present-day Orange Free State] where they all had different views about the path ahead. The point was these divisions did not stop them. Despite the difficulties, they went on to form three Boer republics [in the Transvaal, Orange Free State and northern Natal] and then one united nation after the Act of Union in 1910.'

In other words the *voortrekkers* did not know what lay ahead, but they kept going despite differences between them. 'It is the same story today,' argues Mr Prinsloo. 'We have to keep developing the nation. We cannot go back along the road we have travelled [i.e. back to hardline apartheid]. The Afrikaner has too much courage for that. He is not a tortoise, he will always take up a challenge. Although we are not going to pack our things into a wagon, we are still going to make another trek, and this time it is a trek of changed attitudes.'

Like the original trek, Mr Prinsloo sees the modern Afrikaners' journey into a new way of thinking as very much a venture into the unknown:

> 'Just look at the map and follow the route of the trek leader Louis Trichardt. It winds all over the place. They were obviously divided over where to head next, but they kept going because they knew they had an objective, however uncertain. Their divisions were over the strategy in reaching their final objective. That's why the Afrikaners will keep going today, despite their divisions.'

I suggest to Mr Prinsloo that there might be a difference between 1838 and today in that the objective itself is the point of contention, not the strategy in getting there. Today's hardliners, far from seeking to go forwards, want to put the clock back. Mr Prinsloo has no comment on that, describing the question as 'political'.

Has the time not arrived, however, for the trek celebrations to be downgraded, along with the Day of the Vow? Government attempts to woo blacks into its power-sharing plans are not exactly helped by the celebration of Afrikaner victories reminding blacks of their vanquished status. For Mr Prinsloo the phasing out of the two anniversaries is unthinkable. 'You would not deprive other nations of their historic anniversaries. Why expect that of the Afrikaners?' He says the FAK has taken note of Zulu objections to the Blood River commemorations. In any case the anniversary should not be used for gloating over past victories. Rather, today's Afrikaners should view the occasion as an opportunity to make 'new commitments' which would take into account the cultural feelings of all the country's race groups.

That said, the Great Trek is still an important event in the history of Afrikanerdom which helped define the Afrikaner nation.

But the question has been raised: just how important? Is its significance based on historical fact or is the trek, along with the Battle of Blood River, a gross piece of mythology, deliberately inflated to serve the narrow interests of Afrikaner nationalism?

South Africa would bear little resemblance to its present form were it not for the Great Trek. The Boer War might never have taken place. There might not have been a National Party or the policy of apartheid. There are plenty of 'what ifs?'.

But the trek did take place and it compares in significance with the opening up of the western part of North America. Forsaking their homes in the Cape colony, the Boer men, women and children initiated a movement of population which in just over twelve years resulted in a redistribution of the white population as far north as the Limpopo River (the present border between South Africa and Zimbabwe) and later even further afield. This migration by whites matched the *mfecane* of the black population, the great dispersal of the southern African tribes who fled the horror and brutality of the Zulu empire under Shaka. These separate black and white diasporas meant that South Africa's history would come to be dominated by a racial conflict over the acquisition and partition of territory. In certain respects therefore, the policy of apartheid can be seen as a derivation of the scramble for land at the time of the Great Trek and later in the Boer republics; also of the less formal but nevertheless vigorously enforced segregation under British rule in the Cape.

The Battle of Blood River has been a mighty symbol nakedly exploited to further the political, philosophical and religious cause of the Afrikaner. Only in the past decade or so have Afrikaner historians made a start on the long and arduous academic exercise of debunking the myth and placing the events of that time in their proper historical context. Their findings reveal an altogether different picture to that of earlier researchers. The conclusion to be drawn from these fresh appraisals is that generations of Afrikaner schoolchildren may have had their heads filled with an entirely erroneous view of history, one which has perhaps been deliberately nurtured to further the aims of Afrikaner domination in general and, since 1948, of the ruling National Party.

Two Afrikaner professors, one at the University of South Africa and the other from the University of Pretoria, are responsible for much of the revisionist thinking about the Great Trek and in particular the Battle of Blood River, that moment in history which is enshrined in granite at the Voortrekker Monument and which is carved into the soul of nearly all Afrikaners from birth. Both are radical reinterpretations.

Professor Ben Liebenberg, in a paper entitled 'Myths surrounding Blood River and the Vow', argues that the significance of the battle was blown up out of all proportion by earlier Afrikaner historians. Liebenberg takes them to task for claiming that, were it not for the victory at Blood River, the Great Trek would have failed and the Afrikaner nation would not have been born. He writes:

> This view, that Blood River saved the Great Trek, overestimates the significance of the battle. At that stage, only a section of the voortrekkers were in Natal. The rest were in the present Transvaal and Orange Free State and they wanted to live there. Their survival was not threatened by the Zulus. If the Zulus had won at Blood River, the Great Trek would, at most, have failed in Natal and not in the Transvaal and Free State. It is therefore not correct to say that the victory at Blood River saved the Great Trek.

A second myth which Liebenberg seeks to explode is that Blood River marked the birth of the Afrikaner nation. He dismisses this line of reasoning by arguing that no nation could be born out of one single battle and that, in any case, at the time of the Great Trek the Afrikaner nation had already developed over a period of two centuries: the Boers' striving for independence would not have been extinguished by one defeat. He also challenges that aspect of the myth which is perhaps most pertinent to South Africa's current situation: that Blood River symbolised the victory of Christendom over paganism. Previous historians, seeing immense political advantage in the promotion of such views, had exploited this interpretation to the full. Liebenberg lists some of their arguments: Blood River was 'the beacon at which the Christian faith triumphed over heathendom'; 'those few Boers at Blood River were the bearers of the Christian faith and their settling in the interior would mean that Christendom would find firm footing here'; 'civilisation triumphed over barbarism and orderly society over anarchy and chaos'. The last argument was echoed by P. W. Botha in his controversial 'Rubicon' speech in August 1985 when he dismissed growing international calls for fundamental reform by declaring: 'Destroy white South Africa and our influence, and this country will drift into factional strife, chaos and poverty.' Professor Liebenberg uncouples Blood River from the victory of Christianity thus:

> . . . no voortrekker saw it in this light. The members of Andries Pretorius' commando were not interested in the conversion of the Zulus. They had only one goal in mind – and that was to revenge the suffering that Dingane had caused them. Andries Pretorius' commando was solely and purely a revenge campaign – and quite understandably so, in my opinion. Again, in the following campaign against Dingane, the so-called Cattle Commando of 1840, the conversion of the Zulus never occupied the minds of the voortrekkers. When, at last, they managed to break Dingane's power . . . they began to capture Zulu children on a large scale not to convert them to Christianity, but to make them work as labourers. The strongest argument against the statement, that Blood River serves as a symbol of Christendom's victory over paganism, is the fact that, in the following half-century, the voortrekkers did little to further the spreading of the gospel amongst the blacks. The governments of the voortrekker republics . . . were so frightened that missionaries would preach the equality of all men that they did not encourage missionary work amongst blacks.

Earlier historians had even elevated the 'victory of Christianity' at Blood River to the status of a 'miracle', something 'supernatural'. One wrote that 'Blood River is different from anything in the history of military science. . . . In its inexplicability, Blood River is a miracle . . . Blood River was not a case of merit, it was pure grace, guidance, and act of Providence.' Another had seen the battle thus: 'The physical facts of the military clash do nothing but affirm the miracle of the deliverance and the extraordinary result underlines, indeed, the intervention of God.'

Professor Liebenberg cites Afrikaner historian Dr D. J. Kotze who, writing in 1979, attributed the 'miracle' of Blood River to, among other things, the fact that the mist, which had hung over the battle site during the previous night, dispersed at daybreak, affording the Boers a better view of the Zulu warriors. Far from ascribing this to divine intervention, Liebenberg suggests a more temporal explanation: 'It is after all no supernatural phenomenon that mist clears in the course of the morning.' Liebenberg also disputes the interpretation that Blood River signalled a divine blessing upon Afrikaners, that God had assigned to the Afrikaner nation the task of keeping South Africa white. He recalls an address at the Blood River commemoration of 1938 at which the speaker had inferred the following from the battle: 'The victory here at Blood River shows us . . . that God wants a white civilisation here in South Africa. It is historically incorrect to state that South Africa belongs to the bantu [black] race . . . God gave South Africa to the Afrikaners – it is our country. Here a white civilisation must rule forever.' Professor Liebenberg, notwithstanding the wrath likely to explode in certain quarters of his own people, poured scorn upon such views:

> It is clear . . . that some people interpret the voortrekkers' victory at Blood River as proof that God wants a white civilisation in Africa; that God is against the equalisation of black people with white people; and that God is not in favour of the mixture of races. Therefore, God's intentions with South Africa are inferred from the myth of the miracle that is supposed to have taken place at Blood River. What these people do not understand is that they merely project their own subjective views onto God.

The myth exposed, one then tackles the question of how it has come to occupy such a daunting place in Afrikaner folklore. The Day of the Vow, the anniversary of Blood River, is now a religious holiday in South Africa which all race groups, even the conquered Zulus, are by implication expected to observe. Here one turns to the most recent research by another Pretoria academic, Professor F. A. van Jaarsveld. He maintains that the vow at Blood River, far from being a solemn and binding covenant, was romanticised to serve as a powerful symbol of Afrikaner survival, not during the trek itself, but only years later when the Afrikaner was at his lowest point, defeated and dejected and in urgent need of a history, a tradition and a heritage to cling to. It was only after the first Boer War against the British in 1880, when Afrikaner nationalism came to the fore, that Blood River – the deed itself and the Boer commandos who fought – became the stuff of Afrikaner legend. After the second Boer War of 1899–1902, when thousands of Afrikaners fled poverty in the countryside to compete alongside British and blacks in the cities, the glorified image of the *voortrekker* leaders evoked a nostalgia for what they conjured up as an heroic past, a time when the Afrikaner was forging his own destiny on land which he had made his own. The Boer War had resulted in disruption and discontinuity to the Afrikaner's way of life. He was desperately seeking to maintain his identity. Rewriting history to strengthen Afrikaner nationalism was one way of doing it.

Van Jaarsveld points out that for a quarter of a century after Blood River the Vow had to all intents and purposes been forgotten. Some families remembered the battle in private acts of remembrance but the leader of the Boer commando at the battle, Andries Pretorius, never commemorated the occasion. Still, tales of that day were retold by some *voortrekkers* who had fought and who had made their homes in the province of Natal where they lived to an old age. Their stories of the battle came to the attention of two Dutch parsons, Reverends P. D. M. Huet and F. Lion Cachet, who were preaching in Natal. The former was responsible for the first commemoration of Blood River when he held a thanksgiving service in the Dutch Reformed Church in Pietermaritzburg in 1864. Two years later the Reverend Cachet arranged the first public celebration at the battle site itself. But it was not only whites whom he addressed: Zulus turned up as well, intrigued by the occasion. Together, whites and blacks laid stones as a joint act of remembrance. In 1865 the *volksraad* (people's council) of the Transvaal agreed that 16 December should become a public holiday but it was never celebrated as such until 1879.

After their victory in the Boer War, the British agreed not to alter the status of the anniversary as a token of reconciliation towards the Afrikaners. In 1911, after the Act of Union bestowing dominion status on South Africa, 16 December became an official holiday for the whole of South Africa. From that date on, the day gradually became a platform for overtly racist political speeches by Afrikaner politicians.

In 1894 a submission had been made to the government of the Boer republic in the Transvaal that 16 December should be marked not just as a public holiday but as a religious day with a 'Sabbath clause' attached. This was to prevent its 'desecration' by foreigners who were then arriving in South Africa following the discovery of gold. The Transvaal leader President Kruger refused the request, arguing that a weekday could not be turned into a Sunday. In 1925 the Pretoria government rejected a similar request by the Afrikaner churches on the grounds that not all South Africans felt attached to the anniversary. In 1952, as the policy of apartheid was taking shape, the government passed a law which for the first time linked a Sabbath clause to 16 December in order to 'protect' the 'holy' day. Henceforth it was to become one of the 'religious' holidays of South Africa. 'Dingane's Day', as it had been known, was redesignated as the 'Day of the Vow'. The annual celebration has since taken on the character of a religious festival in which honouring the Great Trek serves as a symbolic and ritualistic reaffirmation of the victory over the blacks, and of the Boers' covenant with God.

Professor van Jaarsveld believes the opinion held by some, that Blood River caused Afrikanerdom to become a nation bound to God, is an historical misconception and a perversion of the biblical account of the Israelites' covenant with God. He refers to a letter published in the Afrikaans newspaper *Rapport* to show how fanatic some still are. The letter read:

> The vow included three things: namely, to build a temple, to keep the day as a Sabbath and that it should remain binding on later generations . . . the Afrikaner who rejects these is not an Afrikaner, even if he speaks Afrikaans, maintains its culture and has a white skin.

Van Jaarsveld has analysed the two most authentic contemporary documents relating to the vow: one drawn up on 9 December 1838 by Jan Bantjes, the secretary of the *voortrekkers'* commando at Blood River, and another by Andries Pretorius, the commander at the battle. He has compared these with the reminiscences of Sarel Cilliers, who presided at the taking of the vow, compiled in 1871 – thirty-three years after the event – when he was seventy years old and on his deathbed. Van Jaarsveld has come to the conclusion that Cilliers' memories reveal significant lapses. He forgot about the building of a church. His claim that 16 December was to be a celebration 'like a Sunday' is not substantiated from the more authentic reports of Bantjes or Pretorius.

According to Bantjes, only the building of a church was promised by those who took the vow, while the celebration of a Sabbath was not part of the pledge. Pretorius, on the other hand, says the religious celebration took precedence over the building of a church. Not surprisingly, perhaps, van Jaarsveld has concluded that, because of the uncertainty about what precisely was promised, there are not sufficient grounds for linking the Sabbath clause to the celebrations of 16 December. If the holiday could be marked between 1865 and 1952 without a Sabbath clause, he argues, why not scrap the clause? This would free 90 per cent of the population who do not feel bound by a traditional Afrikaner religious holiday.

During the late 1930s, prime ministers Jan Smuts and J. B. M. Hertzog tried to unite Afrikaners and English-speakers within a common South African national- ity and therefore had hoped that 'Dingane's Day' would be celebrated by all whites as an 'ordinary' public holiday with speeches and special sports events and the like. After 1948, however, the Nationalist government was not interested in 16 December as an occasion for the binding together or reconciliation of all South Africans: they saw it rather as a tribal Afrikaner 'holy' day. It deteriorated into an annual emotional jamboree for the narrow pursuit and promotion of Afrikaner nationalism. It meant nothing to the vast majority of the country's population.

According to Professor van Jaarsveld, Afrikaner nationalism was historically orientated and had a strong religious base. It arose from the alleged similarity between the Great Trek and the exodus of the Israelites from Egyptian bondage and their settlement in Canaan. The history of the *voortrekkers* was not only theologised but regarded with nostalgia. After the Boer War the defeated Afrikaners came to venerate and romanticise these agricultural pioneers. The myth and the legend afforded legitimacy to the twentieth-century Afrikaner nationalists.

Earlier Afrikaner historians had also taken liberties, according to Professor van Jaarsveld, over the question of who exactly was bound by the Blood River vow. One had written in 1971: 'It was . . . not merely a vow for a particular situation, and also not merely for a specific time or for only a section of the nation, but a vow that stretches into the future and involves the coming generations of the Afrikaner nation until the end of time.' Afrikaners challenged this version at their peril.

Professor van Jaarsveld is one who has dared to question the received wisdom. He asked the question: 'Does the presence of three Englishmen, sixty Zulus and an unknown number of coloureds among the voortrekkers in the Blood River encampment imply that all subsequent English, Zulu and coloured generations are bound to celebrate 16 December? Or, are they considered to have been outside the voortrekker community?' Van Jaarsveld maintains that from historical documents it is clear that only those members of the commando and their families who were present at the battle, together with those charged with protecting other Boer camps in the area were concerned with the 'vow' and not the whole of Afrikanerdom, most of whom had no part in the battle.

This is how he explains his 'radical' interpretation:

'It's a process of mathematics. In 1832, a few years before the trek, there were sixty-six thousand whites in the Cape colony of whom about fifty-two thousand were Afrikaners. Only ten thousand of these moved out as part of the Great Trek. Until 1840 no more than six thousand people had taken part in the trek – ten per cent of whites living in the Cape. Thus forty-six thousand in the Cape – "Queen Victoria's Afrikaners" – played no part in it. In the northern parts an estimated four to five thousand Afrikaners had no involvement in the battle, which means that ninety-five per cent of the Afrikaner people of those days were not involved. A correct reading of the "vow" documents indicates that the vow was to bind only those who were present in Natal and who directly or indirectly took part in the battle.'

By what right then did the few thousand Natal *voortrekkers* (or a commando of 468 Afrikaner men) bind all Afrikaners to celebrate 16 December? Although Professor van Jaarsveld has never advocated the abolition of the Day of the Vow as an ordinary public holiday, he asks why all Afrikaners should be bound to celebrate it today? He states that the religious and cultural guardians of Afrikaner nationalism expect all Afrikaners to celebrate 16 December for the sake of the cohesion of Afrikanerdom and for political motives. In van Jaarsveld's view, any man who is attached to Afrikaner traditions is free to celebrate the day, but it is unreasonable to expect it of someone purely because he happens to be an Afrikaner. The public furore which was unleashed in far-right circles when van Jaarsveld first expounded these views was spirited to say the least. Professor Liebenberg goes further than van Jaarsveld:

The taking of a vow on behalf of someone else who is not consulted in the matter, goes against everything that is reasonable. There can be nothing like it. . . . The answer to the question of who is bound by the vow can therefore only be: only those who took the vow. The present generation of Afrikaners is not bound by the vow. They do not commit a sin . . . if they do not attend a Day of the Vow commemoration. They are free to spend December 16 as they like.

The traditionalists were outraged by this new thinking, especially by the appeal that the religious dimension to the Day of the Vow should be abolished. In a newspaper article in 1982, cited by Liebenberg, one of the 'orthodox' school responded thus:

Even if you as an Afrikaner are not a direct descendant of those four hundred and seventy burghers at Blood River you might be remotely related. . . . It remains a fact that your brother in faith was victorious. If one member is happy, all members join in happiness. If one member suffers, all members suffer together. The question is: what happens if one member makes a promise? We as believers in South Africa share in that vow out of gratitude to the Maker who faithfully preserves His people.

The number of Afrikaners who today commemorate the Day of the Vow is diminishing. But for the keepers of the faith – those who 'trekked' across South Africa with their ox-wagons to mark the hundred-and-fiftieth anniversary – the views of van Jaarsveld and Liebenberg amount to heresy. For thousands of Afrikaners, for entire sections of the ruling National Party, for the right-wing die-hards, there can be no acceptance of the possibility that the central event in Afrikaner history, the taking of a vow prior to a decisive battle, may not have been as important or binding as generations have been led to believe. Without the myths surrounding Blood River many of the political, social and religious arguments advanced by the Afrikaner to justify his role in Africa fall away: the claim made by some that Afrikaners are a 'chosen' people sent by God to civilise the black 'hordes'; the notion of a united *volk* bounded by a common covenant; the superiority of the white man, with God on his side, over heathen blacks. Cracks appear in these philosophical and religious pillars once history is re-examined.

The Afrikaners' struggle in Africa – the trek itself, their bravery in the Boer War against Britain and the endurance of their women and children in British concentration camps, the fight for survival after defeat at the hands of enemies – is acknowledged. There are, for example, very few black leaders who do not accept that the Afrikaners have a place in South Africa and that their history and culture must be accommodated in any future settlement, though not on a racial basis. The achievements of the Afrikaner speak for themselves. The tragedy is, however, that the Afrikaner has chosen as the symbol of his nation an event which has been manipulated by successive leaders for subtle political purposes: an attempt to bind Afrikaners together on the basis of mythmaking so that the commemoration of the *voortrekkers* is now viewed by the majority of the country's population as a sectional reminder of how the white man subjugated the black tribes and has suppressed them ever since. If only the Afrikaners had continued to mark the occasion as it was commemorated at that first ceremony at the Blood River battle site, when blacks and whites together laid their stones as a token of remembrance. . . .

On 29 March 1979 Professor van Jaarsveld, a quietly-spoken academic, began a lecture at the University of South Africa in Pretoria as part of an international congress on the meaning of the Great Trek. His address – 'An Historical Mirror of Blood River' – outlined his research into the limited significance of the covenant which was entered into on that crucial day. He advocated that the Day of the Vow should revert to its earlier status as an ordinary public holiday without the Sunday clause. Suddenly the doors of the lecture theatre burst open and twenty-six youngsters led by an ultra-rightist leader called Eugene Terre Blanche grabbed the professor. One of them was carrying a *sjambok* (whip). They pushed aside a nun who tried to hold them back. Terre Blanche seized the microphone and denounced van Jaarsveld, declaring that he would not permit the sanctity of Blood River to be challenged. He condemned 'liberal politicians, vagabond academics and false prophets' who were 'desecrating and degrading' all that was holy to the Afrikaner 'under the cover of learning and false religion'. Several of the intruders were later fined in court.

On that night, Professor van Jaarsveld endured the dreadful ordeal of being tarred and feathered. Afterwards he wanted to continue with his address but was taken away to have the tar removed when his skin started burning. Not a single member of the multiracial audience lifted a finger to help him. They were stunned and terrorised by an act of extremist white intimidation and violence.

CHAPTER TWO

'One of the most unconquerable races ever seen upon earth'

The Great Trek of 1838 is the epic tale, the focal point, of Afrikaner history, an event which gave the *volk* its first sense of direction after the settlers had drifted aimlessly for almost two centuries. But where did these strange people come from who departed Europe's shores to embark upon the dangerous voyage south across vast oceans, to establish their homes at the foot of what was then an unknown continent?

The first rounding of the Cape by the Portuguese sailor Bartholomeu Dias in 1488, followed a decade later by Vasco da Gama, enthralled the peoples of Europe. In the years following those early voyages a succession of Portuguese sea captains put in at Table Bay at the Cape for brief stopovers. To compete with the Portuguese, English ships landed at Table Bay in 1591. The Dutch followed four years later en route to their East Indies colony of Batavia. Within a few years trading ties with the east, and hence the importance of the Cape, were strengthened with the formation of the *Generale Vereenigde Nederlantsche Geoctroyeerde Oostindische Compagnie*, the United Netherlands Chartered East Indian Company, soon to be known by its Dutch abbreviation, the VOC, or its English title, the Dutch East India Company. The company was headed by a powerful Council of Seventeen based in Amsterdam with outposts in Malaysia, the East Indies, Formosa and Japan. The VOC, a virtual state-within-a-state, was empowered to conclude treaties and contracts with local rulers. Soon the sea links between the Netherlands and Batavia were so well established that the founding of a properly equipped victualling station en route became a priority.

Among those early callers at the Cape was a VOC employee Jan Athoniszoon van Riebeeck. Having been accused – falsely, he claimed – of lining his own pockets while serving as a junior merchant in Japan, van Riebeeck was being recalled to company headquarters in some disgrace. On his return he found life in Amsterdam tedious compared to the splendours of the east. Van Riebeeck strongly recommended the Cape as a replenishment stop and managed to talk the VOC into appointing him to command the new post. On Christmas Eve 1651 van Riebeeck, his wife and son set sail on board the *Drommedaris* with four other vessels under his command. His ship, along with the *Goede Hoope* (Good Hope), reached Table Bay on 6 April the following year, the other vessels making landfall within a month. Van Riebeeck's statue stands on the foreshore of modern-day Cape Town. His instructions from the company were to build a fort, to plant gardens and orchards, to provide fruit and vegetables for passing Dutch ships, to lay in supplies of fresh water and to erect a flag post to help guide the vessels to shore. There was not the slightest hint in the company's orders that the small settlement to be established at the Cape was to become a permanent station.

It was not an easy adjustment for the first arrivals: the settlement was not self-financing and it was an arduous life combating the often harsh weather and sickness and establishing the early bartering links with indigenous Khoi people, also called Hottentots. Nevertheless, after a year, the outpost was able to start resupplying vessels with poultry, vegetables, water and milk.

In his diary van Riebeeck wrote that he had arrived at the Cape with ninety people, a mixture of lowly artisans and gardeners. As the community grew, some were granted independence to set themselves up as farmers providing the station with food in order to defray VOC costs. These 'free burghers' were the very beginnings of the Afrikaner people in South Africa. This departure from the embrace of the company symbolised the Afrikaner's eventual severing of links with the Europe of his birth as he sought out a new future in the forbidding land which he had made his home.

More settlers arrived, fleeing a period of turmoil in Europe. The Netherlands had been subjugated by both Burgundy and the Spanish Hapsburgs and the country had been divided between a Calvinist north and a Catholic south. Wars in Europe had thrown up a generation of displaced people who were easily seduced by prospects of adventure and quick riches in far-flung parts of the globe. It was from these paupers that the settlers and the burghers derived. They were a colony of bankrupts and conscripts often dragooned into VOC service. 'Civilising' southern Africa at no stage figured in their thinking.

A second great European influx occurred in 1688 – the Huguenot protestants who left France, present-day Belgium and Holland after the repeal of the Edict of Nantes in 1685 by the French King Louis XIV. The edict – sanctioned by the Catholic monarchy in 1598 – granted protestants the right to worship according to their consciences and had ended decades of violent feuding between the two orders. But the edict had come under strain during the first half of the seventeenth century and Cardinal Richelieu, a fierce opponent of French protestantism, helped fuel the campaign against the Huguenots. The Catholic clergy refused to accept the edict. Protestant freedom was seriously curtailed and dissidents were tortured. The revoking of the edict became inevitable and nearly half a million French protestants fled their country, scattering to Holland, Belgium, Germany, Scandinavia, Canada and Ireland. Some 40–50,000 went to Britain. For every thousand Huguenots who were to leave France only one made his way to the Cape.

Despite their pitiful state when they arrived, several of the first Huguenot settlers and their successors had been people of standing in France even though they had suffered at the hands of the Catholic monarchy. Deon du Plessis, deputy editor of the *Argus* newspaper in Cape Town, himself of Huguenot descent, says: 'They were a cut above the original Dutch settlers, many of whom were simply VOC soldiers and not terribly bright. After all, two of Napoleon's armies had been kept on the run by the Huguenots. They were an innovative people, a good cross-section: tradesmen, bootmakers, farmers, a baker, a priest and a doctor.' One of Deon du Plessis' ancestors, Jean Prieur du Plessis, was a surgeon and set himself up in 1688 as a doctor; he issued the first death certificate in South Africa to record the killing of a fellow-Huguenot. A certain Marais had been struck by a stone thrown by a Hottentot so that 'the great vein over the heart was drenched in blood', as the certificate described the cause of death. Jean Prieur du Plessis returned to Europe when his wife died, to find himself another Huguenot spouse. Very few in Deon du Plessis' family have married non-Huguenots.

Some of the new arrivals had known the good life. Their early homesteads at the Cape were often primitive huts of stones and leaves. But soon they were building their own farmhouses and cultivating vines, advancing the fledgling Cape wine industry which flourishes today. It was not long before they had reclaimed their respected positions in society, becoming prosperous farmers, doctors, lawyers and businessmen. As the Huguenots moved deeper into the Cape they faced formidable difficulties. It was a wild region and the settlers were continually harassed by local bushmen, not to mention Cape lions. They were also a neglected people. They were assisted for a time by the company, as many had arrived destitute, but the VOC had no interest in developing the colony. Though subject to the bureaucratic whims of the company, the settlers were on their own.

It was a young man of German Huguenot descent who staged the first public protest against the VOC, notably against the tyrannical governor Wilhem Adriaan van der Stel who had tried to corner the entire Cape economy. When van der Stel was recalled to Holland in 1707 by the Council of Seventeen, Hendrik Biebault and some roistering friends galloped on their horses through the centre of Stellenbosch near Cape Town, pulling up in front of the *drostdy* (administrative centre) where Biebault celebrated their victory with the famous words: *Ik ben een Afrikaander* (I am an Afrikaner), the first instance of the European settlers identifying themselves as a new people of another continent, and an early demonstration of the Afrikaners' readiness to rebel against authority if it is usurped. Later a French soldier in the service of the VOC became so angered by corruption and maladministration within the company that he staged an extraordinary one-man rebellion at Drakenstein where many of the Huguenots had settled. For this he was sentenced to be crucified, drawn and quartered, the remaining parts of his body to be impaled at the entrances to the colony as food for the birds.

The tercentenary of the Huguenots' arrival in 1688 was marked by a special festival which brought together members of one of the oldest and largest Huguenot families, the de Klerks. A newspaper advertisement announced: 'This family get-together will take the form of an authentic French Huguenot three-course dinner, at which estate wines will be served emanating from some of the original farms which were granted to the French refugees late in the seventeenth century. The cost of the dinner is twenty-five rand per person.' Fortunately for the organisers not all the de Klerk family turned up.

From an original settlement of 200 in 1688 the number of Huguenots grew during the ensuing 300 years to one million or about a fifth of the white population. At the tercentenary pageant President Botha delivered an address honouring the Huguenots' heritage, observing that their most important contribution had been 'a spirit of freedom which remained a continuing responsibility of future generations.' He went on:

'The Huguenots were hardworking people and creative people. They were people of faith. But above all, they were people of freedom. Their urge towards liberty and their quest for freedom of faith and worship compelled them forever to turn their backs on their country and find a home elsewhere where they could find that freedom. . . . Their urge for freedom is alive in their descendants.'

Botha attributed his own 'stubborn streak' to his Huguenot ancestors, recalling that his grandfather had married Anna Durand, the daughter of a Huguenot settler, and that he himself 'had married a Rossouw' – a reference to his wife Elize, herself from a Huguenot family. The president referred to a 'moving story of endurance' by one of his Huguenot ancestors, Marie Durand, who was held captive in the Tour de Constance in France 'because of her convictions' and because her brother was a protestant preacher. She had been held prisoner for thirty-eight years, said Botha, and every year the inscription after her name in the prison record had read: 'Her faith remains unchanged.' Botha went on to quote Sir Arthur Conan Doyle, the creator of Sherlock Holmes, on the subject of the national characteristics formed by the intermarriage of the Huguenots and the Dutch free burghers:

'Take a community of Dutchmen of the type who defended themselves for fifty years against all the power of Spain at a time when Spain was the greatest power in the world. Intermix them with a strain of those inflexible French Huguenots who gave up home and fortune and left their country for ever at the time of the revocation of the Edict of Nantes. The product must obviously be one of the most rugged, virile, unconquerable races ever seen upon earth. Then, finally, put a finer temper upon their military qualities by a dour fatalistic Old Testament realism and an ardent consuming patriotism.'

Within a generation of their arrival, the French language had died out among the Huguenot settlers. They were not allowed to speak French and their children went to Dutch schools. Together the Huguenots, the Dutch, the Germans and other European expatriates fused into what was to become an 'Afrikaner' nation: Europeans still tied to western ideas, yet slowly detaching themselves from the currents of western history and adapting their beliefs and outlook to the demands of a hostile land. They were a small community: only 37,000 by the end of the eighteenth century. This compounded their insularity, as well as their interbreeding.

It was an irony therefore that, having shed their European connections to forge a new future thousands of miles away, it was again events in Europe which were to provide a crucial turning point in the lives of these people who were already calling themselves 'Afrikaanders'.

In 1795 the armies of revolutionary France moved into the Netherlands, forcing the Prince of Orange into exile in England. The English moved quickly to forestall the French seizing the Cape: its possession by Napoleon would have had serious repercussions for British shipping en route to India. A British fleet set sail and, after minor Huguenot-inspired resistance, Cape Town was captured and became a British colony. Having fled to South Africa to escape despotism in Europe, the Afrikaners were once more subject to a European power.

The Dutch repossessed the colony in 1803 but the British were back three years later to make their occupation permanent. A policy of anglicisation threatened the identity of the settlers as English became the medium in the public service and in the judiciary. The position of the Dutch Reformed Church was respected but was still subservient to the colonial administration. English and Scottish schoolteachers were imported to spread British culture and the English language in Dutch schools and eventually English was declared the sole official language. As English-speakers gradually took over the jobs previously filled by Afrikaners, the Dutch language came under pressure. 'Anglo-Afrikaners' were quite happy to become anglicised but others yearned for the independence which had galvanised their forefathers into fleeing Europe. After all, under the weak administration of the VOC, they had largely been left to their own devices; conquering the land and the climate and withstanding black marauders had turned them into hardy, self-sufficient people, by then accustomed to looking after their own affairs with minimal intrusion from central authority. If there was a growing Afrikaner identity it was not that of an emerging nation; rather a mutual desire among the settlers to maintain the freedom they had fought for and to continue to be allowed to live their own lives without interference.

In 1820 the first group of British settlers arrived to help shore up the eastern borders against the black tribes. Relations with the Afrikaners were amicable; indeed the existing settlers were there to meet them when they landed at Algoa Bay, later renamed Port Elizabeth. There was some intermarriage between the Afrikaners and the British but in general the two communities led their separate lives. Like their Dutch and Huguenot predecessors, the new arrivals were a cross-section of society: soldiers, businessmen, doctors, clergymen, farmers and artisans. Their arrival doubled the number of English-speakers in the Cape colony. The British way of life – cricket, horse racing and afternoon tea – received a fillip. The English jury system was introduced while the *landdros* (law officer) was replaced by English-style magistrates. Newspapers and libraries sprang up for the first time. Above all, the arrival of the British increased the demands for more democracy, with the result that fully responsible government was granted in 1872.

The British occupation of the Cape had brought with it another group of immigrants whose activities irked the Afrikaners: the church missionaries. A few

21

had appeared during the final years of VOC rule but their numbers increased rapidly after 1806. Sponsored by the London and Glasgow missionary societies and fired with the evangelical spirit, these dedicated, somewhat zealous men embarked from a Britain where the debate on slavery was soon to result in the abolition of the slave trade. Some of the missionaries championed the cause of the Khoi people, alleging that they were the victims of murder and ill-treatment at the hands of the settlers. In 1811, in response to the allegations, a circuit court known as the 'black court' spent four months investigating the charges, during which time fifty settlers were summoned and several thousand witnesses questioned. At the end of the proceedings not a single murder charge could be proved: a few of the settlers were fined as a result of minor charges.

Undeterred, the philanthropists continued to press the cause of the Hottentots so that in 1828 'Ordinance Fifty' was passed, which abolished discrimination on the basis of colour for free Khoi and others, prohibited restrictions on an individual's freedom of movement and ruled that no one could be forced into service. The same conditions were granted to slaves freed in 1834. The granting of these rights, together with reforms to the land-tenure system, were seen by the Afrikaners as restricting their freedom. They had further cause for complaint about the role of the missionaries following a series of devastating raids during 1834 by Xhosa warriors belonging to one of the major black tribes which migrated south from other parts of Africa. Over twenty Afrikaners were killed and thousands of horses, cattle and sheep stolen. The governor of the Cape, Sir Benjamin D'Urban, counter-attacked, driving the invaders back across the Fish River, the declared border, and imposing a settlement which ensured that they would stay there. The missionaries disapproved, as did the authorities in London. The frontier agreement was reversed, with the result that the Xhosas drifted back on to the land claimed by the Afrikaner settlers, a final realisation, if any were needed, that the settlers could not rely on the British to defend their interests.

Attempts by British governors, assisted by the burghers, to drive the black tribesmen beyond the Fish River proved to be only a temporary consolidation of the unofficial border. The frontiersmen complained that they were not being afforded sufficient protection by the colonial government and a notorious incident at Slagtersnek in 1815 only strengthened their view. Boer farmers returned from fighting the Xhosa warriors to learn that one of their community, Frederik Bezuidenhout, had been arrested by an under-sheriff at the head of a platoon of mixed-race soldiers of the Cape Regiment. Bezuidenhout's Khoi herdsman had lodged charges of ill-treatment against him. Bezuidenhout had ignored several summonses and in his absence had been sentenced to one month's imprisonment. He took refuge in a cave and while resisting arrest by a search party was shot dead. A small insurrection of the burghers followed, organised by friends and families of the dead man. The rebellion had racial overtones: the settlers were disgusted that Bezuidenhout had been summoned to court proceedings by a non-white and that Hottentots had come to arrest him. Of the sixty or so who rebelled against the *landdros* thirty-nine were eventually tried for treason, of whom five received the death penalty. The treatment of the condemned men was a further source of outrage among the settlers.

One of the accused was a member of the de Klerk family, perhaps one of the most captivating figures in the family's history. A deeply religious man, twenty-nine-year-old Theunis Christiaan de Klerk sought to protect his co-accused at the trial by testifying that the rebellion was mostly his responsibility. He entered a plea for mercy but the court rejected it. His wife petitioned the authorities with a final appeal for clemency. That, too, was turned down. Four days before the execution day de Klerk was allowed to attend the christening of his youngest son. When they hanged de Klerk the rope snapped three times before he was finally executed.

A clergyman, appointed by the British colonial authorities to attend the hanging, told the officer in charge of the execution that 'The English will regret this until the end of time.'

Events such as these forged the defiant spirit of the Afrikaners. Their isolation, arising from the severing of links with Europe, was reinforced as they sought to distance themselves from British rule, a process of alienation compounded by the exhausting wars against the black tribesmen. To the settlers, British policy seemed aimed at treating the Boers and the blacks as equals whereas the Afrikaners regarded themselves as superior and separate.

Three reconnaissance parties called the *kommissie trek* (commission trek) set out in 1834 to explore the territory beyond the colony. They returned with stories of vast uninhabited lands where the Boers could live free of British overlordship. The following year, under their leader Louis Trichardt, the first of the *voortrekkers* loaded their ox-wagons, gathered together their families, their servants and their animals and set off north, linking up with another group at the Orange River. From Grahamstown, Graaff-Reinet, Uitenhage and other towns across the eastern zone similar parties moved off; altogether some 10 to 15 per cent of the white population joined the exodus. In a subsequent document researched by Afrikaner historian F. A. van Jaarsveld they said:

We broke away from British rule and left our mother country, where we were slandered, vexed and humiliated, and with wife and children crossed the very desert and arrived in a savage country where we thenceforth envisaged the possibility of being allowed to breathe the air of independence.

Trichardt's group, having crossed the Orange River, headed further north across the grassy plains of the present-day Orange Free State. They travelled little more than seven miles per day, moving only as fast as their animals could walk. From time to time, when they were exhausted or when their ewes were lambing, they would rest for a few days beside a watering hole, *uitspanning* (outspanning) their wagons into a *laager*, the circular formation which came to symbolise the gritty determination of the Afrikaner to defend himself against his enemies.

When they reached Thaba Nchu beyond the Orange River, they considered themselves to be beyond the borders of British jurisdiction. The pioneers elected their own *volksraad*. Even in their new country the Boers had no respite from the continual thrust and counter-thrust with their black opponents that had dogged their years in the eastern settlements and which 150 years later repeat themselves in South African armed attacks into neighbouring black states in pursuit of black insurgents. The divisions among the *voortrekkers* over where to head next began the tradition of bitter feuding which has punctuated the emergence of the Afrikaner nation. The world may regard the Boers as a granite-like monolith united in their stand against outside forces, but within the Afrikaner *laager* the schisms can run deep. Another of the arrivals at Thaba Nchu, Piet Retief, had drawn up an article, published in the *Grahamstown Journal* on 2 February 1837 before his departure from the Cape, which became the manifesto of the *voortrekkers*, a catalogue of the grievances which were sending them on their way. He wrote:

> We despair of saving the colony from those evils which threaten it by the turbulent and dishonest conduct of vagrants [meaning blacks and Hottentots] who are allowed to infest the country in every part. . . . We complain of the severe losses which we have been forced to sustain by the emancipation of our slaves. . . . We complain of the continual system of plunder which we have endured from the Kaffirs [as the blacks were called] and other coloured classes. . . . We complain of the unjustifiable odium which has been cast upon us by interested and dishonest persons under the cloak of religion [the missionaries] whose testimony is believed in England to the exclusion of all evidence in our favour; and we can foresee as the result of this prejudice, nothing but the total ruin of the country. . . . We are resolved, wherever we go, that we will uphold the just principles of liberty; but whilst we will take care that no one shall be held in a state of slavery, it is our determination to maintain such regulations as may suppress crime and preserve proper relations between master and servant. . . .

How these sentiments are echoed in different language by the leaders of today's Afrikaners! For 'turbulent and dishonest vagrants' and 'the Kaffirs' 'continual system of plunder' read the 'revolutionaries' and 'black Marxists' who are seen as threatening today's peaceful order. Replace the 'unjustifiable odium' conjured up by 'dishonest persons' from England with today's allegations that mischievous foreigners paint a totally false picture of South Africa or that churchmen like Archbishop Tutu of Cape Town meddle in politics under 'the cloak of religion'. For the preservation of 'proper relations between master and servant' based on 'just principles of liberty' read the modern National Party's adoption of the policy of 'group rights' or racially separate political representation in which no one race shall 'dominate' the other and in which 'civilised standards' shall be upheld. How little some things have changed since Retief left the Cape and made his way to the *voortrekker* outpost.

'One of the most unconquerable races ever seen upon earth'

From Thaba Nchu, Retief led the divided *voortrekkers* in fifty-four wagons in an ascent of the Drakensberg mountains heading into Natal, thereby setting in motion the tragic sequence of events which would culminate in the deceit and slaughter at the Zulu headquarters and later the historic battle on the banks of the Ncome River. After they had defeated the Zulus the trekkers pursued the Zulu chief Dingane and his army for a further two years until Mpande, Dingane's younger brother, defected and with Boer support eventually forced Dingane into exile in present-day Swaziland where he was murdered by Swazi tribesmen, an early example of Afrikaners attaining their aims through helpful black leaders 'co-opted' to their cause.

With tranquillity restored to Zululand the Afrikaners could hope for a period of settled living after the arduous trek from the colony. But their new-found independence was to be short-lived. The Boers sought British recognition of their republic which the Cape governor was reluctant to bestow. Citing the Boers' alleged mistreatment of the natives, the governor reoccupied Natal and declared it to be a British colony. Soon the Boers were on the move again, making their way north into the Orange Free State and Transvaal. At the town of Potchefstroom they issued a manifesto declaring the Afrikaners living there to be independent of British sovereignty. But the British were in hot pursuit, diplomatically if not militarily. In 1848 the territory between the Orange and Vaal rivers was annexed by Britain as the Orange River Sovereignty. The Boers could muster only minimal resistance.

But the British had bitten off more than they could chew. Weighed down with administrative problems elsewhere in the colony, they eventually agreed, at the Sand River Convention in 1852, to grant the Boers independence in the Transvaal. Two years later, at the Bloemfontein Convention, the Orange Free State was granted freedom as well. It had taken the Afrikaners almost twenty years since the first ox-wagons had rolled out of the eastern colony to win liberation.

But although the trek into the interior may have been over, the Afrikaners' journey in search of security was not. The twenty years following their departure from the Cape had demonstrated two things clearly: that the relationship with the British and the independence they had been granted were likely to remain fragile creations, while the murderous engagements with the black tribes pointed to a potentially greater problem lying ahead.

The Great Trek had resulted in a fundamental redrawing of the map of southern Africa. The region had been balkanised, with the creation of two Boer republics in the north while Britain retained control over the Cape colony and Natal. It had been a unique development in British colonial history. Attempts at drawing the four territories closer together met no success throughout the two decades which followed the granting of independence to the northern states. At one point the Transvaal and the Free State came close to civil war until the Vaal River Treaty of 1857 guaranteed their respective independence, about which there was considerable concern in Britain.

When vast diamond fields were discovered three years later there was further cause for renewed British interest in the events of the interior. As alluvial diggings multiplied along the Vaal River and around the town of Kimberley, the Transvaal, the Free State and local Griqua tribesmen registered their claims. In 1871 Britain annexed Griqualand West along with the diamond fields, turning the area into a crown colony and thereby depriving the young Boer states of substantial amounts of desperately needed revenue. There were rebellions among blacks living in Griqualand West who had acquired weapons and ammunition. Once again the British were seen as failing to control the black hordes; British policy appeared once more to favour the blacks at the expense of the Afrikaners. The diamond discoveries resulted in thousands of blacks leaving their tribal areas to converge on the towns and cities. South Africa's permanent black urban population was being born. Having trekked from the Cape, in part to escape the encroachment of blacks, the Afrikaners once again found themselves among them; at the same time, the British determined to establish a federation, with all the loss of Afrikaner sovereignty which that would entail. Britain at first attempted to persuade the states to join a federation; when this failed Britain simply annexed the Transvaal, where gold deposits had also been found.

The man who was to emerge as the greatest of the Boer leaders, Paul Kruger, led the Transvaal Afrikaners' struggle against annexation. He travelled to London in an abortive attempt to persuade the British government to revoke the annexation. The Transvaal was in open rebellion and the first Boer War (known by Afrikaners as the War of Independence) broke out in 1880, culminating in the Battle of Majuba in which the British were soundly defeated. A subsequent peace treaty restored independence to the republic though some matters remained under the authority of the British.

But the British were not going to leave matters at that, especially when it became clear that the reports of gold deposits on the Witwatersrand (the area around Johannesburg) heralded the discovery of the world's largest gold-bearing seam. The Transvaal became a potential economic power house. Johannesburg was transformed into a gold-rush city as thousands of *uitlanders* (foreigners), most of them British, converged on the booming mining towns. If Kruger had emerged as the staunch defender of the political and economic interests of the Transvaal, he was matched on the British side by Cecil Rhodes, an arch-imperialist who was determined to obtain for Britain the riches of the north.

Kruger would have none of it, and slowly Britain and the Boers edged towards another confrontation. In seeking to bring the Transvaal to heel, Rhodes exploited the position of the *uitlanders*. An armed British contingent stationed in neighbouring Bechuanaland (present-day Botswana) crossed the border in 1895 with the aim of supporting a planned rebellion by the *uitlanders* of the Transvaal. The uprising never materialised and the raiders, led by Dr Leander Starr Jameson, were intercepted west of Johannesburg and arrested.

Undeterred, a new high commissioner at the Cape, Alfred Milner, resolved to break the back of Boer resistance. In the face of such threats, the burghers of the

Transvaal and the Free State drew closer together, supported by Afrikaners in the Cape. In 1899 the *uitlanders* petitioned Queen Victoria with their grievances about the administration of the Transvaal and their exclusion from the franchise. This was a political gift to Milner, whose message to the Boer leaders was 'reform or war', knowing full well that the former course was most unlikely. With the two countries dangerously circling each other, Milner and Kruger held an unsuccessful meeting on 31 May 1899 to try to agree on a formula for enfranchising the *uitlanders*. The Boer republics increasingly suspected that this question was a Trojan horse, manufactured by the British to conceal their real intention – the subjugation of the Transvaal to British rule. On 9 October the Transvaal delivered an ultimatum to the British government demanding that it give up its claims to the republic, withdraw its troops from the Transvaal borders, turn back British troops on the high seas bound for the Cape and establish an arbitration committee to resolve the differences between the two sides. The British were told that unless they agreed to these conditions by 5 p.m. on 11 October – two days away – the Boers would regard the British silence as a declaration of war. The British failed to respond to the ultimatum and so the Boer War (or the Anglo-Boer War, as South Africans call it) began.

Kruger declared martial law in the Transvaal while President Steyn of the Free State mobilised his forces to support the republic. The *uitlanders* left and the gold mines were closed down. The Boer commandos – largely a people's army of able-bodied men and young boys equipped with German rifles – deployed on several fronts to confront the approaching British units. The Afrikaner army consisted of no more than 80,000 men against a force of 450,000 British and empire soldiers at the height of the war. The British – experienced in other colonial wars in Africa and India – were over-confident; the Boers knew their terrain. They invaded Natal where early battles resulted in the Boers' seven-month siege of Ladysmith in which British forces under Baden-Powell were garrisoned. Similar sieges at Mafeking and Kimberley allowed the British time to send reinforcements. Boer forces entered the Cape to forestall British troop movements and in so doing rallied many Cape Afrikaners to their cause. The British suffered serious defeats at Spionkop and at Vaalkrans. Field Marshal Lord Roberts and a new chief of staff, Lord Kitchener, arrived to take charge and on 15 February 1900 the British forces broke through the republican lines to raise the siege of Kimberley. Bloemfontein was occupied soon after and then the British moved northwards, crossing the Vaal River and taking Johannesburg. Pretoria fell on 5 June. It looked as though the war was over; indeed Lord Roberts was recalled to London leaving Kitchener in charge to bring the war to its conclusion. But the Boers called a council of war and decided to embark upon guerrilla warfare with small mobile groups of commandos mounting hit-and-run attacks on the British and withdrawing before the enemy had time to respond.

To counter these tactics Kitchener launched a two-pronged policy which was to leave a legacy of bitterness between the British and Boer nations, a bitterness which still burns deep within the soul of many Afrikaners. The strategy was aimed at depriving the roving Boer commandos of the food and shelter provided by Afrikaner homesteads while at the same time rounding up Boer women and children, further to deprive the commandos of support. Where it was suspected the Boers had sought shelter, farmhouses were razed to the ground; the buildings were destroyed along with the farm animals, crops and orchards. A network of guard posts, known as 'blockhouses', was erected across the country close to the vulnerable railway lines, linked by miles of barbed-wire fencing, to help monitor the movements of the Boers and then corner them. The blockhouses were supplemented by 'concentration camps', the British thereby earning themselves a place in history as the inventors of this particular form of population control. Conditions were appalling. Twenty-six thousand Afrikaner women and children died, mostly from measles and pneumonia due to poor medical services and inadequate rations. In the House of Commons in London the Liberal leader Sir Henry Campbell-Bannerman accused the British government of employing 'methods of barbarism'.

Despite the continuing Boer resistance, the suffering of the women and children could not be allowed to go on. Moreover there were divisions within Afrikaner ranks. The so-called *bittereinders* (bitter-enders) wanted to pursue the war until the very end while the *hensoppers* (hands-uppers) were willing to surrender. This deep division among Afrikaners was to recur decades later when liberal Afrikaners, willing to talk peace with the African National Congress, were branded as sell-outs or 'hensoppers' by today's 'bittereinders'.

At the town of Vereeniging, south of Johannesburg, a delegation of Boer leaders who met Milner concluded that the very survival of the Afrikaner nation could be ensured only if the war ended. It was assumed however that the acceptance of a peace treaty would merely be a temporary setback in the struggle for Afrikaner independence. The settlement, signed on 31 May 1902, imposed colonial status upon the Boer republics, leaving the British with the task of remoulding the country's four states into a united nation. The total number of Boers killed in the war, either in combat or in the concentration camps, was around 30,000 while losses on the British side were put at about 22,000. One of the clauses in the Peace of Vereeniging read: 'The question of granting the franchise to blacks would not be settled before the introduction of representative government'. The fact that this issue was postponed then, and was pushed aside in the years afterwards, sowed the seeds of the anguish and the struggle of rival nationalisms which would dominate South Africa's politics in the second half of the twentieth century.

The Afrikaners found themselves in a desperate state, their nation almost on the point of extinction. The century or so since the Great Trek had been a wasted period in which they had put considerable effort into identifying their enemies but had made little progress in identifying themselves. These lost souls were not a cohesive socio-cultural unit. Their language, culture and sense of belonging fractured, they began to suffer an inferiority complex. Many were leading strict, austere lives. Once again the spectre of British imperialism had returned to haunt them. In the face of this adversity, the first stirrings emerged of a real Afrikaner nationalism: not the sporadic flurries of cultural pride which had gone before, but the forging of a true national identity which was to sustain the Afrikaners in their darkest hour and later inspire them towards the final establishment of their own country.

During the Great Trek the Afrikaners had journeyed across many of the lands of southern Africa. It was possible, perhaps, to speak of an Afrikaner diaspora. The divergencies among them of culture, class, language and geographical outlook persisted as they explored new territories. The softer climate of the Cape made for a more relaxed view of life than the hard, draining environment of the Transvaal. In the home of many Cape Afrikaners, English was the spoken language. Others, especially the pastors of the Dutch Reformed Church, fought to uphold High Dutch. The emerging *Afrikaans* language – Germanic-based but gradually absorbing the colloquialisms of the mixed-race and slave populations – became the tongue of thousands of the Afrikaner farming community who spoke neither English nor High Dutch. There were moves towards establishing an Afrikaner language and cultural movement. Afrikaners living at the Cape – who had not permitted themselves to fall prey to English influences – got together in the 1870s to form Die Genootskap van Regte Afrikaners (The Society of True Afrikaners). The first Afrikaans-language newspaper, *Die Afrikaanse Patriot*, was founded and helped imbue its readers with a sense of national pride, informing them that they, the Afrikaner people, had a Christian, civilising mission to perform in South Africa.

Then came the founding of the first genuinely Afrikaner political party, the Afrikaner Bond. It was launched in 1879 by S. J. du Toit, a *predikant* (preacher) in the Dutch Reformed Church who called for exclusive Afrikaner control of a united and independent South Africa. He was soon to be challenged for the leadership of the Cape Afrikaners by Jan Hofmeyr, editor of a Dutch-language newspaper *De Zuid-Afrikaan*, who urged the accommodation of English-speakers and defined Afrikaners less exclusively as 'anyone who, having settled in this country, wishes to remain here to help to promote our common interests and to live with the inhabitants as members of one family'. This debate was to recur again and again. In the years after the Boer War, especially following the formation of the Union of South Africa in 1910, leaders like Jan Smuts and Louis Botha pursued a policy of reconciliation with English-speakers. J. B. M. Hertzog, by contrast, adopted a staunchly pro-Afrikaner position. The modern National Party – founded in 1914 to further the political aspirations of the Afrikaner people – has slowly had to attract English-speaking support as Afrikanerdom has become bitterly divided. Large numbers have defected to right-wing parties, some of which are themselves seeking to win English support.

Those early expressions of exclusive Afrikanerdom prompted fond recollections of the years of struggle whose leading figures were suddenly elevated into national heroes. The emigrants who had undertaken the Great Trek to escape British rule were suddenly afforded the name 'voortrekkers', perhaps best translated as 'pathfinders', although this name had not generally been used at the time of the trek itself. The stories of the trek, of Blood River, of the suffering of the women and children were resurrected in the Boers' consciousness to create a sense of history and heritage to sustain them during the years of anguish and humiliation.

Soon after Union, relations with the British came to a head at the outbreak of the First World War when South Africa was called upon to assist the western allies against the German armies. Those whose souls were still full of bitterness over the British treatment of the Boers and who yearned for their own free Afrikaner republics saw in the outbreak of hostilities in Europe a perfect opportunity to rid themselves of British domination. When war was declared, burghers in parts of the Transvaal began arming themselves, their resolve to stay out of the war strengthened when it was learned that South Africa was considering an invasion of South-West Africa (Namibia), then a colony of Germany which had been sympathetic towards the Boers in their war against the British. The government had to crush a revolt mounted, in the eyes of many Afrikaners, by loyal Boers seeking to re-establish their independence from imperial Britain. Who put down the rebellion? Fellow Afrikaners, Botha and Smuts who, from that time on, would be seen by many of their own people as servants of the British crown and traitors to the Afrikaner cause, a perception sharpened in the case of Smuts who, three years after becoming prime minister in 1919, put down a revolt by white miners over wages.

Britain's announcement in 1922 of its intention to return to the pre-war gold standard threatened a loss of one-third of their gold earnings for the South African mining houses. Their response was to reduce the number of white miners they employed in favour of blacks earning lower wages. In the subsequent Rand Rebellion, armed white miners seized the mining compounds on the Witwatersrand. Their action was inspired largely by the Communist Party whose slogan was 'Workers of the world unite for a white South Africa', an engaging irony given that today's South African Communist Party, now backing the black struggle rather than the white one, is branded by Pretoria as a Marxist evil leading a revolutionary assault by radicals to overthrow the state. The rebellion was defeated when Smuts sent in the army and the air force and at least 150 miners died.

Economic conditions forced poor farmers from the Afrikaner heartlands to migrate to the English-dominated cities in search of work. Until 1910 only 10 per cent of Afrikaners lived in the towns; by 1930 their number had quadrupled. In the English cities the Afrikaner once again felt himself to be a foreigner in his own country, a servant of British interests and of Anglo-Jewish capital which was the foundation of the great mining concerns and other industries. Many Afrikaners could barely speak English. For the first time they found themselves having to compete with coloureds and blacks for jobs which Afrikaners had traditionally regarded as *kafferwerk* (kaffir work), the name *kaffer* (heathen or non-believer) used disparagingly by Afrikaners to describe blacks. It is a term still heard today among some sections of Afrikanerdom. The Afrikaner was ill-equipped to compete for skilled and semi-skilled jobs. Cut off from the land and his secure family homestead, his sense of dislocation in an urban environment triggered profound demoralisation. Should he assert his pride in his Afrikanerdom in this fast, aggressive and largely hostile social environment? Or should he rather hide his origins, deny his nationality, and succumb to the prevailing Englishness of the towns?

Rural poverty and the emergence of a 'poor white' problem prompted a three year-long enquiry funded by the Carnegie Corporation of New York. The commission's report, published in 1932, estimated that some 300,000 whites, most of them Afrikaners, were in effect destitute and living below the poverty line. So severe was their plight that people had developed inherent poverty habits, losing all desire to fight for survival and falling back instead on welfare hand-outs. Entire rural Afrikaner communities were poverty-stricken.

And yet out of this utter deprivation there arose a new generation of Afrikaners whose migration from country to town was to mark a second 'great trek'. It was their first introduction to the twentieth century and the ways of the modern world. The Afrikaner seized the opportunity and set about wresting the country from exclusive English control. The abject misery of the urban Afrikaner produced a grim determination to confront 'the enemy' on his own ground. The problem of Afrikaner poverty in the cities slowly disappeared.

Central to the promotion of the Afrikaner's cause was the revival of his language. During the twilight of the Boer republics before the Boer War, Dutch had been the official language in business and education. But many Afrikaners, shrinking from both formal High Dutch and the language of their British conquerors, fell back increasingly on their own Afrikaans tongue, although many educated Afrikaners regarded it as an unrefined patois. The Boers' struggle for survival gave birth to a flowering of Afrikaans poetry. The flood of rural Afrikaners to the cities resulted in the formation of dozens of language movements to ensure the survival of Afrikaans amid the overwhelmingly English environment of the major cities. An enthusiasm for the language spread not just among the newly urbanised poor but also among the professions, in the universities, and in the church. In 1919 the Dutch Reformed Church approved the translation of the Bible into Afrikaans, a powerful stimulus to the language when it appeared in 1933. In 1925 Afrikaans was given equal status with English in the constitution. The language issue was harnessed by those promoting the cause of Afrikaner nationalism.

Attempts at reconciliation between English and Afrikaners in the wake of the Boer War had always foundered. The two Boer generals, Smuts and Botha, had formed a party in the Transvaal to bridge the gap between the two white communities. But any reconciliation was superficial; wounded pride, bitter memories and suspicion of 'the enemy' were too deep. The Act of Union of 1910, granting South Africa self-government as a British dominion, attempted to heal in constitutional form the wounds which lingered from the Peace of Vereeniging. Smuts and Botha returned from the war to discover that their South Africa Party, promoting national reconciliation, had alienated a substantial body of Afrikanerdom which was now backing a National Party under Hertzog. This placed Afrikaner interests first and favoured a separation of the two white

31

populations until the Afrikaners had built up their political and economic resources to challenge the British. Hertzog ousted Smuts in the 1924 general election and secured another victory in 1929.

But the years of economic depression were taking their toll on the country. The gold price had slumped, there was a flight of international capital from South Africa, and many felt that the country should follow Britain's example by forming a 'national government' to steer the country through the crisis. The result, in 1934, was the amalgamation of Smuts' South Africa Party and Hertzog's National Party into the United Party.

Dissidents opposing 'fusion' defected under the leadership of D. F. Malan to form the Gesuiwerde Nasionale Party (Purified National Party). Afrikaner nationalism suddenly became more aggressive, more organised and, most significantly, more ideological. Two political trends characterised this new force in white politics. First was the campaign to turn South Africa into a republic outside the British Empire, an issue which cut to the very heart of Afrikaner and British sentiments and interests. Secondly, the new National Party gave an impetus to the process of Afrikaner 'ethnic mobilisation' – the construction of a network of political, social, economic and cultural organisations dedicated to the uplifting of and eventual *baasskap* (domination) by the Afrikaner in all walks of life. The Afrikaner Broederbond was founded to become an underground wing of the Nationalists, an organisation exploiting nepotism to the full to steer Afrikaners into influential positions. The Dutch Reformed Church was mobilised as a spiritual engine-room for the Afrikaners' advancement. This new brand of Afrikaner nationalism was a revolution in the making.

For Afrikaners the Nationalist victory in 1948 meant the restoration of everything that had been lost since the Boer War. Under the party's auspices the Afrikaners, deprived of industrial skills, slowly filled jobs which were arising in the huge state bureaucracies: the transport, railway, postal and other government sectors. Even in industry the urban Afrikaner began making his mark, progressing slowly from lowly, degrading jobs to blue-collar and then white-collar employment. A few Afrikaners looked to scale the heights of private enterprise. The Afrikaners – hardly Boers any more – were mobilising themselves ethnically to eat away at the domination of English-speaking economic and political interests. But there was another factor. The National Party also voiced an increasingly intolerant and suspicious attitude towards the country's black working population in the cities and on that score had struck a sympathetic note among the Afrikaner *volk*.

'Apartheid' was not invented by the 1948 Afrikaner government if by that is meant the separation of people according to race. Attempts at segregating the white and black communities of South Africa had begun when the first Dutch settlers arrived. Jan van Riebeeck planted a lane of wild almond trees as a demarcation line between the Khoi and white areas. But the white settlers who spread further into the interior intermingled with blacks in everyday economic and social intercourse. Attempts to halt this process focused on the creation of native reserves but in general segregation was more by custom than by legislation.

Then in 1913 the government passed the Natives Land Act, which set aside parts of the country as 'scheduled areas' for black settlement. The lawmakers wanted to maintain a regular supply of black labour to white-owned farms and mines – the political dimension of the legislation was not paramount. But the Natives Land Act was an important turning point in relations between blacks and whites. For the first time the government had formalised the geographical separation of people, and because the native locations would be the only places where blacks could exercise any degree of self-administration – leaving whites to rule in the rest of the country – the concept of blacks and whites exercising political power within segregated racial territories was born. The 1913 legislation was the forerunner of the *bantustans* or black homelands which today form the basis of black political life. The amount of land granted to blacks was subsequently extended (to about 14 per cent of the country) by the Native Trust and Land Act passed in 1936. At the same time though, blacks lost the right to purchase land in the reserves and were restricted to tenure farming.

Other laws passed during the 1920s and 1930s imposed curfews on black areas and controlled the number of blacks allowed to work in urban areas. In 1936 Hertzog, in a 'black manifesto' speech, made clear that South Africa was a 'white man's land'. In the same year blacks lost their common-roll franchise: instead, three white MPs would represent them, while blacks themselves would be confined to an advisory Natives' Representative Council. But still these laws were fragmented, responses to facts on the ground rather than pieces in a huge ideological jigsaw puzzle. All that was to change when the Nationalists came to power.

The National Party slogan in the 1948 election was 'apartheid and guardianship' – the word 'apartheid' having slipped into the political vocabulary following a report completed the previous year of a National Party commission under P. O. Sauer MP, which looked at future race policy. The report of the Sauer Commission was the first substantial exposition of the theory and practice of apartheid. Its starting point was to protect the white race 'against any policy, philosophy or attack which might endanger or undermine its [the white race's] continued existence'. The report spoke of the 'ultimate separation' of the races, with blacks seeking their political future in 'reserved areas' leaving the rest of the country to the whites. Blacks working in the cities in 'white South Africa' would be visitors or 'temporary sojourners' without any political rights whatsoever. They would live in segregated residential areas; no black trade unions would be permitted; education, far from preparing blacks for a western culture and economic system, would be directed instead towards the blacks' own African traditions. But none of this was discriminatory, argued the report. The separation of the races was to allow each to fulfil itself unencumbered by the constraints of the other. Thus was born the concept of 'separate but equal'.

Under the National Party's first two prime ministers, Malan and J. G. Strijdom, the findings of the report began to be reflected in legislation. The Population Registration Act (1950) provided for the racial classification of the country's population. Many couples suddenly found themselves to be of different racial castes with all the social stigma which went with this. The Prohibition of Mixed Marriages Act (1949) rendered unlawful unions between whites and non-whites, while the Immorality Amendment Act (1950) extended the existing ban on sex between whites and Africans to whites and all people of colour, a humiliation for mixed-race people who owed their existence in large part to liaisons between whites and blacks and whose mother tongue was mainly Afrikaans. The Group Areas Act (1950) provided for separate residential zones for the individual races with penalties for those living in a racial area other than their own. The Resettlement of Natives Act (1954) gave the government the power to remove forcibly tens of thousands of squatters living close to white areas. The Reservation of Separate Amenities Act (1953) legislated for what had already been common practice – separate park benches, post-office queues, railway carriages and so on. The Abolition of Passes and Coordination of Documents Act (1952) imposed the hated pass-book system, a masterful example of how the titles of apartheid laws can mean exactly the opposite of what is contained in the acts themselves.

But even while these laws were being enacted the National Party leadership had still not elevated apartheid into the great Utopian experiment it was later to become. Malan saw the policy as a reflection of the differences between people as ordained by God; the ideological dimensions ordained by the party's intellectuals made little impression upon him. Malan, whose political nursery had been the hardships suffered by his people in the first half of the century, still had as his priority the uplifting of the Afrikaners. For him, apartheid was merely a social policy. There was little evidence that he had got to grips with the concept of a grand design to answer the country's race question.

Who better to reflect on the slow encroachment of racial hegemony than the venerable lady who has dominated the parliamentary struggle to thwart the gradual introduction of apartheid? South Africa's longest-serving member of parliament, Helen Suzman, has since 1953 represented the Houghton con-stituency in Johannesburg on behalf of the liberal Progressive Federal Party and before that the United Party and the Progressive Party. For thirteen of those years, hers was the only liberal voice in parliament. Mrs Suzman, then a junior backbencher, remembers the closing months of Malan's premiership. 'He was a dour *dominee* [pastor],' she recalls. 'The debate about the grand design of apartheid was far too elevated for him. It was the same with Strijdom. Apartheid hardly concerned them. All they were interested in was the *swart gevaar* [black threat].' In these early years in parliament, however, Mrs Suzman began to detect the flawed thinking that would later bring such misery to the country. 'The policy was antediluvian. There was absolutely no appreciation of economic develop-ment, for example how wealth should be created, where jobs and industry should be located. They never understood the realities on the ground.'

After Malan and Strijdom, Hendrik Verwoerd was a different animal alto-gether, a messianic figure who, according to Helen Suzman 'scared whites stiff, but gave them guidelines'. Born in Holland and brought to South Africa as a child, Verwoerd had been defeated in the election of 1948 but had entered parliament in the upper house as a senator. Addressing parliament in September of that year he set out what was to become the philosophical basis of his master plan:

'What is the situation as it exists? Europeans and non-Europeans travelling mixed in the trams and in the trains; Europeans and non-Europeans mixing in hotels where meals are served; engaged more and more in taking possession of the theatres and the streets; engaged in devastating the reserves; engaged in seeking learning that they do not use in the service of their people, but which they use to cross the border line of European life, to become traitors to their own people. . .'.

Verwoerd's solution?

'I want to state here unequivocally now the attitude of this side of the House, that South Africa is a white man's country and that he must remain the master here. In the reserves we are prepared to allow the native to be the masters; we are not masters there. But within the European areas, we, the white people of South Africa, are and shall remain the master. . .'.

Verwoerd spent the next eighteen years, first as Minister of Native Affairs and then as Prime Minister, putting the theory into practice. As the Afrikaner historian W. A. de Klerk expressed it in his classic study *The Puritans in Africa*: 'Never in history have so few legislated so programmatically, thoroughly and religiously, in such a short time, for so many divergent groups, cultures and traditions, than the nationalist Afrikaners of the second half of the twentieth century.'

Under Verwoerd the laws came thick and fast with a single-mindedness and ruthlessness which distinguished apartheid from the racial legislation and practices that had gone before. Verwoerd was a driven man whose political obsessions, according to Professor Sampie Terreblanche, were reinforced by a religious conviction born of the failed attempt on his life in 1961 when an assailant opened fire on him at an Easter show in Johannesburg. Says Terreblanche, Professor of Economics at Stellenbosch University in the Cape: 'Verwoerd concluded he had been saved by God. He then realised the religious aspect could be the most important part of politics and proceeded to exploit his escape, though whether this was the result of expediency or a genuine belief that the Almighty had intervened to save him was hard to tell.'

At the centre of the master plan were the black homelands, the territories where the blacks were to be shunted leaving the rest of the country to the white man. The Tomlinson Commission, appointed by Verwoerd two years after the Nationalist victory, reported in 1955 on the future shape of racial boundaries. Integration, it concluded, would only lead to friction. Separation was therefore the answer. Separate development, or apartheid, would consequently be constructed around the creation of the *bantustans*. Initially Verwoerd foresaw only limited self-government for these territories but later, as prime minister, he conceded that the homelands could become fully 'independent' states in a fragmented South African commonwealth. Eventually four homelands – Transkei, Ciskei, Venda and Bophuthatswana – were to become nominally independent.

The grand design did not stop with Tomlinson. Another of the apartheid ideologues, W. H. Eiselen, Secretary of Native Affairs, produced a report in 1955 which resulted in a kind of racial Berlin Wall being imposed upon the country. The 'Eiselen line', as it became known, was an administrative dividing line running north to south through the Cape province. Blacks were banned from the western side of the boundary and the western Cape was declared a 'white and coloured preferential area'. The idea was a nonsense, of course, and the black tide eventually defeated it. But because there had been no proper housing programmes for the blacks in the western Cape the result was the appalling squatter camps that arose at Crossroads and nearby. Not that the coloureds benefited from the 'preferential' treatment either. Under the Separate Representation of Voters Act (1956) they were removed from the common voters' roll.

Yet none of this appeared to conflict with the Afrikaners' Christianity. Far from seeking to 'civilise' the heathen, the Afrikaners' perceived superiority had traditionally steered them towards isolation and separation from the indigenous peoples around them. Under apartheid, though, the Afrikaner was suddenly elevated into a bearer of God's message. The consignment of the blacks to the *bantustans* was not seen as racist: rather, it was an opportunity for the black tribes of South Africa to develop and fulfil themselves within their own protected areas. Such a policy was fully in keeping with the Afrikaner's view of his mission in life and it conformed entirely with what his church told him: that nations were separate but equal. It was the ideal solution. The Afrikaner could assuage his Christian conscience by convincing himself that he was assisting the blacks in their own development; yet he did not have to live with them to achieve it.

Verwoerd eventually revealed himself in his true colours, leading the battlecries of white domination. Despite all the protestations by more recent Afrikaner leaders that their aim is a system of government in which no one group dominates another, their very speeches betray that the protection of the whites is uppermost in their minds. As recently as 1985, President Botha reminded the world that he 'was not prepared to lead *white* South Africans and other minority groups on a road to abdication and suicide. Destroy *white* South Africa and *our* influence and this country will drift into factional strife, chaos and poverty' (my italics).

Says Helen Suzman: 'Verwoerd was the most frightening man I have ever been confronted with. He was extremely dominating, tall, with a streak of grey hair, a high-pitched voice and a rather feminine mouth. He had opaque eyes which looked like peeled white grapes. They didn't seem to have any pupils.' Mrs Suzman says Verwoerd was totally convinced that he had a divine mission to impose apartheid. She remembers a speech in 1958 in which, as native affairs minister, he said that 'by 1978 the stream will reverse itself and blacks will have gone back to their homelands because they will then be prosperous areas which will provide them with a livelihood'. The total impossibility of achieving such an objective was completely lost on him, she says. 'Verwoerd was a remarkable speaker. He would build up his arguments layer upon layer. You sat there like a dolt taking it all in until you realised it was all built upon a false premise.'

But then the Afrikaners are masters of turning logic on its head. Night after night government ministers appear on television putting their case and somehow one finds oneself suspending rational thought because the arguments, often so implausible, appear reasonable. It is one of the achievements of forty years of Nationalism that the power of logic among whites has generally been sur-rendered. The chairman of the giant Anglo American mining company, Gavin Relly, once commented: 'Apartheid has made fools of us all.'

Sampie Terreblanche of Stellenbosch University recalls Verwoerd as an excellent salesman:

'For decades the Afrikaners had not been in control of their political destiny. Verwoerd came along and restored their sovereignty while affording it to the blacks as well, saying the Afrikaners were a chosen people whose task was to bring justice to all the peoples of southern Africa on a separate but equal basis. The Afrikaners therefore accepted that there was a moral justness in apartheid.'

Piet Meiring was news editor of *Die Transvaler* when Hendrik Verwoerd was editor between 1937 and 1948. 'We had to teach him the very principles of journalism, but he was an apt pupil.' Verwoerd regarded *Die Transvaler* as the mouthpiece of the National Party. Meiring fought against him to uphold basic news values; he was unhappy that the paper was simply reporting National Party events. 'We must have news, not just politics,' he told Verwoerd, to which Verwoerd replied, 'You are talking nonsense. We have a job to do. Reporting National Party meetings is more important than covering cricket matches.' It was also more important than covering the visit to South Africa in 1947 by King George VI which *Die Transvaler* dismissed with references to 'busy streets' in Johannesburg and no mention of the royal party whose presence had brought thousands out on to the pavements. Verwoerd wrote the reports of his own political speeches. Meiring remembers him as a brilliant man who had 'guts'. 'But he was still very much a Hollander and had an inferiority complex. He felt he had to prove himself to his followers as an Afrikaner.' Later, when Meiring was appointed head of the government's information services, he again served Verwoerd. They had got on well at first but slowly Meiring began to have doubts. 'He was so bloody certain of his target – the establishment of the republic, the achievement of all that the Afrikaner had been striving for. But one had to ask: where the hell did the English-speakers, the blacks and the coloureds come into all of this?'

In 1966, after the second and successful assassination attempt on Verwoerd, Johannes Balthazar Vorster, an altogether more engaging man, became prime minister. Says Meiring of Vorster: 'I've never known better company on or off the golf course.' Helen Suzman found him truculent though 'with a wry sense of humour'. He was obsessed with law and order, a man who would tolerate no defiance of the laws. Indeed if Verwoerd's premiership witnessed the gradual construction of the giant race scheme, Vorster's period as Minister of Justice and then prime minister was marked by the imposition of sweeping security laws to counter black nationalist assaults on the apartheid citadel. In the wake of the National Party victory of 1948 several black nationalist organisations like the African National Congress had increased their campaigning in support of change. The South African Communist Party (having ditched its earlier defence of white workers in a white South Africa) had placed its support behind the black struggle. During the 1950s protests were called, much to the consternation of the government. The Suppression of Communism Act (1950) had banned the Communist Party, as well as the promotion or propagation of communism. The Public Safety Act (1953) empowered the government to declare a state of emergency, while the Criminal Law Amendment Act (1953) imposed severe penalties on those engaged in certain anti-government protests. The Unlawful Organisations Act (1960), banning the ANC and the Pan-Africanist Congress, was the government's response to what it saw as an insurrectionist threat following the Sharpeville massacre on 21 March 1960, when policemen guarding the township's police station shot dead sixty-nine blacks and wounded 178 others taking part in a protest against the pass laws which regulated the movements of black people.

Vorster, as justice minister, steered through parliament the General Law Amendment Act (1963) with its notorious 'ninety day clause' under which a police officer could arrest without a warrant anyone he suspected of sabotage and detain a person without trial for three months without access to a lawyer. Another clause empowered the minister to continue detaining a person sentenced for a 'political' offence even though he may have served his term of imprisonment. But this proved insufficient for Vorster in his attempts to control black resistance. Consequently the Criminal Procedure Amendment Act (1965) extended the detention period to 180 days. In 1967 the two laws were superseded by the Terrorism Act which finally established indefinite detention without trial.

Says Helen Suzman: 'Vorster goes down in history as the man who brought detention without trial to South Africa. His main concern was not so much the Verwoerd social experiment but the maintenance of white supremacy however that could be best achieved. But he was also a pragmatist and did away with some of the more absurd apartheid laws.' This pattern was to be followed by his successor P. W. Botha, who came to power in 1978 and under whose leadership the National Party was to mark its first forty years in power.

Might things have turned out differently if the National Party's narrow majority in 1948 had gone the other way and if the grand experiment of apartheid had not happened? Would things have been different had Smuts, the United Party leader, won the election?

Immediately following Union, the 'non-white question' had not played a prominent role in the political debate; the fate of the Afrikaner was a far more pressing concern. Gradually though, the issue crept up on successive governments. There was black encroachment into white areas, mainly by squatters; territorial segregation, as reflected in the Natives Land Act; and the removal in 1936 under Hertzog of the already limited black voting rights, became the thrust of government policy. Smuts acquiesced in the passing of the 1936 legislation. An internationalist and a conciliator between Boers and British he may have been, but Smuts was no closet liberal when it came to the question of the blacks. He was firmly of the view that blacks and whites should remain segregated in the urban areas, while the question of a black franchise was not of pressing concern to him. His view of the black problem was essentially a paternalistic one: that the whites had been placed in a privileged position in South Africa and therefore it was incumbent upon them to help uplift the living standards of their black countrymen, particularly in the rural areas and in the townships. He saw far-reaching dangers in integration but was realistic enough to recognise that the flow of blacks to the cities was unstoppable, observing that: 'Segregation tried to stop it. It has however accelerated. You might as well try to sweep the ocean back with a broom.' The findings of several reports in the years before 1948 had supported his view and suggested that an all-embracing solution to the 'native question' might not be the answer.

The Stallard Commission of 1922 had regarded the African presence in the cities as temporary, and therefore viewed the intermingling of the races as undesirable. But there was a slight shift of emphasis a decade later in the shape of the Native Economic Commission of 1932. Its report noted falling living standards in rural areas, with a scarcity of land for black farming; the migration of hundreds of thousands to the urban areas had resulted in 'permanent city dwellers' despite government laws to thwart the trend, a lesson which seems to have gone unheeded by the later architects of apartheid. In 1941 the Van Eck Commission on Industrial and Agricultural Requirements noted that the rural areas could not sustain the numbers living there and that a further move towards the cities was an 'economic necessity'. The migrant labour system was condemned both by the Smit Committee (1942) and in a report on the native reserves by the Social and Economic Planning Council which stated that 'the past half-century has witnessed a decline in the stability of native family life which constitutes a danger to the whole nation – black and white alike – in the spheres of health, of morality and of general social structure, peace, order, reasonable contentment, goodwill and a sense of national solidarity.'

The Fagan Commission – sitting immediately after the Second World War during which the pass laws had been suspended – opposed total segregation but concluded that the migration of blacks from country to city could not be halted. It dismissed as absurd the idea that blacks could be sent back to the reserves. The commission set out three possible options for South Africa's future race relations: total segregation, which it rejected as impractical; a policy of 'equalisation' between whites and non-whites without separation or discrimination, a course it also rejected on the grounds that there were irreconcilable differences between the races which had to be accommodated; and a third 'middle way', which accepted the presence of millions of urban blacks living close to whites but which sought to take account of the differences between them. In supporting the third option the report said:

> We admit that our enunciation of the policy which we have chosen as our guiding principle is very vague and general. That, however, is in our opinion inevitable. A formula with such elasticity leaves us ample scope for judging each particular problem in the light of its own circumstances. . . . The relationships [between the races], too, will always be fluctuating and changing and never stand still – and a cut and dried solution is therefore something that cannot be.

Oh that subsequent attempts at solving the black/white issue had started from such humble beginnings; that a willingness to admit to 'vague and general' principles, 'elasticity' and a wariness of 'cut and dried solutions' had been more in the minds of those who ran the country after 1948. The Fagan Commission was the antithesis, therefore, of the National Party's Sauer Commission which paved the way for apartheid, the specific, non-elastic, cut and dried solution to South Africa's problems.

It is fanciful to imagine that had Smuts won the 1948 election South Africa would have entered a racial paradise. But the healthy uncertainties of the Fagan Commission might have prevailed over the fantasies and single-mindedness reflected in Sauer's findings. There would not have been an immediate political solution – resolving the black franchise question might not have been achieved even by today. But South Africa might have benefited in the ensuing decades had the recognition of realities prevailed over the quest for the complete racial and political order. Time spent in trying to reverse the irreversible might have been better devoted to improving the lives of the millions of blacks who are part of South Africa. At the very least, the enormous hardships suffered by black people might not have been so widespread; the climate for negotiation might have been improved.

In seeking Utopia, the National Party ideologues of the past forty years tried to achieve what most political leaders of the twentieth century have come to recognise as unattainable. Instead of treating politics as the 'art of the possible' the Afrikaner nationalists came to regard it as the 'art of perfection'. Only recently have the Afrikaners begun to realise that their dreams, their fantasies are not going to be fulfilled.

CHAPTER THREE

Inside the Pressure Cooker

'Three die in family shooting.' This was the headline emblazoned on the front page of the *Citizen* newspaper on Monday, 21 March 1988. 'Man kills wife, mother-in-law and himself' said a secondary headline, with a report of an Afrikaner family feud which had led to the killings at a house near Johannesburg. The report went on:

> Two young brothers fled from their house at the weekend when their father opened fire on their mother and grandmother before turning the gun on himself. Mrs Rita Scheepers (41) and her husband Mr George Scheepers (36) were killed instantly. Mrs Scheepers' mother, Mrs Rina van Lingen (59), died later on Saturday in hospital. . . . Police said Mr Scheepers arrived at the house early on Saturday afternoon and tried to persuade his wife to return to him. An argument ensued and Mrs Scheepers was gunned down in the kitchen. She was shot three times – in the chest, leg and arm . . . Mrs van Lingen who apparently tried to intervene during the shooting was then shot. Mr Scheepers then moved to the lounge where he shot himself in the head with a .38 special revolver. Mrs Scheepers' brother said the couple had often quarrelled but that the family had 'not expected it to come to this.' He described his sister as 'an upright born-again Christian woman'. He said he believed the couple had still loved each other despite having separated two weeks ago. 'She said she would go back to him if he stopped his nonsense,' said the brother.

This was not an isolated instance of family slaughter followed by suicide. In another incident an Afrikaner businessman shot his wife and two children with a crossbow while they were asleep, then set fire to their luxury home and finally killed himself with a pistol. On another occasion five teenage boys committed suicide. The city of Pretoria, conservative and solidly Afrikaner, has one of the highest suicide rates in the world. The fact is that Afrikaners sometimes kill themselves in remarkably dramatic circumstances. And when they go, they tend to take others with them.

But why? After all, the Afrikaners are in the driving seat in South Africa, with little immediate threat to that supremacy. Yet large numbers of them feel less than secure. Most are not wealthy. There are a growing number of 'poor whites', victims of depressed economic times, for whom soup kitchens and welfare centres are available, a social service normally directed at deprived blacks. Some whites live in houses inferior to up-market properties in the black townships like Soweto. Many have rarely set foot beyond the towns or farms where they were born, let alone travelled abroad. Among the lower classes, particularly in the rural areas, some Afrikaners are still hillbillies. The women wear 1950s-style frocks adorned with *valletjies* (little falls), layers of frills which constitute 'style'. Safari suits, with short trousers and long socks, are the order of dress for the men, large stomachs often falling over the trouser belt resulting from a vast consumption of beer and barbecued steaks (still relatively inexpensive in South Africa), health warnings about the excessive intake of red meat falling on deaf ears.

Their lives become politically and mentally incestuous, a rigid adherence to received norms of living in which any threat to security or survival becomes exaggerated out of all proportion, where different ways of doing things are discouraged, and where whites and blacks are perceived to have their designated places in an order of things which should not be disturbed. The intrusions of the modern world into an existence that has remained largely undisturbed for three centuries are not easily tolerated or absorbed. The stresses involved in supporting the 'laager mentality' are sometimes overwhelming. When the cracks show – when personal inadequacies or problems coalesce with a general feeling of insecurity – then the Afrikaner is inclined to go over the top very quickly, directing his frustration against those closest to him and causing scores of deaths through family murders; there is also a high level of divorce and alcoholism.

Lloyd Vogelman, a psychologist who describes himself as a 'liberal', blames apartheid. Interviewed by Reuters news agency, he said apartheid increased the feeling of isolation on the part of South Africa's 5 million whites, resulting in hostility from the black community and condemnation by other countries. 'Apartheid,' he said 'is very broadly one of the most destructive elements in South Africa. It is incompatible with mental health and is the primary cause of violence in this country. . . . What we are seeing among whites is a feeling that they are losing power.'

This psychological trauma expresses itself through violence just as, so often in his history, the Afrikaner has had to resort to his rifle to extricate himself from threatening situations. The frontier wars of the eighteenth century against the 'kaffirs' and the battles with the Zulu battalions during the Great Trek have firmly convinced the Afrikaner that attack is the best form of defence. The pursuit of this strategy today is reflected in the not infrequent 'overkill' tactics employed by the riot police against anti-government demonstrators, and in the possession by many Afrikaners of personal weapons which they are not loath to use. Few would think twice about whether to apprehend a burglar or to call the police – they would rather shoot first and ask questions later. It is a brave motorist indeed who disputes the cause of a road accident. There have been occasions when one driver has pulled out a gun and killed the other.

Vogelman points to an authoritarian streak within Afrikaners which leads to a mental rigidity that makes it difficult for them to deal with problems flexibly. This, coupled with a strongly patriarchal streak within Afrikanerdom, results in instances in which fathers believe 'it is their God-given right to take the lives of their families'. Jan van Arkel of the Department of Practical Theology at the University of South Africa told the news agency that 'many whites felt a sense of hopelessness about the future.' He added: 'I think the negative expectation of the future plays a fairly significant role for whites.' Vogelman noted that, by contrast, similar cases of family murders among blacks were rare. The victims of the oppression and the daily drudgery imposed by apartheid appear to be more relaxed about life than those responsible for their misery.

The conclusion is that living within white South Africa can be a strain, and sometimes the strain becomes too much.

The pressure to conform is exerted from an early age with a demand for complete allegiance to Afrikaner culture, the church and the National Party (until the sizeable right-wing split of the 1980s made it respectable to support a party other than the Nationalists). Afrikaner family life is authoritarian and strict; there are well-defined community pecking orders. Conformity is encouraged from the Afrikaner child's first day at school.

The history of modern teaching in South Africa's schools has been intimately linked to the rise of Afrikaner nationalism and its aim of achieving the unity and supremacy of the Afrikaner people. The development of the Afrikaans language and its establishment as the medium of teaching in the country's schools proved an important vehicle in this endeavour. In the old Transvaal republic the Boers (whose Afrikaans language in day-to-day conversation had long since replaced the High Dutch of the early settlers) sought to withstand the growing influence of the *uitlanders* by trying to enforce a 'Dutch-only' policy in education. The *uitlanders* responded by establishing their own private English-language schools. However, after the Boer War, Lord Milner attempted to anglicise the education system as he had already anglicised much of the country's administration. This in turn provoked the emergence of private schools for the Afrikaner providing 'Christian-National education', a philosophy of teaching handed down by the high priests of Afrikaner nationalism and enshrining a view of life rooted in the Afrikaners' austere Calvinist faith. All teaching was in Dutch. It accorded with the creeds and tenets of the three Dutch Reformed churches and instilled into the pupil a strongly nationalistic view of past and present. Young Afrikaners were consequently convinced that their religion was reflected in their superiority as a separate ethnic group and was an instrument for the defence, promotion and survival of Afrikanerdom. Abraham Kuyper, a Dutch Calvinist theologian, had referred to 'sovereignty in one's own sphere' and had declared that each nation's separateness was ordained by divine will. Such ideas became the life-blood of the new Christian-National education administered to thousands of Afrikaner pupils.

In 1906 and 1907, just prior to Union, Smuts and Hertzog managed to persuade the authorities in both the Transvaal and the Orange Free State to reinstate Dutch as a medium of instruction up to Standard Five (age twelve) for pupils whose home language was Dutch. In deference to Afrikaner demands for a strong religious content in education, schools were compelled to begin each day with a religious assembly. This paved the way for the Afrikaners' Christian-National schools to enter the state system; they accepted English and Afrikaners at the same schools, but taught them separately. These were called 'parallel medium' schools. They were established where there were not enough children to justify 'single medium' schools.

But even this compromise did not satisfy the nationalist zealots, who devoted the ensuing three decades to agitating for the promotion of Afrikaans in schools and also for the effective adoption throughout the education system of Christian-National schooling. Their victory came in 1948 in the shape of a pamphlet secretly concocted during the war years under the auspices of the Institute for Christian-National Education. It was to have a profound influence on the future of South African education, paving the way for the National Education Policy Act of 1967 which enforced an existing system of separate primary and secondary schools for English and Afrikaners (although even in the former teaching was to be heavily influenced by the Christian-National philosophy).

The pamphlet also demanded separate education systems for African children (later provided through the Bantu Education Act of 1953) and for coloured and Indian children (which was instituted in the 1960s). It also stated that 'non-white education shall not be financed at the expense of white education'. This foreshadowed the very restricted financing of African education from 1955 until at least 1972.

Efforts to thwart the growing polarisation in schools had failed. In the five years before the Second World War Smuts and Hertzog had sought to unite English and Afrikaners, and a distinguished educationalist Dr E. G. Malherbe compiled a report called 'The Bilingual School', published in 1939. On the basis of interviews with 19,000 schoolchildren, Dr Malherbe recommended that the future education system of South Africa should be based upon 'dual medium' schools where both English and Afrikaans would be the languages of instruction. The Smuts government made plans to introduce such schools in 1948. The Institute for Christian-National Education quickly mobilised to stall the proposal and then kill it off, arguing that parents did not want their children taught in any language other than the mother tongue. It argued that because Afrikaner parents promised at the baptism of their children to bring them up in the spirit of the church, it was their right to demand the same of the schools their children attended. This resulted in an excessively authoritarian discipline which accorded with the narrow constraints of Calvinism.

Not surprisingly, as Christian-National education spread its tentacles the school boards were packed with clergymen. If, as a teacher, you were not 'well in' or you belonged to the wrong church, your chances of promotion in Afrikaans-medium schools were slim. History, geography and biology books were slanted in favour of the Afrikaner nationalists' view of man. It was taught that man evolved after the fall of Adam. Cavemen were a regression of the perfect man. To this day, evolution is not included in the biology syllabuses of South African schools. From their teaching, pupils inferred that black people were heathen and could not be equal to whites. There was heavy stress on conflict between blacks and whites;

blacks were seen as problems rather than people. In history lessons, the youth of Afrikanerdom was instructed that the British were villains who had stolen the Afrikaners' just rights. The study of comparative religion in the senior section of the religious education syllabus was forbidden.

In 1962, South Africa's first Education Advisory Council, comprising twenty-nine members, was set up. Dr Malherbe, who had spent twenty years as principal of the University of Natal and who had turned down the position of deputy-director of UNESCO (United Nations Educational, Scientific and Cultural Organisation) in order to continue devoting himself to South African teaching, was excluded from the committee.

The National Party rarely forgives those who stray from the fold, and it never forgave Dr Malherbe for his dangerous flirtation with non-sectarian teaching.

Instead a system of education evolved which isolated the Afrikaner not only from blacks but also, to a very large extent, from his English-speaking compatriots. The Christian-National insistence on mother-tongue instruction applied throughout the education system. The refusal to allow teachers of different races to be trained in the same institution or to permit non-racial state schools, even where parents favoured them, was likewise an expression of the doctrine.

It is only recently that younger Afrikaners have begun to break free from the constraints of decades of politically-inspired religious education.

Adriana van der Westhuizen (I have changed her name as she is a prominent public figure), now in her thirties and in many ways a 'detribalised Afrikaner', can still recall the pressures to conform to what she calls 'the tripod': Afrikaner culture, the Dutch Reformed Church and the National Party, all three combining to reinforce allegiance to Afrikaner nationalism. 'There was no overt pressure from the National Party,' she remembers, 'but it was always there.' She and her classmates sang strongly nationalist songs and the great Afrikaner leaders were extolled in lessons. 'No one said it out loud, but one was left with the firm impression that the National Party and the government were synonymous.'

Adriana recalls being led to church by her father, he wearing the Afrikaners' traditional dark Sunday suit, she in a neat dress, white shoes and socks, and a bonnet. They left the black servant at home. Adriana can remember asking why their servant was not allowed to accompany them to the same church. Her *dominee*'s response referred to 'differences in the way they [the blacks] worship'. The *dominee*'s sermons on most Sunday mornings had political or racial undertones: there was strong emphasis on the Afrikaners as a chosen race and Bible readings were selected to imply that Afrikaners were comparable to the ancient Israelites.

In school the teaching of history would revolve around the struggle of the Afrikaner. 'History was taught in such a way as to make the Afrikaner look good.' The Boer leaders were heroic figures who made immense sacrifices. They were depicted in a very sympathetic, uncritical light with stories of how the Boer families had trekked barefoot over the mountain tops and with photographs of women and children dying of hunger in the British concentration camps. European history was skimmed over – the French Revolution, recalls Adriana, was dismissed as 'a mob that got angry'. The philosophical dimension of the French Revolution and later European wars of liberation were barely touched on. There was little reference to the rise of African nationalism in what Adriana describes as her 'tunnel vision' schooling.

Adriana, like many South Africans, can vividly remember events when Verwoerd was assassinated in 1966:

> 'They interrupted the radio programmes and school classes were suspended. The teachers and the kids were crying. At the state funeral the troops on duty had tears streaming down their cheeks. Verwoerd had been a father figure for most Afrikaners, a charismatic leader. He was an honest man who told the whites they would be OK and the blacks would be despatched somewhere else. The *volk* were younger then. They needed someone like him, a man who could unite them.'

It was only when she went to university that Adriana's questioning of the political and religious norms of Afrikanerdom turned into rebellion. For the previous generation of whites the Sharpeville massacre of 1960 had been a turning point. Many whites believed their time was up in South Africa, many thought about emigrating, and international economic confidence in the country plummeted. For Adriana, her 'moment of realisation' came in 1975 and 1976 when she was a student at Stellenbosch University. Until then it had been easy for students to ignore the claims for black rights. Most blacks lived hundreds of miles away in the Transvaal or the eastern Cape. The western Cape, where Stellenbosch is situated, is largely populated by whites and coloureds. 'New students would arrive on the campus and on the first day enrol with the National Party student association along with the drama club or the rugby club, or whatever. If you asked them why they were joining the Nats and not the Progs [the liberal opposition Progressive Federal Party], they'd reply "because my father said so".'

The year 1975 was when the problem of black squatters erupted in nearby Cape Town. The settlement of squatters, homeless blacks from the impoverished *bantustans* attracted to the city in the hope of finding work, was accompanied by often ruthless attempts by the police to eradicate their primitive tin and wooden huts. People were forcibly removed from their homes, a policy which was to be used time and time again over the years wherever black communities – 'black spots' in the language of apartheid – had put down roots close to white areas. For young, liberal Afrikaners, already challenging the attitudes of their own tribe, such events resulted in a crisis of conscience, a spur to their hesitant departure from the all-embracing *laager*. The following year saw the outbreak of the riots in Soweto, the black ghetto city close to Johannesburg, after the government ruled that Afrikaans was to be the medium of teaching in black schools. Ministers ignored warnings from those close to the Soweto grass-roots that trouble was brewing. The violence spread to other black and coloured areas and 500 people died. 'Soweto broke out just before the start of the university vacation. I can remember my mother telephoning to order me to give Soweto a wide berth on the car journey home to Pretoria. We therefore had to undertake a long detour to bypass Soweto and Johannesburg.'

The return of boyfriends and fellow-students from the South African invasion of Angola in 1975 (in support of pro-western UNITA guerrillas against a new Cuban-backed Marxist government in Luanda), some of them wounded, many reluctant to talk about their experiences, aggravated Adriana's doubts about the direction in which the Afrikaner-dominated government was leading the country. Her concern grew with the violence of the mid-1980s and the accompanying political stalemate. Moreover, the post-war generation of Afrikaners like Adriana benefited from a standard of education denied their parents. Three or four years studying at university, combined with foreign travel, prompted a new enquiring spirit. Increased prosperity made younger Afrikaners more secure than their parents and grandparents; the more enlightened could afford to look beyond the narrow confines of ethnic nationalism.

In recent history Afrikaners have experienced two major adjustments to their lives. The early part of this century saw their transition from the country to the city, a traumatic upheaval for a people reared on the land, for whom the towns and cities were foreign territory. Their second adjustment has come more recently, as many Afrikaners join the ranks of the affluent. Some have become as prosperous as their English counterparts, their life styles as comfortable.

The family of Deon du Plessis (the journalist with the Cape Town newspaper the *Argus*) also took advantage of the new age of Afrikaner opportunity. His grandfather, J. J. du Plessis, left school in his teens with no money and only half an education. He found a job as a window cleaner in a store in Paarl in the western Cape. He ended up owning the store and hoped that his son (Deon's father) would join him in the business. But the son wanted to be a doctor and studied at the (English-speaking) University of Cape Town. He eventually became principal of the University of the Witwatersrand (also English-speaking) in Johannesburg. He is unusual among his generation of Afrikaners in having spent most of his life in a major city; that is a measure of how recently the Afrikaner has been exposed to the dynamics of modern urban living.

'My generation,' says Adriana van der Westhuizen, 'are the first to become Afrikaner capitalists in significant numbers. Agreed, Afrikaners have made it to the heights of big business before, but their numbers have been few. Today's Afrikaners are now to be found in merchant banking or on the Stock Exchange, the kind of places you would never have found them just a few years ago.' But despite their entry into the world of big money, traditionally occupied by English-speakers, do they remain Afrikaners first?

'They are first and foremost capitalists. They utilise their contacts in government and within top Nationalist circles. They criticise the government because it won't reform apartheid fast enough for their liking. They want the economy deregulated and privatised so as to create more wealth and with it, they hope, stability. If government policies hinder that process then they will call for greater liberalisation. But that is a long way from their contemplating black majority rule.'

The Afrikaner business elite still lead their separate lives, cut off from any significant social contact with English-speakers and blacks.

Nina Overton, Professor of Communications at the Randse Afrikaanse Universiteit (Rand Afrikaans University) in Johannesburg, is a 'new Afrikaner' who has rebelled against the traditions of her parents' generation. Attractive, fashionably dressed and outspoken, she is a world apart from the traditional image of the dutiful Afrikaner woman who keeps her place.

Her maiden name was van Rooyen, a family which her grandfather has traced to the very earliest Dutch settlers. Her father, whose family had settled in Natal, came to Johannesburg and shared the humiliation of the Afrikaners who converged on the big cities in hard economic times. He studied medicine at Witwatersrand University and applied for a postgraduate appointment at a Johannesburg hospital. But his application was resisted because he was regarded as a 'rabid Nationalist'. Says Nina: 'The Afrikaners weren't wanted. They were not good enough: not classy, refined or educated enough for the English-speakers.' They had little to support them. Unlike now, the Afrikaners did not own their own banks or building societies. 'You can understand and sympathise with their anger.' The tragedy, says Nina Overton, is that the Afrikaners who have been in power since 1948 have reinvented the wheel by pursuing a policy to exclude English-speakers and blacks. Nina's grandfather was a founder member of the secretive Afrikaner Broederbond; other relatives have been prominent in the Bond.

But the family has a strong streak of individuality. Nina says she was brought up to think for herself, so that she could look objectively at her parents' staunch Nationalism and question her people's devotion to Calvinism. For Nina, Calvinism represents a religious safe house for insecure Afrikaners. Another rebel in the family was her uncle – a writer and a doctor – who, although a member of the Broederbond, belonged in the 1970s to a group of free-thinking, anti-apartheid authors and poets known as Die Sewentigers (literally 'The Seventiers'). The van Rooyens lived in Victory Park, a Johannesburg suburb which is home to a large Jewish and other non-Afrikaner population. 'We were never a "Boerish" family,' recalls Nina. 'My parents were sophisticated people. They were typical of those Afrikaners who feel they do not want to give up their identity. But this did not prevent them from mixing with others or from travelling.'

As a young student, Nina began questioning her parents' outlook, challenging especially her father's suspected membership of the Broederbond. It was only when she read a book on the Broederbond – exposing its secret membership list – that Nina's suspicion was confirmed. This was in the 1970s, when for many the Broederbond conjured up sinister images of an organisation secretly orchestrating the affairs of state. 'How can you belong to such an organisation,' she demanded of her father, 'with all its rituals, its ceremonies and its exclusive promotion of members?'

Nina's contacts with black people were limited during her early years. 'We were brought up to have respect for our black servants. But we never really knew them.' It was only in 1983 that she first got to know black people on a one-to-one basis during a study trip to the United States with two other South African whites and four blacks. The visit took place shortly after a car bomb had exploded in the centre of Pretoria killing nineteen people and injuring many more. 'I was outraged when the English-speaker in the group informed us that he was in contact with the African National Congress [the main black nationalist movement fighting apartheid].' But after her fellow-visitor patiently explained his reasons for talking to the ANC she understood that by having no contact with the principal black nationalists she was missing a dimension to the South African situation. On the same trip, Nina recalls how the English-speaker in the group used to seek out the company of other whites in the evenings while the blacks and Afrikaners would get together. When Afrikaners make the effort to get to know black people they often find they have a lot in common. As Nina Overton puts it: 'The Afrikaners are a down-to-earth people. Like the blacks we have grown up from peasant stock. We've both had to toil the fields to survive.'

Are Afrikaners Europeans or Africans? Afrikaner politicians often claim to 'understand' Africans. P. W. Botha and Foreign Minister Pik Botha have often talked of the need to solve the region's conflicts on the basis of 'Africans talking to Africans' whether they be white or black. Pik Botha's claim to 'understand' blacks has some merit; he has frequently engaged in discussions with black leaders and, as an informal though tough negotiator, he often hits it off with his black counterparts.

But South Africa's other Afrikaner political chiefs know little of the lives of ordinary black people, as opposed to the often unrepresentative black 'leaders' wheeled into their offices so that they can claim to be 'talking to blacks'. P. W. Botha was once invited to the annual gathering of the Zionist Christian Church attended by hundreds of thousands of blacks, an event portrayed by the government propaganda machine as black South Africa opening its heart to the country's white leader. Botha visited townships in the Sharpeville area and because a few hundred blacks lined the streets and waved, Botha was suddenly transformed into the champion of township blacks. Such political manipulation is an abuse of the natural courtesy and warmth of many black people even towards their political enemies.

Nina Overton says this of the split African/European identity:

'We have more in common with Europe – Britain, France and Germany rather than America – than we do with Africa. Our values are European. But we are not living in Europe any more. We come from a group of European fanatics who fought for their religion and who could not live on in their own country.

We are still fanatic and our rigidity has been made more inflexible because we are a group of Europeans placed in a harsh, unforgiving continent where our lives are dominated by drought, flood and political problems.'

Nina was struck on her visit to the United States by Americans' dedication to causes – 'campaigns against smoking, campaigns against this and that'. 'I asked myself "Why?" The conclusion I reached is that Americans really do not have any serious problems confronting them whereas we Afrikaners – all South Africans – don't have time to fight causes because we are living out our problems every hour of the day.'

Insularity and isolation breed egocentricity. Afrikaners, indeed whites in general, often tend to believe that South Africa and its problems occupy the centre of world attention, that presidents and prime ministers do not go to bed at night without worrying about the latest situation in South Africa. Many Afrikaners still cling to the belief that they are a special or 'chosen' people whose survival is somehow more important than that of other nations in the world. That the international community is not overly worried about the Afrikaners' fate, that their problems are not unique and that people abroad ask why the Afrikaner often considers himself worthy of special treatment are questions shrugged off amid charges about mendacious foreigners.

Afrikaners, even those whose loyalty to the *volk* has weakened, remain constrained by a racially claustrophobic upbringing and by a church which told them that separateness was ordained by God. Any hostility towards blacks can be enhanced by two years' conscription in the army during which time young Afrikaners often confront black insurgents on the border or black demonstrators in the townships. For forty years apartheid was the answer. They would dearly have loved it to work; it was, for them, South Africa's 'ultimate solution'. The fact that, four decades on, the policy has failed has thrown Afrikanerdom into tribal and individual confusion. The *laager* may be under assault from outside – it has been since 1948 – but it is inside Afrikanerdom's drawn-up circle of ox-wagons that the real turmoil is taking place. The confusion has divided the *volk* to the left and to the right. It has left the guardian of apartheid, the National Party, desperately searching for a policy with which to replace it. Afrikanerdom today is in its most fractured and fluid state for years.

Nina Overton puts it like this: 'In the end the Afrikaner knows he cannot fight numbers. Moreover, they know they are living in a pressure cooker.'

The Afrikaner – possibly through his German component – displays a passion for order and compartmentalisation. But Africa is not an ordered continent. It is the continent of the shebeen, not the five-star hotel. The European sense of order rarely strikes a chord in Africa.

The Afrikaners claim to be 'of Africa' but their European roots linger, however detached they are from the mainstream of western ideas and culture. European history has passed them by. The French Revolution, with its Declaration of the

Rights of Man asserting that 'all men are born and remain free and equal in rights', did not filter through to the Afrikaner. Yet the Afrikaners still cling to what they believe are European 'standards'. During British rule the Boers were surrounded by swathes of pink on their map of southern Africa. Now the world beyond the *laager* is black and it is hostile. In being urged to seek a power-sharing accommodation with blacks, the Afrikaners are being asked for the first time to leave the white *laager* for good. For a century and a half the Afrikaners have enjoyed a secure base from which they ventured out to test the temperature of Africa, safe in the knowledge that they could always return to a haven where their European 'values' would be protected. The *laager* is an expression of the Afrikaners' failure to adjust completely to the land in which they live.

The Afrikaners' argument that they are an African tribe wishing to live as Africans among their black compatriots is not convincing. The Afrikaners have never really been able to meet Africa on its own terms. Their language, rich in African idioms, is for blacks the language of the squad car and of the oppressor, not a language of reconciliation between peoples. It is one of the many African tragedies that Afrikaans, spoken by thousands of blacks and mixed-race people, has come to be associated with racial exclusiveness. Blacks speak the language because they have to, whether in response to the security policeman, to the impatient government official or to the white *baas* (boss) or because they have grown up in an Afrikaner environment, not because they want to. Yet Afrikaans could so easily have become a medium of healing between the races because of what it has drawn from the rich soil of Africa. Not for one moment have Afrikaners thought how they might set their language free and remove it from the straitjacket of apartheid ideology so that blacks and others would be proud to use it. Afrikaans is a young language born on the African continent, but a language which might one day be lost because of its identification with Afrikaner power and privilege.

The Afrikaners over three centuries have failed to learn the great African quality of humility, genuine humility before God; they have proved extraordinarily insensitive to the hopes, fears and feelings of black Africans. Afrikaners need to lose their racial arrogance, but that may only come when they lose exclusive political power; such a transition will prove a great racial leveller in South Africa. It may be only then that Afrikaners can truly call themselves Africans. Africa has never really penetrated the minds of many Afrikaners. They hunt, they go on safari, they share with blacks the draining climate and landscape of Africa. The deeper meaning of the continent – its tides, its flows, its way of doing things – have left little impression upon many Afrikaners because, at the end of the day, they return to their European roots. As Zambian president Kenneth Kaunda has observed, the way Africans think is born out of their experiences; it is therefore very emotional and very deep. By contrast the Afrikaners, as Europeans, tend to think rationally or conceptually about the situation in which they find themselves. In a revealing moment during a break in talks in Cairo on resolving the Angolan and Namibian conflicts, Pik Botha – frustrated at getting nowhere during a particularly robust session – exclaimed:

'These people [the Angolans and Cubans] are different to us. They just don't talk like we do.'

The journey deeper into Africa is a relatively recent phenomenon for liberal Afrikaners, who have made the effort to step outside the *laager* in search of their black nationalist counterparts.

The Afrikaner was content as long as his Christian morality could justify apartheid. But once the policy began to fray, the Afrikaner found himself hopelessly disoriented. This confusion was bound to find expression in his politics, culminating in the schisms of the 1980s – the most serious divisions within the Afrikaner *volk* since the last century. Liberal Afrikaners searched for new policies and a new morality. Right-wingers saw nothing wrong with things as they stood: why change the policy of apartheid and the moral order which underpinned it? In between were the majority of Afrikaners still supporting the National Party. They believed that some aspects of apartheid had to be reformed but not its essential race-based principles. This gave rise to a grave moral crisis for the Afrikaner: how could he accept the need to reform elements of apartheid without acknowledging in the same breath the fallacy of its entire justification? The National Party's attempt to address this central dichotomy caused numerous contortions and raised a question for the first time in forty years as to whether the party had a future or whether it would collapse under the weight of its own inbuilt contradictions.

CHAPTER FOUR
Verwoerd's Children

The hundred-and-fiftieth anniversary of the Great Trek was not the only Afrikaner landmark during 1988. On 26 May the town of Parow near Cape Town held a rally to mark the National Party's forty years in power. It was a sorry occasion.

Parow town hall is not the most inspiring of buildings; inside, it is downright gloomy. Somehow this seems in keeping with the mood of the party. The cream of the Nationalist establishment are preening themselves for the party faithful. During the warm-up, waiting for the arrival of P. W. Botha, the audience sings 'When Irish Eyes are Smiling' – a note of solidarity with another old enemy of the British? The hall is packed with Nationalist MPs and their wives; the rest are civil servants bussed in from Acacia Park, the government complex near Cape Town where MPs and bureaucrats live behind concrete walls. The gallery of the town hall is virtually empty. You can count on one hand the members of the public.

P. W. Botha receives a respectful though hardly enthusiastic hearing. He pays tribute to previous Nationalist leaders, reasserts that one man, one vote won't work in South Africa and calls for self-discipline. Foreign Minister Pik Botha closes his eyes, but then he was up at four o'clock in the morning for a live satellite interview on US television. The party leaders appear tired and the party itself ideologically exhausted, a dinosaur left over from a past political age. The gathering may be honouring forty years of Nationalist rule but the party seems woefully short of ideas on how to survive the next forty. A civil servant leaving the meeting says he now knows why he no longer votes for the National Party.

Back in the 1960s when Prime Minister John Vorster began to relax certain aspects of 'petty apartheid' (for example segregated sport and separate bus queues) members of the ruling National Party could be divided into two groups: the *verligtes* (enlightened ones) and the *verkramptes* (narrow-minded ones). The former favoured relaxing 'petty apartheid' race laws. The *verkramptes* opposed this, demanding the retention of undiluted white supremacy. The National Party of today still consists of two broad strains of opinion but the labels have changed. No longer are the arguments over whether 'petty apartheid' should be abolished; the party has to varying degrees gone along with that for some time. The question now is about the division of power. Publicly at least, the National Party recognises that the Afrikaner can no longer wield exclusive control. It is how that power should be shared with the blacks that is the current debate within the party.

Some party members may share the views of the right-wing Conservative Party, which favours a return to the rigid apartheid of the Verwoerdian era, but they would constitute a small minority. The main body of the National Party is committed to reforming apartheid, conceding that the Afrikaners' huge experiment in social engineering, far from allowing the various race groups to fulfil their aspirations, has only stifled them politically and economically and threatened the stability of white South Africa in the process. Hence P. W. Botha embarked on a policy of measured reform at the beginning of the 1980s. But the questions to be asked were: how much reform, what kind of reform, what pace of reform and to what end?

Willem de Klerk, former editor of the Afrikaans newspaper *Rapport*, who first coined the *verligte* and *verkrampte* labels, now characterises today's National Party as consisting of 'conservative reformists', who are by far the majority, and 'liberal reformists', comprising around a quarter of the party's MPs.

The conservative reformists include most of the government. They are committed to the relaxation of apartheid in the economic and social fields, especially where black deprivation leads to discontent. The reform of the pass laws and the desegregation of central business districts in the major cities were examples of reforms carried out because black economic advancement was being thwarted and because the result would not dramatically change the political balance between blacks and whites. As for wider political reforms, the principle of 'group rights' (or political representation according to race) underpins consideration of dispensing power to blacks. The conservative reformists think in terms of an eventual race federation: separate racial authorities at local and regional level with the three-chamber parliament providing a central forum for whites, coloureds and Indians. The blacks would be represented through a central power-sharing body. The MPs in this section of the party are gradualists, concerned more with the pace of reform than with its content.

Two problems confront them. The belief in economic reform before political change rests on the assumption that blacks with more wealth and a higher standard of living will downgrade their political demands. This could prove a profound miscalculation. Far from eroding black political aspirations, the emergence of a more prosperous class of blacks and a new generation of black intellectuals – a genuine black middle class – may only sharpen political demands. After all, revolutions are rarely organised by the underprivileged mobs on the streets; they are simply cannon fodder for the real conspirators, namely the middle classes who have tasted the good life economically but who want their political deserts as well. Moreover, if black leaders continue to boycott racially based politics, how will the government find black representatives without co-opting 'moderates' who will quickly be branded as 'puppets'?

Moves towards a more equitable society are viewed as a process needing delicate handling. Renier Schoeman, MP for the Natal constituency of Umhlanga, calls it a 'social experiment' which must be carried out at the pace determined by the government. 'If the view gains ground that the National Party is not in control of reform – or if uncontrolled, involuntary reform occurs in response to external and internal forces – the party will have cooked its goose.'

Conservative Nationalists speak of 'calibrated reform' in which the political changes in the country build upon one another as the population (mainly the whites) grows accustomed to them. Says Schoeman:

'If in 1979 you had asked any Nationalist whether it was possible that coloureds and Indians would be in parliament within five years, ninety-eight per cent of them would probably have said "no". If the three-chamber parliament had not been introduced there is no way that we would today be discussing bringing blacks into government.'

Schoeman rejects the old categories of *verligte* and *verkrampte*; he regards himself as an 'orthodox' Afrikaner culturally, even though he attended an English-language school and university and has travelled widely abroad. His view is that the National Party is now less ideology-bound than at any time in its history. 'What's important now is arriving at the destination, not the route you take.'

But different routes can lead to different destinations and the point of departure is crucial. The National Party's programme of measured, cautious reform seeks to keep pace with the whites' readiness for change. But the speed of reform is substantially behind the expectations of the 30 million blacks. The conservative reformists at this stage believe the maintenance of 'group rights' to be non-negotiable. Says Schoeman:

'There is a need for accommodating blacks in a way which will not destroy the system. It is vital that white fears are allayed. I must say that one major fear on their part is that moderate black leaders, who are strong enough to withstand radical pressures, will not be forthcoming. There is an almost feverish wish on the part of whites for a strong and moderate category of black leaders who will understand the changes of attitude which whites are undergoing.'

For blacks this is all very well, but all the demands for understanding, patience and compassion are placed at their doorstep. The very people who have suffered at the hands of the minority are now being asked for forbearance until a political solution acceptable to their oppressors is reached. Even the word 'dispensation', used by the Nationalist government to indicate a sharing of power with people of colour, smacks of the white man granting favours to blacks.

Writing in the journal *Leadership* in 1987, Willem de Klerk said:

The conservative reformists want to maintain the status quo in content, tempo and style. There is a kind of messianism among them – that there is only one way, one truth and one life, and that is the current model. One senses a diminished urgency here, in terms of which it is argued that the pre-negotiation stage in which we currently find ourselves should be extended only with the greatest caution. They are prepared to compromise further, but only within the existing framework and with the emphasis on gradual change.

The liberal reformers may comprise a minority in the National Party, but if South Africa's politics become more fluid in the years ahead their role as standard-bearers of more extensive reform may become more influential. Their starting point is that the government should issue a declaration of intent pledging the complete eradication of apartheid as well as genuine negotiations with black nationalists without any preconditions. This group would regard the present government as having a transitional role paving the way towards a wider democracy.

The liberals' most significant point of departure from conservative Nationalists lies in their readiness to drop the whole concept of 'group rights'. Thus the crucial cornerstones of apartheid like the Group Areas Act, providing segregated housing, and the Population Registration Act, racially classifying all citizens, would be thrown into question. The substance of reform rather than its pace is therefore paramount.

One proposal would be to divide the country into fifteen or twenty provinces in which the population would vote on a one man, one vote basis regardless of race. There would be one federal parliament, which would probably result in a black majority government. Where would the protection lie for whites, given that very few would support such a system without cast-iron guarantees? Essentially any federal structure would include built-in protection of individual cultures and language, also a bill of rights, reinforced by a constitutional court, to uphold civil rights and human dignity.

Does this mean liberal Nationalists are prepared to consider unfettered one man, one vote – a complete abolition of 'group identity' upon which decades of Nationalist policy have been founded? Sakkie Louw, one of the new breed of younger Nationalist MPs, says all legally enforced racial segregation must go:

'From a political and a practical point of view it is a good thing that we recognise groups. It is a natural thing for people of similar cultures to gather together but this should not be legislated identity. There is after all a natural differentiation between a Zulu and a Xhosa. It is therefore unwise to believe that you can ignore the group concept. But such differentiation should not be based on law.'

Louw sees the government's plans for a national power-sharing forum (at which black representatives selected on the basis of race would be invited to negotiate a constitutional solution with the country's white rulers) as a starting point only. How would Louw and those who think like him envisage a political settlement which breaks away from the concept of legislated groups? 'Everybody must get his fair share and participate. We must therefore work out a constitutional structure which is not based on race.'

Louw favours a territorial federation or some form of devolved government defined not by race but by geographical boundaries. This is as close to the policy advocated for many years by the liberal opposition Progressive Federal Party as to make no difference. Such a system would almost certainly result in a government with a majority of black faces and a black head of state. 'I don't mind serving under a black president,' says Louw, 'so long as civilised standards and the rule of law are upheld.' South Africa's Foreign Minister Pik Botha was firmly slapped down by President Botha when he ventured similar views.

The question of entrenched protective clauses lies at the heart of the whites' discussions about power-sharing. They look at other African countries where black governments have replaced white and draw one conclusion: guarantees of whatever kind are not worth the paper they are written on. Zimbabwe provides the most recent example: there, as whites see it, President Mugabe scrapped reserved white seats at the earliest opportunity. What they forget to mention is that he abided by the 1980 Lancaster House independence agreement to the letter.

Liberal reformists believe that under a federal system white political parties could forge alliances with blacks sharing similar political attitudes. The thinking is that there are millions of blacks who do not support the ANC, as well as those viewed as 'radical' leaders like Archbishop Tutu or the coloured churchman Allan Boesak, who favour moderate government and who continue to have faith in the capitalist system. A black and white alliance of such interests, they assert, would be a powerful force in a post-apartheid South Africa.

Multiracial politics would therefore be the pattern to follow if the liberal wing of the National Party had its way. It is one of the most damning criticisms of the present government, casting doubt on its claim to be searching for a more equitable system, that after more than ten years of trumpeting its aim of a racially fair settlement, the party has shown not the slightest interest in extending its membership to coloureds and Indians (with whom it already participates in government) let alone to blacks, the target of its continuing power-sharing plans. Some Nationalists are prepared to move faster, insisting that talks with the ANC and other black nationalist organisations are inevitable. MP Albert Nothnagel told parliament: 'You cannot bluff yourself that with guns and violence you can erase the political ideals of [black] people.'

Willem de Klerk, in his *Leadership* article, said of the liberal reformists:

The more radical reformists wish partially to change the status quo by means of a new basic philosophy and new procedures. Their point of departure is that of a multiplicity of possibilities and an openness to a variety of possible models. A sharper sense of urgency results in talk of a leap of reform, to enable a move towards full negotiations as soon as possible. . . . They are still vague on details and exact alternatives, but a core consciousness exists on two points: the rejection of any kind of race federation and the urgent need for a leap of reform to further negotiation.

Speaking of himself and like-minded Nationalists, Sakkie Louw says: 'We are not the children of the Verwoerd era. We are looking at South Africa from a totally different situation.' He concedes that apartheid has caused South Africa an immense amount of harm. 'I cannot defend it. We have made a lot of mistakes.'

Louw admits that the liberals are in a minority in the National Party caucus, the vast majority of whom are still influenced by the ideas of the Verwoerdian era. He

57

believes that many younger MPs share his views on the way ahead. 'I have accepted the basis of reform and I go along with it. I accept its consequences. You cannot take reform to a certain stage and then stop. I have accepted that we will have to share South Africa with all its people. It is impossible to keep apartheid.'

From the mid-1980s onwards, as political violence intensified, there was talk of a group of 'New Nats', between twenty and fifty in number who, unless far-reaching reform was initiated, were prepared to sever their links with the National Party to form a new centrist grouping with the liberal Progressive Federal Party and others. It was hard to find anyone who would own up to being a potential defector, but still the rumours grew that liberal Nationalists were simply waiting for a senior party figure (Foreign Minister Pik Botha was mentioned) to defect and they would follow. Pik Botha himself dampened the expectations. This left the younger MPs in a quandary. As P. W. Botha's control over the party became near-total, the dispirited younger MPs either kept their thoughts to themselves or swallowed their doubts and disillusionment by accepting government positions and the accompanying 'perks'. They justified their acquiescence with the argument that by being closer to the centre of power they could exercise more influence on decision making. Possibly they were deceiving themselves. Not even more senior cabinet members dared to cross swords with Botha.

A formidable intellectual vanguard for the cause of liberal Nationalism lies outside the party, among Afrikaner academics and journalists. Two schools emerged. There were the so-called *neo-verligtes* (neo-enlightened) who came together in 1984 at the annual congress of the Reformatory Movement of South Africa. One of the participants, law professor Marinus Wiechers, explained to the *Financial Mail* political and economic weekly that old-style *verligtes* still believed in some kind of constitutional structure embodying group identification; this he labelled 'dolled-up apartheid'. The *neo-verligtes* were looking at the notion of an open society within a unitary state. At that stage the group appeared to believe that the National Party was still the most effective vehicle for change in South Africa but their loyalties were to be sorely tested in the years ahead. Another group, the *oorbeligtes* (super-enlightened), had at the same time become so disillusioned with the National Party that they had already made the break. Indeed Wiechers transferred his loyalties to the Democratic Party, whose formation was given the go-ahead in February 1989 by the leaders of the three principal anti-apartheid parties – the Progressive Federal Party, the Independent Party and the National Democratic Movement – after months of discussions on merging to form a new liberal movement. Two *oorbeligtes*, Hermann Giliomee and André du Toit of Cape Town University, made contact with the outlawed African National Congress, much to the anger of Botha's government.

One Nationalist politician refused to compromise his beliefs. Wynand Malan could not have come from more solid Afrikaner stock. His mother and father had been active in the *Ossewabrandwag* (Ox-Wagon Fire Guard, a right-wing group which supported Hitler in the Second World War), and both had helped build up the fledgling National Party. Malan was five years old when the party came to power in 1948 and he recalls listening to the election results on the radio. Every time a Transvaal seat fell to the Nationalists the family would burst into a rendering of the anthem of the old republic 'Kent gij dat Volk' ('Do you know that people'). When a constituency in the Orange Free State was won the anthem would be 'Heft burgers een lied der vryheid aan' ('Raise up a song of freedom').

After attending the University of Pretoria, Malan became active in National Party youth politics, joining the party's youth wing, the Nasionale Jeugbond, and a cultural organisation, the Junior Rapportryers, of which he became national chairman. But though a member of the party, his interest in politics dwindled during the mid-1970s because of the government's failure to enact significant reform. Malan flirted with municipal politics in Randburg, north-west of Johannesburg, but resigned from the local party committee in 1977 because of what he says was his disillusionment with politics. Five days later Prime Minister Vorster called a general election and Malan, though unhappy with the party's policies, agreed to stand as a candidate. He accepted that it was perhaps preferable to stay in the party and fight from within. As a measure of Afrikaner tribal loyalty, there had been no question of his joining the Progressive Federal Party despite his dissatisfaction with his own party. 'Belonging to the National Party was like growing up with a mother and father who are alcoholics – you wouldn't disown them.' His objective in entering parliament, he says, was to fight for black political rights.

What made Malan so concerned about black people when the rest of the party was still committed to Verwoerdian apartheid excluding blacks? Says Malan: 'I grew up in a home where justice and fairness were always the guidelines. Also, I had a law practice in Johannesburg. I met lots of black clients, many of whom just came in off the streets and against whom there was considerable prejudice on the part of the white staff. I could not live with the prejudices.'

As an MP Malan occasionally allowed himself to be optimistic about the future, especially when P. W. Botha came to power and called upon whites to 'adapt or die'. Despite the 1983 constitution which left blacks out in the cold, Malan still gave himself room for hope. A parliamentary reply from Botha saying he favoured normal patterns of residential settlement without force of law suggested to Malan that the president was considering the abolition of the Group Areas Act which provides for racially segregated residential zones. Even after the controversial 'Rubicon' speech, in which Botha refused to bow to international demands for far-reaching change, Malan gave him the benefit of the doubt. 'If you looked at the substance of the speech there was still the embryo of reform. But it was the "body language" of the speech – the delivery – that was all wrong. I was hoping P.W. had had an off-night. Knowing the man, that can happen from time to time.'

In 1986 a report by the advisory President's Council recommending the abolition of the Group Areas Act was leaked to the press. Here again was some hope. But Botha made clear that he would not tolerate the repeal of the act. The report was referred back to the committee and Botha told Nationalist MPs that any of them who 'had a problem' over this issue should go and see him. 'Normally

I would have laid low,' says Malan, 'but by this stage I was having a real struggle with my conscience.'

Malan's move towards the final break came over the fate of several black detainees (anti-government activists imprisoned without trial) whom he knew, particularly Vusi Khanyile, chairman of the National Education Crisis Committee which had tried to coordinate black pupil and parent demands in the schools protests of the mid-1980s. Malan considered that black leaders like Khanyile were against violence and committed to opening up parliamentary politics to include blacks. In Malan's view, Khanyile was exactly the kind of black representative the government should have been talking to. Khanyile had been detained, released and then re-detained by the security police. Malan felt strongly that security enforcement was being taken to the extreme; there appeared to be no coordination between the political and security agencies of the country. Malan requested a meeting with Botha, determined to make clear his views on two crucial areas. Firstly, the National Party's policy could not remain focused on separate race groups; Malan felt unable to back such a policy publicly. He also wanted to register his objection to the detention of black activists merely because they were strong political leaders, their views continually interpreted as subversive. An election was forthcoming and Malan knew he could not stand on a National Party platform. He contemplated getting out of politics altogether.

According to Malan, the Transvaal leader of the National Party F. W. de Klerk asked him whether he intended making 'a big fanfare' about leaving the party. Would he deliver a statement to the press outlining his reasons for quitting? Would he stand against the party? Malan told de Klerk: 'I don't intend telling the press that I am retiring for health reasons.' The showdown with Botha marked a turning point in Malan's career. His account of that meeting also provides an insight into the man who had dominated South African politics.

At his crucial meeting with Botha, Malan voiced his concern about the way the government's security policy was being applied. He said tough security laws were being enforced in a political vacuum. 'You cannot expect the bureaucracy to apply sensible security methods if they don't know what the political goal is,' Malan told Botha. Botha restated his position, arguing that Malan was not properly informed. The charge that its opponents 'do not have all the facts' is one frequently levelled by Pretoria to dismiss criticism. Apart from the sheer arrogance of such an assertion, it begs the question: 'Why don't they?'

Says Malan:

'I could not get it through to him that security cannot be divorced from politics. On the concept of "group" politics he wouldn't budge. This remained non-negotiable. The philosophy which came through what he was saying convinced me that I was doing the right thing in leaving the party. It was only then that the agonising stopped. I remember an enormous sense of relief that the burdens were at last off me.'

Following his resignation Malan received telephone calls from numerous supporters, including blacks. Some sent cheques. All conveyed the same message: 'Go back to parliament and fight as an independent.'

Malan says he had a 'feel' for P. W. Botha. 'Botha tried his utmost,' says Malan, 'but he could not understand why people were not falling over themselves thanking him.' Malan suspects that the major flaw in Botha's character is that he does not understand the concept of 'human dignity':

'To P.W. human dignity is not the inner self, not the human need to be, to act, to make decisions for oneself as an individual. To him dignity is all about the conditions that people live in – the norms forced upon people. Upgrading Alexandra township [a black housing area close to Johannesburg] gives blacks human dignity in Botha's eyes. What he is actually saying is: "For my purposes and for my interests, you may have something." He would worry about squatter problems but he would not allow squatters to change their situation themselves; instead, improved conditions are something he has to bestow upon them. When P. W. Botha says, "I grant you freedom of movement or I restore your South African citizenship," then he feels he has given somebody human dignity. He has no understanding that dignity is something which is inherently mine, that I have always had that freedom – along with my arms and my legs – and it is not something I need to thank him for. He is not being malicious in this approach. He is very sincere. Because he believes he is being sincere anyone who disagrees with him must be insincere. According to the extent to which he disagrees with a person, so he determines how far along the scale towards being a Marxist revolutionary he should place him.'

Malan recalls that at a news conference after his resignation Botha was asked about their meeting. The president had replied that Malan was not sincere because, as he had left the meeting, Malan had wept and had said, 'God bless you.' Malan remembers his departure from Botha's office as an emotional moment. After all, he was leaving the family to which he had belonged most of his life, deserting the party for which his parents had worked. He told Botha, 'I will pray for you'. Says Malan: 'Botha could not understand how I could become a political opponent and yet still pray for him.'

Botha's continual need to be thanked for his efforts may be traced to his childhood. He was a *laat lammetjie* (a late lamb) – a late arrival who may well have been spoilt by indulgent parents and elder sisters. Perhaps he was allowed to get his own way a little too often and this stayed with him throughout his political career. His anger can explode if opponents stand up to him. His search for recognition and gratitude made him increasingly unpredictable as Afrikaners – his own people – deserted left and right.

He was born in 1916 in the district of Paul Roux in the Orange Free State. Botha's father, a *bittereinder* in the Boer War, was a well-to-do farmer who took the young P. W. to political meetings, giving him his first taste of politics. His mother had been a prisoner in a British concentration camp. In 1936 Botha cut short his law studies at Grey University College in Bloemfontein without graduating, to become a National Party organiser in the southern Cape. When he later became prime minister, unkind critics pointed out that it was the first time that South Africa had been governed by a 'matric boy'. Having caught the eye of the Nationalist leader D. F. Malan, Botha subsequently filled several other party posts until his appointment as information officer in the run-up to what became the Nationalists' election victory in 1948. In his early days as a National Party organiser Botha earned a reputation as a disruptor of his opponents' political meetings. Later, as chief secretary of the National Party in the Cape province, Botha honed his talent as an organiser and as a ruthless suppressor of opposition. Brought into government by Verwoerd, Botha soon acquired cabinet rank as Minister of Coloured Affairs, enacting much of the political and social apartheid legislation inflicting second-class status upon mixed-race people. Some believe that Botha's part in subordinating the coloureds left him with something of a guilty conscience; perhaps one reason why he brought them back into parliament under his new 1983 constitution.

Later, as defence minister, Botha gained a reputation as a 'hawk', despatching South African troops deep into Angola in 1975. This was a controversial period in his career. The South African public was deliberately kept in the dark about their country's involvement, even when the casualties began returning from the 'operational area'. Botha's role in concealing the extent of South Africa's military operations presaged the wide-ranging clampdown on public debate about military and security issues when he became the country's leader. He adopted a tough posture on national security, cracking down hard on internal subversion as well as on neighbouring states allegedly harbouring insurgents belonging to the African National Congress. He was also impressed with the professionalism of the defence forces. Whatever the flaws of his policies Botha, as prime minister and later as president, fashioned a strongly technocratic government modelled on the efficiency he sees in the armed services. He became a 'hands-on' administrator. It was not surprising that when the government decided in June 1986 to suppress black unrest, the army was accorded an important role in returning the townships to 'normality'. Civil servants had failed, so Botha turned to the technocrats in the army to do the job.

Yet his streamlined administration was still dogged by political and security miscalculations for which no one appeared to be held accountable. Police shootings in the eastern Cape town of Uitenhage in 1985 resulted in the deaths of nineteen black protesters. A subsequent commission of enquiry, though acquitting the officer-in-charge of direct blame, found police procedures in the area to be severely wanting. At no stage, however, was it even hinted that the minister responsible or security chiefs should be held publicly accountable for the actions of the men under their command. Similarly, there was no public accountability when South African commandos were caught raiding the Angolan enclave of Cabinda in an abortive attempt to blow up the country's oil installations. Under Botha, South Africa's government may have improved the efficiency of its internal workings but the cost to the integrity of the public service has been high. On his election in 1978 Botha had committed himself to 'clean government' but his administration became tainted by mounting evidence of widespread corruption.

During the early part of his premiership, P. W. Botha seemed an innovator willing to attack some of the apartheid shibboleths. The rest of the world and his opponents at home may have sneered but, given the history of Afrikaner Nationalist policy, his reforms were almost revolutionary. Out went the barring of black trade unions; laws banning sex and marriage across the colour line were repealed; restrictions on the movements of black people were lifted when the influx control laws were overturned. Botha became the first South African premier to visit the black township of Soweto outside Johannesburg.

Arguably his most significant achievement was to change the nature of the political debate in South Africa. Previously it had been about how to keep blacks out. Under Botha the debate focused on how to bring them in. It is unlikely that Botha had any great master plan or secret agenda, as some suspected. The reforms were inspired less by Botha's concern for black political participation (the blacks' exclusion from the 1983 constitution was evidence of that) than by his resolve to maintain order and stability. This was the technocrat in him. Apartheid laws which threatened stability or whose abolition might help buy more time were quickly dispensed with. Even at the height of the turmoil of the mid-1980s several of these social or economic apartheid laws were removed from the statute book.

The reforms began returning South Africa to where it stood in the 1950s before Verwoerd's 'grand apartheid' took shape. But that was not sufficient. The world had not stood still in the intervening thirty years. The clamour for political equality among blacks and the demands made upon South Africa by the western world meant that the country could not simply return to toned-down racial discrimination.

As demands grew for more far-reaching changes, Botha considered that neither the blacks nor the international community were grateful to him for those reforms he had enacted. Certainly some of his actions had been brave indeed. But some reforms appeared to have been granted grudgingly, and questions of human dignity rarely entered into the argument. If the government had been considering fundamental reforms it might have used its vast propaganda resources to start preparing whites for changing times. All that emerged from Pretoria was a pop video entitled 'We all want a better future' conceived on the basis of dubious ideas about what constituted 'communication'. Public relations slowly edged out policy. The state-controlled broadcasting service – whose role as a propaganda vehicle is crucial in white politics – was deployed to help eclipse opponents.

Although its charter is modelled on that of the British Broadcasting Corporation, the South African Broadcasting Corporation (SABC) – through its news and current affairs programmes – bears little resemblance to the BBC's tradition of impartial and objective reporting. The Corporation was one of the organisations seized by the Afrikaner Broederbond after the Nationalists' election victory in

1948, and it slowly infiltrated its members into top positions. The National Party is thus given free rein to set the agenda for public debate on the nation's airwaves. Attention to opposition parties is often a token gesture – a reassurance to the white electorate that other parties do exist, that accusations of South Africa being a *de facto* one-party state are unjustified.

Throughout the violence of the 1980s a principal black opposition group, the United Democratic Front, was never offered a platform to explain why the black youths of South Africa were taking to the streets. By contrast, 'experts' from right-wing institutions in the United States pontificated on subjects like how the Soviet Union manipulates revolutionary movements including the African National Congress to further the spread of world communism, or how journalists are hoodwinked into spreading insurrection. The SABC also mounted debates and broadcast critical reports on 'liberation theology' (which sees the church acting as an agent of political change) to expose the dangers of revolutionary warfare sanctioned by priests. As for international news, the SABC often focuses on reports of other countries experiencing similar problems to South Africa and resorting to similar methods to deal with them. The SABC feasts on events like inner city race riots in Britain (the SABC's London correspondent delivering the questionable verdict that the riots were inspired by the nightly scenes on British television of black unrest in South Africa) and the imposition of news censorship in the Israeli-occupied West Bank and Gaza Strip. The SABC had a field day with the decision by the British government of Mrs Thatcher to ban broadcast interviews with certain political 'extremists' involved in the Irish question. Reports from other parts of Africa indicating the dire consequences of black majority rule are another favourite. Thus the inter-tribal violence in the Matabeleland province of Zimbabwe was given headline treatment (especially when whites were killed). The antics of former Ugandan leader Idi Amin were, of course, manna from heaven for the SABC.

Yet at one stage in the mid-1980s, when President Botha's reform programme was gathering pace, it looked as though the SABC was about to loosen itself from the shackles of the National Party and open up the political debate. Ensuring the continuance in office of the National Party was still the name of the game, but the government felt confident that its interests would not be seriously damaged by granting the SABC a little more licence. A new nightly current affairs programme called *Network*, launched in 1985, was modelled on the *Nightline* programme on the American ABC network. The *Nightline* team, under its presenter Ted Koppel, had earlier spent a week in South Africa broadcasting five programmes live. Koppel interviewed South African figures across the political spectrum, including P. W. Botha, Pik Botha, Archbishop Tutu and Sheena Duncan of the Black Sash women's civil rights group. The participants often engaged in the kind of cut-and-thrust discussion rarely seen on the SABC, which rebroadcast the programmes after they had been transmitted in the United States.

Apart from its content, *Nightline* also had a slick presentation. The producers brought the set from America, and the colourful, streamlined studio with banks of television monitor screens behind Koppel, hardly revolutionary for most western television services, was new to South Africans.

The conclusion reached by the government and the SABC was that television news and current affairs could be exploited as a powerful medium to prepare white South Africans for the coming changes. *Network* was the result. Interviewed by the *Sunday Times* of Johannesburg in August 1985, as the programme was being launched, an SABC editorial chief, Sakkie Burger, said: 'We intend to present the issues of the day in a more advanced television format. Credibility is the force behind top American television personalities like Ted Koppel, Dan Rather, Barbara Walters and Walter Cronkite. I want that for *Network*.' The programme got off to a promising start with discussions with black American civil rights campaigner Jesse Jackson and the liberal opposition MP Helen Suzman, and a debate on the Conservative Party's alternatives to Nationalist policies. By the following month Burger was quoted in the newspapers as saying: 'South Africans will continue to hear anti-South African opinion as they did with the item featuring Jesse Jackson.' The new approach was welcomed by other media. By October 1985 the television columnist of the *Star* newspaper, Ian Gray, was so impressed by the changes that he wrote: 'It would seem that white South Africans are prepared to pull their heads out of the sand and listen to the sort of views we have been denied on television for so long. Perhaps *Network* should have been introduced a few years ago.' The programme prospered for a few months but then suddenly the shutters came down again.

The swift change of direction coincided with President Botha's 'Rubicon' speech rejecting international demands for swifter apartheid reforms. The government and the SABC concluded that the more liberal approach towards the dissemination of news and current affairs had been an error. The right wing were then on the rise and making political capital out of the appearance of black leaders (however moderate) on *Network* while black rioters were setting fire to the townships.

Political interviewing and reporting were suddenly taken away from those who had fronted *Network*, while the morning news programme *Radio Today*, which had striven to maintain objective journalism, was similarly reined in. In the May 1987 general election campaign, Wynand Malan, standing as an Independent MP, was subjected to an excessive grilling during a *Network* interview. The campaign of another Independent, Dr Denis Worrall (the former South African ambassador to Britain who had just defected from the Nationalists), was recorded but the dramatic nature of his return from London and the manner in which he harnessed the support of the cream of enlightened Afrikanerdom was barely reflected. Increasingly the SABC came to mirror the world as seen by P. W. Botha. Any pretence by SABC chiefs to independent journalism was eventually shattered by what became known as the 'Hendrickse affair'.

The Reverend Allan Hendrickse, the mixed-race leader in the segregated tricameral parliament, led scores of his supporters on to a whites-only beach in Port Elizabeth to challenge the country's race laws. Given that Hendrickse was in the cabinet, one of only two members who were not white, his action was a profound embarrassment to Botha, who was infuriated. After several exchanges Hendrickse resigned from the government. He promptly popped up on *Network* to explain his reason for resigning, in terms that were hardly flattering to Botha. The president was outraged. The SABC's director-general Riaan Eksteen was hauled out of a cocktail party at a Cape Town hotel and virtually ordered to redress the coverage in Botha's favour before the programme went off the air. A statement by Botha was consequently read out at the end of the programme. Having incurred Botha's wrath, Eksteen was on a slippery slope which eventually led to his 'retirement' from the director-generalship with a substantial golden handshake.

The sacking left SABC journalists demoralised. Many believed that given more leeway the corporation could achieve a reputation for objective news coverage by allowing other parties and organisations access to the debate without necessarily surrendering the airwaves to revolutionaries. Instead they became even more frustrated, a frustration born of their brief experience of the SABC's 'Prague Spring'.

The crackdown on free expression resulted from an explosion of township violence. The limited commitment to black political participation became the first casualty of the growing right wing. Imaginative thinking dried up. Botha spoke of 'the outgrown concept of apartheid' but as pressure mounted his earlier reforming zeal was surrendered to the cause of maintaining Afrikaner unity. It was a lost cause, since the hard right had defected and were unlikely to return in the foreseeable future. There was much talk of the National Party writing off its right-wing defectors. Many felt that the party should give up attempts to woo them back and instead construct a new centrist constituency around moderate Afrikaners and English-speakers. Botha appeared paralysed by the right-wing threat, concerned not to go down in history as the man who split Afrikanerdom. The more Botha sought to appease the right wing the more credibility he lent them. Botha became the Conservative Party's most effective recruiting agent.

In a general election in May 1987 Botha virtually placed the country on a war footing to try to steal the right's thunder. Listening to Botha, voters would have believed the African National Congress to be at the gates of Pretoria. The old bogey of *swart gevaar* (the 'black threat' so often put forward by Nationalist politicians to justify the policies of the big stick) was resurrected and exploited to the full, while armed raids into neighbouring states served to fuel white unease, so much so that many did not believe the government had the resolve to defeat the perceived threat. Why have the National Party's *ersatz* version of apartheid and lukewarm defence when you could have the real thing with the Conservative Party? On the night of the election results, with the right wing eating into Nationalist support, Botha was fuming in the presidential office and summoning officials to explain why his election strategy had backfired.

For Nationalists like Sakkie Louw it was unacceptable for the party to kow-tow to the right-wing by slowing down the pace of reform. The Nationalists' task, in his view, is to make the Conservative Party irrelevant by setting a target date for the abolition of apartheid in a few years' time. In the search for a peaceful solution, Louw is prepared to join the increasing ranks of Afrikaners willing to sit down and negotiate with the African National Congress. 'The ANC cannot be ignored. If you ignore it, you cut your channels to most African nationalists. But the ANC must renounce violence. Most whites would rather join up with the right and the ultra-right than talk to an ANC committed to violence and a Marxist-Leninist government.'

Even so, Louw sees no future for a country with increasingly repressive security laws. 'No government will ever be able to maintain the status quo by force. The only solution is a political solution. You can staunch the situation for a while then you have to face up to the facts.'

Botha placed international diplomacy after the appeasement of the right. The few western leaders like Mrs Thatcher who withstood mounting pressure to invoke economic sanctions against South Africa were offered little ammunition to fight their corner, as Pretoria blithely tightened its grip on black nationalist opponents. The effective bannings of seventeen anti-apartheid organisations, including the United Democratic Front, and restrictions on the political activities of the giant labour federation COSATU (Congress of South African Trade Unions), were imposed by Botha in discussion with Defence Minister Magnus Malan and Law and Order Minister Adriaan Vlok, with scant consideration of international ramifications. Diplomats in South Africa's foreign service were exasperated by some of Botha's actions. Their warnings about the damaging effects of some of the government's decisions on international relations often failed to permeate through to Botha's office.

Instead Botha increasingly surrounded himself with 'the good news boys', men who owed their position to Botha. The President became divorced from many whites and insulated from the angry noises on the streets of the townships. That is not to say that Botha, with his shrewd political antennae, could not keep track of the undercurrents within white politics. But he appeared less and less inclined to respond.

Stellenbosch professor Sampie Terreblanche has a poignant comment on what many saw as Botha's isolation. During the twilight of the Vorster years, Terreblanche, then on the board of the South African Broadcasting Corporation, met Botha on a flight from Johannesburg to Cape Town. According to Terreblanche, he and Botha agreed that Vorster's premiership was not going well. Terreblanche suggested that the group of advisers around Vorster was becoming smaller and smaller and that they were telling him only what he wanted to hear. Says Terreblanche: 'P. W. threw his arms up in the air and exclaimed, "That's the problem!"'

Botha symbolised the insularity which characterised his government, a government filled largely with men whose experience of the world outside South Africa, indeed outside the National Party, was alarmingly limited. The yardsticks were missing. South Africa's little political cauldron was all that mattered.

Botha authorised armed raids into three neighbouring black states just as the Commonwealth Eminent Persons' Group (elder statesmen from Commonwealth nations sent to South Africa on a peace initiative) was making progress in mediation efforts between Pretoria and its black nationalist opponents. The raids were a cynical piece of warmongering which left a number of people dead or injured and which effectively scuttled the EPG initiative when there were encouraging signs. The EPG was fast approaching the moment when they would ask both the South African government and the African National Congress to show that their commitment to negotiation was genuine. Pretoria was not prepared to make such a commitment, fearing that it would place South Africa on an irreversible path towards a negotiated settlement and black majority rule. So the whole enterprise had to be brought to an end.

Internally, a system of joint management committees, including police and army chiefs, took control of wide areas of public administration, bypassing parliament and responsible directly to the top-secret State Security Council. Botha's 'total national strategy' or 'total government' to counter the perceived 'total onslaught' resulted in the armed forces being drawn inexorably into the workings of the body politic. The army thus became identified with the policies of one political party, thereby compromising its traditional role as the servant of the whole country and its people. Profound discontent built up within the National Party as MPs slowly realised that power had slipped from their hands and from parliament. Of course the government was still responsible to the legislature; without parliament's approval the budget could not go through. But under the state of emergency, power became centralised in Botha's office. Where the Conservative Party was beavering away at grass-roots level, knocking on doors and listening to people, the National Party had bestowed wide-ranging powers on generals, police chiefs and technocrats at the expense of party workers and members of parliament. Whilst the Conservative Party championed the cause of parliamentary politics, the government moved into the arena of junta politics.

Within the party, frustration built up because the regular caucus meetings ceased to be a forum for Nationalist parliamentarians to influence party policy. MPs emerged from the meetings to ask Afrikaner journalists what was going on in government. There was a strong and growing feeling that Nationalist MPs should be better consulted. After the May 1987 general election the new intake of MPs included several successful professional people. They ignored the party tradition of new members' reticence. After all, were these members expected to sit on the back benches for the next few years without letting their views be known?

Botha ended ten years as South Africa's leader lacking the vision required to complete the job he had started. Unable to see beyond the horizon of 'group rights', unwilling to initiate a debate which would take South Africa beyond its obsession with racial differentiation, determined to retain racially separate housing and education, Botha gave little encouragement to creative thinking in the National Party. Within the younger generation of Nationalists there were voices waiting to be heard. More than one influential Afrikaner figure said privately that with Botha clinging to office South Africa was facing the gravest leadership crisis in its history.

Helen Suzman has never believed Botha to be reformist at heart and regards him as a man of limited intellect. Her distaste for him goes back to the time of Verwoerd's assassination when Botha, in an explosion of anger, said: 'See what you liberals have done'. Through the speaker, she demanded and received a 'grudging apology'. Botha and Suzman never exchanged a word outside the chamber for more than thirty years until in March 1988 when, with her PFP leader, Mrs Suzman went to Botha to plead for clemency for the 'Sharpeville Six', a group of blacks facing the death penalty for the murder of the deputy mayor of the black township of Sharpeville.

Mrs Suzman concedes that during the ten years after Botha came to power there were many changes in South Africa, some of which were not simply cosmetic. Botha, in her view, accepted many economic realities which never crossed the minds of his predecessors, although he was prodded by his economic advisers. But, for her, there were limits to his reforming measures; he would not go along with anything that jeopardised white domination. In Mrs Suzman's view, the reforms came too late and were too hesitant – hence the right-wing surge and the disillusionment of blacks.

'Take the abolition of the pass laws [which regulated the movements of millions of blacks] – the most repressive laws on the statute book. They could have been abolished years ago to improve the climate for negotiation. But it came too late and the laws were repealed within a few days of the state of emergency being imposed, thereby undoing any goodwill that might have been accrued.'

Whatever enthusiasm Botha might have had for sharing power with other race groups was eclipsed when the township revolts began, the right wing emerged and international opinion turned against him. That point could have marked his finest hour. When the nation's fortunes were at their lowest, Botha, like Churchill, had an opportunity to seize the country by the neck and move it forward. He had acquired enough power. The security forces were back in control and the state of emergency had brought him a breathing space to think creatively. Instead that moment became Botha's nadir.

When Botha's new constitution abolished the position of prime minister and turned Botha himself into state president, newspaper articles described the new position as a 'Gaullist-style' presidency. The comparison between the South African and French constitutions was of no particular relevance. But the comparison which might have been drawn was between how General de Gaulle dealt with the Algerian question and how P. W. Botha planned to tackle his country's internal crisis. Of course, Algeria in the 1950s and South Africa today are not comparable; the Afrikaners, unlike the *pieds noirs* French Algerians, are not colonists. But the two leaders' style of crisis management may justifiably be compared.

De Gaulle returned to lead France in 1958, overran all opposition from the *colons* (French and other European settlers) in the OAS (*Organisation de l'Armée Secrète*), quashed an army rebellion and paved the way for Algerian independence. Botha allowed himself to drift, incapable of firing the country's imagination and unwilling to confront the forces ranged against him. Maybe he should have reformed more quickly and more fundamentally by announcing a timetable for black participation in government after admitting coloureds and Indians in 1983. There was always going to be a right-wing backlash of some kind. But some Conservative Party MPs acknowledge privately that Botha could have overwhelmed them if he had acted speedily and more decisively. In other words the pace of reform could have become unstoppable. Speaking in May 1988 Chief Buthelezi said:

'Had the state president in 1983 moved boldly to mount negotiations involving all South Africans to bring about a true democracy, we would by now have travelled a long way towards it and the extreme right wing would have been isolated as irrelevant. It is the weakness in his national leadership that has encouraged people like Dr Treurnicht to believe that the state president can be overcome.'

Instead Botha resented the fact that his reforms had not been appreciated by black people. He felt that blacks should be grateful for what he had done for them. Notwithstanding the imperial trappings of office, he was still the spoilt child waiting to be thanked, still the party in-fighter roughing up the opposition and protecting his own people. Unlike Churchill and de Gaulle, the accolade 'statesman' could not be bestowed upon Botha.

Unable to achieve any kind of settlement of South Africa's internal problems, Botha, perhaps considering his eventual place in history, cast his horizons wider. As he passed his tenth anniversary in power, he initiated a frenzied spate of regional diplomacy. Coinciding with diplomatic talks on ending the conflict in Angola and bringing Namibia to independence, Botha met several black African leaders in quick succession. In pursuit of the 'breakthrough into Africa' which had eluded his predecessors, Botha appeared to be striving for a new era of regional peace as his legacy to his country. It was uncertain however to what extent he could cement new relationships with black Africa. The feeling grew that, no matter what reform cards Botha still had to play, it was time to start a new game. A new leader, a new generation, was needed to take the 'great leap forward' that many considered vital, indeed inevitable.

Botha's wavering left the *volk* with little sense of direction. Deon du Plessis, deputy editor of the *Argus*, met a member of the Citizens' Army (the reserve force) at a *braaivleis* (barbecue) and witnessed grass-roots disillusionment with Botha. As the sun set, the reservist had to leave to take up guard duty. 'We must go and guard Botha's village', he said grudgingly. Du Plessis uses an Afrikaans word of his own invention – *onsheid* (oneness) – to capture the idea of the Afrikaner people moving forward together. That spirit was shattered under Botha, he says.

Another important phrase in Afrikaans reflects an Afrikaner's determination to extricate himself when the going gets tough. Says Deon du Plessis:

'If you're fighting in southern Angola and a tyre comes off the Ratel [armoured vehicle] and the shells are coming in, the troopies will say *'n Boer maak 'n plan* [a Boer makes a plan] and knuckle down to getting out of the situation as quickly as possible. Afrikaners see little evidence that this government has a plan and they don't feel happy with it.'

Nevertheless, P. W. Botha was the only anchor the Nationalists had. Whatever the misgivings about him, Botha was respected as the man who launched the reform programme, holding the party together under formidable pressures. When Nationalists looked left and right, they saw further reasons why they had to stick with Botha. A left-wing alliance would, in their view, have meant a collapse of the nation's security, while a government of the right would have led to a fascist nightmare. For most there was no choice but to stick with Botha during the years of instability in the mid-1980s. But once the violence had subsided and new political initiatives were required, it became increasingly evident that fresh blood was needed. In January 1989 Botha suffered what was officially described as a 'mild stroke'. Two weeks after leaving hospital he resigned as leader of the National Party, to be succeeded by the Transvaal Nationalist leader F. W. de Klerk. But Botha's retention of the state presidency gave rise to uncertainty about the country's political direction.

As long as the National Party led by de Klerk can build upon its more recent image as a reforming, technocratic party it should retain the support of most of its MPs and its voters. Says Sakkie Louw:

'I believe the National Party is the only party that can negotiate a future for the people. P. W. Botha opened up new avenues and in so doing produced a split within Afrikanerdom. He took the risk but got no thanks from the international community. While we were saying "we accept power-sharing", we obtained no counter-recognition from the outside world.'

There is a strong feeling in government that changes to apartheid laws are being hampered by the poor state of the economy. Reform costs money, argue government officials, and the financing of reform is being cut back because of international economic sanctions. There is little attempt in Pretoria to disguise the deeply felt anger at the United States, which is seen as the engine-room of the sanctions campaign.

Information Minister Stoffel van der Merwe says South Africa is now spending vast sums countering sanctions:

'Take the arms boycott. South Africa has withstood the boycott by building up its own arms-producing industry ARMSCOR [Armaments Development and Production Corporation]. We now produce the weapons we require. But, at what cost. There would have been more money for black education and housing and so on, if we had been able to buy our weapons. We are now reaching the point where reformist measures cannot continue at a satisfactory pace because of the lack of money.'

Sanctions and economic pressures permitting, what is the likely direction of National Party policy in the years ahead? Increasingly, government policy seems aimed at decentralising power to the fullest possible extent. Some kind of federal structure would appear to be the target; but not a western-style federation based on geographical division. As many in government see it, this might have been possible under Verwoerdian apartheid when the country was subject to geographical divisions (the 'commonwealth of nations') comprising 'white South Africa' and the black homelands. The population was less mobile in those days so a geographic division was thought possible. Conveniently, the demographic outline of 'grand apartheid' coincided with the country's racial boundaries. But that is no longer possible. Government thinking is that with increased movement of population, especially blacks leaving the homelands for the major conurbations, these divisions have become so blurred that a geographic carving-up of a future South Africa is now unrealistic. A strict racial division is no longer possible either. There are people in the country – black and white – for whom 'race' has lost its legitimacy as the criterion of their political and social aspirations.

On the other hand, there are thousands for whom race remains the yardstick. The government believes that ignoring such racial identities will mean disaster. Says Dr van der Merwe: 'So long as "group" feelings exist and you try to ignore them, then you have a recipe for oppression. You must give adequate protection for groups so that people have a sense of security.' The minister observes that the *Indaba* power-sharing plan, merging the black homeland of kwaZulu with the 'white' province of Natal (which would inevitably have led to a black majority administration), though an encouraging process, did not offer adequate protection for minority groups, especially the whites. Says van der Merwe, one of the younger, reform-minded cabinet members: 'Under the Indaba plan the cultural, linguistic and religious interests of the whites were protected but not their political claims. Their interests could therefore be harmed without their being able to do anything about it.' Van der Merwe reflects the concerns of the majority of South Africa's whites; that once a majority takes over, the minority will be oppressed. 'Oppression is obnoxious. It is unacceptable whether it is by a minority or a majority. The Jews were persecuted by a majority but that did not legitimise it.'

So the government feels it must continue to recognise the separate races as individual cultural and ethnic groups, while at the same time moving away from race as the principal criterion for the country's political arrangements.

If there is a model for how the government intends to readjust national politics to accommodate these competing demands, it lies perhaps in its handling of the sensitive issue of 'group areas' – the dividing up of the country's major towns and cities along racially segregated lines. The government has recognised that in many areas demographic forces have overtaken the law. Several suburbs of major cities have become 'multiracial'. People of different races, either through choice or

72

force of circumstance, are living together in a single suburb. Pretoria's response has been to accept that a certain dilution of the law is inevitable and that the racial divide can no longer be sacrosanct, whilst at the same time upholding segregation for those people who feel they still require the protection of the law to maintain the racial exclusivity of their particular area.

Similarly, in national politics, the government is likely to retain 'group rights' as the basis for sharing power, while at the same time accommodating those for whom race is not an important political or social issue. National Party policy might therefore be heading towards a devolved federal system based on one man, one vote, whose constituent parts will be part geographic, part racial and part economic, with citizens enjoying the freedom to associate or disassociate from the country's multitude of interest groups. In other words, the political system would still rest on the principle of 'group identity' but with a 'get-out' clause for those wishing to shed their group identification.

A National Council power-sharing forum, envisaged by the government as the vehicle for negotiating a constitutional settlement, has received little public support from a range of black leaders because of its racial complexion. So far only a few homeland and urban black representatives have expressed a willingness to serve on the body. Dr van der Merwe is not discouraged by this. 'You have to start somewhere,' he says. 'We cannot wait until everyone comes aboard. Moreover, it should be noted that the National Council has the power to re-compose itself so as to expand the basis of its membership.'

Confronting what is likely to be a long period of gradual change, Pretoria appears alert to the old adage that 'a government is at its weakest when it starts reforming'. Says van der Merwe:

'We have to reform in a phased way. We have to run the process according to what the traffic will take. The dilemma of a reform process is that by uplifting people you create rising expectations. Demands can quickly exceed expectations. The ensuing frustration can bring about revolution.

'We are entering a danger zone. Just like the early voortrekkers who crossed the Orange River, we know that in the short term it's probably safer to stay on this side of the river. We know there are dangerous rapids to cross to reach the other side. But we also know that in the long term our lives will be better once we reach the other side.'

The National Party's hesitant transition from Verwoerd-style apartheid to a more sophisticated form of racial separation has meant that thousands of whites have had to readjust their political horizons. The party followers were nurtured for years on the notion that Afrikaner nationalism – as pioneered by the Nationalist government, the FAK, the Broederbond and others – stood for separate development and the partition of the country into black and white states. The Afrikaner was told he would have responsibility for his own future while 'self-determination' would see to the political aspirations of blacks. These were the arrangements for the future, the Afrikaners were told.

The Afrikaners

The National Party's 1948 election victory was achieved because it won the support of three principal constituencies in white politics: the middle-class, urbanised Afrikaner; working-class Afrikaners; and the Afrikaners living on the *platteland* (rural areas). It was perhaps the working men who were most important to the National Party. Though mobilised by an intellectual elite, the party was essentially a force acting on behalf of blue-collar Afrikaners and cohorts of state employees. It is now seen by blue-collar workers and many junior civil servants as allying itself with capitalist interests and turning into a bourgeois party. The same conviction which drove Afrikaners out of Smuts' United Party (because it was identified with English-speaking finance) is now driving many of the present generation of working Afrikaners into the arms of the right wing because they see 'their' party as having sold out to both Afrikaner and English big business. They feel betrayed. The emergence of the Herstigte Nasionale Party – HNP (Reconstructed National Party) in the late 1960s resulted in a loss of support for the Nationalists among working-class Afrikaners in the cities. The Conservative Party started eating into the *platteland* vote in the early 1980s. This leaves the National Party with its support based predominantly on middle-class Afrikaners and English-speakers. That is not to say that there are not middle-class Afrikaners as well as English-speakers voting for the CP. At the other end of the political spectrum the support of liberal English-speakers for the Nationalists can be volatile.

The party began deviating from apartheid soon after Verwoerd's death. Says Carel Boshoff, organiser of the right-wing commemorative trek: 'After Verwoerd, the development of separate nations was still the government's policy, but not the viable development of black nations.' In other words, Boshoff and his followers condemn the government for establishing black homelands without granting them sufficient resources to sustain themselves. Because they are not going concerns economically, they cannot be self-sufficient politically. Hence, for the right wing, the government has welshed on the grand vision. Without a vision it has no policy. Without a policy it has no legitimacy. As Boshoff puts it: 'The National Party tried to solve physical problems with metaphysical answers.'

'We warned in 1981 what the consequences would be of the National Party's "reforms" under P. W. Botha. We told people that the direction in which the government was heading could only lead to total integration in which the Afrikaner would lose control over important matters like having his own schools, his own residential areas. The government's policy has been a very severe breakaway from how the Afrikaner understood his future would be in South Africa.'

Boshoff focuses on the crucial dilemma now facing the National Party. Just as Britain lost an empire and searched for a role, so the National Party has lost an ideology and is still searching for a policy. Amid that unsettling search for direction many Afrikaners yearn for a return to the old order. The National Party, in trying to steer people towards new realities (however cautious that attempt might be), is finding it to be a monumentally sensitive undertaking. The party is now reaping the rewards of decades of filling the minds of Afrikaners with propaganda about the total separation of the races, the 'black threat', reminders of the exclusivity of the Afrikaner and his sacred mission to civilise southern Africa. Now suddenly he is being asked to share power with the black man.

Afrikaners, not given to swift changes of pace or direction, found it difficult to reconcile these new ideas with the message of the past. They are confused and uncertain. For many the National Party remains the channel for change without whites' surrendering sovereignty over their own future. They see the party as resilient; its 'bulldog' image creates confidence among whites. Moreover they fear what would happen to the country's security situation if Nationalist support were seriously eroded. The party commands immense loyalty; for many, to leave would result in an identity crisis. In America voters support Republicans in one election, Democrats the next. Not in South Africa where voting patterns have been considerably more entrenched.

Can they believe the Nationalist government when it says that power-sharing will not lead to black majority rule? Those harbouring such doubts have proved a rich recruiting ground for the party which has taken up hardline apartheid where the National Party left off. The call by the Conservative Party for the Afrikaner to regain his own land, his own government and his own freedom proved magnetic to thousands of previously Nationalist supporters. No longer was the National Party the voice of Afrikaner nationalism. That role now fell to the CP, leaving the Nationalists to struggle for a new identity.

CHAPTER FIVE

Staring into the Abyss

Take the N3 highway leading south-east from Johannesburg towards Durban. Turn off on to the Route 23 country road after about sixty kilometres, and you are heading into the *platteland*, the conservative heartland of the Transvaal. Driving alongside mile upon mile of maize fields, skirting rows of giant wheat silos silhouetted against the skyline like space rockets on their launching pads, glimpsing isolated black settlements of mud or brick huts, their corrugated iron roofs held down by rocks or boulders against the swirling winds of the Transvaal dustbowl, you arrive after a two-hour journey at the town of Standerton. It is, perhaps, an appropriate place to go in search of the *broedertwis* (brother fighting against brother) that has shaken Afrikanerdom to its core.

On the league table of South African *dorps*, Standerton has a lot going for it: a railway station, a couple of hotels, a twenty-four hour petrol garage. It is a sleepy town. At the moderately fast food restaurant, the visitor from Johannesburg feels like a rare species. Outside the Carnegie Library, with a 'whites-only' sign above the door, is a memorial stone with a viewfinder pointing towards the sky which, according to the former town clerk, enables you to look directly at the Southern Cross. (It was cloudy the night I tried it.)

There are two drinking establishments in town. One is the genteel Standerton Hotel on what passes for the town square where, according to the locals, 'the Nats drink'. Round the corner at the more boisterous Toristo Hotel you'll find the right-wing Conservative Party supporters and the rougher types from the ultra-right *Afrikaner Weerstandsbeweging* (AWB) – the Afrikaner Resistance Movement. In the bar of the Toristo a tiny, bespectacled construction engineer from Scotland, out on contract and slightly the worse for wear after another boring evening's consumption of his native drink, is, perhaps bravely, weighing in with the CP locals. He praises Mrs Thatcher, which leaves them cold because these boys are barely aware of a wider world beyond Standerton, and lauds President Botha, saying everyone should give him the benefit of the doubt. This goes down like a lead balloon with the heavies in their khaki safari suits who are in from the farms for a hard night's intake of a favourite Afrikaner concoction – brandy and Coke. The AWB leader Eugene Terre Blanche once told me Afrikaners were uneducated when it came to drinking – he says he takes an occasional Scotch and water.

It's by-election time in Standerton, which for the locals possibly provides the most excitement in the town since the previous election in 1987, when the

76

Conservative Party seized the constituency from the Nationalists in a major upset. Standerton became one of twenty-two seats in the Transvaal to fall to the Conservative Party in an election which saw the right wing become the official opposition in parliament, displacing the liberal Progressive Federal Party. But then Standerton has always been a cockpit of feuding in Afrikaner politics. The town goes back to 1864 when Adriaan Hendrik Stander, one of the first people to move to the eastern Transvaal, settled on a farm on the banks of the Vaal River just south of what is now Standerton, on the border between the Transvaal and the Orange Free State. He named the farm, which he bought for today's equivalent of about seventeen pounds, *Grootverlangen* (Great longing). Stander was following the practice of many Afrikaner *voortrekkers* who upon finally establishing their homesteads – perhaps on a hillside somewhere, shaded by the trees, with a breathtaking view of the land that is now theirs – gave their new *boerewoning* (farmhouse) a name reflecting the years of struggle and yearning for a peaceful, final resting place on earth: names like *Hemel en Aarde* (Heaven and Earth) or *Rus en Vrede* (Quiet and Peace).

Stander borrowed the money to buy the farm from an English preacher; he shot local game and sold the skins in Durban to pay back the loan. Later, local Basotho tribesmen attacked the farm and killed one of Stander's sons. In 1875 the farm was bought by a syndicate of Afrikaner businessmen, and individual plots of land were sold off. The following year an application for the town to be granted official status was submitted to the British administrator of the Transvaal, Sir Theophilus Shepstone. This was approved in January 1879 after which Stander's Drift, as it had been known until then, became Stander's Town or Standerton.

But Standerton won its real place in Afrikaner history in the 1948 election. Standerton had been the seat of the United Party leader, General Smuts – former Boer leader, member of the Imperial War Cabinet during the First World War, and a principal drafter of the preamble to the United Nations charter, the latter something of an irony given South Africa's later pariah status within the world community. Smuts believed he had Standerton sewn up. But a few days before the election the party organisers sent him an urgent appeal to campaign personally in his constituency. Pre-election surveys were putting his National Party opponent, Wennie du Plessis, ahead. Smuts had to bring forward by a few days his seventy-eighth birthday celebrations in order to head for the constituency. He wrote to friends in England: 'I suppose I will win again, but in order to do that, I will have to campaign myself.'

When Smuts arrived in Standerton he expected to be welcomed by supporters on the outskirts of town. There weren't any. Everything was too quiet for his liking. His first meeting was docile; there were no National Party supporters present to heckle him. He was a seasoned enough politician to realise that their absence was simply intended to lull him into a false sense of security. On the eve of the election the two parties each held a ball at venues on either side of the town square. The Nationalist candidate du Plessis, hearing the music drifting over from the opposing camp, was said to have ventured the remarkably unoriginal comment: 'What do I hear? Is that a violin? Could it be Nero fiddling while Rome burns?' Smuts did not stay for the counting of the votes.

It's doubtful whether Standerton has changed much since Smuts' defeat. Certainly the election campaign could not have been more intense. The crucial battle today is between the Nationalists and the CP. All the trees in Piet Retief Street boast election placards with slogans which go to the very heart of the question: who, today, is a true Afrikaner? The Conservative Party advertisements, in the party's blue and yellow colours, ask, *Die Nattes weer glo*? (Would you believe the Nationalists again?) and call for support *Vir Blanke Voorbestaan* (For White Survival). The National Party displays – in the republic's national colours of white, orange and blue – offer 'realism, moderation and responsible government' as the way ahead compared to a 'dangerous future' with their Conservative Party opponents. *NP bouers of KP brekers* (NP builders or CP wreckers) is the National Party slogan.

The white, orange and blue colour scheme is continued at the headquarters of the NP candidate, Hennie Erasmus, a portly attorney imported from the town of Witbank outside the constituency to try to win back Standerton from the right wing. His office curtains are in the same colours. Mr Erasmus does not look like a winner. Already he is conceding that the result will be 'neck and neck', meaning he knows he's lost and is just hoping that the losing margin won't be much more than the 952 votes by which the CP won the previous time. Mr Erasmus acknowledges the issues which have driven traditional National Party supporters into the right-wing camp. 'There's a feeling that everything is been given to the blacks,' he says.

> 'People seem to believe that there are suddenly more blacks on the streets, more blacks in the shops. The town council has been considering opening up the central business district to all races – that hasn't helped. Plans for minor reforms to the Group Areas Act also worry them. My opponents have whipped up fears over these issues. People are now convinced that a black man opening a shop in the town centre today means black majority rule tomorrow.'

Of concern to Mr Erasmus, indeed to the National Party as a whole, is this: if the CP poll well in Standerton they'll be perceived as winners. 'People like to be identified with winners and not losers,' he concedes, 'and that could set off a bandwagon effect in the CP's favour.' Standerton is clearly an important constituency for the Nationalists to win back. The CP permeation of the farming areas of the Transvaal is already well established. But Standerton is only partly a rural constituency. As Hennie Erasmus explains it, only 20 per cent of the constituents are farmers, while 40 per cent are civil servants and the rest blue-collar employees, mainly miners and electricity workers. All three groups are aggrieved with government policies. The farmers are unhappy about the amounts of relief subsidies during several years of drought while the blue- and white-collar workers feel cheated over a proposed wage freeze. 'Lower white living standards are financing black advancement' is the cry.

Moreover, the whites of Standerton have thrust at them evidence of black progress at their expense even when they are away from their jobs on holiday. The desegregation of beaches in Durban, where many Transvaal whites take their holidays, has angered them. Says one of the constituents: 'There they are on the beaches, the blacks, thousands of them, urinating and fornicating in public.' Poorer whites from the Transvaal, staying in Durban's grim one- or two-star hotels and accustomed to having beaches of their own, feel threatened by blacks because they know that increasingly they will have to compete with them for jobs while the poorer housing zones in which they live might soon be open to blacks if the Group Areas Act is further relaxed. They don't want to be reminded of the blacks while on holiday. A few miles up the coast, however, in the swanky resort of Umhlanga where richer whites from the northern suburbs of Johannesburg go to perfect their sun tans, no such tensions arise. Black children can be seen riding the surf waves and ignoring the shark warnings over the public address system along with the white kids. But neither the white children nor their parents are worried about the blacks because they know that even if group areas segregation were relaxed the chances of a black person being able to afford a house in their area are slim; and anyway, even if he could, he would be a 'nice type of black'.

The traditional National Party supporters in Standerton are more genteel than their CP counterparts. Their candidate, Mr Erasmus, takes me on a drive some eight miles out of town to the farm *Goedgevonden* (Well-found) of Marie and Tol van der Linde. This is big farming business. There are over a dozen tractors lined up in the farmyard while Mr van der Linde's crop-spraying plane is buzzing overhead. Over coffee in their plush modern home, looking out over a *dam* (man-made lake), Mrs van der Linde admits to being scared by the prospect of the Conservative Party ever taking over. She's not worried about the reaction of her own blacks, she explains.

'We all live happily here. But what about the blacks working on the farm of my neighbour who's a CP supporter? It won't be my blacks that come and kill me. But the blacks next door might come over and murder me, just to show how unhappy they are under a CP government.'

We drive from the farmhouse to the small black community on the van der Lindes' farm. The development here is a credit to the couple. Their thirty or so migrant farm workers are allowed to have their families from the homelands living with them, thereby avoiding the disruption of family life that has affected millions of blacks under apartheid's notorious influx control laws which, until their abolition in 1986, regulated the movement of blacks. On a hillside on their 3600 hectares, the van der Lindes have built homes for all their black workers and their families: small houses, each with a couple of bedrooms, a kitchen and a bathroom – better than most of the homes in black townships. At the centre of this very settled black community is a school which was also built from the van der Lindes' own funds, although they are now receiving sponsorship for the school from a local company. The black children are neatly dressed in smart school uniforms. There are three black teachers at the school and a black headmaster. In honour of Mr Erasmus's visit, the pupils sing their school song '*Ubani Ban-*

79

twana?' ('Who are the children?') in Zulu. Photographs of successive National Party prime ministers are mounted on the classroom wall.

Back at the farmhouse, Mrs van der Linde shows me her photograph album which proudly catalogues the history of her black 'family'. There's Josephine with the first of her five children to survive infancy, seen in the photo carrying her baby African-style nestled snugly inside a blanket on her back. 'They never used to go to doctors,' explains Mrs van der Linde, who also shows me a reference book she keeps, with a page for each member of the settlement: a record of which men get drunk, which women are not using contraceptives, etc.

Says Mrs van der Linde: 'We live our separate lives. But we get together at times. Often we have a cup of tea with them.' I ask her husband whether he can foresee a black government in South Africa. 'Look,' he replies, 'there are respectable black doctors and lawyers who don't have the vote, whereas there are rough blue-collar workers among the whites who drink themselves into a stupor and then go home and beat up their wives. And yet they have the vote. So the blacks ought to be given a place in government.' But Mr van der Linde doubts whether there will ever be a black president of South Africa.

Such comments are typical of how well-meaning, paternalistic Afrikaners like the van der Lindes feel about blacks: they are prepared to afford them what they regard as a dignified, albeit separate, life; they are willing to take tea with them at times. They realise that certain apartheid laws will have to go and that blacks and whites do have to exist within the same country. Their convictions rest on the same principles that have guided the Afrikaner through four decades of apartheid: a belief that he has a mission ordained by God to bring Christianity and civilisation to the indigenous peoples. But those same Christian principles also mean the van der Lindes, and others like them, could never envisage the blacks running the country.

It is, though, the mere prospect of whites and blacks coexisting within the same country that has accounted in large measure for the rise of the Conservative Party. The CP candidate in Standerton is Rosier de Ville, who owns a Cape Dutch-style farmhouse, unusual for this part of the country. Unlike the van der Lindes' farm, which has minimal security, the de Ville homestead is surrounded by a twelve-foot fence. Mr de Ville says the fence is to deter petty criminals in the area. Yet one cannot help feeling that he has already battened down the hatches for the revolution.

While Mr de Ville cooks the chunky steaks and *boerewors* (sausage) over a *braaivleis* (barbecue), his wife, wafting away the flies, explains why she defected from the Nationalists to the CP.

'I didn't cross over because of my husband,' she insists, denying the strong political tradition in South Africa of a wife dutifully following her husband into the voting booth to mark her X on the same spot. 'I just went along to a few meetings, studied the Conservative Party policies and compared them to those of the government. I felt the CP had the only solution: that South Africa should become like Europe with each nation having its own government. The same should apply here: separate governments for separate people, not because they are black or white, you understand, but because even the individual black tribes with their different cultures want to govern themselves and not be ruled by other black groups.'

We go inside for lunch, passing a huge leather-bound Bible on a desk in the hallway. 'It's written in High Dutch,' says Mrs de Ville. 'Probably brought out by one of the early settlers.' Mr de Ville clasps his wife's hand to say grace.

As we eat, Mr de Ville explains why he believes the Nationalist government is selling out the whites:

'You cannot allow blacks to have sex with whites, to live with them and to marry them; you cannot start watering down the Group Areas Act so that blacks can move into white areas; you can't give them local government rights and offer them national power-sharing and expect it all to end there. It's bound to result in black majority rule and the extinction of the white man in Africa. There is no other way.'

Mr de Ville excuses himself. He has to shower, change and meet the party leader, Dr Andries Treurnicht, who has driven from Pretoria to address a major CP rally that night. Treurnicht pulls in a large crowd. Party organisers provide closed-circuit television screens for those outside who cannot get in. Across town, President Botha is due to address a Nationalist meeting. Bad weather prevents his helicopter landing, so he has to make the journey by car, arriving two hours late, by which time the master of ceremonies has exhausted the repertoire of Afrikaner folk songs which always precede political meetings in South Africa. In deference to the large number of English-speakers who have recently filled the vacuum in National Party support left by Afrikaner defections to the right, they also sing 'She'll be coming round the mountain when she comes.'

After the Nationalists' meeting I snatch a word with Mr Erasmus. He's looking gloomy: no longer talking about a neck-and-neck finish, speculating instead on the size of the Conservative majority. He says to me: 'If the CP majority goes up from 952 to 2000, I will lose my faith in my fellow-Afrikaners.'

To discredit the Conservative Party, the Nationalists bring up their big guns in the Afrikaans press in a concerted effort to convince white voters that the right wing has been hijacked by the far-right AWB. *Beeld* and *Die Burger* – the flagships of the staunchly pro-government *Nasionale Pers* newspaper group – publish the transcript of a bugged telephone conversation between a right-wing politician and the AWB's deputy leader; this, it's claimed, demonstrates that the AWB has laid down certain conditions to the CP for its support, namely that the CP, if elected to government, should implement the AWB's plan for a *Boerestaat* (Boers' State). The two papers carry the kind of propaganda against the 'CP–AWB alliance' normally reserved for the ANC and the South African Communist Party. It's claimed that several CP members of parliament belong to the AWB. On the CP hustings in Standerton, *Beeld*'s name is dirt. Even the foreign correspondent of the BBC, an organisation which rarely endears itself to white South Africans, is

81

more welcome than the man from *Beeld*, which must register as one of the more extraordinary results of the schism within Afrikanerdom. The press campaign misfires dramatically for the Nationalists. The majority of voters in Standerton are not the least bit bothered about where the CP gets its support from as long as that support helps stop P. W. Botha.

A few days before the poll both parties in Standerton delay the start of their scheduled election meetings to allow voters to tune in to what is billed as 'South Africa's first Kennedy/Nixon-style television clash.' The South African Broadcasting Corporation has agreed to a televised debate between the CP leader Dr Treurnicht and the National Party's Transvaal leader F. W. de Klerk. Both sides are clearly nervous about the debate. Senior government politicians have rarely been confronted with such a challenge. They have never had to develop a slick, American-style TV performance. Indeed one or two cabinet ministers are renowned for being totally incomprehensible on television. In the run-up to the debate, newspapers recall how Richard Nixon, confronting Senator Kennedy in 1960, may have lost the presidential election because he had not shaved properly, not the kind of 'image problem' that South African ministers have had to concern themselves with before. For Treurnicht the debate is an important opportunity to establish himself as a potential national leader although, like de Klerk, he cannot afford to be mauled. The arrangements for the televised debate are the lead item on the morning news. It soon becomes apparent that there is absolutely no risk of de Klerk being embarrassed, since the debate is going to be carefully structured and controlled, with both participants allotted equal time to debate each topic, with no interruptions or cut-and-thrust discussion. An impartial politician will ensure fair play, as Dr Treurnicht refuses to accept one of the SABC's political journalists as chairman, believing they are in the lap of the National Party.

The debate turns out to be more like a championship chess match than a battle of political Titans.

In an opening move Treurnicht warns of the 'red lights flickering' as far as the National Party's vision is concerned. The Nationalists, he says, are

'. . . creating a constitutional system and political structures which will amount to a situation where, in an undivided land and with a universal franchise, with equal treatment and equal opportunities and the right of all these [different racial] communities to make joint decisions at the highest level, which means it will also involve twenty million blacks in the same dispensation, then it is creating a dispensation in which we run the risk of not only coloureds and Indians, but the white community in particular, being swamped, overwhelmed and overpowered by a black majority and a black majority government.'

De Klerk's response is equally assertive but hardly any more intelligible. He condemns the CP's policies as pie-in-the-sky:

'If you admit that you will have millions of people of colour in the same country as the whites for all time and want to give sole sovereignty to whites, the inevitable consequence is that those, who together with you and together with us as whites, will have to live in such a country in an inferior position into perpetuity.'

The debate is now into its middle game, with de Klerk hoping to make some mileage out of the CP's alleged links with the AWB. The Nationalists are pinning their hopes on ordinary white voters being scared off the CP if they think that the CP is involved with what many perceive as neo-fascist bully-boys. De Klerk refers to the AWB's breaking-up of meetings including one recently addressed by himself (an outrageous complaint given that the National Party's own strong-arm boys, using similar tactics, were in no small way responsible for the Nationalists themselves coming to power in 1948). De Klerk goes for the jugular: '. . . the Conservative Party must answer to those of your supporters – decent Afrikaner people, Calvinists – who do not want anything to do with these things [the AWB's tactics and policies]'. The good doctor refuses to be thrown off his stride, declaring: 'I defend the right of an organisation to join me in resisting the dangerous direction you are taking.'

In the endgame, Dr Treurnicht presses home his party's objections to the dilution of the Group Areas Act, particularly in those 'grey areas' of big cities like Johannesburg where blacks have crept into previously white suburbs. The CP leader launches his attack: 'You have neglected to protect those [white] people, their property and their community life and now there is great anxiety – more than anxiety, great resentment – among many people who say "We are not being protected, we are being forced out." When you wake up one morning there are non-whites in the flat next door.' Mr de Klerk's final word is this: 'If we live in the same country, and this is the reality for which your party has no answer, we will have to, unless we stand for continued white domination, we will have to find a way, in which without domination, we also afford those people a fair chance. Fair participation in decision-making.'

Thus the debate drifts towards a stalemate; except, of course, that Treurnicht has really won hands-down by seeing to it that the debate was fought almost entirely around the issue which is the CP's biggest crowd-puller – the freedom of the whites. De Klerk has little opportunity to develop any positive ideas on power-sharing with blacks. He's on the defensive throughout, trying to reassure those drifting to the right.

As the weekly *Financial Mail* observed afterwards: 'For fifty minutes the screen was filled with two Afrikaners engaged in an obscure tussle over what kind of apartheid is justifiable.'

By 1.30 a.m. on Standerton's election night, the Nationalists are nowhere to be seen. Their posters lie sadly in puddles of rainwater. The CP supporters have been celebrating victory for several hours already. The returning officer, fighting to be heard above the white supremacist chanting on the steps of the town hall, announces a CP majority of 2854.

Like Smuts forty years before him, Hennie Erasmus, his faith in Afrikanerdom destroyed, has not bothered to stick around for the declaration.

On the same night that de Ville notched up his sweeping victory, another CP member was returned to parliament in the constituency of Schweizer-Reneke on the western side of the Transvaal. Pieter Mulder is of solid Afrikaner stock. His father Connie Mulder (who died in January 1988) was the information minister at the time of the infamous 'Muldergate' scandal, when it was discovered that his department had laundered vast amounts of public money to finance propaganda drives at home and overseas to improve South Africa's image. The scandal cost Mulder his cabinet job and the position of Transvaal leader of the National Party, a relegation which cast him into the wilderness until he eventually found a new political home when the Conservative Party emerged in 1982.

Mulder's family has a long history of commitment to the Afrikaner cause. Pieter Mulder recounts that his grandfather fought on the side of the Boers, while his grandmother Maria Potgieter was incarcerated in a concentration camp at the age of sixteen. Her mother had died very young and Maria had to look after her four brothers, two of whom died in the camp. She nursed one of her brothers, a four-year-old suffering from measles. 'The lad was afraid of the dark so they kept a small light burning after dark. The British guard came round and ordered "lights out", kicking out the flame as he ignored the pleas of the family. That night the boy died. That story has been told and re-told over the years at family gatherings.' The British destruction of the family farmstead also became part of the Mulders' folklore. Returning to their home after the Boer War, Mulder's mother found the house burned to the ground. Only the charred wooden frame of the front door was still standing. When she rebuilt the home, the frame remained in place as a lasting reminder of the suffering of the Afrikaners.

The Mulders reluctantly accepted the Peace of Vereeniging ending the Boer War, but in the First World War there was a bitter family division when one son fought on the side of the British while his younger brother joined the rebellion against South Africa's entry into the war. For a time the younger brother was on death row, having been falsely accused of killing someone until the supposed victim of the murder suddenly made an appearance. For Pieter Mulder the lessons of the past – of the history of a nation fighting for its freedom – cannot be forgotten in the politics of today:

> 'British South Africa was based on colonial borders. When the British left we Afrikaners found ourselves to be the colonial power faced with the problem of what to do about millions of blacks living amongst us and specifically how to grant them freedom. Because we are Afrikaners we understand what freedom is all about. But the question has to be asked: "Are whites to lose their freedom now?"'

Mulder admits that a political philosophy based on racial groupings may be strange to an Englishman, whose political system places a greater emphasis on the individual. However he notes that India was partitioned on the basis of religious groups. Mulder and his fellow Conservative MPs contend that nowhere in the world has power-sharing worked. Mulder cites the example of Lebanon. He points to Israel's problems with the Palestinians, saying the Israelis should either give autonomy to Arabs in the occupied territories or else admit them to the Knesset (Israeli parliament). The Israelis cannot have it both ways, he believes:

'What would survive under black majority rule? That course is a high-risk policy because if things turn out badly you cannot return to the way things were before. I would be stupid to enter a power-sharing deal. If I were living in Europe or the United States where there is a respect for democracy then I would be prepared to take the risk but not in Africa.'

Mulder argues like most white South Africans when the West calls for one man, one vote. 'Look at the rest of Africa. No capitalism. No moderates. No multi-party governments.'

Traditional western-style democracy is not the answer for Mulder in that 'if we give the blacks power how will we check them?' The danger in the government's plan, he warns, is that if it runs its full course there would be 600 black MPs and 160 whites, which means the whites would lose power and control of the army. Instead Mulder wants partition for South Africa's white and black peoples. He acknowledges that this would mean a smaller 'white South Africa'. 'Each "state" would have its own government and its own powers. They would co-operate economically and militarily – just like the European Common Market.' Does he consider himself a racist by upholding the policy of apartheid, condemned by so many people both inside and outside South Africa? 'The Europeans see racism in apartheid. They knew what Nazism meant and comparing the two is the only way they can explain these strange Afrikaners and their doings.'

Lower living standards for whites have thrown up a champion of the white blue-collar workers in Arrie Paulus, a staunch defender of the economic interests of working- and lower middle-class Afrikaners. Paulus is the Conservative MP for Carletonville, about an hour's drive south-west of Johannesburg, a mining centre where the local white miners live in drab bungalows. Before his election Paulus was secretary of the Mineworkers' Union (MWU), an exclusively white labour organisation which has increasingly come into conflict with the emergent National Union of Mineworkers, representing blacks, led by an accomplished lawyer Cyril Ramaphosa.

After leaving school Paulus worked for a white municipality, then the giant steel corporation ISCOR, finally joining his two brothers in the mines in 1956. For the next thirteen years he worked as a *stoper*, whose job is blasting the gold seam, and then as a 'developer' digging out underground tunnels. Paulus eventually became a leading member of an action committee set up to protect white mineworkers' interests against black demands for parity in wages and conditions. Says Paulus: 'Since 1914 the Chamber of Mines [representing the main mining companies] has tried to bring in blacks to do the jobs of whites. The whites rebelled in 1922 [the Rand rebellion, put down when government planes bombed the miners' headquarters] and again in 1946.'

In 1964, Paulus's predecessor as head of the MWU agreed to an experiment in four mines over a specific period, in which blacks would be allowed to do the work of whites up to a certain level. 'The experiment was extended to other mines,' says Paulus, 'and we realised what was happening.' Paulus joined an action committee which won a subsequent election to the MWU executive, with Paulus as secretary. Over the next decade Paulus ran the MWU, fiercely defending his members' interests in the face of government reforms allowing black trade unions, and the rising clamour by many black miners to be allowed to undertake 'scheduled' jobs – those reserved for whites.

Paulus says the National Party was founded to pursue separate development under which each nation (code word for race group) would be governed by its own people. Each group would be allotted its own land where it would elect its own people. Within the area that comprises white South Africa, the whites must therefore be in charge. Hence the whites must continue to have preference when it comes to the allocation of jobs and opportunities on the mines even though hundreds and thousands of black workers form the backbone of the mining industry and without their efforts several mining concerns would collapse, along with a fair slice of the country's economy. Paulus has no problem with this dilemma. 'Eighty-five per cent of blacks in South Africa's mines are foreign workers [from neighbouring black countries or from the "independent" homelands]. Why must we allow people from other countries to do the work of white people in white South Africa?' After all, argues Paulus, the blacks have their own mines in Bophuthatswana and Lebowa (two of the homelands). There they can run their own mines and obtain blasting certificates and even become mine managers. White mineworkers in 'white South Africa' are even prepared to offer them assistance in their own countries, says Paulus. 'But the Conservative Party still regards blacks as foreigners.'

Paulus has emerged as a strident defender of white interests against government plans to privatise some of the huge Afrikaner-dominated industries and bureaucracies which for years have been employment havens for Afrikaners. It is ironic that a country so bitterly hostile towards Marxism should itself have controlled the economy to protect individuals. Privatisation and deregulation are seen by the government as making the economy more productive in a bid to create jobs for whites but perhaps, more importantly, also for blacks. For men like Paulus this is a betrayal of the whites whose sweat and labour helped build up these giant concerns during the early years of Afrikaner nationalist growth.

For Paulus, government plans for the economy raise the spectre once more of the 'poor whites' – the Afrikaners who fled poverty on the farms in the 1920s only to become the pawns of English capital, as the right wing sees it, in English-dominated towns like Johannesburg. If you privatise the hospitals, says Paulus, then they have to run at a profit. 'If they run at a loss, they will simply put up the fees which means it will become nearly impossible for blue-collar workers among whites to afford hospital treatment because their medical aid insurance schemes cover only part of the charges.' If companies like Anglo American take over ESCOM (the electricity supply industry) then the same rule would apply. Either

Anglo would put up charges to make ends meet or they would shed labour to reduce the wage bill; in either case whites would suffer. Moreover Paulus nurses a fear that companies like Anglo, left in control of key industries, would manipulate the economy to serve their own ends. Such is the future under a National Party government, says Paulus, who sees a dangerous parallel between what the government has done on the political front and what it plans to do with the economy:

'With privatisation, the government is doing exactly the same thing that it did with the constitution. It introduces apartheid reforms without warning the people. Now they are trying to privatise without telling whites exactly what they have in mind. They are trying to bluff people and people don't like it. Sooner or later the government will have to face the music.'

Paulus seems unimpressed by the Thatcher revolution in Britain which, in part through privatisation, has created a new share-owning prosperity for sections of the British population, some blue-collar workers among them. Paulus's view is that if private companies can make industry more efficient, why can't government? Paulus notes that unemployment went up when Thatcher's policies started taking effect. When reminded that the level of jobless subsequently fell, Paulus dismisses this as a short-term recovery. 'The more they privatise, the more they have to create jobs. Where are the new jobs going to come from in South Africa? Where is the finance?' The government, says Paulus, has clearly set its eyes on the black population as a priority for employment opportunities. 'But it's too late for that now. We cannot keep up with the demands. We should have tackled this question thirty years ago by introducing proper birth control.'

Such concerns about the future of his white followers prompted Paulus's decision to leave the MWU in 1987 to stand for parliament:

'I had achieved what I had set as a goal for white mineworkers – better wages, holidays and pensions. I feel that in parliament I can help them more. Without any doubt in my mind, I am the only person in the [white] House of Assembly that knows the white mineworker and can talk on his behalf. Most other MPs are doctors and lawyers'

– the latter remark an unmistakable side-swipe at the National Party and the professional class it now increasingly represents.

How does he regard the man who is now doing for black miners what Paulus attempted for whites – Cyril Ramaphosa, leader of the National Union of Mineworkers? Says Paulus: 'With the blacks behind him he could have achieved much more if he had left politics behind him and fought for his workers. A union must involve itself in bread and butter issues and leave politics to politicians.' Arrie Paulus, unlike Ramaphosa, can feel confident about such a system, knowing that the politics is safely in the hands of white politicians. He sees his task as campaigning for the poorer whites; that means a complete return to an apartheid economy as well as to political apartheid. The Conservative Party is setting itself a formidable task: to turn the clock back thirty years and defy all the forces that turn South Africa's economic wheels. Many believe that should the CP ever come to power it would quickly face reality, which would compel it to jettison most of its policies.

The Conservative Party was formed following a traumatic series of events for the National Party during 1981 and 1982. Botha and conservative elements within his party had been at loggerheads over how the prime minister was interpreting party policy on the mixed-race and Indian communities. The prospect of the two communities being allowed to share power with whites was not to the liking of the right-wingers. On 22 February 1982, at a National Party caucus meeting, twenty-two Nationalist MPs abstained on or voted against a motion expressing full confidence in P. W. Botha. A furious Botha gave the rebels one week to back him. Six of the defectors returned to the fold leaving sixteen who refused to back down. They either resigned from the party or were expelled. Among the rebel cabinet ministers was Andries Treurnicht, who went on to lead the Conservative Party.

It was not the first time that the National Party had lost defectors to the right. An earlier schism in the late 1960s occurred when Prime Minister John Vorster started desegregating sport. He also broadened the base of the party's support by appealing to the country's English-speaking population. Two English-speakers in the party were appointed to the government. But even these mild changes were too much for the right wing to stomach. Albert Hertzog, son of the pre-Second World War prime minister General J. B M. Hertzog, rose in parliament to denounce English-speakers as too liberal. They should not be afforded a prominent role in public life, he contended. In September 1969, at the Transvaal congress of the National Party, the tensions came to a head when the right-wing members refused to back a vote of confidence in the party leadership and its policies. Subsequently they either resigned from the party or were expelled. Within a month the defectors had organised into a new party, the Herstigte Nasionale Party. In the years that followed, the HNP attracted support from hardliners believing the government was going soft on apartheid. It gained its highest level of support in 1981 with 13 per cent of the white electorate. But it has only ever won one parliamentary seat, and under its second leader Jaap Marais proved to be more of an irritant than a political threat. For the National Party leadership the defection of the HNP was traumatic enough. The defections which led to the formation of the Conservative Party were an altogether more serious rupture, one that would prove a far more substantial challenge to the National Party's hegemony.

But the new split did not succeed in uniting hardliners opposed to the government's reform programme. There was immediately rivalry between the CP and the HNP, partly personal and partly political. To begin with, the two parties differed on a number of crucial issues affecting the future shape of South Africa's racial constitution. Both parties favoured a return to Verwoerd's homeland policy in its strictest form, whereas the government had failed to make all ten *bantustans* 'independent' and were allowing homeland blacks into 'white South Africa'. Both parties held that coloureds should have a homeland of their own, joining the blacks in being hived off from 'white South Africa'. But the Conservative Party went further, favouring the creation of an Indian homeland as well, a policy opposed by the HNP because the Indians had 'no moral or historical claim to any part of South Africa'. The fact that the first Indians arrived in South Africa more than a century ago as indentured labourers, long before many English-speakers, appeared to escape the HNP's notice. Another important difference concerned South Africa's official language. The CP, seeking to make inroads into the National Party's broad Afrikaans and English-speaking support, thought the existing policy of having two official languages should continue. The HNP wanted Afrikaans as the only official language inside the country, but conceded that English could be used in foreign relations.

But beyond the political differences, the HNP under Jaap Marais felt bitter that the CP were 'Johnny-come-latelies' whereas the HNP had broken many years earlier on a point of principle and had carried the right-wing flag alone. Marais had spent twenty years in the political wilderness while the CP leader Andries Treurnicht had stayed behind within the security of the National Party benches 'plucking up the courage' to move only when it appeared he had little choice, as Marais told a newspaper. To the outsider, the differences between the HNP and the CP may appear to have a certain 'Alice in Wonderland' dimension to them. The heated row between the two took place with the black townships on fire and lives lost every day, as blacks demanded their political rights. And yet here were two right-wing parties arguing over how many homelands the country should have. Attempts at unity talks were fruitless. The CP seemed intent on seeing off the HNP. On the whole it succeeded, leaving Treurnicht as the undisputed champion of the right-wing cause. Soon he had fashioned the CP into a dynamic party.

Judging by the fanatical views of some of his supporters, one would expect Treurnicht to be some kind of brown-shirted *Führer*. In fact, he is restrained, extremely courteous, well dressed and has an engaging sense of humour. He is a good deal more charming than his rival P. W. Botha. Born in 1921, he was one of nine children. He graduated from the University of Stellenbosch and later became a minister of the Dutch Reformed Church: his master's thesis was on the subject of Calvinist theology and the relationship between church and state. As editor of the church mouthpiece *Die Kerkbode* he waged a strong campaign against the World Council of Churches which attacked South Africa's racial segregation. With conservatives holding sway in the church, Treurnicht soon rose through the ranks to become assessor in the general synod in 1966. Under the guidance of Prime Minister John Vorster, Treurnicht became the editor of a new Transvaal daily newspaper published in Pretoria, *Hoofstad* (Capital City), where he presented a conservative view of the major political, cultural and theological issues facing the country. He did not break with the National Party when Hertzog defected; instead he entered parliament himself for the first time, winning a by-election in June 1971 in the Transvaal seat of Waterberg by defeating the HNP candidate Jaap Marais, a defeat which still rankles with the latter.

Treurnicht edged closer to the centre of power through his chairmanship of the

Broederbond in the early 1970s. From 1979 onwards, after his appointment as black affairs minister, the gradual distancing from National Party policy became discernible. He opposed the idea of other races joining parliament or the cabinet. He objected to a team of mixed-race schoolboys participating in Craven Week, a special training school for enthusiastic youngsters organised by South Africa's rugby chief Danie Craven. His position strengthened by his election as Transvaal leader of the National Party in 1978, the break with the government came closer. When Botha revealed his power-sharing plans, Treurnicht defected.

Interviewed by *South Africa Foundation News* Treurnicht explained his political philosophy thus:

> I am convinced that a realistic political policy for the racial and ethnic diversity of southern Africa can succeed only on the basis of separate independence and self-determination for the various nations. We must acknowledge the reality of their existence and as a consequence their right to the highest political representation, to their own political structures and to their own countries. We have to move away radically from power sharing in a unitary state and we have to take more sincerely group areas and the economic, educational and political development of the nations within their own geographical areas.

If the Conservative Party ever came to power how would the face of South Africa change? The prospect terrifies many whites, not just the traditional liberals who have supported the Progressive Federal Party but also middle-of-the-road Afrikaners, those who don't want to hand over to black majority rule but who at the same time dread what they fear would be a quasi-fascist dictatorship. Ironically, the prospect of the CP coming to power appears to have a less traumatic effect on the country's black people, or at least the anti-apartheid activists among them. They fully expect that life would become tougher, but on the other hand some believe a Conservative government would plunge the country into such chaos – internal turmoil, international isolation and economic crisis – that the old order would come tumbling down once and for all, paving the way towards majoritarian democracy, a process possibly quicker than waiting for the National Party to dispense power as and when it sees fit. The reverse of this argument, of course, is that amid the chaos there would be very little left for a future black government to inherit.

The Afrikaner commentator Willem de Klerk – following his analysis of the present National Party – turned his attention in *Leadership* magazine to how Conservative Party policies would affect South Africa, if the CP ever formed a government. An article by him in April 1988 entitled 'Backwards in Anger' represented perhaps the most wide-ranging and thoughtful scrutiny to date of CP policies and their possible consequences. De Klerk noted certain non-negotiable principles on which CP policy was based: South Africa to be divided into separate national states or fatherlands for whites, coloureds, Indians and the various black tribes, each with their own sovereign authorities. Where there were large black or coloured settlements (like Soweto) within 'white South Africa' these would be hived off as 'city-states'. In other words South Africa would be subjected to partition by legislation passed by a CP-dominated white parliament. This in turn would lead to large-scale relocation of people. One Conservative MP, noted de Klerk, was already on record as saying that 70 per cent of blacks would be back in their homelands within ten to fifteen years once the Conservative Party had assumed power.

A CP election victory, argued de Klerk, would lead to: the abolition of the coloured and Indian chambers under Botha's power-sharing constitution (which might also be jettisoned); the repeal of several laws that have abolished racial discrimination, leading to a reimposition of the bans on mixed marriages and sex across the colour line; separate amenities for the various race groups in hotels, restaurants etc.; the reintroduction of job reservation for whites, influx control laws, which used to regulate the movements of black people, and the pass laws; the abolition of multiracial administrative bodies set up at regional and local level; the loss for blacks of their freehold housing rights; the closure of multiracial central business districts; the banning of multiracial universities; the return of apartheid in sport; and, once again, the prohibition of black trade unions.

De Klerk's conclusions about such an outcome made grim reading. He referred to a 'harsh' scenario in which a CP victory results in a final racial confrontation, a full-scale war. A 'soft' scenario foresees an exodus of whites fleeing the country in either a steady stream or a panic-stricken mass of refugees. He concludes:

> What we are dealing with is a scenario of either hurtling headlong into the abyss, or sliding into it. . . . The retroactive radicalism of a CP government, built upon an unacceptable ideology, in a situation where it will no longer be possible to turn back, will inevitably bring on the national and international breaking point. Therefore the Scenario of the Abyss, in all its variations. Partition could only be achieved after protracted and intense violence. It could not be achieved through negotiation and compromise. In the light of [these] scenarios, a CP takeover is an appalling prospect. It becomes a political absurdity to give it any consideration at all. It will amount to nothing less than pulling down the pillars in an act of self-destruction. But still . . . there are those political prophets who say that South Africa is capable of committing this historic act of idiocy – voting the CP into power.

The rise of the Conservative Party has made respectable a wide-ranging debate about political solutions unthinkable a decade ago. The more the National Party has rolled back the frontiers of apartheid towards a more integrated society, the more the radical right has tried to reverse the process. The Conservative Party wanted a return to Verwoerdian apartheid, with blacks confined to their home-lands. However, Carel Boshoff of the Afrikaner Volkswag, the leading light behind the right-wing trek celebrations, regarded this solution as being as unworkable as the Nationalists' policy of a united South African state governed by a power-sharing arrangement between whites and blacks. Both were morally indefensible and politically unworkable. Black majority rule would be the inevitable consequence. As the township unrest grew in the mid-1980s and as black demands for political rights intensified, Boshoff became convinced that another course was required.

A secession of whites from a black-dominated South Africa was therefore the answer – the creation of a *volkstaat* (people's state). This would be the reverse of Verwoerd's vision. Verwoerd had proposed hiving off black states, but Boshoff believes that such a plan is impossible. Rather than the secession of black states from 'white South Africa', the Afrikaners should retreat from an inevitably black-ruled South Africa. Verwoerd's ideal of a white state dominated by whites would still be honoured but the practicalities of implementing it would be different. The project, it is acknowledged, would involve partitioning the land and the consequent forced removal of millions of people.

So much for the political dimension to the right wing's plans for splitting up the country. What about the economic factors? In the last few years of the twentieth century, is it realistic for an economy like South Africa's – dependent on blacks and whites – to be partitioned into independent racial territories? A foretaste of the problems which could face the CP occurred after it captured a string of town councils in municipal elections in the Transvaal. The newly-elected council in Boksburg promptly reimposed apartheid laws segregating parks, swimming pools, recreation areas, etc. Blacks and coloureds responded through a consumer boycott of Boksburg's white-owned shops and businesses, who were immediately in uproar at their loss of earnings. Some placed signs in their shop windows reassuring black and coloured customers that: 'All races are still welcome here.' Such efforts to counter natural economic forces at local level give rise to serious questions as to the feasibility of the right wing's plan for the national compartmentalisation of South Africa along racial lines.

In the face of such potential economic and political havoc, the question arises: would a National Party government ever allow the right wing to take power? The approach of an election which the CP stood to win could herald South Africa's worst crisis to date. The National Party, convinced that its gradual moves towards power-sharing offer the only pragmatic and peaceful way forward, would be staring right down into the CP abyss at the prospect of the reversal of all its reforms to apartheid. The government of the day would have to consider the stability of the country under a CP government. By that stage, of course, the National Party would be looking liberal. Faced with the prospect of a right-wing government, thousands of coloureds, Indians and indeed blacks would look to the National Party for protection, hard as that is to imagine after more than forty years of oppression.

The security forces would be placed under immense strain both in maintaining law and order and in deciding where their loyalties lay. The police force, many of whom support the Conservative Party, might split, with some backing a CP government and others continuing to serve the existing National Party government. The army would be more inclined to keep the existing Nationalist government in power. Despite their reputation for destabilisation in neighbouring black states, for attacking black nationalist bases beyond South Africa's borders and for clamping down hard on township unrest, the armed forces are generally firmly committed to the government's reform programme. Defence Minister Magnus Malan may be convinced that there is a Marxist-inspired 'total onslaught' against South Africa which demands a tough response, but as far as domestic policies are concerned he believes in reform as a stabilising agent. Would the armed forces therefore be prepared to stand by and watch the reforms of the 1980s thrown overboard by a CP government? Would they agree to the wholesale subjugation of people on a scale not witnessed before, with the removal of people from 'white South Africa' back to the homelands?

It doesn't seem likely. Under present circumstances, the prospect of a CP election victory would be a more likely spark for a military coup in South Africa than would any kind of threat by black nationalists. Martial rule, or at least government by some kind of political/military executive coupled with a suspension of the constitution, could well be imposed to thwart a Conservative Party takeover. At the same time, the authorities would continue to enact limited reforms affecting blacks to maintain a measure of stability. Deprived of power won democratically, sections of the right wing would almost certainly take up arms in a campaign of violence directed against whites and blacks. By that time, they would have concluded that there was no other way of reversing the loss of white sovereignty which they already see in the government's integrationist policies.

How great a force is the Conservative Party in the white politics of today's South Africa? Piet Meiring, the former government information chief under Verwoerd, says: 'The right wing scares me stiff. The Conservative Party is the most dangerous thing that has ever developed in South African politics. They become emotional about things we were emotional about forty years ago. The platteland is becoming subservient to the right. I don't know where it's going to end.'

In several cities where so called 'grey areas' (suburbs where blacks have encroached into designated white areas in defiance of the Group Areas Act) have mushroomed, the Conservative Party is benefiting from, indeed exploiting, the tensions that can arise when people of different races find themselves on a racial front line. In the Mayfair district of Johannesburg, whites living in mediocre houses built sixty years ago have sold them to Indians desperate for housing, at three times their actual value. The whites then move out to up-market suburbs and buy properties they could never otherwise have afforded. When the government announced it was going to legalise a number of 'free settlement areas' (irreversible 'grey areas') it pledged in the same breath to increase penalties for those contravening the Group Areas Act in other suburbs that were still segregated. The tougher proposals, though later dropped, deferred to the right wing which campaigned determinedly against the gradual dilution of Group Areas legislation. Allowing a few 'grey areas' will almost certainly turn them into magnets for thousands of blacks suddenly able to live legally in previously white suburbs close to the city centres instead of in remote townships. Resources in these new multiracial zones – housing in particular – may well become stretched, thereby straining race relations, to the further benefit of the right wing: another case of the National Party doing the right thing for the wrong reason, and too late.

It is not only by returning to the old apartheid policies of the Nationalists that the Conservative Party is exploiting the mood of uncertainty among Afrikaners. The style and approach of the party reminds people of the good old days. Whereas the National Party has become distant from the people, relying on slick public relations to convey its message, the Conservative Party has recognised that politics is as much about hard work at grass-roots level as it is about image. This, after all, was how the Nationalists came to power in 1948. No village council, no school board, no church organisation is too small for the attention of Conservative Party officials. The CP leaders are doing what the Nationalists did successfully in 1948, driving for hours across vast tracts of the country to fulfil a tight schedule of political meetings. Whereas today's Nationalist leaders often arrive in a local constituency and either leave the same night or stay in a hotel, Treurnicht will accept a bed for the night at the home of the constituency branch chairman where a few of the local party supporters might gather for a drink and a chat after a meeting. He will polish his own shoes in the morning, interest himself in the family and the house and local affairs – he comes across as 'one of us' not some remote figure 'up there'. The CP has gone back to the people and made the politics of the *braaivleis* its own. The party thus provides a compelling reminder of the heyday of Nationalism in power – the years 1948–61 – when an objective, the creation of the republic, generated enthusiasm and idealism. The CP recaptured that mood; by contrast enthusiasm, as opposed to support, for the National Party has never been so low.

The Conservative Party has established a firm power base in the Transvaal but still has to demonstrate that it has substantial support elsewhere. The next few years will tell whether CP support will be confined to the farmers and blue-collar workers of the Transvaal or whether it will inherit the mantle of Afrikaner nationalism of which the National Party is slowly divesting itself. Whatever its long-term impact, the Conservative Party has already been responsible for one important change in the white politics of South Africa. Before its arrival, the division was very much between Afrikaners and English-speakers, the former voting Nationalist almost to a man while a sizeable percentage of the English supported the Progressive Federal Party (although many voted Nationalist periodically). Now white voting along ethnic lines is being replaced by a class system cutting across Afrikaner/English divisions. The Conservative Party is generally home to those at the lower end of the economic ladder – the 'have nots'. The Nationalists are the party of the upper and middle classes, urban Afrikaners who have severed their links with the rural areas, and English-speakers who see in the National Party a vehicle to hold back the right wing and stave off uninhibited black majority rule.

How far is the mainstream right wing prepared to go in defending the Afrikaner people if their demands cannot be met through the parliamentary process and if the government continues to initiate reforms which, however cautious, are seen by hardliners as further selling out the whites? Professor Carel Boshoff of the Afrikaner Volkswag says: 'As long as the road is open for negotiation we will use that and prevent any kind of [right-wing] radicalism. But when every road is closed I don't think you will prevent the Afrikaner fighting for his survival. We will fight and die for the freedom of the Afrikaner nation.' There are some further to the right, however, who believe that the taking up of arms in defence of the Afrikaners might come sooner rather than later.

CHAPTER SIX

'You cannot make a slave of an Afrikaner'

The night is pitch black. At a prearranged meeting place, a roadside on the outskirts of the northern Transvaal town of Potgietersrus, several colleagues and I wait, telling ourselves we should feel nervous. The man we are to meet is said to be one of the most sinister figures in today's South Africa, his followers a menacing army of fanatics prepared to stop at nothing to achieve their aims.

We see the headlights of two vehicles approaching. They move fast. As they screech to a halt, their tyres throw up clouds of dust, blinding us. Out jump several 'heavies'. 'The leader will see you now,' says one. 'Come in your own cars,' he orders. 'Stay close behind and be prepared for detours.'

We move off into the dark backstreets of Potgietersrus, not a town where it's possible to take many detours. In fact, you can probably cruise around the whole of Potgietersrus in less than half an hour. Nevertheless we don't recognise where our shadowy escorts are taking us.

At last the cars halt. The heavies jump out and usher us towards a row of shops. We are shown into a restaurant. At a corner table sits the man we have come to see. He's just finishing his meal; he's dressed in a neat silver-blue, three-piece suit and is wearing immaculately polished shoes. He greets us charmingly and we feel more at ease. We are set for the first international news conference granted by Eugene Terre Blanche, leader of the Afrikaner Weerstandsbeweging (Afrikaner Resistance Movement) whose followers send a menacing chill down the spines of those with long memories of events in recent European history. The television crews take over the restaurant, erecting glaring lights and entwining cable around the tables, oblivious to the diners eating their *kabeljou* (fish) or *springbok* steaks. Terre Blanche seems taken aback. Clearly he was thinking in terms of a couple of reporters with notebooks, not all this. But he's got to learn to live with this kind of publicity. After all the right-wing leader is now the focus of worldwide media attention, an international newsmaker. The previous week (22 May 1986) his supporters had broken up a meeting in Pietersburg, also in the conservative northern Transvaal, to have been addressed by the Foreign Minister, Pik Botha, regarded by the right as a virtual communist because of his prediction that, with certain guarantees for whites, there could one day be a black president in South Africa. The pictures beamed around the world of the right-wing hordes in Nazi-style uniforms, waving swastika-like flags had conjured up images of Germany in the 1930s. Those abroad who long suspected that South African whites were fascists took one look at the AWB and believed their views were confirmed. And the man we are meeting tonight is South Africa's Adolf Hitler, fresh from his own Beer Hall Putsch.

The trouble is – one cannot suppress the feeling, deep down, that Mr Terre Blanche and his followers are overgrown schoolchildren playing toy soldiers. And that's the problem in reporting on them. Is the AWB high comedy? Or are Terre Blanche and his faithful to be taken deadly seriously, the face of a new, tougher, more vicious and uncompromising Afrikaner ready to mount a scorched-earth policy rather than surrender to even limited change?

The Pietersburg meeting was broken up by rightist louts many of whom were drunk. Ordinary, decent National Party supporters who'd come to hear Pik Botha speak were insulted by the rightists and told to 'clear off and take the blacks with you.' The AWB men took over the stage, bawling out Afrikaner songs and punching the air with their fists as they chanted 'Ah-Vay-Bay' (the AWB's initials as pronounced in Afrikaans). Searchlights picked out the figure of Terre Blanche as he arrived to celebrate the AWB 'victory' in driving Pik Botha out of town. A young National Party supporter battling unsuccessfully to make himself heard above the din described the scenes as 'a disgrace to Afrikaners'.

What was perhaps more of a disgrace was the reaction, or lack of it, from the police. Had these anti-government protesters been black they would not have been allowed anywhere near the town hall, let alone been permitted to take over the meeting. For some time there had been doubts about the political leanings of certain sections of the police, particularly units based in the conservative northern Transvaal. There were suspicions that some were supporters, if not members, of the AWB. It was only after Mr Botha had been humiliated and the meeting abandoned that the police eventually fired a token tear-gas canister to clear the hall. On the morning after, the government minister due to have chaired the meeting, Pietie du Plessis, launched an unusual attack on the police saying they 'were not capable or did not want to maintain law and order'. He complained that the police contingent on duty had actually escorted Terre Blanche into the meeting hall. The then Law and Order Minister, Louis le Grange, responded to those appalled by the events of that night by promising that the government was 'not prepared to tolerate thuggery and bullying tactics or to allow people such as the Afrikaner Weerstandsbeweging to make use of intimidatory tactics to control the political scene'. Le Grange announced a full enquiry into the Pietersburg fracas, though the police role in the affair was not submitted to public scrutiny. Faced with growing evidence of a right-wing backlash against its reformist policies, the government shied away from nipping the AWB in the bud through the kind of security measures applied to anti-apartheid organisations. Slowly the AWB was allowed to grow, because of the government's paralysing fear of the right. Followers who at first resembled drunken English football hooligans became more disciplined though no less threatening, smartening up their act as Terre Blanche became more alert to the art of exploiting the media.

A week after Pietersburg – on the twenty-fifth anniversary of South Africa's withdrawal from the Commonwealth and the establishment of a republic – right-wing groups staged a rally near the Afrikaner shrine at the Voortrekker Monument, thereby throwing down an emotional as well as a political challenge to the government. The authorities had at first refused to allow the meeting place to be used by the right wing but eventually agreed, on condition that the gathering was a 'cultural event' and not a 'political meeting'. The distinction, a fine one, was exploited by the right-wing leaders including Terre Blanche and Treurnicht, the latter declaring in overtly political terms that 'the Afrikaners were not prepared to be a minority in their own land and wanted to maintain a white South Africa'. P. W. Botha was not mentioned by name, in deference to the restrictions, but the 10,000 present got the message – that P. W. was a 'sell-out'. Speakers recalled the long history of struggle by the Afrikaner, and stones were laid, each representing a crucial moment in Afrikaner history. Some bore the names of the major battles in the Boer War, others the names of some of the 26,000 women and children who died in the British concentration camps.

The government had no answer to the AWB's tugging of the political heartstrings and its exploitation of Afrikaners' uncertainty about the future. Government ministers promoting the concept of gradual reform, yet unable to spell out where those reforms were leading, created a vacuum in which the AWB flourished. There was a near-replay of the 'Battle of Pietersburg' in Standerton shortly before the March 1988 by-election there. The Transvaal Nationalist leader F. W. de Klerk, a strong advocate of measured reform, was confronted by scores of AWB supporters. During the traditional, pre-meeting singing of Afrikaner folk songs, the AWB repeatedly demanded Number 7 on the song sheet (the AWB's swastika-like emblem comprises three interlocking figure sevens). There was a moment's respite from the chanting while a pastor read a prayer calling for tolerance, after which pandemonium broke out again. Rival Nationalists and rightists rolled up their sleeves, tear-gas canisters and stink bombs exploded and a power cut threw the meeting hall and the whole town into darkness. The unfortunate Mr de Klerk was later able to resume his meeting when the lights came back on and after the AWB men, having made their point, had left. Three weeks later Terre Blanche felt confident enough to call for a mass rally in Pretoria to demonstrate that his following was on the increase.

The venue is the city's Skilpadsaal (Tortoise Hall), so called because its roof is shaped like a tortoise shell. Some 6000 have turned up and quite clearly Terre Blanche is no longer attracting militant thugs only. The audience comprises many 'ordinary' Afrikaners – some farmers from the *platteland*, blue-collar workers from Pretoria and Johannesburg – for all of whom it is a family day out. They have brought their picnic baskets and portable *braaivleis* (barbecues) not to mention a healthy supply of beer. Many of these newly-recruited followers have already acquired some of the AWB trappings – the swastika-style emblems on their shirt epaulettes, the AWB flags, the khaki uniforms. Even young children are wearing khaki shirts and shorts while 'stormtroopers' sport paramilitary uniforms – brown shirts, dark brown trousers and black boots. When the AWB chants go up and the singing resounds one has a sense of what the Nuremberg rallies must have been like. The Skilpadsaal's echoing acoustics enhance the effect making it sound as though 60,000 and not 6000 are gathered.

One song is unashamedly entitled 'We sing for apartheid'. The banners stretching along the walls scream out 'We shall soon overcome', 'Let the history of our faith remain eternal' and 'We share power with no one'. A speaker from Natal slams the Indaba power-sharing plan for the region drawn up by moderate whites and blacks. The message is this: whites who vanquished the Zulus at the Battle of Blood River in Natal are not going to share power with them now. In scenes reminiscent of the Nazi book-burnings, copies of the plan are torn up in front of the stage and stamped on by AWB men. There's a chilling moment when the black, green and gold flag of the African National Congress is unfurled and then ceremoniously set on fire by the leader of an AWB 'torch commando' which rides into the hall on horseback to the frenzied cheers of the rightists. Speakers launch threatening attacks on leading anti-apartheid campaigners like Archbishop Tutu and Dr Allan Boesak. The English-speaking universities are branded as nests of Marxists, as is the English press. A speaker demands to know what Pretoria is doing about the Congress of South African Trade Unions (COSATU), the country's largest anti-government labour federation, 'which is run by an Indian' (a reference to COSATU's general secretary, Jay Naidoo). Next in line for attack is the United Democratic Front, the anti-apartheid affiliation claiming 3 million members. Inter-black feuding which has left hundreds dead in fighting between UDF loyalists and the Zulu-based Inkatha movement led by Chief Buthelezi (who is also abused) is cited to explain that the UDF is simply a front organisation for the ANC which is 'seeking to put down the Zulus before they attack us'. 'P. W. Botha is incapable of defending Afrikaners against the ANC,' declares another speaker 'The AWB is the only organisation which can overcome the ANC. Who's the greatest danger to the country – the AWB or P. W. Botha?'

Then it's time for the grand entrance of Terre Blanche himself. The AWB's public relations officer, who's been acting as master of ceremonies and leading the singing (he's got a very good voice) delivers a vocal fanfare. 'Ladies and gentlemen, the leader of the Afrikaner Weerstandsbeweging, Mr Eugene Terre Blanche,' he announces as though he's introducing the United States president. The reaction is tumultuous as the leader's stage-managed entrance brings him to the podium surrounded by his newly-established uniformed bodyguard unit, taking their role terribly seriously. Terre Blanche acknowledges the cheers with Hitler-like half-salutes. He's wearing the familiar shiny grey three-piece suit. His balding hair is swept back. He's already perspiring heavily under the glare of the television lights.

Eugene Terre Blanche is one of three South African political figures who stand head and shoulders above their contemporaries when it comes to public speaking, the others being the former ambassador to Britain, now independent politician, Dr Denis Worrall, and Dr Allan Boesak – and even they often speak from notes. Not so Terre Blanche who addresses audiences for up to ninety minutes without reference to a single piece of paper, his only prop being a neatly-folded handkerchief to wipe away perspiration or, when he becomes really emotional, his tears. His speeches are a symphony to listen to: a quiet beginning, then the introduction of a melody which repeats itself at various pitches and at various decibel levels, and a grand finale. He never rants, he never hams it up. His words just roll out naturally, enthralling his audiences with their power, their imagery and their drama.

The occasion of the meeting is the anniversary of the Battle of Majuba during the first Boer War in 1881 at which a force of 200 Boer fighters, crawling on hands and knees to avoid drawing fire, stormed the Majuba ridge and overpowered the British contingent who had occupied the seemingly impregnable position. Ninety British soldiers were killed in the attack by the Afrikaners, who lost only one.

In his speech Terre Blanche takes up the theme of scaling daunting mountains. 'There are those who choose the difficult road of struggle and those who choose the easy path of negotiation,' he begins. 'The government of P. W. Botha has chosen the way of negotiation and already communism is embracing them. The AWB, by contrast, is pursuing a dangerous and difficult road which nevertheless will lead to a volkstaat [people's state] for whites into which P. W. Botha will not be admitted because he is a traitor to the Afrikaner.'

'The new state will have no need of blacks,' continues Terre Blanche. 'We will govern ourselves with our own superior white genes. In our volkstaat we will return to the white nation that was lost. Despite struggle and death in the concentration camps the Afrikaner was never asked before to make so many sacrifices as now under Botha.' Terre Blanche almost spits out the name of the president. There follows a thinly-disguised attack on Jewish capital, symbolised for Terre Blanche by the former head of the giant Anglo American empire, Harry Oppenheimer, as well as by the giant Rothschild family. Government plans to privatise huge Afrikaner-dominated industries are bitterly repudiated by the AWB leader. 'Botha and [Finance Minister] Barend du Plessis have no right to sell off our property,' he declares. 'Selling it off to Indians and blacks.'

Then comes the clincher, the menacing threat that reveals it is perhaps wrong to dismiss the AWB as a pack of jokers. 'The AWB has to prepare for the night when he, the Afrikaner, in violence, will claim what is rightfully his.'

His speech over, Terre Blanche leads a convoy of cars to the Union Buildings, South Africa's historic seat of government perched on a hilltop overlooking Pretoria. With guns tucked into their waistbands and truncheons dangling from their belts, the AWB cohorts hand in a petition for President Botha demanding their *volkstaat*. A policeman is photographed shaking Terre Blanche's hand as he accepts the petition. Three days later Archbishop Tutu and scores of other anti-apartheid churchmen are either hosed down by water cannon or arrested, or both, for trying to present a petition to parliament in Cape Town. Once again the government demonstrated its reluctance to employ measures against the right which they have no hesitation in using against the left. An emergency debate in parliament on the churchmen's arrests brings a scathing attack on the govern-ment's double standards from Helen Suzman. 'I want to know,' she demands 'who instructed the police major to wield the big stick. Could it be that this ridiculous overkill was . . . designed to demonstrate that the government was not soft on law and order except, of course, when it came to dealing with the violent armed men of the AWB who, shouting slogans and sporting brown shirts with Nazi-like emblems, arrived at the Union Buildings in Pretoria unchallenged by the police. No water cannon for these model citizens!' The Law and Order Minister, Adriaan Vlok, defends the police action but announces an investigation into the AWB under the terms of the Internal Security Act. Terre Blanche dismisses this as a joke. Within a few days his brownshirts are rallying again, this time in the town of Krugersdorp west of Johannesburg, with the AWB leader again rousing the faithful with sonorous warnings of the extinction of the white man.

'And so it grows. . . .'
'Throughout the Transvaal, the Cape and the Free State, the resistance grows. The black power of Dingane [the Zulu king whose men murdered Piet Retief] will not take us over. Too many tears have been shed on the Afrikaners' path through history.' Tears come to the eyes of Terre Blanche himself as, in a subdued voice, he reminds his spellbound audience of the women and children 'dressed only in rags' who endured cold winter nights in the concentration camps. He warns Law and Order Minister Vlok not to contemplate banning the AWB. 'You cannot touch the AWB,' he predicts. 'How do you ban a people, a history? A people who fight for an ideal greater than itself can never be destroyed.'

Tonight Terre Blanche has two plain-clothes security guards, a new addition to the inventory of acolytes who now follow him. They stand behind Terre Blanche while he's seated on the stage and then accompany him across to the podium when he delivers his speech. They scan the audience earnestly, expecting an assassin to appear at any moment. The brownshirts are also there, manning the wings and keeping a close eye on the audience, trying desperately to look important. One senses that they would give anything for a real incident which would allow them to demonstrate their toughness. Tonight they are in luck. A bad earth connection in the public address system sets off a buzzing noise, which rather detracts from Terre Blanche's ringing words. For the boys in brown this is clearly a Terribly Serious Matter and they're looking around for scapegoats. Suspicious eyes are cast upon the television teams with their miles of cables. Whispers between the brownshirts are overheard, suggesting that one of the television cables is causing the interference. The heavies assume a tough posture. The fists are knotted tighter, so that the knuckles turn white. But the AWB bouncers are torn. The looks on their faces suggest they would dearly love to wade in and sort out some innocent cameraman allegedly responsible for the buzzing. But that would further detract from their leader's speech. They decide to live with it.

A right-wing newspaper is distributed. Among the articles is a condemnation of the international 'propaganda' attacks on the Austrian president Kurt Waldheim over his wartime activities. The writer comments:

By carrying out his duties faithfully and striving after firm principles, he

[Waldheim] became a world leader in the field of international politics. . . . Because he does not allow the money powers to dictate to him, he is called guilty of 'knowing of war crimes'. The fact that he does not yield to the propaganda which wants to discharge him from his office, in my opinion makes a better man of Kurt Waldheim.

An attractive lady in the front row steals the evening. She's dressed in a fetching red beret, a khaki blouse and skirt and matching red shoes and handbag – the AWB colours. Clearly AWB 'designer outfits' have arrived.
'And so it grows. . . .'

A few days after his controversial Pretoria rally in February 1988, Eugene Terre Blanche, a man whose political outlook is in no small measure formed by his detailed historical study of the suffering of the Boers in the war against Britain (he refers to the concentration camps in nearly every speech), affords a courteous and warm welcome in his office to myself, from the BBC, and to my colleague from *The Times* of London – more British you cannot get.

Terre Blanche greets us by praising Britain's recapture of the Falkland Islands from Argentina in the South Atlantic war of 1982. He commends Prime Minister Margaret Thatcher's despatch of the naval task force as an heroic stand by a proud nation determined to defend its interests and never to give away what is justifiably its own. For the AWB leader, there is a parallel with the task now facing the Afrikaner nation:

'You want me to give away my land to the African National Congress who are not a nation, not even Zulus or Xhosas, but are just a bunch of communist-inspired murderers right from hell? The ANC cannot claim land just because they are black. They are the real racists. Would you British hand over your country to all the West Indians you've let in?'

Terre Blanche appears to enjoy a love-hate relationship with the British. The hardships of the Boer War are scorched deep into his soul, yet he clearly admires the gritty qualities of the British which have seen them through two world wars. Perhaps also it is the long history of the British nation which he respects, a history and a place in the world which he would like to achieve for his own people.

'I like the British. They are good fighters, a civilised people. They gave us Shakespeare.' Which of the great plays has he read? *Hamlet* and *King Lear*. Perhaps Terre Blanche sees himself as an heroic Shakespearean figure. ('I will do such things, what they are yet I know not; but they shall be the terrors of the earth' – *King Lear*.) 'My grandfather's mother was an English lady', he tells us.

Terre Blanche is speaking to us in his comfortable office in the AWB's new headquarters in the plush Pretoria suburb of Waterkloof Heights, whose luxurious houses and spacious gardens are home to upper-class Afrikaners (hardly a happy hunting ground for the AWB) and the diplomatic community. Clearly the AWB is on the march financially as well as politically if it can afford the new HQ, which contrasts noticeably with the dingy offices in downtown Pretoria it occupied until a year previously. The new offices, next to an up-market boutique called 'Executive Touch', are air-conditioned, with a thick carpet whose rich, woven colours recount the history of the Afrikaner and his struggle – the Voortrekker Monument, the establishment of the republic in 1961 and the Union Buildings in Pretoria are all depicted. On the reception desk is a model of an ox-wagon, the symbol of the Great Trek; a larger reconstruction stands on Terre Blanche's desk. On the wall behind him are pictures of the great Boer War leaders whom Terre Blanche respects as true heroes: the brilliant guerrilla strategist Christiaan de Wet who fought a cat-and-mouse game of harassment against the British military overlord, Lord Kitchener; Piet Cronje who led the western Transvaal commando unit and confronted Baden-Powell at Mafeking; the dour Koos de la Rey, deeply religious, never without a Bible in his pocket. Which of the Afrikaner leaders does he admire the most? 'Paul Kruger,' he replies unhesitatingly, recalling the man who confronted the might of the British empire under Cecil Rhodes in the last half of the nineteenth century and who, in the Transvaal, created for the Boers their first recognised Afrikaner republic.

Terre Blanche expands on the kind of exclusive Afrikaner state for which he is striving: 'You can never make a slave of the Afrikaner. My forefathers fought for land in Africa. We don't want the whole of South Africa – just the land which they struggled for, land which is the sole property of my people – dear land, too expensive to give away just because we have to be good to black people.' The Transvaal and the Orange Free State would form the rump of Terre Blanche's *volkstaat*. The independence of both was recognised by Britain at the Sand River Convention (1852) and the Convention of Bloemfontein (1854) respectively. 'Those conventions were international law,' says Terre Blanche. 'The Afrikaners have a rightful claim to those territories. It is the task of the United Nations to see that every nation has its own land without interference.' Terre Blanche also lays claim to that part of northern Natal which formed the basis of the land deal between the Zulu king Dingane and Piet Retief before the Boer commando and his followers were slaughtered by the Zulus. 'That deal was a legal contract,' he declares, 'signed by kings and leaders. It was Boer land.'

'I am not claiming land because I am a white man,' he insists. 'I am not a white colonialist.' Only Afrikaners and Christian English-speakers who identify totally with the Afrikaner cause qualify for full citizenship in his Boer Utopia. Somewhat negating his denials that the AWB is neo-fascist, Terre Blanche makes it clear that Jews would be welcome only if they converted to Christianity. Says Terre Blanche: 'Jews do not want to be part of Christianity. I cannot compromise with my God. We Afrikaners fled Europe as Christians and survived. We believe we will still survive because God will help us.' As for the blacks, they would be admitted to the *Boerestaat* as *gastarbeiter* (foreign labourers) only. Terre Blanche reveals his contempt for President Botha and his plans for power-sharing with blacks, a contempt mixed with sorrow that an Afrikaner could have strayed so far from his own people:

'I'm sorry an Afrikaner can be so wrong, sorry he doesn't know the realities of

African politics. I do not hate Botha as a person. He was a good minister of defence and member of the National Party. But he has changed to such an extent that today you can hardly see the difference between the Nationalists and the Progressive Federal Party. P. W. Botha will vanish from history.'

The AWB leader is reluctant to reveal much about himself. He plays down his image as a messianic leader come to deliver his Afrikaner people. 'I'm just doing my job, being true to myself.'

His family ties can be traced back to Etienne Terre Blanche of the French city of Toulouse who married Marie Lefevbre, emigrating to South Africa with the Huguenots in 1769. Unlike many Afrikaners with the same name, the AWB leader has not changed his to the diminutive of 'Terreblanche' or 'Terblanche', preserving the purer form of 'Terre Blanche' because it means 'white earth'. Eugene Ney Terre Blanche was raised in the western Transvaal. His father, a farmer, was a lieutenant colonel in the army. 'I had a wonderful father.' He attributes his powerful oratory to his father's schooling. 'He taught me to speak and how to love my own language. From him I learned to state what I am and what I believe in.' Recalling his father, tears come to Terre Blanche's eyes. 'He was a big influence in my life, a hell of a man. In the end he did not become what he could have been.' Terre Blanche does not amplify on this. Indeed he provides very few glimpses into his private life. He denies absolutely a personal hatred for black people. 'Whenever people come to visit me at my farm in Ventersdorp and don't know the way, I tell them to go to the garage in town and ask the black attendant there for directions to "Eugene's house". He knows me, we are friends.'

Why all the Nazi-style trappings? 'How the hell can I be a Nazi? I am simply being true to my forefathers, to my country and to my God with whom we entered into a vow at Blood River.' He insists, somewhat unconvincingly, that the AWB emblem, a swastika-style arrangement of three black sevens within a white circle against a red background, is not inspired by the Nazis. The three sevens, according to an AWB policy document, represent the biblical prophecy of 'the final and absolute triumph in and through Jesus Christ.' The three sevens stand in direct opposition to the three sixes which are the sign of the beast and of the Antichrist in the Book of Revelations. The eagle with outspread wings which surmounts the emblem – another striking reminder of the German Reich – is said to represent the eagle referred to in Deuteronomy and Psalms.

'Our main task is to be there when this government sells out the country, to restore law and order when it vanishes, to ensure our women and children are not maimed and raped by ANC murderers. In the meantime we give our full support to the Conservative Party. If the CP comes to power, I'm going home, back to my farm and my people. I'm here because I have to be. I will fight as long as I have to, in order to save my people. No force, no might can stop me in that.'

Is there a trait within Afrikanerdom which reveals itself in frequent outpourings of neo-fascism? The National Party itself is compared by its severest critics to Nazi Germany or Stalin's Russia. Yet despite a history of discrimination and suppression, the ruling Afrikaner-dominated party – though certainly authoritarian and increasingly repressive – still has some way to go to match the evils of the European tyrannies of the 1930s and 1940s. But is there, nevertheless, on the far right of Afrikaner nationalism, a compelling attraction for the fascist doctrines of racial purity that caught the imagination of several European peoples when they themselves felt threatened?

Of course, the entire policy of racial segregation was founded on the principle of a distinctive Aryan white blood, but this notion was not presented by the scientists of apartheid in any aggressively supremacist sense, at least not publicly. After all, the Afrikaners, in constructing separate development, were following God's calling: providing each race with its own destiny on an equal but separate basis. According to National Party doctrine, the genes of whites were not superior to those of the natives, they were just different – hence separateness was justified.

A streak of racism revealed itself in the early part of this century in the shape of a cartoon figure in the Nationalist press called Hoggenheimer, depicted as a Shylock-like, Anglo-Jewish capitalist supposed to represent the Oppenheimers and others whose wealth had been acquired, in the view of ardent nationalists, through the sweat of poor Afrikaners slaving away in the mines. During the 1930s opposition built up in some areas to Jewish immigration to South Africa from Nazi Germany. A movement known as the Greyshirts emerged in 1933, attracting support from some rural Afrikaners whose frustration over their own economic deprivation was occasionally vented on Jewish traders. The Greyshirts made little impact on the political stage except to embarrass the National Party who numbered Jews among their supporters. But the increasing number of Jewish refugees arriving in the country compelled the Nationalist leader D. F. Malan to take a stand. He backed a party proposal that all Jewish immigration be stopped. The campaign was joined by the future Prime Minister Hendrik Verwoerd who, as editor of *Die Transvaler*, proposed a quota system to control Jewish entry into certain professions. Despite these anti-semitic rumblings, however, a campaign against Jewish people was never a major plank of National Party policy. In the general election campaign of 1938 – when the full effects of Jewish immigration were being felt – the Jewish issue did not figure prominently. After all, South Africa's Jewish community may be one of the largest in the world outside America and Israel but the 'problem' they presented was marginal given that the Afrikaners were surrounded by 30 million blacks. Moreover, the Jews are white.

Nevertheless events in Europe during the 1930s were not without repercussions in South Africa, giving rise to what – until the AWB – was South Africa's only example of a significant rightist movement outside mainstream politics. Even so, the parallels with Nazi Germany were hazy. The movement arose out of the 1938 Great Trek commemorations and expressed itself in the desire to maintain the momentum towards Afrikaner liberation which had infused the celebrations at the Voortrekker Monument. The Ossewabrandwag (OB, the Ox-Wagon Fire Guard) was established to perpetuate the spirit of the commemorative trek. In words strikingly similar to those used today by Terre Blanche, the OB sought to 'protect and further the religious, cultural and material concerns of the Afrikaner and to bring together all Afrikaners, women as well as men, who endorsed these principles and were willing to strive for them.' The organisation met for military training, torchlight rallies and such like, its members clearly inspired by the rise of National Socialism in Germany with its emphasis on the ethnic purity of the Aryan race. Jews were naturally excluded from the movement.

The Nazis' racial policies clearly attracted some Afrikaners, not principally because of their anti-semitism but because Hitler's search for a cleansed identity for the German people helped bolster the Afrikaners' arguments in favour of their own nationhood and the establishment of an Afrikaner state untainted by non-whites. Whereas Hitler's dreams rested on the principle of creating *Lebensraum* (living space) for the German people in conquered European lands, the Afrikaners sought their political future within a retrenched exclusivist white state, and recognised that blacks would require their own territories as well. That said, the later forced removals of black people living in 'black spots' in white areas to the consolidated black homelands resembled in concept, if not in their final horrific outcome, Hitler's attempts to rid the face of Europe of the Jewish people. Several Afrikaner leaders, with little loyalty towards Britain, calculated that an Afrikaner republic would be achieved more quickly after a German rather than an Allied victory. During the war the OB attracted several hundred thousand followers who frequently engaged Afrikaner army conscripts in street fighting and bar brawls.

Some OB members, disgruntled with what they regarded as the organisation's hesitant policies, formed themselves into an elite group known as the Stormjaers (Stormtroopers) who planned a more active role in assisting Nazi Germany by sabotaging the Allied war effort and channelling intelligence information to the Germans. Telephone lines were cut; electricity lines, pylons and railway lines were blown up. Two Stormjaers, Julian Visser and Hendrik van Blerk, were sentenced to death in 1942 for killing an innocent bystander when they planted a bomb at the post office in the town of Benoni east of Johannesburg. Malan, as prime minister, later commuted their sentences to life imprisonment. Forty years later this act of clemency was cited by Helen Suzman when she appealed to President Botha to grant a stay of execution to the 'Sharpeville Six'. According to Mrs Suzman, Botha expressed interest in her allusion to the Stormjaers' case. But this failed to change his mind. Although he later reprieved the six, on that occasion he refused to grant a stay of execution. Had it not been for a successful eleventh-hour appeal in the Supreme Court the six would now be dead.

Members of the police force were believed to share the OB's anti-war policies and over 300 officers were dismissed. Many of the OB members were interned, among them the future prime minister of South Africa, John Vorster. His own confinement might have eased any nagging doubts two decades later about locking up his leftist opponents under increasingly extensive security powers, especially the 90- and 180-day detention laws. After the war Vorster was turned down as a candidate in the 1948 general election by Malan because of his OB connections. Vorster was not the only would-be Nationalist leader to leave a skeleton behind in the cupboard of the Second World War. P. W. Botha was himself briefly a member of the OB but left when it began its violent activities and when it was made clear that OB membership precluded joining the National Party.

The ending of the war and the election of the National Party resulted in the eventual decline of the Ossewabrandwag. With the Nationalists victorious and the policy of apartheid guaranteeing Afrikaners' nationhood and freedom, there was little further need for an ultra-rightist group. Until, that is, the policy of complete racial separation was relaxed; until the search for absolute ethnic separation came face to face with the political and economic pressures of the twentieth century.

By the early 1970s the devotees of total apartheid were becoming distinctly uneasy. Notwithstanding both the tough crackdown on black organisations like the ANC in the wake of the Sharpeville massacre of 1960 and the growing resistance to the kind of international pressure reflected in the famous 'wind of change' speech delivered in Cape Town by the British prime minister Harold Macmillan, dilution of some aspects of apartheid was beginning. South Africa established relations with the black African state of Malawi with the result that a few black diplomatic families were given special residence status in the white areas of the capital, Pretoria. There were a few hesitant nods in the direction of mixed sport; the government started turning a blind eye to the infringements of minor race laws classified under 'petty apartheid'.

This relaxation of apartheid – no matter how trifling to the outside world – was earth-shattering for Afrikanerdom even though the implementation of 'grand apartheid', by way of the establishment of the black homelands, was proceeding apace. It was at this time that the divergence between *verligtes* (enlightened ones) and *verkramptes* (narrow-minded ones) emerged. By 1969 some Afrikaners had come to regard Vorster as a traitor.

Eugene Terre Blanche was in his mid-twenties at that time. He had previously been a policeman and was a member of John Vorster's bodyguard, which might explain his love today of surrounding himself with security personnel. He then became a farmer, writing drama and poetry as a hobby. According to a newspaper report, one of his plays *Sybrand the Watermaker* was once a set book on the syllabus of schools in the Cape.

In 1973 he and six other 'concerned young Afrikaners' launched the Afrikaner Weerstandsbeweging, meeting in a garage in the Transvaal town of Heidelberg to 'begin the search for an alternative to a Westminster system of government' as AWB literature recounts. For more than a decade the organisation's activities resembled those of school pranksters rather than of a movement preparing itself for the final defence of its people. Several AWB members were convicted of planning to infest the Sun City hotel and entertainment complex with syphilis germs (presumably because the leisure centre is multiracial) and of storing weapons illegally at a Transvaal farm. Terre Blanche, one of the accused, was given a suspended jail sentence. Only later did Terre Blanche mould this rag-tag-and-bobtail collection of misfits into a force to be reckoned with. Such was Terre Blanche's charisma that he survived a challenge to his leadership following reports linking him with an attractive female columnist on an English-language newspaper.

The rise of the AWB cannot be attributed to a latent fascism within Afrikanerdom. The clue lies elsewhere: in the collapse of 'grand apartheid' and the failure of the National Party to replace it with a new philosophy; the uncertainties created by the ideological vacuum; the desire for an anchor, a sense of belonging, when traditional points of reference are being shed.

On the political level, the deviation from exclusive white privilege alarms those on the bottom rung of the Afrikaner ladder. The National Party has increasingly become the terrain of upper-class Afrikaners who can afford to be more generous to blacks, whereas the right wing attracts the support of those who see their positions threatened by 'upwardly mobile' blacks, especially on the shop floor. The government's turning a blind eye to infringements of the Group Areas Act created 'grey areas' where whites find themselves living cheek-by-jowl with blacks – places like Hillbrow in Johannesburg. On the economic front, government moves towards privatisation appear further to endanger white security as does increased racial integration in the workplace.

The number of registered black apprentices increased eightfold between 1981 and 1985. The position of white blue-collar workers was further jeopardised by automation in industry. The early part of the 1980s also witnessed the worst economic recession for whites since the 1920s. The figure for registered white unemployed in 1981 was just over 6000; by 1986 it had risen to 32,000. Salaries fell; more white-owned businesses collapsed; insolvencies quadrupled in the four years up to 1985. Against this background the ultra-right was picking up support from the working class, the blue-collar workers, the minor civil servants having to deal with blacks on an everyday basis, and the debt-ridden farmers; all felt distressed by their personal setbacks and transferred those grievances on to a government which in their view had betrayed the white man. The Afrikaner Resistance Movement was there, ready and waiting for them.

Is the AWB the face of future Afrikanerdom, the naked display of raw racism eclipsing the more enlightened, sophisticated Afrikaner who has emerged in recent years? Are the modest protagonists of liberalisation to be shouted down by the raucous demagoguery of the right?

In politically fluid times it would be dangerous to put a ceiling on far-right support; by the same token it would be premature to write it off. The AWB is not typical of the mainstream of Afrikaner nationalism. Even at their most assertive, the parties representing Afrikaner interests have always sought to achieve their objectives through the established political and parliamentary channels. Despite all the assaults in recent years on human rights, the Afrikaner remains committed to a parliamentary system. The Conservative Party and the HNP still conform to this constitutional model – it is here for the moment that they part company with the AWB, with its commitment to a militant and possibly armed pursuit of its objectives. Terre Blanche's powerful use of symbols and banners and emblems is also not part of the Afrikaners' political tradition. Nor is the idea of Terre Blanche as a kind of *Führer*. While the Afrikaners have always supported strong, commanding leaders, these were figures who emerged from within the *volk* and were not imposed upon them. Although the National Party itself stands accused of using AWB tactics in breaking up opponents' meetings during the 1940s, the ultra-right's ugly pursuit of white supremacy outside parliamentary boundaries is foreign to the Afrikaner's understanding of democracy.

Nevertheless the AWB is playing a not insignificant role in the current shifting sands. In the country areas and the poorer white towns they have paved the way for the Conservative Party, mobilising support and creating the emotional climate for the right wing to prosper. Several AWB members have already won seats in parliament under the CP flag, a worrying 'Trojan horse' strategy for those concerned about maintaining the vestiges of democracy. The dismissal by Law and Order Minister Vlok of the AWB's more outrageous demonstrations of armed militancy, claiming they were not actually breaking the law, only served to enhance the organisation's image further. Mr Vlok may have overlooked the fact that Hitler came to power 'legally'.

In a way the National Party and the AWB have become partners in a self-destructive, chicken-and-egg situation. The Nationalists' wavering in part created the right-wing. The government's fear of the right in turn stifled creative, far-reaching reform. When television around the world shows Eugene Terre Blanche and his brownshirts barking out their 'Ah-Vay-Bay' slogans, the government can turn to the international community and say: 'Now you know what we are up against.'

The Afrikaner Weerstandsbeweging is the backstop for militant Afrikaner nationalism. Its day would come if South Africa ever slid into Latin American-style anarchy with a government drowning in a sea of violence involving the armed services, black nationalist insurgents and white paramilitary forces of the right. Barring that eventuality, the majority of Afrikaners would not support the use of right-wing violence to further political ends. Most Afrikaners express a profound distaste for the AWB, described to me by one enlightened Afrikaner as 'low-brows with a good leader'. So it is questionable whether the AWB, as a body, would court a tough government response by engaging in violent acts. The danger is that individual members might elect to do so. Some members are former policemen trained in the use of weapons. Some have volunteered for service in the war against Namibian guerrillas based in Angola so that they could kill blacks. A young Afrikaner, Hendrik Strydom – a former policeman and, according to the police, a self-confessed member of the AWB – appeared in court after six black people died in a shooting spree on the streets of Pretoria at the hand of a white gunman.

The AWB is a natural haven for fanatics. It offers them a home and affords them legitimacy in their own eyes. It is among such types of individual that the perpetrators might be found, if the day should come when white 'sell-outs' as well as black people start disappearing from their homes in the middle of the night, their bodies turning up next morning in grimy back alleys.

CHAPTER SEVEN

Wrestling with the Scriptures

The call comes in the middle of the night. The pastor drags himself from bed and drives through the dark streets of the black township. He finds an innocent black family standing in the road, their home destroyed by a firebomb. The perpetrators are usually black vigilantes – suspected of being government agents – whose victims oppose the state. Often they bomb the wrong house by mistake. The family inside may suffer death or injury – at the least their home is burnt to the ground and they lose all their meagre possessions. 'What is happening to us?' they ask the pastor, who has no answer. In despair, he can only ask himself: 'What is going on in this country?'

The township is Mamelodi near Pretoria; the pastor is Nico Smith, who left a senior position at Stellenbosch University to become minister in Mamelodi. Smith also left the white Dutch Reformed Church after years of mounting unease over its support for apartheid, to join the racially segregated black Reformed church. At first he lived in a white suburb a few kilometres from Mamelodi. Sensing that he was regarded as a 'white stranger' by his black congregation, he applied for and was granted special government permission to live in Mamelodi itself among the people whom he serves.

It is not only when black families need his help that the phone rings. Very often the calls are from whites, abusing or threatening 'the white who now lives among the kaffirs'.

Nico Smith's long journey to Mamelodi took him from the bosom of Afrikanerdom to the heart of the black community, an act of treachery in the eyes of many of his own people. The journey began on a tramcar in Germany in 1963 when Smith was returning from a meeting with the famous Swiss theologian Karl Barth who had opposed the Nazis, and who told Hitler that he owed a higher loyalty to God than to the *Führer*. Barth had asked Smith two questions: 'Are you free to preach the gospel in South Africa?' and 'What if you have a biblical insight which is contrary to that of your friends and family – are you still free?' Because of the strictures of apartheid, Smith's only answer could be: 'I don't know.'

In the years that followed, Smith worked at missions in Pretoria and in the black homeland of Venda, his discomfort growing as the grip of apartheid tightened. In 1975 came his first break with the *volk* when he resigned from the Broederbond. This followed the defection from the government of the far-right Herstigte Nasionale Party (HNP) several years previously, the first political schism in Afrikanerdom since the National Party had come to power. The

111

Nationalists and the Broederbond were determined to prevent any further rifts: thus all Broeders were required to sign a document pledging loyalty to the National Party. Smith refused, explaining to his Broederbond 'cell' leaders: 'How can I do this? I am a theologian.'

Later at Stellenbosch, Smith taught his students that the gospel called for the equality of all races. He was accused of preaching heresy. Smith recalls: 'At Stellenbosch they were threatening me at so many levels, it became impossible.' Then the black community at Mamelodi called him to their ministry. Says Smith: 'I just knew I had to go. I was not going to change anything among whites. I decided I would rather give my energies to the blacks – the downtrodden and the rejected. I don't know why they chose me. It must have been God's will.'

The first Dutch and German settlers who arrived at the Cape in 1652 belonged to the Dutch Reformed Church, an offshoot of the protest against Catholic France inspired in Geneva by the theologian John Calvin, one of the most important figures in the protestant Reformation of the sixteenth century. Calvin's Geneva was an austere place. Frowning on extravagant or self-indulgent behaviour, while monitoring all ardent and worldly desires of its members, Geneva society became a puritan enclave of the Reformed church. Calvinism was firmly rooted in the scriptures and held that all things were predestined by God, that man therefore had to accept that certain aspects of his life could not be explained. The culmination of Calvin's teaching was contained in his massive work *The Institutes of the Christian Religion*, published in 1536, which dealt with man's 'inward soul' where he sought redemption and eternal life, and with 'civil government' to regulate man's relationships outside his inward life. Calvin was clear that a government should not attempt to determine man's spiritual life as this would become, in modern terms, an ideology. Calvin's teachings were often misunderstood in the Low Countries. By the time they had arrived at the Cape the way was open for further revision.

The first settlers under van Riebeeck were not accompanied by a minister of religion. Dutch ministers en route to and from the East Indies would administer the sacraments but in general the settlers' spiritual requirements were attended to by 'comforters of the sick'. The first resident minister arrived in 1665 and so this date marks the formal establishment in South Africa of the Nederduitse Gereformeerde Kerk (NGK), the Dutch Reformed Church, though it was still a department of the Dutch East India Company.

The settlers had brought with them a fundamentalist form of Calvinism which, in the still untamed frontier country thousands of miles away from Europe, remained unrefined. Consequently, the twists and turns of Afrikaner history acquired a religious significance, if not at the time, then certainly later when the leaders of Afrikaner nationalism delved back into history for evidence of a divine calling for the Afrikaner people.

Calvin influenced the religious formation of the Afrikaner people, but later neo-Calvinists whose teachings in Europe and America also reached South Africa were altogether more rigid. They reinterpreted Calvinism as a philosophy of natural theology according to which God revealed himself both in nature and in history. The moment the revisionists reached that conclusion, their logic was that God must be recognised in everything. From there it was a short step to believing that the *will* of God was also apparent in all things. The existence and development of the Afrikaner people became an 'act of God' and, because God had created the nation, it had to continue. Another logical argument was that God had willed that there should be separate nations and races.

The preachers who joined the colony were there for the benefit of the settlers; there was little evidence of their conveying the teachings of the Bible to the indigenous people. The Calvinist tradition was not explicit about the need for missionary work. The notion of the Afrikaner bringing religion to the black people of southern Africa mainly emerged with the arrival of Scottish Presbyterians in the 1820s.

When the settlers trekked north, the only book they carried with them was the Bible. When they arrived in the Transvaal and found a river thick with reeds, they turned to the scriptures, read about the baby Moses cast adrift in the rushes and concluded that they had discovered the source of the Nile. They named the spot Nylzijnoog (Eye of the Nile) and the town they established nearby is to this day called Nylstroom (Nile stream). The Bible also told them that the Israelites had been commanded by God to annihilate the Canaanites. Was there a lesson here for the Afrikaners, they asked themselves, as they journeyed deeper into lands peopled by strange heathens and pagans?

The Scottish Presbyterians brought to South Africa a spirit of pietism which resulted in their ministers working actively among the non-white population. The Sendingkerk (Dutch Reformed Mission Church) was formed as the 'sister' church of the NGK serving the mixed-race people; the NG Kerk in Afrika (Dutch Reformed Church in Africa) was established for black worshippers. Those belonging to the pietist school represented a reaction against the stagnant, impersonal faith embodied in Calvinism. The most powerful influence during the nineteenth century was Dr Andrew Murray whose benign presence in the church opened up many new frontiers, particularly in education and missionary work. The NGK therefore became a more missionary-minded church. Second in importance was the Gereformeerde Kerk based in Potchefstroom, which sought to re-establish Calvinism. Originally seen as rigidly Calvinist, the Gereformeerde Kerk became the most open of all the Afrikaans churches, rejecting attempts to see state, nation and *volk* as demi-Gods. For them God alone was sovereign. A third church, the Hervormde Kerk, is still uncompromisingly dedicated to apartheid.

What mattered to the NGK was the salvation of the soul, not the visible fellowship of believers in a single body of the church. Hence the NGK's ninth synod held in 1857 was a crucial turning point in church history, as it paved the way for the racially segregated churches which still exist within the 'single family' of the Dutch Reformed Church. The synod of 1857 passed the following resolution:

> The synod deems it desirable and scriptural that our members from the heathen be received and absorbed into our existing congregations, wherever possible; but where this measure, owing to the weakness of some, should prove to be an obstacle in the furtherance of the cause of Christ among the heathen, the congregations from the heathen shall enjoy their Christian privileges in a separate building or institution.

The 'weakness of some' (i.e. the refusal of Afrikaners to share Christian, human fellowship on a non-segregated basis) prevailed.

Until the end of the nineteenth century the church maintained a separate identity from the Afrikaner *volk*, possibly because of the influence of the Presbyterians. Slowly, though, the church became the captive of the Afrikaner people. The Boer War, or rather its aftermath, was a powerful impetus for this. Nico Smith's grandmother died in a British concentration camp, his mother was a camp inmate and his father a British prisoner-of-war in Ceylon. When his parents returned to their farm after the war, they discovered it had been burned to the ground. They propped up pieces of zinc sheeting against a wall for shelter. Thousands of people were in a similar plight. Says Smith: 'The Dutch Reformed Church stepped in and told them "It is not the end of the world. We are still a chosen people." The church took them into their care. It launched major financial schemes to help; the church became very, very involved.'

By the time the Afrikaner government came to power in 1948, the Dutch Reformed Church had lost contact with the original teachings of Calvin and in so doing conveniently provided the theological foundation for apartheid. Calvin would never have condoned the virtual deification of the nation or the absolutism of the state or of race. The Nationalists' policies led to the elevation of apartheid to a civil religion in which the secular notions of *volk*, culture and politics became prominent features. In so doing they went beyond the bounds of justifiable civil government set down by Calvin; they entered man's inner soul and tainted his spiritual being with political ideology.

In the wake of the Nationalists' victory, hour upon hour of scriptural research was devoted to reconciling apartheid with the Bible. From the pages of the scriptures it was inferred that God had ordained a divergence of languages and therefore of nations. For example in Genesis 11 (the tower of Babel):

> the Lord did there confound the language of all the earth: and from thence did the Lord scatter them abroad upon the face of all the earth.

In Acts 17 it was discovered that:

> From one single stock he not only created the whole human race so that they could occupy the entire earth, but he decreed how long each nation should flourish and what the boundaries of its territory should be.

It was at a church conference in Bloemfontein in 1946 that members of the Dutch Reformed churches formulated their support for the policy of apartheid. A paper presented by Professor J. D. du Toit of Potchefstroom developed the concept of God as 'the maker of differences'. In the same way that God had created differences in plants and in animals, he argued, so with the human family. Articles in the Dutch Reformed Church newspaper *Die Kerkbode* by other theologians supported this view. Theologian Johan Heyns, appointed in 1986 as moderator of the Dutch Reformed Church, concedes that: 'The church did not only support apartheid theoretically, it gave the policy a biblical and ethical justification. The church provided apartheid's theology.' As a result the church played an important role in the general election of 1948. Nationalist politicians on the hustings were able to say to ordinary Afrikaners: 'Even the church supports us'.

Nico Smith, then a third-year theology student preparing for the ministry, can recall the 'hour of triumph' when the Nationalists won the election. He and his fellow students ran through the streets of Pretoria singing freedom songs like: '*Hoor jy die magtige Dreuning?*' ('Do you hear the mighty rumble?'). The rumble was the thunderous arrival in power of the National Party. Smith was absolutely convinced that God wanted a separation of peoples.

'The NGK should have realised there and then that the Afrikaners had reached salvation, that they were now OK. The church should have resolved to tell the volk: "We are a church. We should not be linked to one people. We have a prophetic witness to fulfil. We must speak up when things go wrong".' Instead the church was slowly sucked in by the National Party's tentacles, ceasing to have an independent voice. With 90 per cent of the government NGK members, the church found it impossible to take an objective stand.

The NGK submitted itself to an ideological marriage of church and state which not even its effective excommunication from the world ecclesiastical movement could deter. In 1960 the World Council of Churches met at Cottesloe in Johannesburg to discuss racial tension in South Africa in the wake of the Sharpeville massacre. Its conclusions were that all unjust discrimination should be rejected. The Cottesloe conference affirmed the equality of all races; opposed the exclusion of people from churches on the grounds of colour; declared that there was no justification in the Bible for the ban on racially mixed marriages; condemned the migrant labour system that separated hundreds of thousands of black workers from their families, the low wages paid to black workers, the system of job reservation and laws under which people were detained without trial.

Several leaders of the Dutch Reformed Church in the powerful Transvaal and Cape synods were happy to associate themselves with this attack on apartheid and racially based religion. But then Prime Minister Verwoerd, fearing a serious rupture in the ideological base of apartheid, set about lobbying the NGK's rank and file till the regional synods rejected the conference findings. Verwoerd spread the impression that during the Cottesloe conference the NGK church leaders had somehow left their powers of reason at home. After all, to go along with the conference rulings was contrary to everything the church had been preaching since the Nationalists came to power. The church leaders were humiliated and forced to recant. The white church was soon barred from the World Council of Churches. The NGK's acting moderator in the Southern Transvaal, Beyers Naudé, resigned as a minister and proceeded to form his own Christian Institute, a home for dissident NGK members seeking a non-racial future for South Africa. Gradually it admitted black members. The institute was banned in 1977; Naudé himself was subjected to various bannings and periods of house arrest.

Subsequently, church theology on race became enshrined in a document adopted by the 1974 general synod called *Ras, Volk en Nasie* (Race, People and Nation), the result of many years of scriptural study. Its conclusion was that separate nations had been ordained by God; the individual lived out his religious, social and political life within this context.

The first signs of a review of this policy emerged during the early 1980s at about the same time that Botha was enacting his first reforms to apartheid. A document submitted by the church to the 1981 edition of the *Race Relations Survey* (published by the South African Institute of Race Relations) spoke of the NGK as 'convinced that in a *multi-national* situation, the church must preach the norms of God's word for the mutual relationships of various *groups* of people' (my italics). Shrinking from mentioning the word 'apartheid', the document nevertheless committed the church to alerting government to the harsher aspects of the policy:

> The NGK must serve as a warning to the nation, drawing attention to poverty, low wages, poor housing, and other socio-economic problems which may arise among the various population groups. The church should bring to the attention of the authorities and all other relevant bodies the needs and distress that exist in the homelands. . . . Although the migrant labour system is not considered by the NGK to be contrary to the teachings of the Bible, it should be eliminated as far as possible in South Africa to avoid its disruptive consequences in family life.

In a memorandum submitted to a commission of enquiry into security legislation the NGK said:

> With regard to the Mixed Marriages Act, the NGK considers that while such marriages are undesirable, their prohibition is an extraordinary measure and should be reviewed. The NGK does not subscribe to the view that squatter settlements on the outskirts of towns are unavoidable. It has helped to minister to the material needs of squatters and in its magazine it openly criticised the pulling down of shacks by the authorities, especially in the cold and wet winter season.

In other words, the church was not departing from the fundamentals of apartheid but now substantially agreed with the Cottesloe conference almost two decades previously as far as some of the iniquities of the system were concerned.

Professor Heyns, a liberal in comparison with most in the NGK, was on record as rejecting the Mixed Marriages Act and Article 16 of the Immorality Act (the latter banning sex across the colour line). 'Afrikaners don't need laws to protect their identity,' he told a newspaper interviewer. Such *verligte* views led to his being ousted in 1982 from the moderature of the NGK's general synod. The following year though, Heyns was elected moderator of the church's Northern Transvaal synod, a surprising appointment perhaps given the highly conservative nature of religion and politics in that part of the country. Heyns proved that he was not going to be tamed by the conservative environment in which he now found himself. He condemned a gathering in Pretoria in 1983 by some 200 conservative *dominees* protesting against the new constitution admitting mixed-race and Indian people to parliament.

Heyns had studied for his degree at Potchefstroom University and later at the University of Pretoria. From there he embarked on a trip to Europe which was to have a profound effect on his views. A spell at the Free University of Amsterdam was followed by a period of study at Basle University in Switzerland under Karl Barth, the same theologian who had changed the life of Nico Smith. Heyns was in his early twenties and as he recalled in the same newspaper interview:

> This was an important experience which would influence me for a lifetime. Whereas I had grown up with blacks who were always culturally, socially and academically beneath me, in Europe I met blacks who were on a similar level. I realised that the colour black need not be a symbol of inferiority. I experienced communion with them in the same church and this was a shocking experience for a *Boereseun* [Boer's son].

During a succession of academic posts back in South Africa, Heyns' views were some distance ahead of the church establishment.

Still Heyns faced an uphill struggle in attempting to wean the NGK away from support for hardline apartheid, particularly within his own Northern Transvaal synod. Hardly had he been appointed moderator than Heyns and fellow liberals were defeated when the synod refused to discuss the opening up of all-white churches to worshippers of other races. But within some congregations there was beginning a 'wrestling with the scriptures', as Heyns puts it, over whether the Bible contained any justification for apartheid. The more liberal Western Cape synod called for reforms including the desegregation of churches. Such deliberations were bringing about what Heyns calls a 'ripening of thinking'.

But the NGK's hesitancy in coming to grips with the theological approval of apartheid aggravated its relations with the other Reformed churches. The NGK has over 1·5 million white members; the Sendingkerk representing mixed-race people has around 700,000, the Indian Reformed Church in Africa has just over 2000, while the NG Kerk in Afrika (for blacks) has a membership of just over a million. All four Reformed churches, though 'sisters' in a 'single family' are constitutionally independent, while sharing the same doctrine.

Relations were strained in particular with the Sendingkerk which in 1982 drafted a confession of faith at Belhar in the Cape declaring apartheid a sin and its theological defence a heresy. It also stated that continuing links between the Sendingkerk and the NGK would only be possible if the latter 'confessed its guilt for providing the moral and theological foundations for apartheid'. The Belhar Confession was a landmark document which in effect challenged all the Christian churches in South Africa to review their position on apartheid. The NGK had replied to this by asking the mixed-race church to drop the Belhar Confession, claiming that the white NGK had acted 'under the guidance of the Lord' in creating separate churches for separate race groups. A letter referred to the 'implications' of the Sendingkerk's adopting the confession, describing the document as an 'act of challenge and conflict' which made 'new polarisation' inevitable.

The revolt of the Sendingkerk was led by one of the most prominent members of the anti-apartheid movement, who became a thorn in the side of the white church. Dr Allan Boesak was one of eight children whose father had died when Boesak was six years old. He thinks he is descended from a Khoi tribal leader who launched a slave rebellion against the British rulers at the Cape in the early nineteenth century. His ancestor's rebellious spirit had clearly infected Boesak. He was instrumental in the expulsion of the NGK from the 70-million strong World Alliance of Reformed Churches of which he was elected president in 1982. His role was crucial also in the formation in 1983 of the United Democratic Front comprising over 600 anti-apartheid groups. Under his leadership the Sendingkerk formally adopted the Belhar Confession, Boesak declaring that 'the Sendingkerk has finally broken with the hurtful history of apartheid'.

A similarly independent stand was emerging from the black NG Kerk in Afrika whose leader the Reverend Sam Buti had himself been in the front line of South Africa's increasing racial turmoil. Buti helped win a reprieve for the black township of Alexandra close to Johannesburg, which under Verwoerd had been destined to be reduced to a hostel city for migrant black workers, with all the other residents of the disestablished township to be deported to the homelands. Buti fell foul of local activists however when he served on the Pretoria-imposed local black council in an attempt to secure funding to improve the area. His house was petrol-bombed and he was forced to retire from active politics.

The black church was calling upon a recalcitrant white church to join a united family comprising all the racially separated Reformed churches. The call was a direct challenge to the NGK to state its position on racial segregation in the church. In response, the NGK was able to exert its own pressure through its control of funding for many of the black churches. The NG Kerk in Afrika (NGKA) established a special fund to assist black ministers who fell foul of the NGK authorities because of their outspoken views. The message from its sister churches soon permeated the ranks of the NGK. Some church quarters began a fundamental reassessment of the NGK's position on certain apartheid laws, notably the ban on interracial sex and marriage.

The NGK had been instrumental in the government's imposition of these laws.

The 1936 meeting of the Cape synod passed a resolution saying that: 'Convinced of the unwholesome results of marriages between whites and coloureds, this honourable synod urges the Committee for the Combating of Social Evils to urge the government, in the name of the synod, to introduce legislation in this matter.' Forty-seven years later a doctrinal commission of the same synod asserted that 'the NGK apparently exceeded the boundaries of its prophetic witness with its representations to the authorities to set up these laws.' The commission challenged the view of the 1982 general synod which had declared that 'the complicated South African society still justifies the Mixed Marriages Act'. The synod admitted that the church had provided theological justification for apartheid; it now declared that all forms of racial discrimination in the church should be abolished, adding that it was difficult for the synod to part company with the 1982 Belhar Confession. The commission was paving the way for a significant rethink of policy by the Dutch Reformed Church. Compared to what had gone before, the synod's findings were revolutionary. Theological teachings, arguing that the separateness of peoples was central to the gospel, were increasingly challenged. But would the ten other church synods follow the lead given by the Cape congregations?

Liberal elements within the church called for a far-reaching review of church thinking. Hardliners mustered their forces to preserve the old order. The scene was set for what came to be called the 'watershed' general synod of the Dutch Reformed Church in Cape Town in October 1986.

The synod was recognised by Heyns and other church figures as an important turning point not only for the church but for Afrikanerdom in general. For the NGK leaders the pressure to review the church's justification of apartheid was balanced by a concern to maintain church unity. Any decisions reached could have a profound effect on the politics of Afrikanerdom. Though the church rejected any suggestion that its deliberations were mirroring the national political debate, quite clearly a defence of the old order would assist the right wing while the adoption of a revisionist stance would assist the government in its attempts to push ahead with reform.

Prior to the Cape Town synod the NGK commission had drawn up a sixty-six page report to be submitted for debate. It was entitled *Kerk en Samelewing* (Church and Society) published in October 1986, and it appeared to mark a significant departure from the existing theology as embraced by *Ras, Volk en Nasie*. The new document had as its premise the essential unity of the human family, in that each and every individual had been created in the image of God regardless of nationality, race, colour or creed. The tabling of the report was accompanied by demands from certain quarters that the synod should formally condemn apartheid as sinful while expressing regret that the NGK had for so long sanctioned it. In advance of the debate, conservative elements were already making known their opposition to any such confession.

The document was the most important pronouncement of the Dutch Reformed

Church in over a decade. Many of its clauses set out a new doctrine for the church, one which sought to distance the NGK from racially discriminatory laws. It tackled many of the issues which had previously divided the church from its sister bodies and from the world movement of reformed churches. 'Church and Society' spoke of the church as a 'universal community', adding that 'the church, as the one universal people of God, may not be restricted exclusively to one nation or group, nor may it exclude anyone on the basis of origin, national allegiance, language or culture.' On the church's view of the relationships between various ethnic groups, the document referred to 'the human race as a unity'. It went on: 'This ideal of the fundamental unity of the human race is of immense importance when it is related to the biblical view of every person. It also precedes all national diversities as such.'

'Church and Society' appeared to diverge from previous doctrine in that race was no longer to be the denominator by which people were separated. The report stated:

> 'Race' is mainly a biological concept related to hereditary traits such as blood relationship, hair, eye, skin, colouring and the shape of parts of the body etc. . . . . Racial characteristics other than blood relationships receive only passing attention in the Old Testament. The Old Testament is indeed aware of the biological factor in the composition of human groups, but it does not describe the origins, the characteristics, or history of races. It most certainly knows no race problem. In the New Testament the concept of race plays no part whatsoever.

Far from being a source of racial conflict, the diversity of peoples was 'within the framework of God's acts of mercy' which highlighted 'the magnificence and the glory of God's all-embracing salvation'.

There followed a denunciation of racial discrimination, the like of which had never been heard before from the organs of the dominant white church:

> Whoever in theory or by attitude and deed implies that one race, people, or group of people is inherently superior, and another race, people, or group of people is inherently inferior, is guilty of racism. Racism is a sin which tends to take on collective and structural forms. As a moral aberration it deprives a human being of his dignity, his obligations and his rights. It must be rejected and opposed in all its manifestations because it leads to oppression and exploitation.

The document sought to distance the church from the government, another remarkable departure given the old cliché about the Dutch Reformed Church being 'the National Party at prayer'. It stated that 'the church is not hostile to the nation, but neither is it the nation's employee.'

Confirming the opposition of previous church conventions to the Mixed Marriages Act, the report stated simply: 'As far as racially mixed marriages are concerned, the fact is that according to the Bible they are permissible.'

On the crucial issue of whether the white church should unite with its sister churches the report hedged its bets. It said that of all other churches the NGK was closest to its sister bodies because they shared the same 'Reformed confession'. The report recommended that 'the biblical doctrine of the unity of the church, and the Reformed view about the visible unity of the church, calls us thereto to bring the unity of the family of NG churches always clearer to expression.' But in the same breath 'Church and Society' stated that: 'The family of Dutch Reformed Churches are essentially one church because of their historical bonds. . . . In reality, however, they are institutionally separate.' In other words the churches were to be embraced by the broad umbrella of the Dutch Reformed movement, but the individual churches were to continue as racially defined bodies. However, the report opened the way for white churches to admit people of other colours by stipulating that 'faith in the truth of God and his revelations in the scriptures is the only condition to be a member of the church of Jesus Christ' and that 'the admission of members from other churches is in principle and practice a matter for the local congregation.' A minority recommendation from a conservative theologian proposed that 'only condition' be replaced by 'fundamental condition', thereby leaving a loophole to allow individual congregations to bar the admission of blacks to white churches. There would, however, be no ban on mixed congregations by the NGK's ruling body.

Then, towards the end of 'Church and Society', the NGK at last tackled the question at the heart of its theological anguish: apartheid. In a minority report Heyns and other liberals admitted that the 'elevation of apartheid to a religiously coloured ideology was an error' and although not intended 'its practical application contributed to much sorrow and suffering and bitterness. Of this in all sincerity before God and the people we must confess.' But this was counterbalanced by more conservative viewpoints indicating that the church as a body could not go so far as to repent its theological justification of apartheid. The NGK's position was stated thus:

Following the reflection that has taken place through the years in church periodicals, conferences, committees and synods concerning the policy which has become known as apartheid, the conviction has gradually grown that a forced separation and division of peoples cannot be considered a biblical imperative. The attempt to justify such an injunction as derived from the Bible must be recognised as an error and be rejected. The Dutch Reformed Church is convinced that the application of apartheid as a political and social system by which human dignity is adversely affected, and whereby one particular group is detrimentally suppressed by another, cannot be accepted on Christian-ethical grounds because it contravenes the very essence of the neighbourly love and righteousness and inevitably the human dignity of all involved.

Although the Dutch Reformed Church, in 'Church and Society', took the revolutionary position that there was no biblical justification for apartheid, still the church could not commit itself to uniting with its sister bodies. The separate

121

racial wings of the church remain. Apartheid still exists for the NGK, though in a different form. Discrimination can no longer be condoned but the national structures under which blacks are distanced from real political power can still be tolerated. The notion of the Afrikaners having a religious trusteeship sanctioned by God has not been jettisoned. The recognition that there is no moral basis for Verwoerdian apartheid does not mean an out-and-out commitment to one man, one vote. Thus the tricameral parliament is supported as a way of 'granting' reforms favouring mixed-race and Indian people, while the government's attempts at power-sharing are seen as the vehicle for offering blacks a voice in politics. But such a stance is still based on the concept of 'we the whites' carrying out reforms on behalf of blacks. Still the Afrikaners through their church appear not to have forsaken their belief in themselves as a chosen people. The government speaks in terms of 'group rights' and adheres to the notion of the separate nations that the later Calvinists believed were ordered by God. The concept is watered down only by Afrikaner benevolence.

The view of former theology professor Carel Boshoff of the right-wing Afrikaner Volkswag is that the Dutch Reformed Church has lost its moral basis:

'If we say we are prepared to share power, land etc. . . . we cannot then still continue to place restrictions upon people. We cannot prevent people from enjoying the rights of full citizenship. The church should realise that before everyone else. The church should realise that an open society with residual discrimination, with white minority rule and with laws like the Population Registration Act still on the statute book, is untenable. In a common society you should open up everything to people of all races, otherwise you are not being Christian. You have no moral basis.'

Heyns' response to this charge is that not to start the process of reform would be immoral.

Just how significant a departure was 'Church and Society' from the traditional theology of the Dutch Reformed Church? Was the church making a fundamental break with the policy of apartheid or simply playing with ethical arguments surrounding the policy?

Claims were made after the general synod that the Dutch Reformed Church had abandoned apartheid in church and politics. Three reasons were cited: the decision to open church membership to all races; the statement that there was no biblical justification for apartheid; and the fact that a group of right-wingers had broken away to form their own church indicated the extent to which the NGK had moved away from old dogmas. But a counter-claim came from a conservative in the church, Professor J. J. de Klerk of the theological faculty of the University of the Free State in Bloemfontein, who had been one of three theological advisers to the general synod. Seeking to reassure right-wingers that the NGK had not rejected the political model of apartheid, de Klerk wrote in *Die Kerkbode* sixteen months after the Cape Town gathering:

The general synod refused to express itself on political models. Whether it is the model of separate development or that of integration. Only the scriptural demands of fairness and justice were stated. The general synod indeed did not express itself against the model of separate development. It did however express itself against the wrong handling of it when it would have done injustice to people or would have been in conflict with the principles of neighbourly love and justice. [But] such a demand could have been made with regard to all political systems where powers are wrongly used.

Such views convinced liberal critics that the NGK had not taken a principled stand against apartheid. Wasn't it still supporting the system of black homelands as well as racially segregated housing and schooling? It was argued that Heyns and other *verligte* leaders of the NGK had been deliberately ambiguous over the general synod's move away from apartheid, in order to convey a liberal image for domestic and international consumption.

Sam Buti of the NG Kerk in Afrika says: 'As far as I am concerned there has been no shift.' While conceding that the abandonment of the biblical justification of apartheid means a lot, Buti believes that the NGK has said only that its churches are always open. 'But what does that mean? Are they talking about open membership? This appears to be another matter altogether.' Buti believes the NGK has not addressed the practical implications of church unity. He is convinced that moves towards the merging of the churches will grow, with or without the NGK. As Buti sees it, there is a crisis within Afrikanerdom over church issues: some feel the church should be an open institution not tied to any race, while others accept that principle but at the same time insist that each race group should worship in its own area.

Heyns is insistent that in 'Church and Society' the NGK rejected both the ideology of apartheid and its application. By apartheid he means enforced or legislated racial separation. For Heyns the decision to open membership to all (local congregations permitting) was the real break with the past, overturning a practice in force since the 1857 synod voted in favour of separate church facilities. Since then the Dutch Reformed Church had been an exclusively white church. So why was the NGK unable to go the whole way by supporting the unification of all its member parts, as the sister churches were demanding? Says Heyns:

'A major obstacle is at congregational level with the language and cultural differences between the four churches. Moreover, how can you change four churches immediately? Here in South Africa we are in a process of transition towards a society based on free association. We are opening up the possibilities of having an open society.'

Sam Buti regards Heyns as 'a fine, open man – theologically sound', an important figure in the current development of the church. 'He is far ahead of his own church. He is tied by "Church and Society". When he interprets the document it is in his own way. He would like to go further. Heyns has no problem with church unity except he knows the Afrikaners are not yet ready for it and he has to tread carefully.'

Heyns, a contemporary of Nico Smith, was the first person to whom the rebel pastor unburdened his feelings about his resignation from the Broederbond. Heyns had replied that he shared his concerns but said they should remain within the fold to try to convince people from within – what Heyns had termed 'critical solidarity'. Smith recalls: 'The trouble was, people accepted the solidarity but not the criticism.' Despite their differences, Smith still respects Heyns. He recounts that in 1982 when he attended the general synod as an observer (having already broken from the NGK) many of the pastors did not want to look him in the eye. But Heyns called Smith to a vacant chair beside him. 'He wasn't afraid to show he was my friend.'

In many ways Heyns is a refreshing figure in the Afrikaner establishment. His affirmation that the church is committed to ending racial discrimination may not convince his opponents to the left, but he does not shy away from the rock face of political issues. He does not reply to sensitive questions with a 'no comment – that's a political question'. Heyns sees his role as depoliticising the Dutch Reformed Church. This does not imply that the church should distance itself from political realities and issues or be silent in the political debate. 'After all,' says Heyns, 'the church has a divine calling to make explicit political pronouncements on the principles of social justice, human dignity and human rights. Only recently we had a three-hour meeting with the Law and Order Minister to express our concerns about the detention of children without trial.' By depoliticising, he means uncoupling the church from its forty-year-long identification with the ruling National Party and from party politics altogether. 'It should be possible for the church to have as its members those who belong to the National Party, the Conservative Party and the Afrikaner Weerstandsbeweging.' That is no easy task. Many congregations in conservative parts of the country have switched their political allegiance to the right wing; thus they tend to be more not less politicised in their religious outlook. There remain many members of the Dutch Reformed Church for whom a separation of religion and politics is alien.

There was a question mark also over the extent to which Heyns could divorce himself from party politics. As a leading member of the Broederbond, with its close links to government, Heyns like other prominent figures is intimately involved in discussions within the Nationalist establishment about the future of the Afrikaner.

A reflection of the more liberal climate within certain circles of the NGK came in the columns of *Die Kerkbode*. An editorial asked whether the presence inside Angola of South African troops was not morally and ethically wrong. This was an unprecedented challenge to the South African Defence Force, which was not accustomed to having the morality of its actions questioned, especially by the Dutch Reformed Church. The NGK's Head of Ecumenical Affairs and Information Dr Pierre Rossouw said the church was entitled to ask searching questions on moral and ethical issues. A joint statement published by the military after a meeting between Heyns and defence chiefs left the impression that the NGK moderator had repudiated *Die Kerkbode*'s article until Heyns himself corrected the impression, saying: 'The questions raised in its [*Die Kerkbode*'s] editorial are perfectly legitimate. Those are the questions in the hearts of our people. Political and military considerations aside, we nonetheless wonder whether the government would not be acting ethically if it withdrew its troops completely from Angola.' (These events took place a short while before South Africa withdrew its units from across the border.)

Simultaneously with Heyns' stand, a small group of ministers in the NGK – albeit on the fringe of the church – asked whether the NGK should withdraw its chaplains from the SADF. Insisting that the church should not be associated with any of the warring parties in South Africa but should rather act as an 'unattached peacemaker', the ministers called for the 'complete disengagement of the churches from the military and the police'.

A book published by a *dominee* in Pretoria, Dr William Nicol, argued that the concept of state security had been elevated to a holy war and that this was in conflict with the church's peacemaking calling. Nicol was one of three NGK ministers who attended an ecumenical conference in Lusaka organised by the World Council of Churches and the South African Council of Churches (the latter comprising the main English-speaking churches); this was also attended by representatives of the two main exiled black nationalist organisations, the African National Congress and the Pan-Africanist Congress. A subsequent regional synod strongly condemned Nicol's participation in the meeting and a motion was passed forbidding NGK members from holding talks with the ANC or attending international conferences at which ANC members were present. Nicol rejected such circumscription of his actions, insisting that talking to the ANC was 'the debate of the future'. His unrepentant stand had uncovered another raw nerve within the NGK, which was no more willing to proceed ahead of the government on this question than on any other. Even Heyns was forced to defend himself against similar charges after a passing encounter with an ANC executive member Thabo Mbeki at a seminar on disinvestment in New York. The two men were briefly introduced; afterwards Heyns made plain he had not known Mbeki would be present.

A further sign that the NGK was conducting a more rigorous examination of official policies came with government plans to reinforce parts of the Group Areas Act in the face of widespread opposition. While acknowledging that the Group Areas Act had 'sometimes prevented even more tragic circumstances' and had 'brought order where chaos would have prevailed', *Die Kerkbode* maintained that the church should guard against party political arguments, and demand instead that Christian principles of justice, fairness and brotherly love be applied in the making and application of laws. The publication noted the 'division and unhappiness caused by the proposed new laws', adding that 'it cannot be denied that the Group Areas Act caused suffering and disruption in the past.' The article was hesitant in its view of the laws; the significance of the article was that church criticism was being made public. The church was entering a public debate with the government, something it had previously shied away from.

125

Heyns comments that at a time when he is trying to make his church less politically doctrinal, the leaders of other churches are increasing their involvement in a politically committed struggle. 'The trouble with Archbishop Tutu and his colleagues is not that they are less biblical as theologians than any other church leaders, but that they have become too political.' Attempts by the Dutch Reformed Church to open a dialogue with the Anglican church and others were thwarted by arguments over the place of the church in the anti-apartheid struggle. How high a profile should the church adopt? Was the Dutch Reformed Church doing and saying enough to condemn apartheid? Were the member bodies of the South African Council of Churches sanctioning violence as a necessary though regrettable course of action for those fighting to overthrow an unjust system of racial oppression? Should the church support the 'just war'?

On this last point Heyns is unequivocal, and his words suggest that there can be little hope of bridge-building between the main Afrikaans and English-speaking churches. Asked whether, if he had been a *dominee* at the time of the Afrikaner struggle during the Boer War, he would have supported the guerrillas' armed struggle as part of a 'just war', he pondered silently for a long time and then said:

'That question touches on a modern concept – that of "liberation theology" – and applies it to a period of history when it did not apply. Naturally I would have been against the British invasion of my small country; naturally I would have been against the British use of concentration camps. I do not have any problem with civil disobedience as a last resort. But I do not believe I would have propagated a revolutionary response on the part of the Boers. I am convinced that you cannot change a situation in a revolutionary, violent way especially when the doors are still open for negotiation. My problem with Tutu and others like him is that they do not use the open doors'.

With such words Heyns placed a clear distance between his church and those clerics from other churches who in 1985, at the height of the violence in black townships, contributed to the Kairos Document ('Kairos' is Greek for 'crisis') which urged churches to adopt a less neutral stance in the struggle between oppression and liberation. The Kairos Document accused the Afrikaans churches of practising 'state theology' and of providing 'theological justification of the status quo with its racism, capitalism and totalitarianism'. The church had to enter the fray on the side of the oppressed, argued the document, adding: 'The present crisis challenges the whole church to move beyond a mere "ambulance ministry" to a ministry of involvement and participation.' By contrast, Heyns sees no role for the priest in the front line of the country's political struggle.

Heyns is convinced that the answers to South Africa's problems do not lie in politics or in a struggle for power. 'The problem is not political. It is biblical and ethical. It is about the transformation of the hearts of people. It is about the acceptance that we are all human beings created in the image of God. It is in this area that the Dutch Reformed Church can contribute towards a change of heart.' Partly for this reason Heyns has desisted from joining the queue of enlightened Afrikaners who have made the trip to Lusaka to talk to the African National

Congress. He believes that the church cannot have a role in talking to the ANC; such discussions should be left to the politicians. 'I have no problem with talking to the ANC so long as it's undertaken by the politicians. South Africa is engaged in a political struggle with the ANC. Therefore I do not see an opening for churchmen or academics to enter that sort of dialogue.' On the terms under which such talks should be held, Heyns disagrees with the government: 'I cannot defend the view that you make a condition of such talks the ANC's renunciation of violence. That way you are making a pre-condition of something that could be a result of the talks.' The sister churches appeared to ignore Heyns' advice about talking to the ANC. A delegation from the NGK in Afrika, representing black people, travelled to Lusaka, a dramatic symbol of the wide gap between the white church and the other member bodies of the South African Reformed movement.

The NGK found itself in the same position as the National Party: convinced that old-style racism and discrimination had to go but unwilling to jettison the concept of group differentiation. While the NGK was talking in terms of joint synods, and joint regional bodies and committees (i.e. interracial cooperation at a senior administrative level), the black and coloured churches were calling for one united church with an open membership traversing all racial boundaries. One minister in the black church put it like this: 'The white church uses the language of the secular world. They talk about "doors" that should be opened. We believe that there are no doors to be closed or opened because there should be no walls or doors separating Christians.' Moreover the Belhar Confession of the Sendingkerk continued to divide the churches. In 'Church and Society' the NGK had refused to go so far as to condemn apartheid as 'a sin and a heresy' as the Belhar document had done.

Nico Smith says that after the 1986 synod he met Heyns, who told him that '"Church and Society" was the Holy Spirit at work.' Smith had replied: 'How do you distinguish between the Holy Spirit and the spirit of the National Party?' Says Smith:

'If you study the document carefully, it is a parallel to Botha's reform programme. In the same way that there cannot be one parliament, rather separate racial chambers, so there cannot be one church, instead separate constituent bodies. Therefore "Church and Society" was the theological expression of the policy of the National Party.'

In that sense the document was a victory for the Nationalists over their rightist opponents. At the 1982 synod, says Smith, the NGK was moving speedily towards the Conservative Party. Heyns was swept aside. The Broederbond must have realised they had a lot of work to do to prevent the NGK being captured by the CP. 'I believe that from 1982 until 1986, the Broederbond worked overtime. When I heard that Heyns had been elected moderator I knew the Broederbond had done its homework.'

'Church and Society' represented the NGK catching up on the government's reform plans. The church had never been out in front preparing the theological ground. Had it been ahead of the government in reformist thinking, the document would surely have contained at least one sentence on scrapping the Group Areas Act and the Population Registration Act. The National Party had not exploited the church to acclimatise the *volk* to changes, realising perhaps that religion was an extremely sensitive issue. The church had spent four decades telling God-fearing Afrikaners that the Almighty subscribed to racial separation. If the church had suddenly rejected this view it would have confused worshippers, and many more might have broken away to the right. The NGK was simply not the appropriate vehicle to blaze the reformist trail.

Nico Smith describes 'Church and Society' as one of the best statements the NGK has ever made – 'good theology, rich and strong' – but full of contradiction. Its deficiency, he says, lies in its application. The church, says Nico Smith, 'failed to understand the age in which we live'. It lacked a 'gift of discernment'; it was unable to distinguish between what was essential and what was non-essential. Nico Smith regards Heyns as a conservative Afrikaner theologian still obsessed with his concept of 'critical solidarity'. For Nico Smith, it was totally the wrong concept for the times. 'You cannot always stand among the people, convincing yourself that you can carry them with you. Sometimes you have to step outside and say "I cannot agree with you. We have to repent".'

Says Nico Smith: 'The church should have spoken out loudly and said: "You cannot reform sin – and we have sinned".'

Left-wing critics of the Dutch Reformed Church may have viewed the adoption of 'Church and Society' as a mild rebuke to the policy of apartheid, but to the more conservative elements within the church it represented a fundamental departure from the theological tenets they had grown up with. They were not prepared to accept such a dramatic change of course and were quick to mobilise opposition. The apartheid purists launched Die Vereniging Bybel en Volk (the Association of Bible and People) to act as a watchdog body guarding conservative interests in the NGK. A meeting between the hardliners and Heyns failed to resolve their differences. Two thousand NGK members held a protest meeting in the Skilpadsaal (Tortoise Hall) in Pretoria. Heyns refused to bow to demands for a special general synod to reject open church membership and mixed marriages.

Heyns and other church leaders were denied permission to address the gathering, which proceeded to adopt a two-point action programme. A resolution stated that:

> all efforts will be made to submit objections, according to church procedure, to congregations, church councillors, circuits and the general synodal commission [the NGK's highest authority when the synod is not in session] . . . simultaneously, preparations are to be initiated to launch a new Afrikaans church where objector members could find a happy spiritual home.

The conservatives planned to withdraw their financial support for the NGK and launch a special appeal to finance their new church. A Continuation Committee of Dissident Members was formed to channel the opposition to open church membership and to counter the condemnation of apartheid. The leader of the rebels, Dr Willie Lubbe, wrote: 'What ministers and elders should realise is that the NGK is facing the most serious crisis in its history, a crisis that could have disastrous consequences for its unity, unless the right of dissident members to differ from synodal decisions is frankly acknowledged. . . .'

The dissidents responded to 'Church and Society' with their own report entitled *Geloof en Protes* (Faith and Protest). It argued that 'the separate existence and development of nations is in accordance with scripture'. Thus the treatment of apartheid in 'Church and Society' was regarded as 'incomprehensible'. Mixed marriages were unacceptable, while the Afrikaner people had the right to reserve membership of their church for their own kind. With a healing of the division seemingly out of the question, the rebels made their final break to form a new right-wing church called the Afrikaanse Protestantse Kerk (APK, Afrikaans Protestant Church), with the sub-title 'Church of Christ among white Afrikaners' – the first split within the Afrikaans church since the end of the last century. The schism mirrored the right-wing breakaways in the National Party, the Broederbond and other Afrikaner cultural organisations. Those had been serious enough for the cohesiveness of the Afrikaners but a schism in the Dutch Reformed Church was almost unthinkable.

A last-minute intervention came from the Conservative Party leader Dr Treurnicht, once described as the 'crown prince' of the NGK when at the age of forty he was appointed assessor, the church's number two position. Treurnicht urged church leaders to exercise patience and to accept that many church decisions were not final. He appealed to the dissidents to 'use all the channels within the church to obtain a revision of the decisions before considering the establishment of a separate church.'

His appeals fell on stony ground. But in the months immediately following the revolt, the schism proved to be less shattering than elsewhere within Afrikanerdom. The new church could boast only 30,000 or so members after its first year. Sixty *dominees* served 150 congregations, with some pastors administering up to six parishes. The NGK denied the new church all access to its premises, so that the APK had to fall back on school buildings and private houses for their services. In any case some of the regional synods of the NGK were staunching the flow of conservative defectors by conveying to their congregations a distinctly illiberal interpretation of some of the general synod's decisions. At a regional synod of the Western Transvaal, the hardliners won a small victory with an agreement that 'boundaries' and the 'ministerial needs of congregations' would be considered in any decisions on admitting blacks. At a Southern Transvaal synod a split in the NGK was averted when a compromise motion was accepted that: 'The NGK recognises the need for visible "structural" NGK unity without abolishing cultural diversity.'

Moreover some of the right-wing political leaders like Treurnicht stayed within the Dutch Reformed Church, cannily gauging that many Afrikaners, however conservative, would think twice before leaving their religious home. He did not wish to court a charge of dividing the NGK. The rebels were disappointed at

Treurnicht's stand, declaring: 'If Dr Treurnicht had come out in open support of us we would have had six hundred thousand Afrikaners who had voted CP all with us.' Clearly it was easier to rebel against one's party than against one's church.

The head of the new church Dr Willie Lubbe, a classicist who had taught at the universities of South Africa and Pretoria, had also been editor of *Die Kerkbode*. For ten years he had been a minister in the church. Recounting the build-up to his defection, Lubbe explained that 'for quite a few years before "Church and Society" was adopted I had been noticing what I would describe as "a tendency towards liberalism" within the Dutch Reformed Church. We stayed within the church even though we were alarmed by this new direction.' The split might have come earlier, but the Dutch Reformed Church was the last of the Afrikaner bastions to experience a schism, mainly because it was only in 1986 that the general synod convened to approve the new policy. For the conservatives 'Church and Society' overturned the old order as embraced by 'Race, People and Nation' with its support for racial separation. 'For decades it had been the policy of the NGK to form separate churches for the different ethnic groups,' says Lubbe. 'They denied they were moving towards integration but there was no doubt about it. They were moving away from the position where each worshipper could pray to God in his own church, in his own way. The NGK was formerly against mixed marriages but then said there was nothing in the Bible against it and so they then approved such liaisons.' He focuses on what he regards as a central anomaly of the new doctrine: that the NGK is now sanctioning children of all races worshipping together in church and in Sunday school, while still supporting racially segregated schooling during the week whereby white children remain subject to the ethnic exclusivity of Christian-National education.

Lubbe says that in the wake of 'Church and Society' the Dutch Reformed Church has become 'internationalised', surrendering its character as a church for the white Afrikaner people. In his view it is the NGK which has broken away, not he and his followers. Moreover Lubbe believes that if the NGK wants to be faithful to 'Church and Society' and to implement the policy fully, it should invite black people into the white congregations and not wait for them to apply. 'Why should we have to mix? Why cannot we have the freedom to be with our own people?'

Would South Africa not be a more harmonious society, perhaps, if institutions like the church did more to encourage racial integration? Lubbe's reply returns straight to the heart of the argument over whether or not the Bible upholds the principle of the existence of separate, definable peoples. Asks Lubbe:

'Why are we different if God did not mean it to be so? Why must we be the same people? The peoples of Europe share the same culture and heritage and yet they do not want to be one state. And yet the rest of the world expects us to be one country. We must take the world as God made it. Apartheid means separateness with justice. We Afrikaners have been here three hundred and fifty years. We know the people of this land. We know the country. We are not going to be told by people outside how to do things. We can think for ourselves.'

Lubbe turns for support for his views to the Book of Revelations: 'The believers *from each nation* [his italics] will enter heaven.'

If a black man were to enter one of his churches would he be thrown out? Lubbe says that would be something for the individual congregation to decide. 'Our membership is for white Afrikaners and also English-speakers who feel they can associate themselves with the Afrikaners.' Why can't blacks join the APK if they too 'associate themselves with Afrikaners'? Replies Lubbe: 'No, the blacks are too different.' Lubbe clearly fears that quiet Sunday mornings at Dutch Reformed churches in white suburbs are about to be disturbed by hordes of black Christians pouring in from the townships. But is this a realistic fear? After all, so complete is South Africa's system of racial segregation that under the Group Areas Act black housing zones are usually located miles away from the nearest white suburbs. Does he really expect that black worshippers in Mamelodi outside Pretoria are going to spend several hours on a bus every Sunday travelling to the city simply for the privilege of worshipping in a white church? 'They'll come,' he replies. 'Left to their own devices they wouldn't. But the blacks are always being instigated to mix. There are so many liberals around who just will not leave people alone. They instigate people who don't think for themselves. The liberals have a lot to answer for. This country was going along nicely until the death of Verwoerd in 1966. Since then it's turned in a liberal direction.'

So the Dutch Reformed Church became the last significant Afrikaner institution to crack. Other pillars of the *volk* had experienced a rift as the government's policies changed from rigid apartheid to neo-apartheid. Despite reforms in many areas of economics, social life, sport and cultural activities the framework of political apartheid remained. The limited political changes were enough to catapult many Afrikaners towards the right, and the same had happened in the church. At its general synod the NGK had committed itself in the religious field to no more than the government had undertaken in the political arena: it had removed the basis for the more hurtful and humiliating aspects of racial discrimination. Like the government though, the church had been unable to consign apartheid to the dustbin lock, stock and barrel. Arguing that its role was not political, the NGK had pulled back from the brink; it had failed to denounce all aspects of racially motivated policy and call instead for a democratic society for all.

In adopting such a position, the church was falling in line with the National Party and those other organs of Afrikanerdom which were inching away from 'grand apartheid' but were not quite certain which path to follow. The former biblical justification of apartheid had been cast aside but the NGK could not foresee a new order. The complications of South Africa's divided society had confused the issue and although some like Heyns would no doubt like to push the church further, the NGK – bound by decades of association with the cause of Afrikaner nationalism – could not suddenly break through into a new age. Moreover, like Nationalist politicians, they were continually looking over their right shoulder. But at least 'Church and Society' had opened up a new debate within the church about the possibility of wider reforms in the same way that Botha's power-sharing initiative had inevitably prompted discussion about bringing the blacks into central power.

Like the National Party the NGK had realised that the old order had to change. The general synod signified that it had caught up with the government's reform plans, but like the government could not make the final break with the past.

It still had to take account of the same 'weakness of some' which was acknowledged by the 1857 synod as, in deference to white isolationists, it set the Dutch Reformed Church on a path leading to religious apartheid.

While the NGK and the Afrikaners agonise over what degree of apartheid the Bible sanctifies, Nico Smith, at his home in Mamelodi, is at peace with himself. His house is much smaller than the spacious home he enjoyed in the white suburb of Pretoria and considerably less salubrious than the charming home he left behind amid the cloistered oak trees of Stellenbosch. His office is part of the dining room, which in turn overspills into the kitchen. His books are crammed into every nook and cranny available. He has a caravan in the garden serving as an extra office. But when he steps out into the street, the only white in a township of half a million blacks, he is among friends.

'It is not an easy life. The easy life is in "white South Africa" – a place like Stellenbosch, where I used to teach, with its beautiful homes and stunning countryside. My life is a struggle. But I have gained on two fronts. I am now a free person and that is a wonderful thing. Also, although I am a westerner, I am now part of this country's people. For the first time in my life I can say "I have become a white African".'

CHAPTER EIGHT

'The greatest risk is to take no risks at all'

'Do you realise what a powerful force is gathered here tonight between these four walls? Show me a greater power on the whole continent of Africa! Show me a greater power anywhere, even in your so-called civilised countries!'

This was the ringing climax to a speech delivered in 1968 on the fiftieth anniversary of an organisation which is almost solely responsible for the dominant position of the Afrikaner today. The speaker, H. J. Klopper, had been the first chairman of the Afrikaner Broederbond. He declared:

'From the time the Afrikaner Broederbond picked up momentum, it has given the country its governments. It has given the country every Nationalist prime minister since 1948. However indirectly, its efforts gave the Republic to our [Afrikaner] nation. . . . We are part of the state, we are part of the church, we are part of every big movement that has been born of the nation. And we make our contributions unseen; we carried them through to the point that our nation has reached today.'

Klopper's remarks were reported in a book published in 1978 entitled *The Super Afrikaners* by two South African journalists Ivor Wilkins and Hans Strydom, after a Broederbond member had defected with a wealth of secret documents and membership lists which had never before been published. Wilkins and Strydom concluded: 'The South African government today is the Broederbond and the Broederbond is the government'; furthermore, the Broederbond 'cannot, and have no wish to, make any significant changes'. The authors recorded the words of the Broederbond chairman in 1934 Professor J. C. van Rooy who, in a confidential note to members, wrote: 'The primary consideration is whether Afrikanerdom will reach its ultimate destiny of domination in South Africa.' The authors commented: 'Probably more than any other single statement in its history, this sums up the organisation's fervent purpose.'

It is a measure of the changes within Afrikanerdom and within the Broederbond in the short period since *The Super Afrikaners* that its present chairman Professor J. P. de Lange was able to tell me, in a rare interview, that: 'We cannot now promote Afrikaner interests without promoting the interests of others.'

The Broederbond (League of Brothers) was formed in 1918 on the Witwatersrand at a time when Afrikaners' fortunes were at their lowest following the defeat in the

Boer War and the inferior status of 'poor white' which had descended on them. The Broederbond's concern was the alienation of the Afrikaner in the English-dominated cities. There was also the question of the link with the British crown whose flag, flying from official buildings, reminded the Afrikaner of his humiliation. A creeping awareness of the 'native question' reinforced the fear that the Afrikaner, already a second-class citizen compared to his English-speaking counterparts, was facing another threat from the hundreds of thousands of blacks who, like him, were converging on the urban areas. The Broederbond, in confronting these issues, helped to unite Afrikanerdom and reinvigorate a depressed people with a new sense of identity. It would be no exaggeration to say that during the 1920s the Broederbond helped rescue the Afrikaners from the threat of extinction as a definable people.

By the 1930s, when Afrikanerdom was beginning to recover, the Broederbond ceased to be a mere first-aid station for the *volk*. It could begin exploring an altogether wider role, instilling aspirations of nationhood into the Afrikaner people. The Broederbond's constitution described members as those 'who strive for the ideal of an everlasting and separate Afrikaner nation' and who would create a 'consciousness among Afrikaners concerning their language, religion, traditions, country and volk'. Exploiting a network of 'cultural' front organisations, the Bond spread its tentacles into every corner of Afrikanerdom, an elite mobilising an entire people in the service of Afrikaner nationalism. It founded the Federasie van Afrikaanse Kultuurvereninginge (FAK, the Federation of Afrikaans Cultural Associations) in 1927; by 1937 its constituent bodies of cultural organisations, church councils, youth and student groups, etc., had grown to 300. Soon it was infiltrating and taking control of chambers of commerce, school boards, farming cooperatives and church committees.

Its recruits were from among the cream of Afrikanerdom; it became an exclusive, secret and sinister body, with members meeting in closely-knit 'cells', not knowing the membership of other groups. They gathered after midnight. They swore an oath of loyalty to the organisation, addressed each other in prescribed ways and used a secret handshake. The Broederbond paved the way for the National Party's election victory in 1948. Having secured political victory, it set about assisting Afrikaners in scaling the economic ladder. It was instrumental in establishing huge Afrikaner business concerns and finance houses. The Afrikaanse Handelsinstitut (Afrikaner Trade Institute) was founded to compete against the traditional economic overlords – the English. Federale Mynbou (Federal Mining) challenged the great English-owned mining houses like Anglo American. At the same time, the Broederbond exploited contacts in government to ensure that members of the *volk* employed in the civil service enjoyed a job for life. Still today, in any English-speaking suburb of Johannesburg, the local post office is staffed predominantly by Afrikaners. It rallied too behind the promotion of Christian-National education, calling for teaching in Afrikaans in single-medium schools. Hardly any institution of state or area of economic activity escaped the Broederbond's attention.

By the late 1950s, with Verwoerd as Prime Minister, the Broederbond was at the height of its power. The chairman of the Bond, Dr Piet Meyer, was a close confidant of the Premier. He was also chairman of the South African Broadcasting Corporation, establishing at an early stage the close link between the Bond and the country's state-controlled broadcasting service. Very few senior appointments went to non-Broeders, whether it was to the cabinet, parliament, provincial councils, the SABC, the church, the civil service, the defence force, police, sports bodies, universities, Afrikaans newspapers – the list was endless. Within fifty years of its establishment the Broederbond had achieved its objective – wresting power from the English. The Bond fuelled the campaign for the founding of a republic, an ambition achieved in 1961 when Verwoerd pulled South Africa out of the Commonwealth. The organisation helped spread the ideology of apartheid. At the same time its membership grew.

Though linked to the ruling National Party it would have been misleading to describe the Broederbond as the secret government of South Africa, despite Broeders forming the majority of those in power. Influential it certainly was, but not manipulative of government. Its task was rather to assist the National Party into power, and once there provide an intellectual environment in which apartheid and Afrikaner nationalism could flourish.

Its coherence was sorely tested during the 1970s, however, when the debate between *verligtes* and *verkramptes* broke out. The Bond began to reflect the wider divisions within Afrikanerdom, and the divergent views of its members could no longer be contained within the sanctified realms of the secret meetings. *Verkrampte* members of the Broederbond, Treurnicht among them, became uneasy about the 'liberal' direction of the policies of Verwoerd's successor, Vorster. Such divisions undermined the effectiveness of the Bond as a power behind the throne.

The first signs of a Broederbond rethink became evident. The Soweto riots of 1976, growing international isolation and general sense that Verwoerdian apartheid was leading the country into a backwater prompted a fresh debate. Occupying the chairman's position at the time was Gerrit Viljoen, who is almost universally recognised as one of the most brilliant of today's Afrikaners.

Viljoen was born in Cape Town in 1926. An exceptional scholar, he matriculated with seven distinctions. He passed all four major subjects for his BA degree at the University of Pretoria, with distinctions in each. He was awarded MA degrees in classical languages at Pretoria and at Cambridge University in Britain. After lecturing at the University of South Africa he was appointed at the age of forty as the first rector of the Rand Afrikaans University (RAU), Johannesburg's first Afrikaans campus. He became chairman of a Broederbond front organisation known as the South African Bureau for Racial Affairs (SABRA) and in 1974 chairman of the Broederbond itself, in which position he was able to extend his power and influence within Afrikanerdom. Viljoen clashed with Prime Minister Vorster because the former advocated a homeland for mixed-race people, contrary to National Party policy. Viljoen was emerging as a champion of the *verkrampte* cause. But by the mid-1970s he appeared to have undergone a transformation, adopting a staunchly *verligte* stance. He promoted dialogue between Afrikaans students and young people from other race groups. In 1979 Viljoen relinquished the Bond chairmanship to become the South African-appointed administrator-general in Namibia, returning to the cabinet in 1980 to gain a reputation as a man of far-reaching views on reform. He became the unquestioned choice of leading intellectual Afrikaners as a future state president, although his low political profile caused some to wonder whether he had the steel for the political fray. Under his leadership the Broederbond began shedding its more sinister image and helped prepare the political climate for the debate on power-sharing with coloureds and Indians which was to reach its height in the early 1980s.

The Broederbond was not spared the ructions which followed the right-wing revolt in the National Party in 1982 and the subsequent establishment of the Conservative Party. It became another entry on the casualty list of Afrikaner institutions to divide as Botha's reforms took effect. Carel Boshoff, elected chairman of the Bond in 1980 after Viljoen, announced his resignation. The Broederbond's executive council declared that Boshoff had become 'contentious' because of his simultaneous chairmanship of SABRA which, contrary to the Bond, had come out openly against Botha's power-sharing measures. In a resignation statement, Boshoff said that the new constitutional plans would stimulate rather than ease racial conflict because they did not 'conform to the requirements of exclusiveness and equality'. Every race group, he added, should have its 'own geographical sphere in which it can exercise authority'.

In other words Boshoff was reasserting the fundamentals of Verwoerdian apartheid. Rather than inviting the coloureds and Indians into central government on a power-sharing basis, albeit a limited one, SABRA was calling for the two communities to be allotted separate homelands just like the blacks. Boshoff was replaced by J. P. de Lange, rector of RAU, who two years previously had been a member of a commission of enquiry which recommended that universities should be free to admit students of all races. The transition from Boshoff to de Lange appeared to formalise the Broederbond's changing character.

Boshoff meanwhile took his campaign outside the corridors of Broederbond headquarters to the wider meeting places of Afrikanerdom. He said it was clear the Broederbond was now to be used largely to promote reform in which the whites would no longer have sole power over themselves. He told a newspaper: 'The Broederbond executive has inevitably removed itself from the views and standpoints many of its members hold on political matters. I think a new organisation for Afrikaners will sooner or later have to be formed to strive for the ideal of a white state as a non-negotiable.' Conservative Party leader Andries Treurnicht, himself a former Broederbond chairman, voiced the view that by supporting the new constitution the organisation had 'signed its own death warrant'.

'The greatest risk is to take no risks at all'

J. P. de Lange says that of the Broederbond membership (roughly 14,000), 10 per cent resigned in the wake of the right-wing revolt. It was the result of a leadership struggle, culminating in 1982–3, over two opposing views of South Africa's future. Says de Lange:

> 'Those who resigned were the same group who were not able to move with the new power-sharing constitution – they were not willing to go along with new concepts. They favoured a "closed" model of society and spoke in the idioms of the previous fifty years. The majority were looking at an "open" society and were thinking much more creatively and inclusively.'

The new thinking was that the Afrikaans language, for example, should become less exclusive, less identified with narrow Afrikaner nationalism; it should be the language of anyone of whatever colour who chose to speak it. It was recognised too, says de Lange, that 'the interests of the Afrikaners were intertwined with those of everybody else' – hence the conclusion that Afrikaner interests could not be furthered without promoting other groups.

There was also a process of redefining the nature of Afrikaner nationalism. The view emerged that those who wanted to make their future in South Africa were the true Afrikaners. Moreover, says de Lange, there was a realignment of the power base of the political parties. Says de Lange 'There is not a single party today which is exclusively Afrikaner. In political terms Afrikaner nationalism has become a much wider concept.'

The rethink has meant that the Afrikaner Broederbond, though still a highly secretive organisation and a powerful vehicle for Afrikaner self-advancement, is less sinister and nepotistic than in the past. It has transformed itself into an agency of *verligte* Afrikaner thinking. The new role developed very quickly after the right had broken away as the Bond became instrumental in bringing new ideas to the fore. It refined its research into new political initiatives – its recommendations became fewer but more substantial. In any case, with power after the late 1970s very much the preserve of P. W. Botha, the influence of the Broederbond could not have remained as extensive as before.

The Broederbond now serves as a channel of communication between the government and Afrikanerdom's elite. But with the elite itself divided, it is harder for the organisation to present a common front. With the government tangled in so many political log-jams of its own making, it is unlikely that innovative proposals from the Bond would be accepted. Moreover it has been reduced to only one of several interest groups seeking to influence government; its role as an extended arm of the government has been eclipsed by the rise of the powerful state security system with its formidable influence on national, regional and local administration as well as its pivotal role in setting political and strategic targets.

De Lange says of the new role:

> 'We must accept that we are no longer the only input into the decision-making process. But the quality of our input is very important. The fact that a member

of parliament or a civil servant, for example, is also a Broeder means he has a depth of knowledge at his disposal. With this background he can approach issues on a more informed basis. We are a learning society.'

Broederbond members still meet secretly and at night ('because that's the most convenient time,' says de Lange). The promotion of Afrikanerdom is still on the agenda but the Bond believes the future of Afrikanerdom can no longer be divorced from that of other races. Critics of the Broederbond argue that Afrikaner protection is still a dominant factor in the organisation's thinking; one described the Bond's policies as 'pragmatic racism'. Though much of its activity remains secret, de Lange is prepared to give an insight into its current role. 'What is true of the Afrikaner Broederbond is that through its network of roughly eleven hundred cells around the country it is actively directing itself towards the promotion of co-operation across the colour lines.' The Bond has therefore come a long way since the days when Afrikaner domination was the aim. The organisation will use its members in key institutions – chambers of commerce, agriculture unions or committees – to explore links with blacks. 'People know those taking the initiative are Broederbond members.' The groups involved may be small, but their concern is to get initiatives started or else to support the initiatives of others. That such a change in outlook and strategy should have occurred over so short a time is a remarkable testament to how Afrikaner institutions can regenerate themselves when they seem to have run out of intellectual steam. The transformation in the National Party which opened the way for the new constitution, and the kinds of change undergone by the Broederbond, may not impress Afrikanerdom's critics in South Africa and abroad. But compared to what went before, they are almost revolutionary.

J. P. de Lange puts it like this: 'We Afrikaners cover a huge spectrum. We have unity with a greater diversity than ever before in our history. We are giving expression to what it means to be an Afrikaner in very diverse ways. Culturally, this has brought about variety, not division. The divisions are largely political.'

'The net result of this is that Afrikaners are less aggressive about being Afrikaners than they used to be.' That would appear to be the case across the spectrum. Among the Nationalists and even in the Conservative Party, white nationalism is slowly replacing Afrikaner nationalism. That said, the Afrikaner remains very aware of being an Afrikaner. 'That's part and parcel of living among a multiplicity of peoples – it's not something that would be important to a nation like the English.'

The transformation of the Broederbond has been possible in large part because the Afrikaners, or certain sections of them, have come of age. When the Broederbond was formed, the Afrikaners were newly-urbanised, an aimless people searching for a place in the world. Like black people who converge on the big cities today, the Afrikaners arrived poorly-equipped. The Broederbond gave them the tools to rebuild themselves. But two or three generations have passed since then. *Oupa* (grandfather) may have been a farmer who had to work as a railway shunter when the Afrikaners were forced to leave their land. His son may have gained matriculation (the school-leaving examination) but the grandchild might be a university undergraduate at RAU, Pretoria or Stellenbosch. There is now a section of Afrikanerdom that can say: 'We made it!' Whereas their parents' generation would have sought jobs in government service, today's 'yuppie' Afrikaners are in the professions like banking, law, architecture and medicine. They are a different kind of people to their parents and grandparents: more modern, recognising that the country will have to change and that organic change is in the nature of society. The debate within Afrikanerdom has consequently loosened up despite the best efforts of the government to contain it.

It is this new elite of Afrikanerdom that the Broederbond today increasingly represents. No longer is it a vehicle exclusively devoted to the uplifting of the Afrikaner, rather it is a forum where the upper strata of Afrikanerdom are debating where to go from here. The debate is quite simply – how can the Afrikaners survive?

As part of this debate the notion of 'group rights' is being tested. Many have already concluded that politics based on group identification is not the answer to the country's problems, since this is rejected by the vast majority of blacks. Others believe some kind of group protection will have to remain.

A remarkable insight into the extent of the current debate within the Broederbond about political alternatives came in a Bond discussion paper circulated among members in September 1986 and leaked to the press. Marked 'strictly confidential', the report was entitled 'Fundamental political prerequisites for the survival of the Afrikaner'. The title itself – referring to 'survival' – was an indication of how the role of the Broederbond had changed. 'Survival' was the question back in the 1920s when the Afrikaners were confronted by the English. Now, as the Afrikaner embarks on the long journey towards an accommodation with blacks, 'survival' is again the watchword.

The paper's introduction spoke of the 'meaningful survival of the Afrikaner' in terms of a 'healthy, balanced realism'. The paper outlined the following prerequisites for the survival of the Afrikaner:

> To maintain Christian values and civilised norms, recognising freedom of religion and worship; to maintain the independence of the judiciary and equality before the law; to maintain law and order; to promote the happiness and the spiritual and material wellbeing of everybody; to honour and protect everybody's human dignity, life, freedom and property; to honour, promote and protect the self-determination of national groups and peoples.

In addition the Afrikaner's survival would be dependent upon the recognition and protection of language and cultural rights; private property; freedom of conscience, of speech and of expression. 'If there are no other impediments, a system or process that can realise these, should be broadly acceptable.' The maintenance of separate residential areas, though necessary for a while, was not in itself 'preconditional for the survival of the Afrikaner' while voluntary 'grey areas' (multiracial suburbs) did not necessarily threaten the Afrikaner's future. The dismantling of statutory apartheid laws was not to be viewed as 'concessions made under pressure, but as a condition for survival'. Ethnicity was important but 'this did not imply that group rights have to be made absolute.'

The report then tackled the central issue of sharing power with blacks and how the Afrikaners should adjust to such an eventuality. The paper stated that: 'the exclusion of effective black participation from the political processes to the highest level is a threat to white survival which cannot be averted by maintaining the status quo or by a further consolidation of power in white hands.' Then came a crucial passage:

> . . . everybody must be able to serve at the highest legislative and executive levels, whatever the future political system may be. This can, indeed, also mean that under some models, the head of state and/or government need not necessarily be white. . . . The office, however, must be circumscribed and limited by the executive in such a way that the power connected to it cannot be used for group domination.

Two messages emerged starkly from the confidential Broederbond document. Firstly, it was not the inclusion of blacks in the political process that threatened the survival of the Afrikaners, but rather their exclusion. Secondly, a black-dominated government, with appropriate protection for other race groups, was by no means improbable. This contrasted with President Botha's slap-down of Foreign Minister Pik Botha who made the same prediction in public.

The report concluded on a note of challenge, asserting that changes would have to come and that the Afrikaner had better be prepared for them: 'we must be aware that, humanly speaking, no guarantees exist. We must think in terms of probabilities and calculated risks. The greatest risk we run today is to take no risks at all. Our will to survive as Afrikaners and our active strength and faith is our strongest guarantee.' That again was a departure for the Afrikaner, who so often has seen any concession to black political power in terms of receiving cast-iron guarantees. Though still referring to separate 'national groups' and self-determination, here was a prominent Afrikaner suggesting that the Afrikaner's own creativity and intellectual vigour would secure his future, not reliance on paper guarantees.

The debate has not stopped with this paper. The thrust of Broederbond discussions today is whether South Africa can move to a federal system of government in which all race groups will be involved. The whole spectrum of possible federal solutions is now open to discussion. The Bond is even looking seriously at the kwaNatal Indaba (the power-sharing plan for kwaZulu and Natal) described by de Lange as a 'very important process' in contrast to its dismissal by certain members of the National Party.

Still the Broeders are grappling with the problem of how the Afrikaner can be protected. De Lange believes that somehow protections will have to be built in.

'What is true is that any eventual constitutional dispensation which ignores either group or individual rights is in for a hell of a lot of trouble.' What parameters of protection will the Afrikaner require? 'I do not think it is possible for the Afrikaners to be in a situation where they are at the tender mercies of others, where they have no power whatsoever to create space for their own identity to flourish.' The government and its black opponents are still poles apart on the question of political rights, the former insisting that individual groups must be protected on the basis of race, the latter calling for racial definition to be submerged by a broader South Africanism. De Lange says: 'Both positions are rather unreal. In my own mind I would accept a situation where ordinary social and economic forces define groups. Such forces are much more powerful than legislation and are more viable in the long run.'

In other words if the economic forces can themselves help break down racial barriers, the political models are there to play with. The ANC's ignoring of group rights, says de Lange, is very much a convenient instrument for the time being – but eventually, he says, there will have to be compromise. 'We have to think in the long term. It will be a rough road.'

De Lange does not share the government's out-and-out opposition to white South Africans meeting the ANC. He believes such meetings have limited importance but agrees that more and more Afrikaners are making the journey north. 'It could bring the time nearer when the ANC rejects violence,' he says. 'Talking to the ANC is not a bad thing. There has to be some preparation.'

In 1986 de Lange attended a conference on education at Long Island, New York, in his capacity as rector of RAU and as former chairman of the de Lange Commission. Also present were several members of the ANC. De Lange spoke of the need to bring peace to the country and for a solution acceptable to all people. One of the ANC delegates launched a scathing attack on de Lange and vowed that he and other prominent Afrikaner figures would be placed on an assassination list. Two other ANC delegates, Thabo Mbeki and Mac Maharaj, embarrassed by their militant colleague's diatribe, left the room. By the time delegates went for their buses at the end of the session, tempers had cooled. The fiery ANC delegate approached de Lange and hugged him, and the pair exchanged farewells – in Afrikaans!

CHAPTER NINE

The New *Voortrekkers*

'Do not rouse the lion in the Afrikaner.'

These words were delivered at a graveside by a survivor of a landmine explosion which had killed several members of a white family. It had been one of several attacks in the South African border area. The African National Congress justified the attacks by saying that in the border regions local farmers and other whites were effectively part of the security network, helping the local police and army to spot insurgents. The attacks sent ripples right through the white community, and the graveside oration was a warning to the ANC that the whites could strike back hard.

There was, though, a small but growing number of Afrikaners who believed that, instead of showing its claws, the Afrikaner lion should seek to get to know the other animals in the jungle in the hope of living peacefully among them.

At their forefront was the former leader of the liberal opposition Progressive Federal Party, Frederik Van Zyl Slabbert. His search for rapprochement between white and black South Africans was to take him and others on a historic journey to the other end of the African continent, thereby courting government action and incurring the charge of 'traitors' from their own people.

Slabbert had already defied government attempts to prevent whites from travelling outside South Africa to talk to the African National Congress. As leader of the Progressive Federal Party he had led a small group of his MPs to Lusaka in 1985. Little new ground had been broken; after all, the PFP delegation was in no position to open negotiations with the exiled black nationalist organisation. Nevertheless, the discussions established a pattern, which Slabbert encouraged, of whites, especially Afrikaners, making the trek north. At the Lusaka meeting the ANC had criticised the PFP for participating in a parliament which excluded blacks, an argument which was to leave a deep impression upon Slabbert.

Later that same year, a second group of prominent whites had met the ANC; among this group was the chairman of the Anglo American Corporation, Gavin Relly. The talks were hosted by the Zambian president Kenneth Kaunda at his country retreat at Mfuwe. At first the white delegation and the ANC representatives sat opposite each other, until the ANC leader, Oliver Tambo, pointed out that they were all South Africans. They then rearranged their seats to reflect their shared nationality.

Slabbert has always been a free spirit and a free thinker; a man prepared to flout the codes of his Afrikaner people. He possesses a determined streak of individuality. He is always searching for fresh channels through which to express his undoubted energy. Such traits were evident in his revealing autobiography *The Last White Parliament*, published in 1985 while he was leader of the opposition. The stifling conventions of Afrikanerdom, his search for some kind of role in a troubled society and the disillusionment with party politics leap out from the pages. The general election campaign of 1974 which brought him into parliament as MP for Rondebosch in the Cape demonstrated for him the 'obligatory ritual of public life'. Slabbert wrote: 'I was off my mind to let myself get trapped into it.'

Of his university days at Stellenbosch, Slabbert wrote disparagingly of insular Afrikaner student life. He describes his fellow-students' obsession with the national game of rugby, while at the same time they buried their heads in the sand with regard to the country's problems. Of his rugby-playing days, Slabbert wrote:

> . . . it was the sub-culture which most disillusioned me; the post-mortems after the game with pot-bellied, beer drinking 'experts' from way back; the sight of players continually ingratiating themselves with sporting correspondents for some coverage; the pseudo-patriotic ethos that pervaded discussions on the importance of rugby in our national life; seeing successful farmers grovelling at the feet of arrogant second-year students simply because we were 'Maties' [Stellenbosch students] on tour in their vicinity. Mentally it was not only escapist, it was a social narcotic to anything else going on in our society.

By rejecting the claustrophobic environment of South African rugby Slabbert had in effect desecrated a shrine of Afrikanerdom, so hallowed is the game. He also travelled overseas, a broadening of the horizons unusual for Afrikaners, for many of whom the next *dorp* is 'foreign'. His travels took him beyond London and New York, where wealthier whites go for their annual 'top-up' of western culture and from where they return convinced that the world does not understand their country. Slabbert travelled to Zambia to meet Kenneth Kaunda, recalling in his book that this incurred the reprimand from then Defence Minister P. W. Botha that he had consorted with 'rapists and murderers of our wives and children north of our borders'. From Zambia he travelled to Kenya and Nigeria, a rare safari for an Afrikaner.

As PFP leader, Slabbert had campaigned hard against the 1983 constitution, believing it to be deeply flawed, a 'hotch potch of contradictory and divergent constitutional principles'. Frustrated at being unable to influence the course of political events, Slabbert signalled even then that he was casting around for a role outside the constraints of parliament:

> It is the present government which has made it constitutionally impossible for the majority of the people subjected to its laws to consider parliamentary strategies for change. Therefore those thus excluded have no option but to

consider extra-parliamentary strategies. It is pure hypocrisy and downright provocation on the part of the government to equate all extra-parliamentary strategies for change with unconstitutional and even subversive strategies.

In early 1985 Slabbert entertained three National Party MPs to dinner in Cape Town: Wynand Malan, Albert Nothnagel and Leon Wessels (later appointed to the government), all on the liberal wing of the party. Slabbert voiced his frustration over the political deadlock in the country. According to Slabbert, one of the MPs told the gathering that 'everybody is terrified of P. W.'. The other dinner guests concurred. The conversation turned to how Slabbert could get through to Botha, how he could convey to him the depths of the crisis facing the country and the urgency of initiating far-reaching changes. Malan floated the idea of Slabbert trying to work out a 'special relationship' with Botha. 'Why don't you spend a whole weekend together to try to get to know each other as fellow-Afrikaners?' suggested one of the MPs.

Slabbert consequently wrote to Botha who responded in a fairly friendly manner. The PFP leader decided that there was little point in launching into a head-on confrontation with Botha; instead he chose to adopt an *oom/nefie* (uncle/nephew) approach, a young Afrikaner talking to one of his elders, without being obsequious. As Slabbert recalls: 'It was a comfortable relationship. There was no acrimony.' Over three or four meetings the two men discussed a wide range of issues including a removal of the ban on the African National Congress, the question of the release of Nelson Mandela and the crucial issue of how to get negotiations with blacks off the ground. Botha, along with Justice Minister Kobie Coetsee, also responded to Slabbert's pleas for an early release of the Afrikaans poet and convicted ANC member Breyten Breytenbach, jailed for terrorism. Slabbert appeared to be making more headway in the face-to-face meetings than in exchanges across the floor of the House of Assembly.

But these encounters could not distract Slabbert from the dawning realisation that he was being manipulated by the government, filling the role, as he saw it, of a token leader of a token opposition allowed to function only to afford legitimacy to the whole flawed system of parliamentary politics. 'What propelled my disillusionment,' says Slabbert, 'was my deteriorating relationship with the military. Their briefings were very often straightforward deception.' A turning point came at a later stage when the then Chief of the Defence Force General Constand Viljoen briefed Slabbert on an undercover operation inside the northern Angolan province of Cabinda in which two South African commandos had been killed and a third, Wynand du Toit, captured. The raid was aimed at blowing up Angola's oil storage tanks along the Cabinda coastline. The South Africans insisted that the operation was mounted to reconnoitre ANC training camps though, as far as was known, the ANC did not have any bases in the area. This, though, was the version Viljoen fed to Slabbert, who felt he was being treated like a 'mental idiot'.

Relations were also strained with the Defence Minister General Magnus Malan who, says Slabbert, 'treated the PFP like an extension of the End Conscription

Campaign [a protest group which, before its restriction by emergency laws, campaigned for an end to the system of military conscription]. Nothing made me feel more manipulated than the way in which Magnus was treating parliament and the opposition.'

But if Slabbert thought the military establishment was pulling the wool over his eyes, he soon had evidence that the foreign ministry was also exploiting his position, or else was ignorant of what was really going on in the region. During 1985, says Slabbert, Foreign Minister Pik Botha invited him to his office to ask whether he would intervene to defuse the deteriorating situation in the Crossroads squatter camp outside Cape Town, where scores of people had been killed as they defied government attempts to move them. The Crossroads violence, together with the appalling conditions in which the squatters were living, had become an international issue of serious embarrassment to the South African government. Slabbert pointed out that his hands were tied so long as the government kept on detaining the real leaders of the Crossroads community, and while troops and police were bulldozing people's homes. Pik Botha, says Slabbert, also appealed to him to help save the Nkomati Accord, the peace pact drawn up in 1984 between South Africa and Mozambique. It had become severely strained following repeated allegations by the Maputo government that Pretoria, in contravention of the treaty, was still supporting the RENAMO resistance movement engaged in a devastating civil war against the government. Slabbert says he told Botha: 'The trouble is I don't know where foreign affairs ends and the defence ministry begins when it comes to regional policy.' Botha firmly denied that the South African armed forces were involved in the destabilisation of the region, for example by continued help for RENAMO.

Convinced that the PFP had become irrelevant to the political process and feeling ever more manipulated by Nationalist politicians, Slabbert and his parliamentary colleague Colin Eglin embarked on a tour of Australia and New Zealand. On the plane Slabbert told Eglin that the party could not carry on as it was; a new political strategy had to be adopted.

In Australia, where the nightly television pictures of South Africa's township violence were putting pressure on the Canberra government to invoke wide-ranging economic sanctions, Slabbert and Eglin met Prime Minister Bob Hawke. According to Slabbert, Hawke pleaded with the PFP leaders, saying: 'Can't you persuade P. W. Botha to release Nelson Mandela? We don't need to have one man, one vote tomorrow, but something which can be held up as progress.' That night, with Slabbert's political career rapidly approaching a milestone, he telephoned Botha's office in South Africa to seek an urgent appointment with him on his return from Australia, a last-gasp attempt by Slabbert to obtain some sign of hope from the government that might cause him to rethink or at least delay his resignation.

After a twenty-six hour flight back to South Africa, Slabbert was received by Botha. Of the meeting, Slabbert says that there was one point when he finally realised his resignation was inevitable. It came when Botha said to Slabbert: 'You have to understand that the majority of blacks support me.' Slabbert recalls: 'I then concluded once and for all that I was wasting my time.'

Slabbert took a short break at the farm in Swaziland owned by his wife's family, a tranquil retreat where Slabbert often retires to think through his ideas. While at the farm he received further devastating evidence that he had been deceived by the Botha government. It was the last week of December 1985 and Slabbert read an article in a South African newspaper about the 'Vaz diaries', documents discovered by the Mozambican army at a base they had captured from the RENAMO rebels. The diaries revealed that the South African Defence Force was still supporting the rebels despite the Pretoria government's peace accord signed on the banks of the Nkomati River. Having listened to Pik Botha reassure him that Pretoria was not engaged in destabilisation, Slabbert could not believe what he was reading. He immediately telephoned the Mozambican capital, Maputo, and arranged a meeting with the minister of state security. A week later, Slabbert and his father-in-law chartered an aircraft from Manzini airport in Swaziland and flew straight to Maputo where President Machel 'briefed us on the whole show' concerning South Africa's involvement on the side of RENAMO. Machel's words to Slabbert were: 'Tell P. W. Botha that they can kill us if they want to at any time. But tell him to remember that Hitler invaded Russia and his war ended in Berlin. Botha's war will end in Pretoria.'

Back in Swaziland, Slabbert read the entire transcripts of the diaries. They covered the very period when he'd been in Pik Botha's office listening to reassurances about South Africa honouring the Nkomati treaty. 'I realised,' says Slabbert 'that while I was talking to Pik the South Africans were still sending supplies to RENAMO.'

Slabbert set to work, drawing up a confidential document reflecting his conviction that politics 'PFP-style' was going nowhere and outlining an alternative strategy.

The document, which Slabbert showed Eglin and other PFP MPs, began with these words:

Unless the government gives a clear and acceptable indication [at the opening of parliament in January 1986] that it intends restoring freedom of choice on a non-racial, non-ethnic basis for the purposes of participating in the constitutional, social and economic spheres of South Africa, I intend resigning my seat at the end of the no-confidence debate. By restoring 'freedom of choice' and 'clear and acceptable indication', I mean repealing the Population Registration Act [classifying people by race] in so far as it serves to impose involuntary racial and ethnic membership for political, social and economic purposes. It also implies the repeal of all consequential legislation which purely on the basis of race or ethnicity prevents any South African citizen from exercising freedom of choice.

The paper went on to recall how the PFP had opposed the new constitution of 1983 because it had excluded the majority black population but had nevertheless participated within the system to exploit the possibilities of constitutional change.

Slabbert concluded: 'I am not prepared to carry on as before. According to my own light and wisdom I have done whatever can be done with the available opportunities and to continue as before I would be bluffing myself and others.' The document was a devastating indictment of the government's policies at every level:

> From the concept of independent homelands to the tricameral parliament, the constitution of South Africa has been unilaterally designed by this government on an involuntary and ethnic basis. Only those who have been prepared to accept this basis, for whatever reason, have enjoyed the patronage of the state – including the PFP.

Slabbert's proposal for a new strategy was that all PFP members of parliament should resign their seats, forcing by-elections in their respective constituencies. The MPs, argued Slabbert, should seek from the voters a mandate not to return to parliament until the government clearly committed itself to dismantling apartheid completely.

Slabbert's recommendation meant that 'if the PFP caucus acts in the above manner it will cause a constitutional crisis and could have a galvanising effect on the whole tricameral system . . . we move from individual political symbolism to what could be the beginning of a strategy to apply constitutional leverage towards a non-racial democracy.' Expressing all Slabbert's feelings of frustration and of being manipulated, the document concluded: 'I believe, strategically, the country is ready for an initiative of this kind. It may be the last opportunity for an opposition such as ours to precipitate incisive political action. In any case, I prefer to go out with a bang rather than to whimper along in the slipstream of the government's repression and incompetence.'

During the first week of parliament, which Slabbert had already marked down as his make-or-break moment, he went to Pik Botha's office and confronted him with the evidence the Mozambicans had handed to him. Slabbert was not satisfied with Botha's explanation. He got up from his seat, said to Botha 'Thank you for your time', walked out of his office and one week later resigned from parliament and from the leadership of the Progressive Federal Party, describing parliament as a 'grotesque ritual in irrelevance'. A senior civil servant, sitting in the public gallery, privately described Slabbert's resignation as the greatest speech he had ever heard in the white chamber. The PFP had not been prepared to back Slabbert's new strategy. Says Slabbert: 'They refused to go along with it for good reasons. It was without question a "high risk" strategy. I don't think they believed I would resign.'

Slabbert's resignation left the PFP in disarray. He had been a charismatic leader who had commanded a good deal of personal support. Being an Afrikaner, he had in part overcome the PFP's image as a party of English-speakers. Several of the party's MPs were bitter at the manner of his departure. Says Helen Suzman:

> 'Slabbert was a very good MP – a marvellous personality. But he had no staying

power. He had become bored with parliament. And what has he been able to achieve since he left – conferences, meetings, speeches to foreign backers? No doubt he has fulfilled a role in keeping open lines of communication between whites and blacks. But he was doing that before he left parliament. After all, he was talking to the ANC before he walked out of the House of Assembly. The manner in which he quit was unforgivable. I don't think the captain of the bloody team walks off the field when the big game is just starting.'

But what big game? After all, hadn't parliament proved itself irrelevant to the wider struggle in the black townships? Mrs Suzman replies that Slabbert quit at the beginning of a parliamentary session which saw the scrapping of the pass laws so that 18 million blacks were 'suddenly able to walk the streets without sixteen-year-old white cops molesting them' – a most important reform, she argues, which could not be dismissed as of little or no consequence. Therein lies the great divide between staunch parliamentarians like Mrs Suzman, who believes that throughout the difficult years of transition which lie ahead parliament must remain sovereign, and people like Slabbert who doubt its relevance, at least in its present form.

In the political wilderness, Slabbert was not certain what course to follow. He was convinced there was little future for political parties which lacked support outside parliament. Slabbert had already voiced the view that the South African political scene was dominated by a struggle between the extra-parliamentary opposition (the African National Congress and the United Democratic Front), which was leading the township protests, and an extra-parliamentary executive comprising political, police and army chiefs on the powerful State Security Council with a prominent role in policy making. Ignoring the extra-parliamentary forces, he concluded, would be to ignore the dynamics which would shape South Africa's future.

Together with Alex Boraine, another PFP member of parliament who had resigned, Slabbert formed the Institute for a Democratic Alternative for South Africa (IDASA), which set out to explore how democracy could be widened within the country. The institute required funding, and Slabbert approached several leading benefactors in the United States including the African–American Institute, the Ford and Rockefeller foundations and the Carnegie Trust. The campaign for sanctions against South Africa was at its height and black activists from South Africa were fêted abroad while whites of whatever political complexion were regarded with suspicion. 'The response we got was: "Wonderful idea but wrong colour,"' says Slabbert. Eventually the Norwegian representative in South Africa and the Friedrich Neumann Foundation in West Germany came forward with funding.

In its first few months IDASA adopted a low profile, showing no desire for publicity. Slabbert disappeared from the headlines for several months, roaming the country launching quiet initiatives to facilitate discussion between young

P. W. Botha *(above left)*, elected South African prime minister in 1978 and later the country's first executive president. Under Botha, previously unthinkable apartheid reforms were enacted, but black protests, international economic sanctions and right-wing Afrikaner defections overtook his earlier reforming zeal.

Andries Treurnicht *(above right)*, leader of the Conservative Party which captured the votes of right wingers fearing black majority rule because of Botha's policies. Treurnicht's party ate into traditional Nationalist support and in 1987 replaced the Progressive Federal Party as the official opposition in parliament.

Frederick Van Zyl Slabbert *(opposite)*, former leader of the liberal opposition Progressive Federal Party, who resigned to open channels of discussion with black nationalists. Slabbert led a group of liberal Afrikaners to Dakar in Senegal for a controversial meeting with the African National Congress.

Eugene Terre Blanche *(above)*, leader of the ultra-right Afrikaner Resistance Movement (AWB). Under the spell of Terre Blanche's charismatic leadership, the AWB became the militant voice of extreme Afrikaners.

Denis Worrall *(opposite)*, former South African ambassador to Britain, who resigned to form the Independent Party, committed to a wider peace process than that of the government. Worrall's return to South Africa helped ignite a rebellion by liberal Afrikaners in the 1987 whites-only general election.

Liberal opposition MP, Helen Suzman
(above left), a staunch defender of human
rights and civil liberties. She has waged
many battles in the struggle against the
imposition of sweeping security laws
imposed by successive Afrikaner
Nationalist governments.

Soweto activist, Dr Nthato Motlana *(above right)*, a prominent opponent of the South
African government. A supporter of the
African National Congress and the United
Democratic Front, Motlana and other
black leaders dismissed the government's
plans for limited power-sharing.

Stoffel van der Merwe *(opposite)*,
appointed South Africa's Information
Minister when international hostility and
black protest were at their height. Van der
Merwe became an articulate exponent of
his government's power-sharing plans for
blacks and whites.

Sampie Terreblanche *(above left)*, Professor of Economics at the University of Stellenbosch. The university was traditionally a reservoir of Afrikaner intellectual support for the ruling National Party until Terreblanche led a rebellion by academics against what they saw as the party's slow pace of reform.

Nina Overton *(above right)*, Professor of Communications at Rand Afrikaans University, Johannesburg. A 'detribalised Afrikaner', Professor Overton says of her people: 'We come from European fanatics. . . . We are still fanatics . . . a group of Europeans placed in a harsh, unforgiving continent. . . .'

Rebel Afrikaner André Zaaiman *(opposite)*, son of a staunch Afrikaner family who rebelled against his people and refused to serve in the army.

Professor Johan Heyns *(opposite)*, moderator of the Dutch Reformed Church. Under Heyns, the church shed its previous position that apartheid was justified in the Bible. Still, though, it would not commit itself to a united, non-racial church.

The Voortrekker Monument *(below)*, Pretoria, 16 December 1988. Afrikaners gather to mark the hundred-and-fiftieth anniversary of the Great Trek, their forefathers' epic journey on ox-drawn wagons into the interior of South Africa to escape British rule at the Cape.

Wynand Malan *(above left)*, former National Party MP who defected, convinced that the government's policy towards black South Africans held little prospect of winning support. Malan campaigned to unite anti-government forces both inside and outside parliament.

Arrie Paulus *(above right)*, Conservative Party MP and former leader of the white Mineworkers' Union. Paulus is a staunch defender of the interests of working-class Afrikaners.

Willem de Klerk *(opposite)*, former editor of the Afrikaans-language newspaper *Rapport*. He resigned the editorship, citing pressure to conform to the government's line.

The Reverend Alan Hendrickse *(above)*, leader of the Labour Party, representing coloured people. His decision to participate in the racially segregated parliament angered many anti-apartheid groups, though he later became a bitter enemy of President Botha.

J. P. de Lange *(opposite)*, leader of the Afrikaner Broederbond. Founded in 1918, the Broederbond was a secretive network pledged to Afrikaner advancement. Under de Lange, the AB has explored ways of ensuring Afrikaner survival on a less exclusive basis.

Former government official, Timo Bezuidenhoud *(above)* addressing squatters in the Crossroads shanty town near Cape Town in 1984. Condemned by both black radicals and fellow white officials, Bezuidenhoud battled to improve the squatters' living conditions against resistance from the Afrikaner bureaucracy.

Dr Nico Smith *(opposite)*, Afrikaner pastor in the Dutch Reformed Church, who rebelled and joined the church's black section, unable to reconcile apartheid with his religion. He left his home in an exclusive white area to become a priest in a black township.

Afrikaners and young blacks on the question of furthering democracy. Slabbert was anxious that the liberal cause should be reasserted despite the growing polarisation within South African society. IDASA sought to inspire Afrikaners in particular towards a greater flexibility. The institute's message was that the Afrikaners' survival was not dependent upon their remaining an immovable granite edifice like the Voortrekker Monument. Slabbert terms this 'the fallacy of misplaced concreteness', and argues that 'you cannot freeze a group into a static force and then accommodate them.' Slabbert, seeking to extend the debate beyond the notion of 'group rights', advocated the politics of 'free association' which rested on traditional liberal-democratic values, placing the rights of the individual first; once those rights had been firmly established in the community then the individual could choose to be identified with any particular group – racial, political, cultural, etc.

The institute established regional offices around the country, but their bridge-building efforts between blacks and whites resulted in IDASA's being dragged into parish-pump politics in the black townships. They were called upon to settle feuds within the United Democratic Front, time-consuming exercises which detracted from IDASA's chief concern – influencing the minds of whites.

Early in 1986 Slabbert attended the same meeting in New York where J. P. de Lange, head of the Broederbond, was threatened by a member of the African National Congress. Slabbert took ANC executive member Thabo Mbeki aside and urged him to take seriously the genuine dilemma facing Afrikaners, particularly academics, who wanted to break with Nationalism and apartheid. Mbeki was advised not to underestimate the dynamics involved in such schisms within Afrikanerdom. Out of this conversation emerged the idea of a meeting between the ANC and liberal Afrikaners from within South Africa. The problem was: where?

A short time later, Slabbert attended a cultural festival on the Senegalese island of Gorée, a former staging-post in the slave trade, a mile or so off the west African coast. Danielle Mitterrand, wife of the French President and the dissident Afrikaner writer Breyten Breytenbach, now living in Paris, were also there. One evening the self-exiled black South African singer Miriam Makeba sang for the invited guests. Her performance – a black South African singing to a white South African many miles from their common fatherland – gave Slabbert the idea of where to hold the gathering of blacks and whites from his country. He turned to Breytenbach and said: 'Wouldn't it be fantastic if I could bring fifty or sixty Afrikaners here to meet the African National Congress.' And so the plan took off. Slabbert travelled to Lusaka to explain to ANC leaders the role of IDASA and to explore the possibilities of debate. He also laid out tentative plans for a meeting of black and white South Africans. Central to his thinking was the fundamental question: 'What does an Afrikaner who has rejected apartheid do?' In a nutshell the problem was this: how could a politically aware Afrikaner, nurtured on years of anti-ANC government propaganda and constrained by laws forbidding a meeting with the ANC on South African soil, break through the wall of prejudice to understand at first hand the men who were undoubtedly major players in the country's future? Having won the ANC's agreement to a meeting, Slabbert returned to South Africa and began marshalling his group of liberal Afrikaners willing to undertake a journey which would inevitably lead to their ostracism by certain sections of their own people. The arrangements were made in great secrecy for fear that the security police would seize their passports. It was only a few hours before they flew out of Johannesburg airport that news of the impending meeting broke.

One of the most prominent members of the Dakar delegation was Hermann Giliomee, Professor of Political Studies at the University of Cape Town and a respected commentator on the country's political affairs. Like many others who went to Dakar he had been brought up in a solid Nationalist family. But the break from the party became inevitable the more he explored South Africa's political landscape.

His grandfather had fought in the Boer War and in the 1914 rebellion against South Africa's support for Britain in the First World War. His father, a history teacher, had become a member of the Broederbond at the age of thirty-five. The family knew the architect of the National Party, D. F. Malan, and had a sense of direct involvement in the Nationalist awakening.

At Stellenbosch University, Giliomee, already questioning government policies towards coloured people, somewhat reluctantly joined the National Party. This was for one year – 1961 – when South Africa became a republic. He allowed his membership to lapse after leaving university. During a later teaching post at Stellenbosch he took part in intense debates with fellow academics, including Slabbert, about apartheid and its ethical foundations, without formulating any substantial alternatives. In 1970, Giliomee wrote to his parents saying: 'For the sake of the children the time has to come when one has to say good-bye to the old things. It is better to do this now than later. Our ways had to part.' He was trying to prepare his parents for what was coming at the end of the letter: their son was deserting the National Party to vote for the PFP in the election of that year. Never having conceived of such a possibility, his parents, until they reached the end of the letter, believed he was referring to an imminent divorce from his wife, a telling insight into how the National Party can command loyalties among Afrikaners which are as strong if not stronger than those binding families.

Giliomee moved from Stellenbosch to the University of Cape Town because he believed his path to a senior academic post was being blocked by arch-Broederbonders. Giliomee was one of several Stellenbosch professors who had openly held views directly opposed to those of the university establishment. By 1986 – with violence sweeping black townships and with the political impasse unresolved – Giliomee was to be joined by other dissidents who were finally making their break with the National Party. When Giliomee was approached by Slabbert to join the group to visit Dakar he had no doubt whatsoever about accepting the invitation, even if it meant the government taking away his passport.

André du Pisani had been attending a funeral in Johannesburg when he received a telephone call from Slabbert three days before the departure to Dakar inviting him to join the mission. Du Pisani, a research fellow at the South African Institute of International Affairs, was also disillusioned with the National Party. He was born in South West Africa/Namibia, the territory which South Africa captured from the Germans during the First World War and which they subsequently controlled in defiance of United Nations resolutions. His father was for a time a schoolteacher in the German *Hochschule* (high school) in the territory's capital of Windhoek while his mother worked for a German company. The family spoke Afrikaans, German and English.

In 1964 the South African government imposed the Odendaal Plan on the territory, which in effect extended apartheid to Namibia through a political constitution founded on separate ethnic groups. The move raised doubts in du Pisani's mind about the viability of racial separation, doubts enhanced after several months travelling around the territory with his father, a part-time farmer forced off the land because of drought, and then working as a census officer. Du Pisani travelled with his father to many parts of Namibia 'from farm to farm, counting people, goats and chickens'. He observed at first hand the effects of government policies: the hardships imposed by the migrant labour system which brought thousands of Ovambo tribesmen from the far northern border region near Angola to jobs further south with no legal status or protection, discriminated against with regard to salaries and subject to the whims of government bureaucrats.

Says du Pisani:

> 'I was profoundly influenced by what I saw. The inequalities were so stark that I came to realise the folly of the Odendaal Plan which had been imposed without consultation with the people of Namibia and had been dictated by the political interests of South Africa not by the interests of the people of the territory. It was based on ideological precepts and could never work.'

Later, at Stellenbosch University, du Pisani remained within the Nationalist fold as a member of the party's university branch. But then a series of events propelled him towards his inevitable break with the party. At Stellenbosch, du Pisani attended a lecture by an exiled South African academic Jan Loubscher who had left the country in the 1950s and had studied Afrikanerdom from afar, in Vancouver. His lecture, entitled 'The Impossibility of Afrikaner Nationalism', argued that it was simply not viable to sustain the myth of Afrikaner nationalism in the face of demographic realities (the growing black population) and of South Africa's weakening international position. Du Pisani described Loubscher's address as a 'profound and evocative lecture'. In 1969 the university received a visit from the leader of Malawi, Hastings Banda, who was then in South Africa as a guest of the government; this was the heyday of Prime Minister John Vorster's policy of detente with black Africa. The visit made du Pisani realise 'there was a black world out there which I knew little about'. By that time du Pisani was approaching his break with the National Party as a result of his involvement in student politics. The Students' Representative Council at Stellenbosch wanted to affiliate with the National Union of South African Students (NUSAS) which mainly represents English-speaking campuses and takes a strong stand against the government's apartheid policies. The students also wanted to establish closer ties with the University of the Western Cape, which is reserved for mixed-race students. These moves were all part of an attempt by Stellenbosch students to transform their campus into an open, non-racial university. The university establishment rejected their demands, against the wishes of most of the students. At this point du Pisani broke with the National Party.

In 1974, after graduating at Stellenbosch, du Pisani studied for a Master of Sciences degree in International Relations at the London School of Economics, his first exposure to a broader world of ideas beyond the often suffocating and parochial academic atmosphere in South Africa. For the first time also, du Pisani met black students from South Africa on an equal basis, sharing with them university courses, sports activities and halls of residence, engaging in conversations which helped to focus his criticism of the South African government and its policies. While he was in London, South African troops invaded Angola and he saw television coverage, denied his countrymen at home, of the intervention. 'Back home,' says du Pisani, 'white South Africans had no inkling of the extent of our involvement in Angola. They were kept in the dark. There had to be something wrong with a system which manipulates the flow of information to such an extent.' While at the London School of Economics, du Pisani began work on a book about Namibia which became a standard work on the territory. His research brought him into contact with members of the South West Africa People's Organisation (SWAPO) which was fighting a long bush war against South African control of the territory. 'Here were people from my own country whom I couldn't meet at home. We talked passionately about Namibia.'

Back in South Africa after completing his studies in London, du Pisani was appalled by the violence of 1976, the bannings of black organisations a year later and the detention of leading black activists from the Black Consciousness movement of Steve Biko who died from serious head injuries while in police custody. Du Pisani protested publicly in a letter to Prime Minister John Vorster. In 1983 he voted against P. W. Botha's new constitution which he describes as 'historically very unfortunate'. The political stalemate since then attracted him to the new channels of discussion offered by the Dakar mission.

In the delegation were several favourite sons and daughters of Afrikanerdom, figures highly respected in their fields. They included the writer André Brink; Theuns Eloff, a student chaplain at Pretoria University; Lawrence Schlemmer, Director of Policy Studies at Witwatersrand University; film director Manie van Rensburg; Johan van Zyl, board member of the Small Business Development

Corporation; and the actress Grethe Fox. Slabbert had assembled a genuine cross-section of enlightened Afrikanerdom, even though not all its members could be regarded as Afrikaner heavyweights.

For Slabbert the mission to Senegal was a mixed blessing. The expectations surrounding the gathering were inflated, with some reports suggesting the Afrikaners were travelling to Dakar to negotiate with the ANC on a political settlement for South Africa and that the discussions would constitute 'talks about talks' prior to wider negotiations with the Pretoria government. Slabbert himself had no such ambitions for the meeting. During a stopover in London en route to Dakar, Slabbert made it clear that the group was not intending to 'negotiate, mediate or do Pretoria's work for it'. The South African delegates were not seeking a 'false consensus' and there would be 'no nice-sounding platitudes' at the end of the discussions. His aims were threefold: to introduce Afrikaners to Africa, to introduce Afrikaners to the ANC and to make Africans aware that 'not all Afrikaners go around shooting blacks'.

It was of course a stark reminder of their country's isolation that the Afrikaners had to undertake a two-day journey via Europe to travel from white South Africa to black west Africa. An overnight flight from Johannesburg to London was followed by a flight to Paris, then onwards via Rome to the Senegalese capital. Travelling with them, I noticed a sense of slight trepidation among the less well-travelled members of the team. They were not certain what to expect. How would black Africa treat these 'white racists' from the south? Slabbert had met the ANC before but for most this would be their first encounter with an organisation branded by the Pretoria government as 'murderous terrorists promoting a communist-inspired revolution'.

The government's Bureau for Information had published a booklet the previous year (1986) entitled 'Talking with the ANC' which contained a dire warning to those who, in the government's view, allowed themselves to be seduced by national liberation forces linked to communists:

> In Vietnam there was a national front, the FLN, which included non-communists. Other democratic elements, including academics, Buddhists, Catholics and students were also vociferously involved in anti-government agitation. However, as soon as the 'national liberation' had been achieved the vanguard element of the front came to the fore and quickly eliminated its former democratic and liberal allies in the front. Many of them found themselves in re-education camps. Many were forced to flee. And many were killed.

The implied comparison between the liberation fighters of Vietnam and the cadres of the ANC was clearly aimed at dissuading the kind of links the Afrikaner group were about to embark upon. Moreover, in January of 1987, just six months before the Dakar initiative, the ANC leader Oliver Tambo, speaking on the organisation's seventy-fifth anniversary, had gone out of his way to invite whites to join the anti-apartheid struggle. The Pretoria government, he had declared, is 'terrified at the prospect of the black and white masses of our country coming together to say "we shall as equals, compatriots and patriots, act as one, to bring the apartheid system to an end and foster the birth of a new South Africa". As surely as the regime of terror has lost its political control over the black masses, so also it is set to lose its political control over the white population. The day of "the new voortrekkers" has come!'

The welcome at Dakar airport took the Afrikaners' breath away. The night-time arrival saw dozens of Senegalese officials and ANC members on the tarmac to greet them. The chaos of Dakar airport did not appear to unnerve them. André du Pisani had visited other African states, so the trip to Senegal was not such a new experience as it was for some of his companions. He recalls: 'The reception as we stepped off the plane was unbelievable. There was a feeling that we all belonged to Africa and that we had been allowed to come close to touching its bosom.' Du Pisani, too, noted the irony that the group had had to travel all the way to Europe and then back to Africa to talk to fellow South Africans, for him a measure of the polarisation within his country's society. 'I realised most of the barriers in South Africa are man-made and that there is no reason why they cannot be undone by man.'

Slabbert wrapped his arms around Thabo Mbeki, the ANC's publicity chief, whose father had spent almost a quarter of a century in South African prisons. Mbeki, a gentle pipe-smoking man, is one of the ANC's ablest talents. After meeting Mbeki some time earlier, a prominent South African businessman remarked that he would be quite happy to see him as his country's foreign minister. It is, perhaps, one of the tragedies of South Africa's recent history that Thabo Mbeki, an urbane, gifted man, has been denied a chance of contributing to his country's unfolding history. His country is the poorer for it.

The opening of the talks was elevated by President Abdou Diouf of Senegal into something approaching a state occasion. Clearly seeing an entry on to the world stage for his tiny country and at the same time anxious to encourage dialogue in South Africa, Diouf laid on a colourful pageant of tribal dancing and singing, with Diouf himself chairing the opening session of the talks. It seemed more like the start of an historic conference to decide the destiny of a nation than a meeting of two dissident groups. In an opening address Slabbert said he hoped the meeting would 'seize the minds of white South Africans by making them realise they are part of Africa'. President Diouf described apartheid as a 'crime against humanity which could not be forgiven.'

When the two sides got down to discussions, an early point of debate was the question of violence and the ANC's use of arms to overthrow apartheid. The Afrikaners were aware that this was a sensitive issue which exposed them to attack back home. What were they doing sitting down and talking to the men of violence? After all, the names of some on the ANC side read like a hit-list of the South African security services; men like Mac Maharaj, an ANC executive member who had spent twelve years on Robben Island, the prison near Cape Town; Steve Tshwete, who had also spent fifteen years on the island, and who had fled South Africa in 1985 after helping to launch the anti-apartheid United Democratic Front; and Howard Wolpe, a white ANC member who had escaped from a South African jail in the early 1960s. The ANC were challenged on why they fudged 'hard' and 'soft' targets. ANC policy had always been that it would attack economic or strategic targets and not civilians, while adding that it was regrettable if civilians were killed or injured 'in the crossfire'. Too often though, bombs had been planted in places which were unquestionably civilian targets with very little economic or strategic value.

The debate was led by André du Toit, Professor of Politics at the University of Cape Town, who presented a paper accepting the 'historical reality' of the ANC's use of violence. He said the Afrikaner group was impressed that the ANC had postponed 'to an unprecedented degree' its recourse to violence and since 1960 had tried to limit its attacks to sabotage and 'hard targets'. But, continued du Toit, he was not satisfied with the ANC's position on 'uncontrolled violence' – killings, and bombings in which civilians were killed. He believed that the political struggle would be severely compromised by indiscriminate killings of civilians:

'Not only does it tend to frighten the more conservative groupings and the majority of whites politically into the government's and the National Party's laager, but it also creates the kind of conditions in which the stage can unleash its massive powers of repression with greater impunity and turn loose vigilante groups and reactionary forces to wreak havoc in local communities.'

Du Toit argued that 'strategically it was quite unrealistic and cynical of the government to require the ANC or other resistance movements to renounce violence as a precondition for negotiation.' But, he went on, 'the overriding requirement must be to devise, and contribute to, possible political initiatives which might begin to open the way to a secure future'. The South African state, though finding its coercive powers unchallenged, was forfeiting even the basic legitimacy that enabled it to rule. The challenge facing opposition groups, therefore, was to 'generate meaningful political initiatives' instead of 'providing a reactionary and destructive coercive showdown'.

Explaining the ANC's position on violence Thabo Mbeki outlined why the ANC could not call a halt to the armed struggle. He said that if the South African government were to indicate its intention of entering into 'serious, meaningful negotiation but that all that was holding it back was the fact that a couple of bombs went off, then it becomes possible to say "OK, let no bombs go off for the next three months to give Botha the possibility to move". Otherwise a moratorium has no meaning.' Mbeki referred to a meeting between the ANC and Conservative MPs in Britain who had advised the organisation that

'with their [the British] experience of decolonisation, their advice to the ANC would be never to agree on a moratorium on violence because it is too easy for one's opponents to set off bombs exactly to demonstrate that you are not in control of your forces and there are radical elements who want to continue the armed struggle.'

Mbeki sought to convey to the liberal Afrikaners the reluctance with which the ANC had adopted the armed campaign:

'In principle the ANC has no problem about [negotiating an end to violence] because in the ANC there is no philosophy of violence, no romanticising of it. It has no problem about negotiating the cessation of violence in order to enter into a negotiating process.'

The Afrikaners' concern about indiscriminate violence was shared by the ANC, argued Mbeki. After all, it made no strategic sense for the ANC to conduct an armed campaign against white civilians when the ANC was trying to win over these same white compatriots to the cause of a non-racial South Africa. But there would be mistakes, as had happened at Amanzimtoti near Durban in 1985 when an untrained unit had planted a bomb in a shopping mall killing five people and injuring sixty-one.

Another ANC delegate said he accepted how difficult it was for the Afrikaners to explain the armed struggle to white South Africans who 'benefit from apartheid'. He said the ANC refused to cease hostilities because President Botha was not interested in negotiations. The argument was taken up by ANC executive member Mac Maharaj. He stressed that the ANC had never ruled out a negotiated settlement. But it would not countenance the proposal that it should disarm itself to 'bait P. W. Botha to the negotiating table'.

'That's the first time in the history of man's struggle across the world that those who have taken up arms in response to state violence, oppression and exploitation are required first to disarm themselves on the grounds that that would persuade the oppressor to come to the table. We ask you: is that a realistic demand?'

This, clearly, was not good enough for the Afrikaners, who left the session on the use of violence dissatisfied by the ANC's position. At a news conference, Professor du Toit expressed their doubts:

'I don't think they have answered this to our satisfaction. This concerns not only the proliferation of uncontrolled violence. It concerns the actions of all those people who claim to act on behalf of the ANC whether or not they are part of an organised and a disciplined hierarchy of political control. What is happening more and more in the emerging civil war in South Africa are all the ambiguous cases, all these cases where it is not clear who should accept responsibility for, for instance, the bombing which took place earlier this week in Johannesburg. In that context I think what we are seeking from the ANC is a clearer statement: if they are in general, as they say, committed to an armed struggle not aimed at civilians then, in these cases, these dubious cases, they must be prepared to take a clearer stand on repudiating and renouncing where civilians do become the victims.'

The discussions became so intense and wide-ranging that the two sides could hardly tear themselves apart. On the second morning the Afrikaners and their black fellow-countrymen were invited to visit a cloth-making factory some distance from Dakar. There was little enthusiasm for the trip; it was an unwelcome intrusion into their discussions and the delegates would rather have kept talking. But in deference to their Senegalese hosts they went. But they could not leave the question of a future South Africa behind them at the conference centre. Against a background of noisy textile machinery, and with the factory manager valiantly trying to interest them in the details of his trade, black and white South Africans continued their obsessive conversations as they walked around the complex. Debates on 'power-sharing', the 'armed struggle', 'entrenched clauses' and a 'bill of rights' were conducted above the din. It was a remarkable and intense reunion of men and women separated by many long years of apartheid. It was like long-lost members of a family suddenly meeting again and catching up on all the family news. But more than that, it became a rigorous examination of what each side stood for. As one of the Afrikaners said to me: 'There's a realisation that we've got to get beyond the mere repetition of rhetoric.'

A crucial issue for Slabbert's team was whether the Afrikaner people – their heritage, language and culture – would be secure should the country be governed by a black majority. The talks therefore moved on to discuss how South Africa's ethnic diversity might enrich rather than impoverish the country in a post-apartheid society. The ANC, believing in a common South African nationalism, refused to consider minority guarantees for whites, as in post-independence Zimbabwe. However, a senior ANC delegate, Pallo Jordan, gave an assurance that the Afrikaner's language and culture would not be sacrificed. The debates spilled out of the conference centre into the hotel restaurants and lobby. Take this exchange alongside the hotel reception desk between Hermann Giliomee and Pallo Jordan:

Giliomee: 'I agree that we should strive for a single South African nationalism. I would join you in that. But you have to recognise the power of Afrikaner nationalism. Should we not aim for a bi-communal system in which Afrikaner and African nationalisms would be accepted? I should like to call it a "sad compromise".'

Jordan: 'But that would be a shabby compromise. The aim must be to bring everybody together into one South Africanism.'

Giliomee's contribution in Dakar proved to be one of the most controversial aspects of the entire mission. Prior to the Senegalese visit he had spent three months in Israel where he had concluded that the Palestinians were for the first time discussing the concept of 'bi-communalism' within one state, given that the

Israeli government was showing little intention of withdrawing from the occupied West Bank and Gaza Strip. At Dakar Giliomee extended this idea to the situation in South Africa, arguing that instead of black nationalism and Afrikaner nationalism trying to suppress each other, the two should combine to create a system which recognised 'bi-communalism'. The ANC's response, said Giliomee, was that 'their future government would recognise a wonderful freedom for all. So many of the white delegates swallowed this in the Dakar talks.'

Giliomee was criticised afterwards by several other Afrikaners for having devoted his presentation to a concept which still embraced separate ethnicity. Giliomee sensed some annoyance at his introduction of such a discussion into a forum which aimed to demonstrate to whites the merits of the ANC's non-racial politics. But, says Giliomee, 'the chances of whites accepting an ANC government and their promises are minute. Whites will not enter a competition in which the highest vote-winner comes out on top.' Giliomee sought to gain an acceptance of this reality, as he saw it, and from there to move on to discuss a compromise solution, one which would recognise and accommodate both the main nationalist tendencies within South Africa. As well as Israel, Giliomee had also studied Northern Ireland, where again there were two broad nationalisms competing with each other. Both the Israeli and Ulster situations had convinced Giliomee that instead of searching for a sweeping settlement, negotiators should put their minds to establishing a framework in which competing nationalist demands could be dealt with. Such moves would take as their starting point that neither a successful revolution nor a long period of sustained repression were feasible and that the concept of a single majority was meaningless. Giliomee had been impressed with the Anglo-Irish agreement signed in 1985 between the governments in London and Dublin, viewing it as a first step towards establishing the kind of framework which could eventually accommodate Protestant and Catholic demands.

The ANC delegation was unimpressed with Giliomee's arguments, regarding them as a reincarnation of race-based politics. But Giliomee considered the ANC's response inadequate. 'They were talking "the politics of redemption" – emphasis on "good" and "evil" and the "horrors of apartheid" – whereas I wanted to move the discussion on to how two nationalisms could be accommodated. The ANC was not thinking clearly about the basics of our society and about what kind of compromise might be necessary.'

Giliomee's views were discomforting to some of the other Afrikaner delegates who appeared to have been won over by the ANC's reassurances about the Afrikaner's place in a post-apartheid South Africa. One of Giliomee's colleagues took issue with his contention that the Afrikaners, like the Jews, viewed themselves as an endangered species. The delegate rebuked Giliomee:

'I cannot agree with the comparison made between the Jews and the Afrikaners. I think we haven't been listening to what we have been hearing over the last few days. There is no threat presenting itself. Nobody is talking about wiping out the Afrikaner. I cannot understand why at this stage we are still entertaining this illusion or strengthening the fear that this could be the case. We here, after two days, can't still think of this as a reality.'

André du Pisani regretted Giliomee's reference to Israel. Although the Stellenbosch professor might not have intended it as such, du Pisani believed Giliomee left the impression that Afrikaner nationalism could be compared to Zionism, the implication being that both South Africa and Israel were 'permanent homes' for 'chosen people', to the detriment of the Palestinians who had been driven out of their country and of the blacks who had been denied political rights. 'It was the symbolism of this comparison which did not go down well,' says du Pisani.

Seeking to drive home his point that the Afrikaners would not require a special dispensation in a post-apartheid South Africa, Pallo Jordan turned specifically to the question of the Afrikaner's concern about the survival of his language. He rounded on Giliomee, saying:

'I must reassure Hermann about the cultural rights of the Afrikaner. I think his remarks display, sadly – and I regret having to say this – abysmal ignorance of life among black South Africans. If I were to take you to ANC camps now, anywhere, ANC training centres, you will be amazed. In ordinary conversation the language that young people, also some of the older generation, use is Afrikaans. What greater reassurance do you need about the survival of your language? These people are communicating in Afrikaans!'

But what of the issue central to any discussions with the African National Congress? Are they prepared to allow for constitutional protection for whites during a transitional period and possibly beyond, a concept which conflicts entirely with their philosophy of a completely non-racial South Africa free of ethnic definition? Du Pisani gained the impression that for the ANC cultural rights were not entirely anathema. After all, he says, they were granted in countries like Switzerland and Belgium to accommodate the rights of population groups speaking different languages. He goes on: 'They don't want the notion of group rights to be abused by a white minority in order to maintain political and economic privilege. Their constitution would already provide for individual rights and as groups are comprised of individuals there would be no need for separate protection of groups.'

Whether other parties would be allowed to function in a post-apartheid South Africa was another question raised by the IDASA delegates. Mbeki's reply was that the ANC's call was for a united, non-racial and democratic South Africa and that for negotiations to be meaningful all participants would have to agree on that starting point. He went on: 'When the ANC talks about a transfer of power, they have never said there should be a transfer of power to the ANC. One will not find that in a thousand documents of the ANC. They have always asked for a transfer of power to the people.'

His differences of opinion with the ANC notwithstanding, Giliomee was impressed with the quality of the debate in Dakar. 'It was the first time that most of us had met highly articulate blacks who were confident and extremely patriotic. One sensed that we were meeting our black peers for the first time, especially in the case of Thabo Mbeki.'

André du Pisani had mixed feelings about the discussions with the ANC delegation. For him the value of the talks lay in a demonstration that rational debate was still possible. This was the most important lesson which he took back to South Africa; that 'given goodwill there could be a victory for reason.' His impression was that the ANC did not present themselves as having a monopoly of the truth or a unique insight into the problems of South Africa. To him they appeared uncertain themselves about the way to solve the country's problems; they realised that the social processes at work in South Africa were often unpredictable. Moreover the ANC doctrines appeared to be diverse. 'The ANC did not conform to the image of the organisation which is promoted inside South Africa. I think it is a total oversimplification to view the ANC as a monolithic, Marxist group bent on violence.' Du Pisani inferred from the meetings that there was no single dominating ideology within the ANC. He viewed the organisation as essentially middle class, believing in social democracy. It accepted the idea of a South African population without reference to race. The leadership was committed to the concept of the country's resources belonging to all the people. There was a strong emphasis on human rights, and du Pisani was surprised by how much research the ANC leaders had done: for example, they had studied the possibility of a bill of rights and had drawn a clear distinction between the protection of rights and the retention of privileges.

But one area of the talks left du Pisani disturbed. He concluded that ANC economic policy was its weakest point, that they had little understanding of the workings of a modern sophisticated economy. He was disappointed by their views on issues like the role of the state in the economy, the position of private enterprise and the redistribution of wealth; on the latter point the ANC had not been able to suggest any mechanism for achieving this objective, saying that they had not given economic policy much thought and that the party which eventually governed South Africa would decide upon economic matters. This did not satisfy du Pisani, who had hoped to hear more about the relation of resources to demography, the use of manpower, foreign investment and so on:

'They did not seem to realise that the South African economy does not have the capacity to support more than eighty million people [a figure which will be reached early in the twenty-first century unless birth control programmes take effect]. The experiences of other African countries should have compelled them to study matters like uncontrolled urbanisation, the use of investment capital, resources allocation, taxation and the relationship between politics and the economy.'

Despite the gaps which du Pisani detected in the ANC's policy thinking, he found the organisation's leaders extremely impressive. 'They had an eye for argument. They were well educated. They had been well exposed to a wider world of ideas.' Two impressions left their mark. Firstly, the ANC's commitment to its cause was very deep. 'They believe their struggle is right and their philosophy comes very close to the doctrine of a "just war".' Secondly, in du Pisani's eyes, they demonstrated a deep understanding for the dilemma facing whites who were seen as 'captives of the system'. They recognised the risk the Dakar group had taken in going to Senegal. 'What they demand from whites is some demonstration that they do not condone the system.' This could be shown in different ways: in the case of academics, attacking apartheid in print, or simply making clear their opposition in discussions with students; business and labour should make their voices heard too. 'The ANC was sensible enough to realise,' says du Pisani, 'that during a long phase of transition it will have to develop a relationship with white economic power even if it is not prepared to come to terms with white political power.'

Many issues were left unresolved; some were not tackled. What did the ANC mean by its concept of social democracy: the west European model in which the will of the people was expressed through individuals, or that of eastern Europe in which the will of the people was expressed through the state? Had the ANC used the Dakar meeting to further its diplomatic efforts to win support internationally? Certainly, the ANC leaders who attended the talks were from the organisation's 'moderate' nationalist wing rather than its Communist Party allies. Absent also were men like Chris Hani, chief of staff of Umkhonto we Sizwe (Spear of the Nation), the ANC's military wing, who a year after Dakar threatened to carry the armed campaign into white city centres, in seeming contradiction to the ANC's attempts to reach out to whites. Moreover, in the euphoria of the Dakar meeting, some of the delegates did slip into the kind of 'false consensus' that Slabbert had warned of, leaving the intellectuals among them to maintain some critical distance between themselves and their ANC discussion partners.

Nevertheless, black and white South Africans had debated the future of their country in a manner perhaps never witnessed before. The final communiqué said that the meeting 'had been invested with an overwhelming atmosphere that this was part of the process of the South African people making history'. Some of the Afrikaner participants knew that they were accused back home of an act of betrayal to both the South African state and to Afrikanerdom. The final communiqué totally rejected this allegation. It accused those in power in Pretoria of obstructing a negotiated settlement and expressed understanding of the conditions that had generated a widespread black revolt. It said that further contacts with wider sections of the South African people were now necessary to 'dispel misunderstanding and fear'. The final communiqué nevertheless recorded the differences between the two sides, for example over the question of violence, reflecting Slabbert's concern that the talks should not aim for an artificial detente. But the communiqué still embodied the spirit of search for a common South African identity.

Immediately afterwards, several of the Afrikaner delegates were asked by South African newspapers to summarise their impressions of the talks. The language they used had rarely been heard before from members of South Africa's ruling ethnic group about their black nationalist opponents. One said: 'I now have a greater appreciation of the moderation of the ANC leadership.' Another compared the 'meaningful talks' with the 'whites' neurosis about such contacts', adding: 'I am looking with new eyes at the liberation struggle. The talks have provided room for me and other Afrikaners opposed to apartheid to make a contribution.' In an attempt to pre-empt the government's inevitably hostile reaction to the talks, Slabbert said he hoped the initiative would not be 'rubbished for cheap and petty domestic politics'. The campaign of vilification had already started however, with the state-controlled South African Broadcasting Corporation referring in a radio commentary to 'political terrorists and political impotents coming together in Dakar', an ungenerous slur on a group of men and women who represented the very best of Afrikanerdom and who were as appalled as most other South Africans at the use of violence to further political ends.

After the talks formally closed, both delegations boarded a boat in Dakar harbour to make the half-hour crossing to Gorée Island, where a year previously Slabbert – to the singing of Miriam Makeba – had hit on Dakar as the venue for the gathering. The visit was deeply symbolic for the Afrikaners. It was from Gorée Island, at the western tip of Africa, that some 20 million slaves had been shipped to America. The Afrikaners were shown the slave house, built by the Dutch in 1776, with the slave master's quarters on the first floor. Beneath them were the dingy cells in which the slaves groaned and sweated in cramped and squalid conditions as they awaited transportation. The walls of the slave house are today plastered with posters attacking racism and apartheid. The visit made a deep impression on the white South Africans, who must have been struck by the realisation that theirs was the last country in Africa in which, because of the colour of their skin, people are still not totally free.

When the Dakar delegation returned to South Africa, one of the accusations levelled against them by their opponents was that they had been naïve, that they had been hoodwinked by the smooth-talking ANC members put up front and that the hard men of the military wing would hold entirely different views. After all, argued the critics, look what happened elsewhere in Africa when black governments took over. What happened in those countries to all the guarantees about white survival and prosperity for all? The point unquestionably needs answering. The response of André du Pisani is that care is required in equating South Africa with other countries on the continent. Certainly, he says, there are deep parallels which cannot be discounted. But South Africa, he explains, has a more pronounced class structure. Blacks and whites in large numbers share urban values. The social rifts do not run as deep as elsewhere because of the communality of religion and language. Somehow a system will have to be found, he says, where cultural rights can be exercised, but not at the expense of individual rights. 'For this to happen the whites will have to make sacrifices. The only way that some level of cultural rights can be guaranteed is for whites to accept that they have to share not only political power but also economic and social power.'

In retrospect, says Hermann Giliomee, 'Dakar brought home the extent to which one is so weighed down by the burden of apartheid and a burden of guilt.'

For Slabbert, the impressions of the Afrikaner group fell into three categories. 'In Senegal there was an infatuation with the place. The group appeared surprised by the sophistication of French-speaking Africa. One of the group, Hardy Botha, an artist, told me that the three days he spent in Dakar changed his whole life. He never went to bed; he just walked around the city the whole night long. He loved it.' In Ghana, which the group visited after Senegal, the mood was less enthusiastic, Says Slabbert: 'Ghana came as a shock. All the signs of post-colonial decay were so evident. "What a dump" was the general reaction. The place confirmed all the worst stereotypes about what could go wrong in Africa.' Burkina Faso, their final port of call, faced similar difficulties, as far as the Afrikaners could see, but they admired what Slabbert calls the 'boyish enthusiasm of the place', or the 'spirit of festive socialism' as another of the group described it. Captain Thomas Sankara, the country's leader, appeared keen to play a role in Africa, says Slabbert, and took a firm line with the ANC delegates, asking why he should give them arms when they had not even got close to Pretoria. As if to underline the uncertainties of Africa, Sankara was killed in a military coup just a few months after the visit by the liberal Afrikaners.

As for the talks between the Afrikaners and the ANC, Slabbert believes the ANC obtained a clearer impression of the genuine dilemma facing Afrikaners who have deserted apartheid: they were not going to fall in line behind the ANC but did wish to broaden the struggle. 'These kind of issues were given a good airing in Dakar,' says Slabbert. After Dakar, he says, the whites became an important element in the liberation struggle. 'The ANC discovered that Afrikaners have minds also.'

Dakar marked the first significant occasion when Afrikaner and African nationalists sat down at a table to discuss the future of their country as equals. There was no sense of the black man being summoned to the white man's table to hear what the white man had planned for him, the mistake which had dogged most attempts by the Pretoria government to reach an accommodation with blacks. The Afrikaners had been able to examine the ANC's policies, forcing the organisation's leaders to be on their mettle. The dissident Afrikaners had to come clean on whether they were willing to submit to a united South Africa. There was no major breakthrough towards peace; that had not been the object of the talks. But it was nevertheless a landmark. If one day the South African government does decide to negotiate with the ANC, it may only be possible because the Slabbert delegation, and others following, have paved the way. The mission to Dakar was the beginning of a process which will slowly make it acceptable and respectable for Afrikaners to talk to the ANC. Indeed, the following year, a broader group of Afrikaners met the ANC in West Germany for talks also attended by officials from the Soviet Union, whose participation was itself a significant breakthrough. Who knows whether this process will produce results? But the business of talking must surely be an improvement on the log-jam of the previous four decades. Subsequent claims by Pretoria that such dealings should be left to the government, and that 'innocents' like the Dakar delegation only make real negotiations harder, would be convincing if Pretoria displayed anything approaching the same kind of imaginative flair that had brought about the gathering.

Perhaps more important than all the issues discussed, was the atmosphere of the gathering. For after the initial reticence had broken down, the meeting in Dakar became a very natural occasion. Free of the shackles of apartheid, black and white South Africans rubbed shoulders in an environment where there was no racial discrimination and where it suddenly struck the Afrikaners how normal it was for blacks and whites to mix and how abnormal was the system of apartheid which had malignantly permeated every area of life in their own country.

As Professor André du Toit put it afterwards: 'I think in the lives of all of us the Dakar meeting will probably be a very important watershed.'

When the group returned to South Africa, the ultra-right AWB mounted a protest over the Dakar talks at Johannesburg airport. Had black rather than white extremists staged a demonstration on the airport concourse, the police would probably have arrested them all. But this one was allowed to continue. One of the white demonstrators wore a white overall splattered with red paint to symbolise 'the blood of Afrikaners which would be spilt because of the Dakar talks'. A white air stewardess carrying a black child off another plane was subjected to vicious abuse by the white extremists.

The Dakar group could have been forgiven if the exhilaration of their time in west Africa had quickly given way to despair when faced with the reality of the racial claustrophobia of their own country.

CHAPTER TEN

The Cradle Rocks

Apartheid, through its geographical compartmentalisation of people, has made more stark the political, economic and social divisions that characterise South Africa: divisions that are not unique to the country and which would to a large degree remain even without racial segregation. The miserable, degrading hovel that is Alexandra township (only recently improved after years of neglect) is located close to ostentatiously palatial residences in the wealthy white suburbs of northern Johannesburg. Luxurious hotel complexes like Sun City are to be found just a few miles from rows of tin toilets awaiting some unfortunate black community forcibly removed from their homes hundreds of miles away.

The contrasts are nowhere more striking than in the hinterland of Cape Town. Driving out of the city along the main highway – following the footsteps of the early Dutch settlers – D. F. Malan airport (almost all of South Africa's civilian airports are named after the country's white prime ministers) is on the left; to the right of the highway is the place which has become identified worldwide with the inhumanity of apartheid – Crossroads. This huge sprawling squatter camp, whose residents construct their primitive shacks from corrugated iron fencing, wooden boxes or any materials they can lay their hands on, resulted from years of government attempts to halt the flow of blacks to Cape Town from the impoverished homelands. The thinking was: stop building houses for the blacks and they will stop coming. The plan was of course futile. Blacks searching for work continued to arrive in droves. Attempts to thwart them reached their most absurd when busloads of blacks from the Transkei would be turned back at the Cape only to return some days later to try once more to infiltrate the ideological cordon. The policy eventually collapsed and Crossroads became the sponge that absorbed thousands of homeless black migrants. Partly because of inter-black feuding and also because of government policies during the 1970s and 1980s, much of the Crossroads shanty area was destroyed while some parts were upgraded.

Soon after this advertisement for apartheid is a political and cultural time-warp, another world altogether: the rugged mountains, the fertile valleys and the rich vineyards further inland from Cape Town. The drive takes you past Eerste Rivier (First River), so named because it was the first river to be crossed by the early explorers venturing inland. In the distance is the Helderberg mountain, 1224 metres high, home to black eagles and peregrine falcons and one of the few peaks in the Hottentot-Holland range that is not regularly shrouded in clouds.

The Afrikaners

One kilometre before the town of Stellenbosch is the farm *Libertas* (Liberty), the estate of the largest of the region's wine producers, Stellenbosch Farmers' Winery, where visitors sample the wares after a guided tour demonstrating the wine-making process. The estate originally belonged to Adam Tas who led a revolt in 1709 against the corruption of the Dutch governor Willem Adriaan van der Stel (son of the founder of Stellenbosch). Tas was jailed. Upon his release he renamed his farm *Liber-tas*. The first vines imported from Europe were planted soon after van Riebeeck's arrival. Seven years after the 1652 landings, he wrote in his diary: 'Today, praise be the Lord, wine was made for the first time from Cape grapes.' Later arrivals, especially the French Huguenots among whom were skilled vintners, brought with them new cultivars from the noble vines of Europe. They took advantage of the Cape climate with its high annual rainfall of 600 mm and reliable hours of sunlight, as well as sufficiently fertile soil and a south-east winter wind known as the 'Cape doctor' said to clear the air of all pestilences thereby preventing diseases of the grape. At harvest time the streets of Stellenbosch are as they might have been 300 years ago, with tractor-drawn carts bulging with grapes on their way to the winery, some bunches falling off to be squashed by a passing car, a modern intruder into this idyllic setting.

Stellenbosch itself is the second oldest and best preserved town in South Africa. Known as 'the town of oaks' because of the ancient trees lining its streets, the town boasts sixty national monuments and five museums. Stellenbosch is famous for its Cape Dutch architecture: homesteads and wine farms constructed by the early settlers and notable for their brilliant white facades, a stark silhouette against the deep green colours of the surrounding countryside. Rows of terraced houses in Dorp Street, with doors and window frames built from local yellow-wood and stinkwood, today house antique shops, boutiques, art galleries or small museums recapturing the lives of the early European immigrants.

But the real centrepiece of the town is the university. It is arguable whether any student anywhere in the world could wish for a pleasanter setting. In the shadow of the nearby mountains, the university is the epitome of what young white South Africans can enjoy: a relaxed campus with immaculately cut lawns, spacious student accommodation and recreational facilities, and sweeping drives along which students can bicycle to their lectures, at least those students who don't drive up-market cars which they park in the shade of neatly arranged trees.

Near the university is a country hotel famous for its rooms with antique furniture and private gardens filled with bougainvillaea. Many students and lecturers retire to the hotel in the evenings to drink wine or beer al fresco as the sun sinks behind the mountains.

This is a world far removed from the harsh climate, natural and political, of the Transvaal. Here the political debate is conducted in more genteel tones. The people of the western Cape live at a less frenetic pace than those in the north. They are different people altogether in the Cape. These, after all, were the Afrikaners who did not trek, men and women who were less agitated about living under British rule, and more prepared to co-exist with the British. They have lived side by side with coloureds for centuries and are perhaps more tolerant towards

166

blacks. Their more relaxed outlook is partly explained by the fact that fewer blacks live in the Cape than in the Transvaal, where the presence of huge black townships like Soweto gives an edge to race relations.

In this university town is some of the most agreeable company and stimulating conversation that Afrikanerdom has to offer. It was in the tranquil surroundings of Stellenbosch – 'the cradle of Afrikanerdom' – that an academic rebellion took place against the old order. It was not like the Sorbonne in 1968 or the American campuses of the 1960s. It never exploded into violence with students taking to the streets; it was, rather, a quiet revolution but no less shattering for the nation's political masters, who had come to rely on the learned men of Stellenbosch as the ideological think-tank of apartheid.

Stellenbosch is named after Simon van der Stel ('Van der Stel's forest') who arrived in the Cape in October 1679 as governor of the colony. Then the population totalled almost 800, comprising officials of the Dutch East India Company, free burghers who had been released from service to farm their own land, and their families. The colony was not self-supporting; very few colonists had turned to agriculture and there was a pressing need for wheat. Within a month van der Stel began tackling this problem, journeying inland and establishing a new settlement on the banks of the Eerste Rivier. Stellenbosch expanded around the site of the governor's camp. The number of settlers slowly increased so that within a few years the community was contributing a substantial slice of the Cape's wheat requirements. Stellenbosch became an emerging frontier town from where commandos set off further into the interior in early encounters with the indigenous Khoi and the black Xhosa tribesmen.

It was an arduous life for these pioneers, dominated by hard work: farming, building their homes, making furniture. Their families and friends were their only comforts, the Bible their sole source of inspiration. Their departure and eventual isolation from the stimulation of the Netherlands and from a Europe which was soon to experience its age of enlightenment meant that the colony became an intellectual backwater ignorant of the new ideas of Descartes, Locke and their contemporaries. The explosion of liberal ideas that accompanied the French Revolution – concepts of justice and equality – passed them by. The Afrikaners produced little literature, art, music or scientific enquiry. Library facilities were scant; there were no journals or newspapers. The intellectual development of the Afrikaner was meagre.

In 1685 churches were established at Stellenbosch and at four other centres in the Cape. For over a hundred years the church was the only medium of education, apart from a few itinerant teachers. The commitment to learning was negligible and the level of teaching elementary. Remote farm communities leading primitive lives saw little need for scholastic self-improvement. During the Dutch period not a single high school of note was established at the Cape. This was a sign of the community's neglect at the hands of the Dutch, a neglect which contributed to the Afrikaners' slipping behind the rest of the world. It was not until the latter half of the eighteenth century, by which time visiting clergymen and academics had at last begun to infiltrate a few ideas from Europe's period of enlightenment, that there was a significant burgeoning of learning.

A theological seminary was founded in Stellenbosch in 1859 for the training of *dominees*, its founders inspired by the teaching at Dutch universities where they had studied. Stellenbosch University College was established, soon renamed Victoria College to mark the British monarch's fifty years on the throne. It was only after Union in 1910 that Stellenbosch and other colleges began to acquire full university status, 250 years after the first Dutch settlers had arrived. By contrast Harvard University was founded in 1636, just sixteen years after the Pilgrim Fathers had landed in America.

Still, by the early part of this century Stellenbosch was beginning to catch up on lost time, proving itself throughout the 1930s, 1940s and 1950s the most important and influential of the Afrikaans-medium universities. Part of the reason was its proximity to the seat of government and parliament, and therefore power, in nearby Cape Town. All of South Africa's prime ministers except its first and last, Louis Botha and P. W. Botha, were students at Stellenbosch University. When D. F. Malan became the first National Party prime minister in 1948 the majority of his cabinet members came from the Cape.

The university's most famous son was Verwoerd, a doctor of philosophy at the age of twenty-nine. Even at this early stage in his career, his search for the perfect ordering of society was apparent. In 1935 he attended a conference in Kimberley convened to follow up the Carnegie Commission report on the poor whites. Verwoerd delivered the principal speech, one of his first open justifications for a policy of discrimination towards South Africa's black population. The priority, he told his audience, was to raise the living standards of whites and only then to give attention to the political and economic wellbeing of other racial groups. Perhaps sensing, even then, Verwoerd's fanatical pursuit of a scientifically structured, racial master plan, a Stellenbosch colleague offered him friendly words of caution on the eve of his departure for Kimberley, saying: 'Try not to solve all the country's problems, Hendrik.'

Verwoerd ignored the advice, proceeding dogmatically with the creation of contrived homelands where the country's majority black population could fulfil its political aspirations; and passing harsh laws isolating those blacks required to live within 'white South Africa' because of the white man's labour requirements. The South African Bureau of Racial Affairs (SABRA) formed in the 1950s was charged with constructing the philosophical pillars of apartheid. In a statement of policy shortly after its establishment, SABRA declared: 'By a policy of free and separate development we must understand the territorial separation of European and Bantu, and the provision of areas which must serve as national and political homes for the different Bantu communities and as permanent residential areas for the Bantu population or the major portion of it.' SABRA was the perfect ideological assembly line for the nationalist government. The race laws went in at one end in their raw political form; at the other end out came their philosophical justification. At SABRA's congress in Stellenbosch in 1960 the Minister of Bantu Administration and Development M.C. de Wet Nel explained to delegates that apartheid was not the same as the segregation which had existed before the election of the National Party government. Rather, he said, it was a more comprehensive system aimed at regulating relations between the various colour groups and at allowing blacks self-determination.

Stellenbosch academics formed the backbone of SABRA and several of its professors contributed to reports drawn up in the 1950s, 1960s and 1970s which paved the way for the principal apartheid laws. But already one begins to detect the seeds of an earlier Stellenbosch revolt, a challenge to the way in which academic advice was translated into National Party doctrine. Unlike the later rebellion, this Stellenbosch revolt was contained within the party fold. Moreover the protests were not on moral grounds so much as on what the academics saw as the unworkability of Verwoerd's schemes. Tensions surfaced in the wake of the first enquiry to which the Stellenbosch academics contributed: the report of the commission under Professor F. R. Tomlinson which met between November 1950 and October 1954 and whose recommendations formed the blueprint for the entire policy of creating black homelands. The report's conclusion was that integration of the races would simply lead to racial conflict; therefore whites and blacks had to develop as separate 'groups', the word that has become a punctuation mark in the language of apartheid. The commission proposed that the existing 260 scattered tribal areas should be consolidated into separate ethnic 'homelands' each populated by one particular black tribe. The commission's members acknowledged that such a policy could work only if the proposed black states were fully developed: they had to be viable, it was argued, and huge investment would be required for these territories to sustain themselves economically. It was on this point that the Stellenbosch members clashed with Verwoerd, then Minister of Native Affairs, who was more interested in politics than economics.

The commission had recommended that over £100 million be spent during the first ten years on the development of the homelands' infrastructure and in creating jobs. The government disagreed and an initial budget of £3 million covering one year only was all that was available. Verwoerd also opposed the commission's proposal that white businessmen and manufacturers should be allowed to set up industries inside the homelands. He argued that this would lead to an unacceptable racial crossover, which would conflict with the policy of apartheid. It would not be beneficial, he maintained, to afford too much help to the Bantu (blacks – the word a derivative of *abantu*, meaning 'people'). Addressing parliament in May 1956, Verwoerd declared:

'The Bantu must start on a small scale. Psychologically he is not adapted to industrial life and certainly not to private enterprise, to be able to start on a big scale. Nor would he be in a position in ten or twenty years' time to take over big industries which have been developed there if his relationship towards industry has been simply that of the recipient and the outsider.'

Verwoerd told MPs that blacks would not improve themselves if 'the spoon-feeding which has been so disastrous in the past in the rural sphere is applied in this [industrial] sphere'. In such sentiments originated the often impoverished and squalid conditions, the corruption and rule by ruthless oligarchies that are the hallmarks of several of the homelands today.

Verwoerd extracted from the Tomlinson report the parts he liked, while ignoring the rest. Within Afrikanerdom, the Stellenbosch academics were now assuming a liberal position. When they tackled Verwoerd on the homelands policy he virtually threw them out of his office. Verwoerd organised a Broeder-bond coup to eject the dissident professors from the SABRA board, installing his own conservative cronies in their place.

The disillusionment of the Stellenbosch liberals intensified under Verwoerd's successor, John Vorster. Again, the grievance was over how the government received a report in which Stellenbosch academics were involved: that drawn up by a commission of enquiry chaired by Stellenbosch sociology professor, Erika Theron, appointed in 1973 to investigate 'matters pertaining to the coloured population group'. The committee, which comprised six coloureds and twelve whites, was charged with investigating the development of the mixed-race population at all levels.

The commission's long-awaited report was submitted on 18 June 1976, two days after the outbreak of the widespread rioting in Soweto. The government accepted most of the report's 178 recommendations but rejected those which compromised the principles of apartheid. The commission concluded that the coloured community was not a 'nation in the making' and could not therefore conform to the government's separatist plans for the various race groups. The lines of 'parallel development' between coloureds and whites should be narrowed. Provision should be made for the coloureds to be represented at various levels of government and in the country's decision-making bodies. Reacting to the recommendations of the Theron Commission, the government stated that the coloureds could not be granted direct representation in parliament or in local bodies. However, the government was prepared to amend the existing Westmins-ter-style constitution to allow greater autonomy for coloureds. The matter was referred to a special cabinet committee under the then Minister of Defence P. W. Botha, a move which eventually resulted in the new constitution introduced in 1983 under which the mixed-race people now have their own parliament, legislating for their own affairs but with only a limited voice in the principal organs of state.

For Sampie Terreblanche, Professor of Economics at Stellenbosch University, his experiences on the Theron Commission and the government's response to its findings were devastating.

'The Theron Commission changed my life. It opened my eyes to the fact that apartheid was wrong, that it was an inhuman policy.' Professor Terreblanche's investigation into the coloured population left him with the firm view that the political system in South Africa meant that entrenched poverty was the plight of at least half of the coloured community. Such people, he concluded, were consigned to a life of permanent misery. The country's political structures prevented them from breaking out of this apartheid poverty trap. Of the three years Terreblanche spent working on the commission, the most crucial period for him was in May and June of 1974 when the commission visited the town of Springs on the East Rand, east of Johannesburg. 'Slowly but certainly I began to change my views.'

The commission first visited the town hall in Springs, 'a luxurious building,' says Terreblanche, 'or, rather, glittery but cheap taste'. He compared the building (almost entirely occupied by white officials) to the conditions he found in the nearby coloured township 'where the poverty was shocking'.

'There were no lavatories except for what were called "slip toilets", so named because the sanitation was so appalling, with urine overflowing everywhere, that you had to "slip in" and "slip out" in order to use them.' A resident of the coloured township complained to Terreblanche about the absence of effective political representation for his people. This was the time when many Portuguese were arriving in South Africa from Mozambique, as Portugal's African empire began to crumble. 'Those Portuguese are as black as we are,' protested the Springs resident 'and yet after five years in this country they, unlike us, are allowed to have a vote.' On the following day the commission visited two coloured areas in the nearby town of Nigel where Terreblanche had another dispiriting encounter. The coloured man guiding the commission members around the area on an official bus, in between describing the area, began talking to himself. But he had forgotten to switch off his microphone. His words were heard by all on board. 'The coloureds don't have a place in this country,' he said. 'We will always be on the losing side.'

Was there one experience that tipped the balance? Professor Terreblanche recounted how, one Christmas, he and his wife had driven their coloured maid home to her designated mixed-race township a few miles from Stellenbosch on the Cape coast. After dropping her off, the couple paid a visit to the nearby beach reserved, under apartheid, for coloureds. 'I'm keen on swimming and I enjoy the beach and the sea. But the coloured beach consisted only of rocks with limited beach and swimming facilities. I realised there and then that a coloured man could be born here and could die here and never have the opportunity to surf in his own sea. I said to myself: "This is discrimination in its worst form".'

Terreblanche says that during the Theron Commission he once asked a mixed-race man why the coloured people had so many children compared to whites. The man's reply was: 'The only pleasure we have is pleasure.'

But Terreblanche still did not make an open break with the government even though the limited extent of P. W. Botha's reforms was clear. Terreblanche explains that despite being 'very depressed' he remained a close confidant of Chris Heunis, Minister of Constitutional Development and Planning, who was emerging as the architect of the new constitution which would grant a limited share of power to coloureds and Indians. Terreblanche exploited his channels to government to try to encourage broader and faster reforms. When the right wing broke from the Nationalists in 1982 to form the Conservative Party, Terreblanche sent a message to Prime Minister Botha urging him to ignore the right-wing split and to continue imaginatively along the path of reform. 'Cometh the hour, cometh the man,' he told Botha.

Still, though, government policies were racially-based both in central government and in regional and local authorities. The concept of a shared South African polity embracing all race groups was not on the agenda. Terreblanche was edging closer to a break. 'By remaining within the National Party and trying to influence policy from inside I was practising brinkmanship. But for brinkmanship to have credibility you must be prepared to go over the brink at a certain time.' Terreblanche was still writing many of Heunis's public speeches. But he soon came to realise that he was not altering policy, 'only changing the rhetoric'. Throughout 1983, however, Terreblanche and his fellow Stellenbosch academics worked hard to sell the new power-sharing constitution, convinced the plan was a start, a first step, towards a political settlement involving all South Africans. The group contributed to radio and television discussions and strongly advocated the new proposals in influential Afrikaans-language newspapers like *Die Burger* and *Rapport*.

Another prominent Stellenbosch academic had by this time also fallen out with the National Party establishment – Professor Willie Esterhuyse. Esterhuyse's links with the National Party had always been informal. He had been a member of his local National Party branch and during the 1970s had occasionally been involved in addressing the party's youth congresses. In 1978 all that changed following the publication of his book *Apartheid Must Die*, which addressed the entire moral issue of apartheid and racial discrimination. The book's publication, and the hostile reaction, spurred Esterhuyse's break with the Nationalists, although informal contacts were maintained.

The growing rift between the government and the Stellenbosch academics represented the tip of the iceberg of liberal discontent. The relationship between the two sides had always been informal, not an institutionalised arrangement. But for minister Chris Heunis in particular, the contacts were very important and he had gone out of his way to use Stellenbosch as an intellectual reservoir providing the orthodoxy of reform for the National Party. Esterhuyse himself had made significant contributions to the debate on the abolition of the Prohibition of Mixed Marriages Act, section 16 of the Immorality Act and the influx control system which enforced the harsh pass laws regulating the movements of blacks. Newspaper articles and reports by him and others helped prepare the public for the eventual repeal of these laws.

In retrospect, says Terreblanche, it was a terrible mistake to bring into parliament the coloureds but not the blacks. It was no coincidence that violence in black townships broke out on the very day that the new parliament met for the first time, erupting in Sharpeville, itself the very symbol of black resistance. Many coloured and Indian townships were also caught up in the violence, members of both communities resenting their second-class political status and protesting against the political sidelining of the blacks. Telling the blacks that they could enjoy their political representation in the homelands appeared to be a signal from the government that the blacks were permanent aliens in their own country. 'For thirty years,' says Terreblanche, 'the official status of the coloureds had deteriorated. They'd become *verkaffired*, as the term had it [reduced to the level of the kaffirs]. The blacks observed this and they could not understand why the coloureds were being given a share in power while they were excluded. In the view of the blacks, there was no difference between the two groups. The violent protests began once this was realised.'

On 16 December 1984 – the Day of the Vow – Terreblanche wrote a newspaper article calling on the government to issue a declaration of intent to abolish apartheid. The Stellenbosch professor, a gracious and hospitable man distinguished by his chalk-white hair, slowly found himself being cut off from the government's inner circles and ostracised from National Party functions of any importance. 'I became persona non grata,' he recalls. 'I'd always gone personally to Heunis's office whenever I had a speech ready which he had asked me to write. Suddenly he would start sending a driver round to collect the speeches.'

Then came 15 August 1985, arguably a watershed in the history of modern South African politics. With violence erupting in the black townships of nearly every major city, and with international confidence in South Africa haemorrhaging, the word went out that President Botha was to deliver an historic speech at a National Party congress in Durban, in which he would finally take the country 'across the Rubicon' by announcing far-reaching reforms. Here was the opportunity for Botha to demonstrate he was a head of state in the Gaullist mould, a statesman, a leader for all South Africans. But on the night, the 'Rubicon' speech turned out to be a damp squib. With parts of the country in chaos, all Botha could do was wave his finger at international opinion and declare his resolve to protect white interests.

Sampie Terreblanche, watching the speech on television at home, could not believe what he was hearing. 'I was ashamed. Sitting there I could not get up I was so shocked.'

Within two months the dissident Stellenbosch academics had formed themselves into an action group.

Eight thousand miles away in London, another man was watching Botha's televised speech that evening. Denis Worrall, South Africa's enlightened ambassador to the Court of St James, had realised in advance the speech's crucial importance. While on holiday in the south of France a short time before, he had spent hours in the lobby of his small hotel waiting for a telephone call to South Africa to register his view that the speech had tremendous potential to signal an imaginative move forward. He wanted to contribute to the drafting of the speech, but his efforts were to no avail. 'I spoke to one cabinet minister in particular who also understood what was required, only to be told that "they" had decided.' Cutting short his holiday, Worrall returned to London to be on hand on the night

Botha delivered his address. He arranged to watch the speech in the offices of the British Broadcasting Corporation in central London in order to brief BBC journalists immediately afterwards and to appear on radio and television programmes to explain to the British public the significance of what Botha was saying. The expectations of Botha's speech in Britain and elsewhere were intense. But as BBC editorial chiefs, joined by Worrall, listened to the speech in a live satellite link between Durban and London, it soon became evident that it was a disaster. The hoped-for breakthrough into a new era when apartheid would be thrown out of the window was clearly not about to materialise. Worrall put a brave face on it, but left the BBC offices that night a bitterly disappointed and disillusioned man.

Since arriving in Britain, Worrall had patiently and effectively sought to explain Botha's reform programme to an impatient British establishment, to a media not given to understanding the nuances of the South African situation and to a British public confused by the issues. Despite the odds stacked against him, Worrall conducted himself with dignity in radio, television and press interviews. He could never hope to convince his audiences that Botha's policies meant significant change, but at least the public was prepared to listen. Had Worrall not been there as ambassador, South Africa's international image would have suffered a lot more. After the 'Rubicon' speech, however, even he realised that he was trying to sell the unsellable.

Recalling those days, Worrall says the speech was a tremendous let-down. 'The government had no understanding whatsoever of what was at stake. There was no sense of occasion. It should have been a brilliant speech. Even if there were to be no major announcements, the speech could at least have been inspirational.'

His frustration did not stop there. In early 1986 Worrall returned to South Africa for the visit of the Commonwealth Eminent Persons' Group (EPG). In London the ambassador had already helped to smooth the EPG's path. After discussions with the Nigerian representative Olesegun Obasanjo, Worrall had obtained an assurance from his government that the team would be allowed to see the jailed leader of the African National Congress, Nelson Mandela. The EPG mission to South Africa went better than most would have expected. Slowly they were edging close to an agreement under which the ANC would suspend its armed struggle in return for Pretoria releasing Mandela and opening negotiations. On what was to be their last Friday in South Africa, the EPG held a successful meeting with Mandela. Over a light lunch, says Worrall, Foreign Minister Pik Botha, backing the initiative, advised the EPG on how to handle a scheduled meeting the following Monday with the government's Constitutional Committee under Heunis. Events were gathering pace and although Worrall was not satisfied with all aspects of the EPG proposals, there was a sense that suddenly a real opportunity for negotiation had opened up. P. W. Botha and Heunis knew it too. Quite clearly they were being drawn into a vortex that neither wanted. Overnight on the Sunday, South African defence units raided three neighbouring black states in pointless military exercises whose political purpose was to kill off the EPG initiative. That night the Commonwealth team returned home, their mission torpedoed. There could not have been starker evidence that P. W. Botha and Heunis had no intention of opening negotiations with their main black nationalist opponents.

Worrall decided it was time for him to end his diplomatic role in London, despite the importance of the post at a time when the international campaign to impose economic sanctions upon South Africa was gaining momentum. At the end of 1986 he returned to Cape Town to take soundings about the future. There are differing accounts of what transpired on this visit. Worrall says that he wanted to learn from cabinet ministers, especially Heunis, exactly where the government was taking the country. Worrall had been profoundly shocked by a statement from the Home Affairs Minister Stoffel Botha (also leader of the National Party in the province of Natal), who had dismissed the Indaba plan, drawn up by white and black leaders in Natal and the neighbouring black homeland of kwaZulu, for a joint regional administration based on one man, one vote with certain guarantees for racial minorities. Stoffel Botha rejected the plan because, he said, it did not afford sufficient guarantees. He meant of course that the plan, despite its protection clauses, would result in a black-dominated government. For Worrall this was exactly the kind of experiment in power-sharing which the government should have been encouraging rather than rejecting out of hand.

Worrall's opponents in government, perhaps out to discredit his eventual highly-publicised defection from the National Party fold, later put the word out that his trip to Cape Town had been to learn whether he was to be offered a senior cabinet post in a government reshuffle. It was only when he found out he wasn't, said his critics, that he decided to rebel. Whichever account is accurate, the source of Worrall's disillusionment with the government was in no small measure his bitter antagonism towards Heunis, whose policies Worrall viewed as the cause of the political stalemate. The two had clashed almost a decade before over constitutional matters, after which Worrall had been despatched as ambassador to Australia, the post he held before moving to London.

With a whites-only general election likely to be called, Worrall, during the last few weeks before he left London, consulted with his supporters in South Africa as to which constituency he should fight. Some of the leading sugar barons of Natal, owners of the province's giant plantations, were behind him. In Natal Worrall was virtually guaranteed victory in a liberal-orientated constituency where the Progressive Federal Party would be prepared to stand aside for him. But the wealthy wine estate owners in the Cape, particularly in the valleys around Stellenbosch, also saw in Worrall a hope for the future. They too let it be known that they would back him if he stood in a Cape constituency.

One of them was Jannie Momberg, a former National Party stalwart and one of the South African athletics chiefs who had helped runner Zola Budd on her path to international fame. Momberg had been at Stellenbosch University in 1952, where he was secretary of the National Party's student branch. From 1957 to 1985 he alternated between chairman and secretary of his party branch. In 1981 he was awarded the Erasmus Prize for service to the party. But the signs of his eventual dissidence had been evident as far back as 1963 when he wrote several letters to the Afrikaans press objecting to the government's handling of the coloured people, who by then had been removed from the common voters' roll. Momberg's flurry of letters had been prompted by a group of coloured children being thrown out of a concert in Cape Town. Like Terreblanche, Momberg had always convinced himself that it was more fruitful to work within the party. But like Terreblanche and the others, Momberg also reached a watershed.

It came in September 1985 when he was attending the National Party's Cape congress in Port Elizabeth. A motion was put forward demanding a more stringent enforcement of the Group Areas Act. Momberg opposed the motion and spoke in favour of the act's abolition, saying: 'The Afrikaner does not need laws to preserve his identity.' He was slapped down by P. W. Botha, after which, says Momberg, 'I was going through the motions of supporting the National Party.' By January 1987 he had decided not to vote in the forthcoming election, concluding that the government was simply trying to modify apartheid, not to scrap it. Says Momberg: 'No builder starts reconstruction work on the ruins of the old house. He clears away the debris first. And as far as I am concerned when you still have the Group Areas Act, the Population Registration Act and the Separate Amenities Act on the statute book, then you still have apartheid.' At a cricket match in Port Elizabeth, Momberg spotted a newspaper headline saying 'Worrall quits'. From his hotel Momberg telephoned Worrall in London to offer him his support and to urge him to stand against Heunis in the Cape constituency of Helderberg. A successful campaign against Heunis, argued Momberg, would send the National Party a clear signal that the country was ready for change.

Worrall's return electrified the election campaign, particularly in the Cape and in academic circles at Stellenbosch. It was here, rather than in Natal, that Worrall's intellectual soul resided. He recognised that Stellenbosch epitomised a new class of Afrikaners: intelligent, sophisticated, not bound by the handed-down folklore and increasingly prosperous. Such people had grown up with the National Party but, like him, were frustrated with the slow pace of change. On the other hand, many of them were not happy with the PFP, which was seen as being 'soft on security' and as primarily representing English-speaking interests despite some Afrikaner MPs and members. Worrall also understood that power in South Africa rested with the Afrikaner: gathering support from English-speaking liberals was not going to break the mould. His task was therefore to carve out a new channel in liberal politics, somewhere between the liberal wing of the Nationalists and the PFP, in the hope of establishing a political home for enlightened Afrikaners as well as similarly-disposed English-speakers. The irony was that it had taken an English-speaker to spot the political ground of Afrikaner politics that was lying vacant. Worrall was also careful to ease the psychological passage of those contemplating a desertion of the Nationalists. At an airport news conference on his return he stressed that his mission was to 'give the National Party a real mandate for reform'. In other words, the National Party was still going to be in government after the election; a strong showing for the independent cause would send a signal to Botha that whites were demanding faster change. For many disillusioned Afrikaners Worrall's standpoint was attractive, a comfortable political cause behind which they could rally.

Worrall decided to take the bull by the horns by standing against Heunis in the Cape constituency of Helderberg, which includes part of Stellenbosch. Heunis was sitting on a healthy majority and had the National Party's powerful Cape machine to back him. By contrast Worrall was starting from scratch with teams of willing volunteers, among them Jannie Momberg. It appeared to be a David and Goliath struggle, but as the weeks wore on it became evident that Worrall's cause was far from hopeless. Both candidates' headquarters were on the main street in the town of Somerset West near Stellenbosch. Heunis's, in a two-storey house, was a joyless place; by contrast, Worrall's base in a rented office was abuzz with excitement. Worrall, publicly reluctant to raise expectations which he could not fulfil, nevertheless admitted in private moments that he believed the seat was 'winnable'.

Worrall linked up in the independent campaign with the earlier defector from the National Party, Wynand Malan, member of parliament for the Transvaal seat of Randburg near Johannesburg whose constituents included many newly-prosperous Afrikaners. Malan, standing over six feet tall and with broad shoulders, is a quietly spoken, sensitive man whose politics are firmly rooted in his Christianity. Writing in *Leadership* magazine in early 1987, the former liberal Nationalist explained his view of the deadlock which had caused him to go out into the political wilderness:

> What is negotiation? The Progressive Federal Party seems to view it as a process involving the easiest and least painful way to place your future in the hands of another. The National Party, on the other hand, seems to view negotiation as a process in which you control the agenda, enabling you to manipulate discussions and their final outcome. Negotiation is rather like playing tennis. One should preferably take the initiative and try to serve first. Serve deep by all means, but don't go for an ace. On the other hand, don't keep serving the ball into the net. Your opponent will simply leave the court if you don't play the game. The game should be played in such a manner that it can continue, but the problem in our country today is that the PFP wants an ace to be served to it; the National Party wants to serve the ace. Neither is negotiating.

Malan recalled in the article that he had been 'born into the National Party', but added that:

> . . . leaving has nothing to do with being a rebel or a hero. I did not clash with the National Party. I clashed with my conscience. And in the end, conscience wins against party.

Despite their political allegiance Malan and Worrall were not natural kinsmen. Worrall, an ambitious politician with a sharp political instinct and a firm grip on the dynamics and practicalities of power, believed it was unrealistic to pursue policies which did not win the confidence of whites, the key power-brokers. Malan was more concerned about the moral and philosophical foundations of his policies. For him the campaign was more an act of self-cleansing, a process, partly inspired by his strong religious commitment, through which he could discover a new identity for himself outside the National Party's Afrikaner establishment. It was noticeable that on public platforms Malan, though demonstrating absolute solidarity with Worrall, displayed more warmth towards Stellenbosch business-woman Esther Lategan who had decided to stand as a third independent candidate. Malan and Lategan, both Afrikaners, often held hands for mutual support as they enjoyed the exuberance of the public meetings and nervously tested new political waters. It was not surprising that after the election Worrall split from Malan and Lategan, the latter two forming the National Democratic Movement while Worrall transformed his loosely organised independent movement into a fully-fledged Independent Party.

The branches of the Afrikaner tree were further shaken when stalwarts of the powerful Afrikaans press announced that they were quitting their posts because of unacceptable interference by the government. The major Afrikaans newspapers have never strayed far from the traditional National Party line but several prominent journalists had tried to encourage an open, critical debate about where government policies were leading the country. One of these was Harald Pakendorf, editor of *Vaderland*, who was given his marching orders for allowing the debate to stray too far. Then in March 1988 Dr Willem 'Wimpie' de Klerk resigned as managing editor of the Sunday newspaper *Rapport* which perhaps more than most had carefully scrutinised government policies. In April 1985 de Klerk had already signalled in *Rapport* that he was ahead of government thinking on the way to resolve the country's problems particularly over Botha's rigid adherence to the maintenance of 'group rights'. De Klerk called for:

> . . . the retention of group involvement in politics and society as a point of departure, but with the express intention of extending very resolutely fully-fledged shared responsibility from the local to the national level of government. A say in one's own affairs without co-responsibility is totally untenable. This co-responsibility must give all the opportunity to take decisions on common issues. . . . A fresh look will have to be taken at the group laws like the Group Areas Act and all related laws. Not, please note, so as to eliminate group rights, but to take the discrimination out of them, to scrap the violation of human rights inherent in them. One such violation, for instance, is the ban on free association, i.e. free choice about which group one wishes to associate with.

Such calls for the scrapping of key race laws were anathema to a National Party government which, after its early flourish of reform, appeared to have lost its way and was striking out at those carrying the debate further. In his resignation statement de Klerk made it absolutely clear that political interference had made his job impossible:

> There is a decisive political reason for my resignation. With several confrontations in the past two years and more recently, I am being placed under increased pressure from National Party politicians. It has been made clear to me . . . that many of my political insights, accents, arguments and appeals have aroused resistance among Nationalist politicians. . . . This intolerance and rejection of criticism and investigative journalism and reasonable political reportage inhibits my political freedom, integrity, honesty and openness.

Interviewed the next day, de Klerk was asked what sort of pressure had been brought to bear. He replied: 'The sort of pressure that *Rapport* must function very much strongly politically in favour of the National Party and that things which might harm the party should be played down very strongly.' Allegations of government meddling in the press were nothing new of course, but for a journalist of de Klerk's stature to substantiate the charges was astonishing. After all the former *Rapport* editor is the brother of F. W. de Klerk, then leader of the National Party in the Transvaal and in February 1989 elected as the party's national leader. Equally damaging, perhaps, was Willem de Klerk's judgement that 'twenty-two per cent of National Party supporters were dissatisfied with the content of reform, its style and tempo.' Although de Klerk did not ally himself openly with the independent movement after his resignation, still hoping that the Nationalists would change their ways, his resignation showed how enlightened Afrikanerdom was distancing itself from Botha. As de Klerk put it: 'I would not feel at home in the National Party if it failed to accommodate the feeling of those to the left of it.'

Another Afrikaner press giant had also concluded that the National Party was no longer his home.

One week after de Klerk's resignation Nasionale Pers, the Afrikaans press group which owns the government mouthpiece *Die Burger*, lost a senior board member and former managing director. For many years Dawid de Villiers had been held in high esteem in Nationalist circles. Now he, too, had had enough. When I spoke to him shortly after he announced his resignation, de Villiers ('Long David' as he is known, because of his height) explained that he was quitting the press group to support the independent candidate Esther Lategan fighting in Stellenbosch. He left little doubt that *Die Burger*'s one-sided coverage of the election had finally prompted his departure, arguably a bigger shock than de Klerk's. De Villiers said the independents wanted to send 'a message to the government that voters were ready for more visible, more incisive and faster movement towards creating a just political system for all South Africans. It would be a message for those who'd lost hope.' He said he could not support an independent candidate and remain within Nasionale Pers while its newspapers backed the National Party to the extent of completely opposing the independents.

After his resignation de Klerk chaired many of the independents' public meetings addressed by Worrall, Malan and Lategan. The trio brought a new dimension to Afrikaner electioneering. In the north, in the dour heartland of the Transvaal, audiences at National Party meetings were still singing the same old Afrikaner folk songs like '*Sarie Marais*', evoking the longing for home and family of the Boer commandos fighting hundreds of miles away. In Stellenbosch, at the opposite end of the country, the Worrall organisers warmed up the audience with Bruce Springsteen music. Worrall and his fellow independents entered the meeting hall to rousing music from *Rocky* and *Chariots of Fire*. But how much substance was there beneath the razzmatazz?

The three independent candidates published a manifesto saying 'the time has come for all our people to reason together in order to determine their approach to reform.' The manifesto outlined 'starting points' for 'new initiatives.' These were: the chief justice or a senior judge to draw up 'all available constitutional options . . . in order that all political groupings may use them . . . for constitutional dialogue'; black politics to be freed by ending the clampdown on black organisations, while retaining the emergency powers 'to secure stability during the transition period'; and the lifting of all discriminatory laws and restrictions on the news media. The three candidates said their manifesto represented a 'flexible programme'.

The morning after Worrall's first speech at Stellenbosch town hall one of the university's rebel academics told me he was disappointed. The manifesto didn't specify how a non-racial, political settlement could be worked out. For many, the programme was too vague while Worrall, suspected by some of being a political chameleon, still appeared to be hedging his bets.

Although Worrall's highly-publicised return and the excitement surrounding his campaign had highlighted the depths of discontent within enlightened Afrikanerdom, the Stellenbosch revolt against the government had been gathering momentum some time before the election campaign. During 1985, with the country gripped by township violence, the government let it be known in Nationalist circles that it was keen to gather reports from distinguished political and social scientists and others outlining possible constitutional models to accommodate the black population.

Notwithstanding their diminishing influence with Botha's government, Professor Terreblanche and his colleagues submitted a report in January 1986 urging the government in effect 'to go back to square one'. The report said that ministers had to change their perceptions of the crisis facing the country; that South Africa could not go it alone politically or economically in defiance of world opinion; that to attribute the widespread violence to a revolutionary conspiracy orchestrated by Moscow was simplistic; that there could not be a final settlement without the involvement of the African National Congress. The report argued that after almost four decades of National Party rule all kinds of conceptual blockages had occurred and that the time had arrived for the government to rethink the entire South African situation. According to Sampie Terreblanche, Heunis paged through the report and dismissed it, saying: 'We do not have all the facts.' The

Stellenbosch group concluded that there was little point in meeting the constitutional affairs minister. In any case, they were not called in for any more
discussions.

In growing desperation the academics sent a letter to Botha in June 1986
expressing the hope that it would not be necessary to invoke a state of emergency.
In August six of them met Botha, but got nowhere. Then on 20 February 1987, as
many at Stellenbosch were rallying behind the Worrall campaign, twenty-eight of
the dissidents went to see Botha. According to Terreblanche the meeting was a
disaster.

The group spent the first forty-five minutes of the meeting outlining the new
political initiatives which they had been calling for during previous months.
P. W. Botha spent the ensuing ninety minutes responding to each point, after
which he announced that the meeting was at a close. Terreblanche recalls that his
reply was one of exasperation. 'But it can't be,' he told Botha, insisting that he and
his colleagues had questions to put. Botha's reply, says Terreblanche, was that if
he gave the academics another chance to speak, he would have to respond again.
'But that's why we are here,' replied Terreblanche. The meeting broke up in
acrimony, according to Terreblanche, with both sides shouting at each other.

Shellshocked, the twenty-eight academics, more accustomed to refined debates
in tutorial rooms than the rough-house of politics, adjourned to the nearby Mount
Nelson Hotel, where Terreblanche calmed himself by immediately downing two
whiskies. The group decided there and then to end what Terreblanche calls their
'subservience within the system' by publicly denouncing government policies.
The day after the meeting with Botha, those of the dissidents who belonged to the
National Party resigned, at last cutting the political strings. Sampie Terreblanche
says he can remember the date when he made up his mind to resign: 15 May 1986,
when Botha sealed the fate of the Eminent Persons Group after the South African
raids. Botha told the EPG, in effect, that his government, and not they, would
oversee any negotiating process. It took Terreblanche some time, however, to
make the final break. 'I was a member of a tribe,' he says. 'It took nine months.'
Ten days after they had met Botha, the dissident group issued a statement calling
on the government to issue a declaration of its intent to abolish apartheid and to
open negotiations on meaningful power-sharing.

In the wake of the showdown with Botha, the pro-government media, not least
Die Burger from which de Villiers had resigned, attacked the academics as an
insignificant minority within the university. Of course the group did not
represent the entire academic establishment because many professors, lecturers
and students had little interest in politics. But attempts to dismiss the academics
as irrelevant backfired with a vengeance. Within three days, 301 signatures were
obtained for a petition supporting the original group. This meant that more than
half of the academic staff at Stellenbosch were now behind the dissidents. The
signatories noted 'with indignation' the attempts by *Die Burger* and others to
misuse the protest by the original group.

The night Worrall announced his defection the Stellenbosch group were
pursued by newspapers wanting them to declare their support for the new

181

candidate openly. Many, including Terreblanche, said publicly that if Worrall wanted to break the reform deadlock he would have their support. That weekend Terreblanche received a telephone call from Heunis ('One of the most unpleasant experiences of my life') who appeared devastated that Stellenbosch University was slipping away from him. After the forty-minute call the gap between the two men became unbridgeable.

Momberg was convinced that Worrall's fight against Heunis would be neck-and-neck, since Worrall was picking up support in all parts of the constituency: the English-speakers in Somerset West, the young Afrikaners at Stellenbosch, the blue-collar workers in Brakenfels, and retired people in Gordons Bay. Momberg says he tried to warn Heunis, 'for old times' sake', to prepare himself for possible defeat. He conveyed the warning to a mutual friend who passed it on to Heunis. Says Momberg: 'The warning was laughed off. Heunis's people lied to him. One week before the election they were telling him a majority of three to four and a half thousand was the likely outcome.' The result when it came shattered Heunis.

On the night of the result, Heunis made the biggest mistake of his political life. After watching the count, in which he and Worrall were running neck-and-neck, Heunis emerged from Somerset West town hall to hear the returning officer announce he had defeated Worrall by just thirty-nine votes. Worrall received the result with a resigned smile; Heunis panicked. He fumbled an interview with the South African Broadcasting Corporation, pathetically blaming his near-defeat on foreign interference, an insult to the thousands who had campaigned and voted for Worrall because in their eyes Heunis represented everything that was wrong about Botha's government. In those few moments the man betrayed a stunning absence of political steel: his performance that night, coupled with the humiliating result, sent his political fortunes into a free-fall.

Without the Stellenbosch revolt Denis Worrall and Esther Lategan might not have cut the National Party majority so substantially. The government had tried to tempt the academics back into the fold but had failed. Professors, lecturers and students had demonstrated their disillusion with Botha's government and served notice that enlightened Afrikaners wanted to break the old mould to search for political cohabitation with their black fellow-countrymen. I recall at the time speaking to a young Stellenbosch student who recounted how he had been walking along the main road in Stellenbosch when a black man had driven towards him on a tractor with a cartload of apples. The student said he had smiled at the black man, who had then waved to him and thrown him an apple. 'That's the kind of mutual respect we have to foster in this country,' he said.

But politics is rarely about respect; it is about power. With Worrall and Lategan defeated and only one independent MP (Malan) elected, the independent cause went into a reflective period, concentrating on party organisation at grass-roots level. The hullabaloo died down. The academic revolt was again confined to the quiet sanctuary of the university campus. One or two distinguished dissident professors, having flirted with alternatives, drifted back to the National Party, convinced that there was no future for fringe groups on the left. They felt that South Africa essentially had a two-party system, that the second principal party was now the Conservative Party and not the PFP and that the National Party was the home for those wanting reform because it was the only realistic vehicle for change. Professor Esterhuyse, who resumed informal contacts with the government, concluded that more could be achieved from within. Efforts were made to woo back other dissident academics; where that failed, the National Party turned outside Stellenbosch for intellectual support.

But that still left many academics out in the cold; intellectuals who had made the break and were not prepared to return to their previous role of legitimising government race laws. Suspicion remained that a university like Stellenbosch would be reduced to an academic rubber stamp for Pretoria's policies. A National Party MP in Natal dismissed the rebels as 'confused Cape-based liberal academics' but the university establishment appeared concerned about the links between the state and the university. P. W. Botha completed his term as chancellor of the university and it was decided not to elect a political figure as his successor.

The 'Discussion Group of Eighty-Five', though sidelined within Nationalist circles, continued its campaign. Its members were convinced that 20 per cent of Afrikanerdom had become 'detribalised' like themselves and now questioned the direction of government policies. The dissidents' task was to mobilise this section of the population, aware that the National Party was extremely effective in destroying any political movement to its left. In early 1988, one year after the election, the Stellenbosch group issued a declaration stating that their earlier call for a move away from apartheid had not been answered. There was 'not merely no progress but the situation has obviously deteriorated'. Commenting on the National Party's imposition of the state of emergency the group stated that:

> The apparent calm and 'law and order' is dangerously misleading, as it depends entirely on the vigorous maintenance of draconian emergency regulations. At most, these regulations may enable the government to keep the symptoms of its loss of legitimacy and of the widespread polarisation of our society under control in the short term. The state of emergency arises from an absence of policy and vision and a failure to address the fundamental questions which underlie the political crisis in South Africa. These are: how to accommodate the legitimate aspirations of the voiceless majority of South Africans in a system of government which is not based on race, and how to allay the fears of the privileged minority in a dispensation that is not based on race.

The document referred to the 'government's dangerous and short-sighted approach'; it castigated the crackdown on anti-apartheid groups, the silencing of 'virtually the last legal and authentic voices of the extra-parliamentary majority'; it described the effective news censorship in force as 'to the detriment of the open debate which is essential for peaceful, negotiated solutions to our problems'. The document was a reassertion by the cream of Afrikanerdom that the National Party was not, and under its existing leadership could not become, the vehicle for the kind of change needed to ensure a peaceful and more equitable future for South Africa.

The rebellion had undoubtedly shocked the government. It suddenly realised that it could not take for granted the support of the intellectuals; there was a lot of dissatisfaction on the left. Until then the National Party had been convinced that despite criticism from its liberal wing it could rely on the traditional intellectual pillars. With the Stellenbosch revolt, that idea was blown to pieces. The defections were undoubtedly damaging to the party. After all the Nationalists had to market their reform, and this could not be undertaken by politicians alone. There were two reasons for this. For a start the Nationalists had been less a political party than a tribal/cultural movement for the promotion of Afrikanerdom, with a considerable network of support systems of which Stellenbosch had been a principal component. Secondly, over the previous ten years, the National Party had relied heavily on academics to advance Nationalist ideas' appeal to English-speakers, whose support was needed as more and more hardline Afrikaners drifted away to the right. The academics had helped create a new political atmosphere in the country as well as a new image of the Afrikaner and of the National Party. On the other hand, perhaps the intellectuals were no longer so important to the party whose original support systems were being eclipsed as the technocrats took over.

How, then, does one assess the revolt on the left of Afrikanerdom: Slabbert, the Worrall campaign, the Stellenbosch academics, the ordinary 'thinking' Afrikaners contemplating their future in a polarising society? This was not a momentary act of defiance against authority. It represented instead a thorough-going review of where the Afrikaners in particular, but also whites generally, were heading. The various liberal groupings differed on various issues, for example whether or not to talk to the African National Congress, whether parliament had a role to play and the future shape of the country's political system. Some simply felt that a new way had to be found but had no clear idea of which path to follow; they were groping forwards in the political dark.

What united these various anti-Nationalist factions was a conviction, tortuously arrived at, that the future of the Afrikaner was not dependent upon the continued maintenance of a system in which he was defined by race alone. These were not people naïvely contemplating a hand-over to unadulterated one man, one vote. But they did not believe that they should fulfil a political role determined by the colour of their skin.

These Afrikaners were searching for a solution which would allow them to embrace their black compatriots as equals, unlike the government's policy which, in their view, increased rather than eased race divisions and whose ideas of power-sharing rested upon the co-option of 'tame' blacks seduced by vast salaries and perks but who were no more representative of black opinion than P. W. Botha himself. For some of the rebels, the answer lay in some form of federal solution, with strong regional government devolved so that the political demands of each race group could be accommodated, with a non-racial government at national level whose head, by force of numbers, would inevitably be black. Others sought to establish cross-racial alliances following the abolition of the Prohibition of Political Interference Act (1968) which had banned multiracial political parties. The key to the various approaches was the notion of 'free association': that whites and non-whites should be able to identify with their fellow-countrymen regardless of colour, which could lead to non-racial parties of blacks and whites sharing political aspirations. For liberal Afrikaners this would mean a recognition of the black man's overwhelming demands for his just political rights while accommodating too the whites' desire for survival.

The dissident Afrikaners recognised that there was little hope for an agreement with the vast majority of blacks unless the principle of 'free association' was accepted. They believed that this did not have to result in undiluted black majority rule, but that after abolishing the division of people by race, South Africans could then start talking about a future non-racial system. Some recognised, though, that at the end of the day some form of racial protection might be necessary to ease the path of whites into a more majoritarian form of government.

That aside, they were in broad agreement that those things most precious to the Afrikaner – his survival, his language, his schooling, his culture – did not require his racial separation from other people. The Stellenbosch revolt also reflected profound unease about the style of leadership of P. W. Botha. The dissidents were uncomfortable that their country's head of state seemed so unsophisticated. The atmosphere of quiet debate pursued by the Stellenbosch academics contrasted with Botha's hectoring tone. There was concern, too, about the whittling away of democratic freedoms amid the President's increased power. Said one dissident, frustrated that his warnings were not getting through: 'They cannot stand to be told the truth. They simply kill the messenger.' In similar vein, the Stellenbosch group, the Dakar delegation and the Worrall supporters were convinced that South Africa dismissed international opinion at its peril. The contempt which government ministers often heap upon the outside world was completely counterproductive, they believed. Moreover, they sensed that the increasing political and economic isolation of South Africa might induce a short-lived defiance within the *laager* but would eventually result in South Africa slipping into chaos.

But where could the dissidents find a satisfactory political home? Worrall had returned like a white knight in shining armour to rally the dissidents, linking up with Wynand Malan, an Afrikaner who expressed all the frustrations and doubts of those on the left. The subsequent rift between the two men, with Worrall forming the Independent Party and Malan his National Democratic Movement, was a devastating blow for those who had been caught up in the liberal Afrikaner revolt against Botha. The tensions were revealed at several meetings between the two men. Says Malan:

'Worrall wanted to work within the fish tank of the present system of parliamentary politics. But I thought the tank was too small. You cannot have a small fish bowl hoping that the big fish from outside will come in. I think real politics lies in both parliamentary and extra-parliamentary politics, thus creating a new fish tank.'

Malan subsequently concentrated on making contact with forces outside parliament, like the United Democratic Front, while Worrall devoted time to seeking alliances with parties already represented in parliament or within the political mainstream. Malan says in retrospect: 'Joining forces with Worrall was the most serious mistake in my political life. I worked like hell for a convergence of our differences. At the end of the day, though, I was living a public lie.' Worrall believes that Malan is misguided in trying to spread his political net so wide.

Afrikaners who had broken from the National Party had looked to the two men as hopes for the future; they were now disillusioned. The National Party was the only winner as a result of the schism; the impact of the new movement was diluted by the two leaders going their separate ways. As Esterhuyse puts it: 'The rebels will want some pretty firm guarantees before again attaching their cause to one particular party or group.' With the left in some disarray, Worrall and Malan began to bury their differences as discussions intensified during 1988 and early 1989, leading to the announcement that a new Democratic Party was to be formed aimed at uniting liberal, anti-Nationalist forces. While Malan, Worrall and the Progressive Federal Party searched for common ground, Slabbert continued his efforts to remould the mind of the Afrikaners.

The dissidents were under no illusions about the formidable nature of National Party rule, particularly under Botha. They had courted ostracism and suffered its consequences. With South Africa in a comparatively fluid political state, there was no telling what fresh schisms there might be within the white constituency in the years to come, when Afrikaners would at last come face to face with the loss of their supremacy. That prospect could be some years away; for now, their brief shining moment of liberal thinking had been overcome by the all-powerful Nationalist machine.

But their visions did not die. They were way past the point of submitting to Botha's daunting presence. Indeed, of the eighteen delegates from inside South Africa who met the ANC in West Germany in 1988, in a sequel to the Dakar gathering, twelve were either lecturers at or former students of Stellenbosch. Their revolt, therefore, was an intellectual deposit in the bank balance of South Africa's future, a statement of intent which is on record to guide the country's leaders if and when they decide to cross the real Rubicon into non-racial settlement.

For Sampie Terreblanche, the Stellenbosch revolt was as much a personal journey as a political odyssey. 'We questioned the legitimacy of this government. In so doing we may help our children and grandchildren. A solution could be a long way off, but we have to speak out now. Like the opponents to the Nazis, we have to make our stand clear at this time for history to record.'

CHAPTER ELEVEN

The Lost Sons

On Thursday 17 March 1988 a huge car bomb exploded outside the magistrates' court in the town of Krugersdorp, west of Johannesburg. Three people were killed and twenty injured, including a baby thrown out of its pram by the force of the explosion. The bombing occurred just a few hours before a Supreme Court judge granted a stay of execution to six black people known as the Sharpeville Six, who were due to hang the next day following their controversial conviction for the murder of the Sharpeville deputy mayor.

Within hours of the explosion the police had published the name of the man they suspected of involvement in the bombing. The alleged bomber did not conform to the traditional picture of the committed anti-apartheid terrorist. He was not one of the 'children of Soweto' who fled the country in 1976 after the riots of that year, returning after military training abroad to seek revenge against the South African state. He was not one of the black radicals of the 1980s who had been politicised by the unrest in the black townships and by the authorities' tough response. The man whose face appeared on the wanted posters after the Krugersdorp bombing came instead from the very bosom of Afrikanerdom. Heinrich Grosskopf was the son of Professor H. J. Grosskopf, head of the Department of Journalism at the University of Stellenbosch and former editor of the Afrikaans newspaper *Beeld*. His mother was Santie Grosskopf, a well-known Afrikaans author. His uncle was a Supreme Court judge; his brother worked for ARMSCOR (the Armaments Development and Production Corporation), which manufactures weapons for South Africa to circumvent the international arms embargo against the Pretoria government.

The naming of Grosskopf as the suspect in the bombing unleashed a wave of hysteria which rendered the principle of 'innocent until proved guilty' virtually worthless. The newspaper *Business Day* accused the police and the Law and Order Minister, Mr Adriaan Vlok, of mounting a 'trial by minister' while Grosskopf's father complained to the Media Council that some newspapers had freely described his son as the perpetrator of the bombing without his arrest, let alone his trial. Any respect for such legal niceties was eclipsed by a widespread sense of outrage. How could this Afrikaner son turn against his own people in this way?

The newspapers devoted thousands of words to recounting the life of 'a brilliant young man, with all the makings of a member of the Afrikaner elite, except for one thing – he was an individualist who tended to question rather than accept the traditional thinking of his community', as one newspaper described him. The media documented how as a boy he had regularly attended the Dutch Reformed Church in Linden, Johannesburg, where 'his questioning mind was evident in his decision to withdraw from his catechism two weeks before he was to be confirmed.' They recorded how Grosskopf had been elected junior mayor of Johannesburg from among seventy-one candidates, after impressing the judges with an address on the theme of 'friendship'. The papers tracked down his wife whom he had deserted along with his parents, when he had fled into exile two years before to embark upon his 'amazing transformation'. The Afrikaans newspaper *Rapport* labelled him '*die verlore seun*' ('the lost son').

But Grosskopf was not the first wayward son of Afrikanerdom to desert the *volk*. The gradual imposition of apartheid may have satisfied the majority of Afrikaners but it troubled a growing number of disillusioned intellectuals and rebellious youngsters, who fled into exile to join the ranks of the ANC, with the aim of returning home to help the violent overthrow of the government. The alleged bomber Grosskopf had been preceded by a string of young Afrikaners convicted of terrorist activities. In 1983 Carl Niehaus and Jansie Lourens were imprisoned for attempting to blow up the gasworks in Johannesburg. Niehaus told the court that his political outlook had changed when he became involved in mission work in Alexandra black township near Johannesburg, where he was confronted with the appalling squalor in which thousands of black people lived. Lourens, a mathematics teacher, was the daughter of a respected psychologist. Another dissident young Afrikaner was Marius Schoon, son of an Afrikaans teacher, jailed for twelve years for an attempted explosion at a Johannesburg police station.

Before them, in the 1960s, there had been Braam Fischer, the highly gifted son of the judge president of the Orange Free State whose grandfather had been prime minister of the Orange River Colony. Braam Fischer could have anticipated a brilliant career in National Party politics. Instead he became the leader of the South African Communist Party. He had been an ardent Afrikaner nationalist until his student days, when he began to challenge policies based on racial discrimination. Fischer was a Rhodes scholar at Oxford University and later qualified at the bar in Johannesburg, later becoming chairman of the Bar Council. He became a communist in his thirties, believing that Marxism was the only solution to the scourge of racial injustice. As Queen's Counsel, Braam Fischer defended black nationalists in several of the major legal battles between the government and its opponents, notably the Treason Trial of 1956–61 when 156 dissidents including Nelson Mandela were eventually acquitted, and the Rivonia Trial in 1963–4 in which Mandela and seven others were sentenced to life imprisonment. Shortly after the Rivonia Trial Fischer went underground, chairing the central committee of the South African Communist Party and approving the formation of Umkhonto we Sizwe, the ANC's armed wing. He was arrested in 1965 and sentenced to life imprisonment under the Sabotage Act and the Suppression of Communism Act. He died of cancer in 1975.

Most remarkable of all, perhaps, was the case of the famous Afrikaans poet and author, Breyten Breytenbach. One of his brothers is a photo-journalist, another a senior officer in the South African Defence Force, a founder of the crack Thirty-Two Battalion which has fought covertly inside Angola, and one of the country's foremost specialists on counter-insurgency. Breyten Breytenbach had outraged Afrikanerdom by marrying a Vietnamese princess with whom he could not live legally in his own country because of race laws. In exile in Paris, Breytenbach helped form a group called Okhela, a faction within the African National Congress comprised mainly of whites. In 1975 he returned to South Africa disguised as a priest to establish an underground network, was betrayed and then arrested at Johannesburg airport as he was trying to slip out of the country. Breytenbach served seven years in prison and continued to write. He arranged for some of his poems to be smuggled out of the prison, including these lines from 'The Struggle for the Taal [Language]' filled with desperation at the suffering his Afrikaner people were inflicting upon their fellow-men:

> For we are Christ's executioners.
> We are on the walls around the locations
> gun in one hand and machine-gun in the other:
> we, the missionaries of Civilisation.
>
> We bring you the grammar of violence
> and the syntax of destruction
> – from the tradition of our firearms
> you will hear the verbs of retribution stuttering.

Not all dissidents, though, chose the path of violence or subversion. Christiaan Frederick Beyers Naudé, whose father took part in the Afrikaners' rebellion in 1914 against South Africa's support for Britain in the First World War, and who was one of the most senior figures in both the Dutch Reformed Church and the Broederbond, rejected apartheid and founded the Christian Institute, which was pledged to reconciliation with blacks. It was eventually banned, with Naudé himself subjected to a seven-year-long banning order severely restricting his movements. Naudé's journey from the very soul of Afrikaner nationalism to a life of resistance against his own people was emulated by many as apartheid revealed itself in widespread suffering. Despite, or perhaps because of, the limited race reforms introduced by P. W. Botha since the early 1980s, there has been no let-up in the number of Afrikaners undertaking that same long journey, for whom unquestioning membership of the tribe no longer sits comfortably with their Christian conscience.

In August 1988 144 young whites announced their refusal to serve with the South African Defence Force. About half of them were students, the others were mostly in the professional classes. The majority had completed their initial two years' military service. They were refusing to take part in the subsequent periods of reserve duty required under law. Announcing their stand at news conferences, under a banner reading 'We won't fight in the SADF', these conscientious objectors were staging the most serious challenge to date against both South Africa's system of military conscription and the role of the country's armed services. Previously there had been isolated instances of such protest; an organisation called the End Conscription Campaign had tried to mobilise disaffected youngsters despite stringent curbs on its activities. The large group of 'refuseniks' included eight commissioned officers, among them a twenty-eight-year-old Afrikaner André Zaaiman, described by his senior commander as 'one of the best I ever had'. That young whites should be refusing military service was serious enough for the defence force. The fact that a talented young Afrikaner who had proved himself in the thick of battle should also be rebelling set the alarm bells ringing, particularly as Zaaiman was the tip of an iceberg of those refusing conscription or fleeing the country to avoid military service – Afrikaners prepared to reject a government and its armed wing both of which, in their eyes, are illegitimate.

Like many other Afrikaner rebels now challenging the values of their own people, André Zaaiman does not come from a family with a long tradition of political dissidence – quite the reverse. His background lies in the very heart of conservative, rural Afrikanerdom. He grew up on a farm near the town of Kroonstad in the Orange Free State, where he used to ride to school barefoot on his bicycle. His father was principal of the local agricultural school and his mother a teacher. It was a very closed Afrikaner environment.

Later, at Grey College in Bloemfontein, where teaching is in both English and Afrikaans, Zaaiman was exposed for the first time to other influences. His passage into the world beyond narrow Afrikanerdom was gentle, whereas his brother was catapulted from one extreme to the other, with traumatic results. Zaaiman's brother had attended the Afrikaans university at Stellenbosch after being head boy and a leading rugby player at his Afrikaans school. While at Stellenbosch he followed his girlfriend to West Germany where she was studying. It was the classic case of a young innocent from a backwater let loose in the real world. It was supposed to have been a short visit to Europe but he stayed two years and, as Zaaiman puts it, he 'freaked out'. When he returned, he refused to speak Afrikaans and for two years, amid growing tension within the family, spoke only English.

After completing his studies at Grey College, André Zaaiman went to the Infantry School in Oudtshoorn. There was no questioning then of the role of the South African defence forces. 'I was very diligent,' he recalls. 'I was just an ordinary Afrikaner.' Zaaiman had to find the money himself to finance his subsequent studies at the University of the Orange Free State. While studying he won a public service bursary and was recruited by the Department of Foreign Affairs as a cadet (trainee) to be groomed as a diplomat.

'This was a most difficult time for me. It was the first time that I became aware of my growing feelings of dissidence from Afrikanerdom and expressed it openly.

I could not fit into the bureaucracy.' At that time the Foreign Affairs ministry was confronting the problems of Namibia, where Zaaiman had twice seen military action. He believed that the diplomats tackling the territory's problems were dealing with things they knew nothing about. The foreign service officials with whom he worked were liberal, he said, but were caught up in a huge bureaucracy; to go against the bureaucracy was seen as betraying the country itself. Says Zaaiman: 'Other cadets used to talk in the tea-room about how things were wrong. But they would never say anything in front of the officials.' Having exhausted the proper channels, Zaaiman eventually presented his doubts to the director-general of the Foreign Affairs department, which led to a huge controversy. He was summoned by the head of administration and told he was 'the worst public servant I have met'. Zaaiman was told he was too outspoken and that even if he stayed in the department for his entire career he had no future. Certain responsibilities were taken away from him. He was assigned tasks on the Transkei and Ciskei desks, created as part of the fantasy that Pretoria enjoys 'diplomatic relations' with these 'independent' states. For Zaaiman, both South Africa's diplomatic ties with these tribal *bantustans* and his own part in them were 'pathetic' and he left the department soon after.

Three years of reflection followed. Employed as a game ranger at the Mala Mala safari camp in the eastern Transvaal, a job he had always wanted, Zaaiman spent the long days and nights pondering his place in South Africa under apartheid. 'This was an important time in my life. I came to realise that there was no way I could conform to the institutions of the Afrikaner establishment. When I left Foreign Affairs I threw off all the Afrikaner baggage you have to carry with you and I was free.'

At Mala Mala the trackers he worked with every day were all black. He built up deep friendships with them, friendships forged in the unique environment of the African bush, where the sunrises and sunsets, as the animals head for the watering holes, provide a stunning reminder of man's mortality. His black friends, with whom he went fishing and drinking, were not well educated like him but he felt a great empathy with them. 'We had good conversations. My suspicions were confirmed that I had been lied to about black people; they did not conform to stereotypes.'

During 1986 Zaaiman took an eight-month leave of absence from the camp to travel to Europe and the Middle East. At Mala Mala there was no television, so in Europe he was confronted for the first time with the true picture of what was happening in the black townships in his own country. In London he stood outside Buckingham Palace thinking: 'These were the bloody colonists of my country and the damned Afrikaner has gone and copied them.' At Versailles he had the same feeling of imperial exploitation. 'I was very naïve, perhaps, and the symbolism was totally wrong. But I realised we in Africa had imported all our ideas from Europe.'

In Holland he met a coloured South African exile, Vernon February, who was a professor at Leyden University. Zaaiman unburdened himself of all his doubts about himself and his country. February helped him to focus his thoughts about apartheid, telling him it was unacceptable and morally wrong. February explained the 'warped history' of the previous four decades and offered an alternative, humanist credo.

'One evening I went round to Vernon February's flat. His wife and family were out and we sat there talking. He prepared Kaapse Kos [Cape food] a Malay curry. There were just the two of us. I sensed how homesick he was and I felt the unfairness of his exile. Vernon said to me: "I have broken with apartheid. Have you?" It was on that night that I decided to become an academic and to write about the things we had discussed. I came away from that evening with my mind clearer about the issues confronting me. I thought to myself: "If only I had had somebody to guide me earlier in my life, this wouldn't have taken so long nor been so agonising." It was on that night too that I was convinced that I could never again do military service. I had lost a good friend who was killed in action in Angola. I had told myself he'd died for his country. But now I asked myself: Had he?'

Zaaiman returned to South Africa to begin an honours degree at the Free State University. In tutorials on South African politics he challenged the handed-down wisdom about the African National Congress and the United Democratic Front. He was banned from classes and visited by the security police, but obtained his degree despite such obstacles. From Bloemfontein, Zaaiman continued his studies at Cape Town University under André du Toit (one of the Dakar group) where the atmosphere and political debate were more free. Says Zaaiman: 'The Afrikaans universities are not educational establishments. They are there to train Afrikaners to be unquestioning public servants and to draw them into the right mental framework.'

Zaaiman's dissidence caused strains lasting several years within his family. His mother supported him. His father, he believes, suffered professionally. He was working as an official in the joint management system of security agencies established to restore calm to the black townships after the widespread violence. His security clearance was downgraded because of his son's activities, and he was passed over for promotion at work.

Zaaiman still faced the most difficult dilemma of all. Given his complete break with the Afrikaner establishment and its support for apartheid, Zaaiman asked himself: 'Am I going to serve in the army?' He was reluctant to join the End Conscription Campaign, feeling he had already left one oppressive society and did not want to conform to another system. 'You have fought for your individual freedom so that the state cannot steal your conscience. You don't immediately want to hand it over to somebody else.' In May 1987 he announced to his commanding officer that he would not undertake another period of reserve call-up; moreover he was dropping his officer's commission. The officer thought he was mad and said so during a formal interview. In taking this stand, Zaaiman laid himself open to a prison sentence of two years or more. But he has no doubts whatsoever about his decision; he could no longer serve a government or an army that upholds apartheid.

'Under apartheid people are treated unfairly and they are powerless to change it. When I was in the army our senior officer had to leave base and I was chosen over a coloured guy as temporary base commander. We decided to rotate the job. But the white soldiers would not obey the coloured officer.'

Does Zaaiman consider himself to be an Afrikaner still?

'I am an Afrikaner. But a small group of my people used the ideology of apartheid to manipulate the Afrikaners, saying they wanted to liberate them, when really it was due to the self-interest of a few. I don't hate other Afrikaners. They've been misled. It is my duty to tell them that and to shift the parameters of their debates.'

For Zaaiman the National Party since 1948 has perverted social dynamics: 'control' is now the preoccupation:

'Apartheid has driven morality out of the public debate. They think only strategically. When I did my national service there were no cross-border raids that I was aware of. We would never burn down kraals; we would respect the village headmen and take a beer with them. In my time it was not SADF policy to get involved in South Africa's internal affairs. The change came in 1980. When I went back on my first reserve duty there had been a remarkable change in army philosophy. Now we no longer respect borders.'

Zaaiman is concerned that most Afrikaner dissidents – especially writers and artists – have turned to Europe when going into exile or when searching for ideas to counter the prevailing racial orthodoxy at home. One of Zaaiman's heroes is Adam Tas, the seventeenth-century burgher who helped overthrow the corrupt Dutch governor at the Cape, van der Stel, together with his European influence. 'The Afrikaner is going through an existential crisis,' says Zaaiman. 'He is beginning to reject apartheid but has no reference point. We must give a context to the Africanness of the Afrikaner. He has to decide whether he wants to be a European or an African. If he chooses for Europe, his language, so important to the Afrikaner, will disappear.'

For André Zaaiman, now working for Van Zyl Slabbert's IDASA organisation, the only Afrikaners who will survive are those who see themselves firstly as human beings, secondly as Africans, thirdly as South Africans and only lastly as Afrikaners – and then through their language only, nothing else.

'The Afrikaners will become an insignificant little group of people within fifty years because they did not take the opportunities when they were there.'

These are the words of Timo Bezuidenhoud, until his retirement in 1987 the Chief Commissioner of Cooperation and Development for the Western Cape. Stripped of its bureaucratic language, the job title means that he was the government official who presided over the Crossroads squatter camp outside Cape Town which, during his tenancy, experienced some of its worst moments of violence. Now working voluntarily for a Christian organisation, Bezuidenhoud has time to reflect on those torrid years when Crossroads revealed apartheid at its worst. His experiences tell him that black majority rule is inevitable and that there will be no room for the Afrikaner, in part because he has squandered the years since 1948.

Unlike André Zaaiman, Bezuidenhoud is not a 'detribalised Afrikaner'. He attacks people like Van Zyl Slabbert for 'crawling in front of the African National Congress', saying: 'I'm not against the ANC because I am an Afrikaner, but because I am against terrorism. It clashes with my values.' Nevertheless, if the measure of an Afrikaner rebel is the degree to which he serves others before his own people, then Bezuidenhoud ranks among those who have moved ahead of the *volk*. But instead of leaving the *volk* behind, as some have done, he has tried to drag it along behind him.

During his time at Crossroads Bezuidenhoud became identified with a government department which, in the eyes of the squatters, was intent on rooting them out and despatching them back to the remote homelands. It was a relationship of mutual hostility which resulted in killings, burnings of shacks, violent protests and tough action by a local police force little concerned about people's appalling conditions. All this came as an immense shock to Bezuidenhoud whose relationship with black people until then had been warm.

But that had been in the more relaxed setting of South Africa's rural areas rather than at the racial front-line in the cities and their black ghetto satellites. Bezuidenhoud's father had been an adviser to the late King Sobhuza of Swaziland and Bezuidenhoud had been raised in the town of Piet Retief close to the Swazi border. After studying law at university, times were hard and he found it difficult to obtain work. But eventually he became a magistrate, travelling across Natal, Zululand and the homeland of QwaQwa dealing with rural blacks. 'I had so many good, honest, sincere friends,' says Bezuidenhoud. He became the secretary for justice in the government of Chief Buthelezi in kwaZulu and later trained local black politicians in Namibia. From there he was to have moved to the homeland of Bophuthatswana as justice department secretary, but instead was summoned to Cape Town by the then black affairs minister, Piet Koornhof, to take charge of the growing problem of hundreds of thousands of 'illegal' migrant blacks settled at the Crossroads site.

'I had had no experience of working in an urban setting and I could not believe what I saw. The place was in a hell of a mess. The hatred and the antagonism were overwhelming.' Bezuidenhoud spent three months learning about every aspect of the Crossroads situation and came up with revolutionary solutions which were extremely unpopular with the government and the security forces, whose answer to Crossroads was quite simple: destroy the camp and return black squatters to the homelands. His predecessor had been very conservative. The situation had deteriorated. Bezuidenhoud fought his own battle within the Afrikaner *laager*, a quiet struggle in which he sided with thousands of black people against the apartheid bureaucrats. 'For thirty-four years draconian measures had been used and they didn't work. Verwoerd has to take much of the responsibility for what happened.'

Bezuidenhoud's first action was to install electricity and other facilities to improve the people's everyday lives. 'They began to trust me,' he says. There was rising opposition to such measures from inside his own department; Bezuidenhoud was passed over for promotion because his seniors did not think he was handling the situation properly. Bezuidenhoud aroused further antagonism when he said that, in his view, Crossroads was too small for its 200,000 squatters; he pressed for a new township at Khayelitsha a few miles away. He then had both the government and the squatters against him, the latter suspicious that a move to Khayelitsha would be a stopping-off point in their deportation back to the homelands.

In 1981 Bezuidenhoud delivered an address at Stellenbosch University proposing a radical new approach to the squatter problem, one guaranteed to increase official hostility. He suggested that instead of shunting the blacks back to the homelands, they should be recognised as permanent and have a proper infrastructure to support them – clinics, hospitals, schools, roads, sewerage, etc. His message was: 'Give a man a piece of ground and he will build his own home. Never mind what it looks like, if it means stability. As his situation improves, he will slowly upgrade his home or even sell it and buy somewhere better.' Bezuidenhoud was speaking like an estate agent in a white suburb; talk of blacks 'buying and selling', of 'improving their homes' was not what the government wanted to hear. After all, weren't these squatters 'temporary sojourners'?

Despite near-universal opposition, the go-ahead for the construction of Khayelitsha was eventually agreed. Bezuidenhoud was then faced with the task of persuading the Crossroads residents that moving to the new township would not result in deportation back to the homelands. He said to the government: 'Let's start with twelve thousand sites [plots of land].' They told him he was mad, that they would never be filled. Says Bezuidenhoud:

'They gave me four thousand seven hundred sites. I called meetings with the squatters and explained what the move would entail, how their living conditions would be improved. I told them we needed to vacate the Crossroads area to rebuild it. Within two months the people started moving. The four thousand seven hundred sites were filled within three weeks and I had hundreds more who had broken down their shacks ready to move. I did it by myself without the police. I could have cleared Crossroads to upgrade it properly if they'd given me enough sites.'

Bezuidenhoud tries in vain to disguise his anger over the actions of the police, the local black affairs office in Crossroads and government officials who gave him little or no backing. 'There was one occasion when some radical blacks were trying to occupy a school. Officials of the local administration [black affairs] board were leaning against their vehicles, not lifting a finger to stop it. They wanted chaos, so it would be seen as my doing.' For the government, the idea of one of their own officials trying to improve the lives of people who had confounded the apartheid system was difficult to swallow. Very few of Bezuidenhoud's colleagues appeared to share his view that blacks should be treated as human beings. At times Bezuidenhoud took his life in his hands to try to defuse explosive situations, knowing full well that the police backed by the apartheid book-keepers were waiting for an excuse to destroy the Crossroads shanty area once and for all. His fears proved prophetic when, after his retirement, black vigilantes, allegedly supported by the police and the government, were allowed to run amok, torching homes and killing scores of people who opposed government policies.

In February 1985 the squatters were convinced that their forced removal from Crossroads was imminent. Bezuidenhoud recalls: 'It was very clear to me that something was in the air but I was shot down in flames by officials.' On Monday 18 February Bezuidenhoud went into Crossroads to try to calm the situation. He refused to go under armed police escort but drove in a battered old van with stones and petrol bombs raining in all around him. In the centre of Crossroads he passed the clinic where the doctor, Ivan Toms, advised him to go back, as he would be killed. Bezuidenhoud managed to get a message to the protest leaders to meet him the next day. He returned for the meeting and for three hours tried to persuade the blacks to halt the violence. But he was getting nowhere. There were about sixty of them confronting him. 'I was very scared,' says Bezuidenhoud, 'but I didn't show it. I just talked and talked and talked. I told them they had no water, no food lorries were getting in, their small children were suffering. I promised them that good news was coming that would ease their fears about being removed. Their eyes were hard. There were youngsters at the back of the crowd shouting "Let's kill him now!" I shouted to them: "If you want to kill me, come to the front and say it to my face!" We carried on talking for three quarters of an hour and eventually we reached an agreement under which the police would pull back and the youngsters would clear the streets. That afternoon the riots were over.'

'The rioting had cost eighteen lives. I made a decision late on a Friday night that I would have to make my views heard. I telephoned [black affairs] minister Gerrit Viljoen to tell him that I was going to see President Botha himself. The director general of the ministry told me I couldn't do it. But I am a fighter. I was one hundred per cent ready to go to P. W. Botha. I didn't care two hoots about my future.'

In the end Bezuidenhoud's urgent recommendations were dealt with speedily. They resulted in an agreement that Crossroads squatters would not be removed by force; that the shanty town would be upgraded; that three other Cape Town townships due to be destroyed would be saved; and that black squatters would be given ninety-nine-year leases. It was a remarkable victory for Bezuidenhoud. Single-handedly he had taken on bureaucrats whose entire outlook was to implement apartheid. Bezuidenhoud had rolled back an apartheid frontier. He had placed common sense and simple humanity before ideology; hundreds of thousands breathed a sigh of relief as a result.

As the official responsible, Bezuidenhoud was detailed to receive US senator Edward Kennedy who wanted to tour Crossroads during a visit to South Africa.

At the shanty town Kennedy condemned Bezuidenhoud for the conditions there. Says Bezuidenhoud:

'I asked Kennedy what he was going to do for these people. He became cross. I told him he should go back to America and canvass industrialists to put money into this area to provide jobs for people. With all his family millions, Kennedy did not do a thing for the people of Crossroads. That's why I am not a liberal. Liberals have many theories. But they never do anything to help people. If you really want to help people, you have to toil, you work, you fight and you dirty your hands. You don't just talk.'

Bezuidenhoud says that his religion helped him through many of the darkest times in dealing with Crossroads. On his retirement he joined Mfesane (a Xhosa word meaning 'compassion'), a group putting Christianity into action, helping black people in the Transkei, the Ciskei, the eastern and western Cape. The organisation is building a school for deaf children in Khayelitsha.

For Bezuidenhoud the post-war years have been a period of missed opportunities. He feels the government should have talked to the ANC before it became 'a radical organisation':

'We should have spent the time uplifting the blacks, so that economic and social forces would now cut across ethnic boundaries. The Afrikaner is in his present position because he never gave the black man the opportunity to develop. The blacks remained static. This led the Afrikaner to believe that the black man could not improve or adjust – that he hadn't got any talents. He never thought about the black man as a person with ambition, hope or a desire to achieve. Instead, only three to five million blacks [from a population of around thirty million] are developed to the standards of western civilisation and therefore fit to govern. The others are divided among the various ethnic groups: the Zulus will never submit to the Xhosas and vice versa. I know these black chiefs in the tribal areas – they are the important people. And they are very hard men. Hereditary tribal leaders will fight it out and the Afrikaner will be squeezed.'

Bezuidenhoud does not belong to any political school. He is a loner; he cannot be labelled. He was perhaps a typical Afrikaner civil servant, until he came face-to-face with the results of apartheid bureaucracy. Having observed the tragedies at first hand he could not live with the consequences; he tried to change the machine. In that he was successful, a small but important dent in the body of Afrikaner ideology.

Culturally he is still rooted in his own Afrikaner people. Politically he has moved ahead of them. An Afrikaner in limbo.

The grandfather of Braam Viljoen fought against the British in the Boer War and was captured and despatched to a prisoner-of-war camp in Ceylon. He returned convinced that Afrikaners and British had to work together to build a new South

Africa and to that end supported General Smuts. Viljoen's father also reacted against exclusive Afrikaner nationalism. He was one of those Afrikaners who did not go along with the Nationalists. For Braam Viljoen's father the final breaking-point came over the issue of South Africa's support for Britain in the Second World War, when the Dutch Reformed Church refused to confirm South African soldiers in uniform. Braam Viljoen never joined the Nationalist cause; he has even deserted the Dutch Reformed Church and now describes himself as an agnostic.

Braam Viljoen's convictions took shape during the early 1950s as a theology student at the University of Pretoria, where he could not associate himself with the academic community's slavish devotion to the National Party. At Pretoria, Viljoen first came into contact with a man who was to have a profound influence upon his life and his thinking. Ben Marais was a theologian who was equally distressed with the church's role in exploiting the scriptures to provide theological justification for apartheid. Having found their own freedom, argued Marais, the Afrikaners were repressing others. For Viljoen, Ben Marais was a sounding board for his own doubts about the growing implementation of apartheid and about the role of the Dutch Reformed Church. Ben Marais had been one of thirteen academics who in 1955 had come out with a strong condemnation of the proposed removal of the coloured population from the common voters' roll. On a visit to the western Transvaal to attend an ordination ceremony, Viljoen was able to speak to Marais frankly for the first time about his own feelings of confusion.

By 1963 Viljoen was so alienated from his own church that he helped form Beyers Naudé's Christian Institute. His real crisis of conscience had come in 1960 with the Sharpeville massacre. Having completed his military service, Viljoen was on the 'A' reserve list of officers liable to be called up in the event of a state of emergency. At that stage Viljoen was preparing for his final theology examinations. He approached the dean of his faculty to enquire whether he could use his influence to delay his call-up, but to no avail. His call-up in the wake of the Sharpeville massacre meant the postponement of his doctoral degree in theology.

'I had very close relations with black people,' says Viljoen.

'During the emergency there was a day when I pulled into my local garage wearing my army conscript's uniform. I had a black friend there who used to fill up my car. The sight of my uniform had a devastating effect upon him. "I see you've joined," he said, and suddenly I realised what must be in the mind of a black man seeing that. I was his friend and now he was thinking that I had joined in the suppression of black people.'

The banning of the African National Congress which followed Sharpeville disturbed Viljoen too, in particular the government's charge that the ANC was the vanguard of a communist conspiracy. His friend Ben Marais had known the then ANC leader, Albert Luthuli, for twelve years. 'If they make a communist of Albert Luthuli then something is seriously wrong,' Marais told Viljoen.

A few months after the Sharpeville emergency Viljoen left South Africa on a study and lecture tour of the United States, visiting seventeen seminaries in as many weeks in the south, the mid-west and the north. He was exposed both to

America's incipient student movement which was to explode in the late 1960s and to the depth of hostility towards the actions of the South African government. He would arrive at a new seminary each Monday morning to be greeted by the inevitable enquiry from the students as to where he came from. 'When I said I was from South Africa it was like igniting a fire,' he recalls. By the Thursday of each week the seminary had come to understand that he was not an advocate of apartheid, and Viljoen became accepted in his own right. 'But on each Monday morning, at a new seminary, I began the whole process over again.'

From the United States Viljoen moved on to the Netherlands, continuing his search for a theological response to apartheid. The Reformed churches of Europe had undergone their own profound theological crisis during the Second World War. At the University of Utrecht he met Professor J. C. Hoekendijk whose research into the abuse of the church in Nazi Germany gave Viljoen an insight into how apartheid, though justified on biblical grounds by its architects, was a corruption of human values, a transgression of everything he understood by religion. Hoekendijk had written a thesis entitled 'Church and People in German Missiology', a powerful indictment of how German Christians had surrendered to the principle of a people or *volk* determined not by theology but by romantic, emotional notions of patriotism exploited by the political philosophy of the day. Viljoen learned from his Dutch mentor the concept of a church of God that could not be adulterated by base notions of a *volk*; also how the principle of 'love your neighbour' was in total contradiction to the principles of apartheid. Hoekendijk's attack on the German churches was pertinent. There had been a close affinity between the German theological position and that of the Dutch Reformed Church. Indeed, many NGK ministers had been trained in Germany.

Hoekendijk recounted to Braam Viljoen his wartime experiences as a leading member of the Dutch Resistance. One story, in particular, stuck in Viljoen's mind and helped him in his own decisions on how he should confront apartheid. During the Nazi occupation of Holland, Hoekendijk and his fellow Resistance fighters were hiding a group of Jewish children in a safe house. Food was scarce; coupons were needed to buy provisions. The Resistance could not declare the children and so were unable to obtain coupons to feed them. Members of the Dutch Students' Christian Association, who formed a strong contingent in the Resistance, decided they had reached a dead end in their efforts to feed the Jewish children. They resolved that one member of their association should sleep with a German officer. Having seduced him, she killed him, stole his coupons and bought food for the children. Viljoen was under no illusion that the girl's actions had contravened one of the ten commandments. 'But it brought home to me the problem of how you resist evil. What is legitimate resistance? My conclusion was that you have to allow for emergencies where normal standards can no longer apply, even though such actions might go against your conscience.'

While abroad, Viljoen kept abreast of the deliberations of the World Council of Churches at the Cottesloe Conference. He wrote to the editor of *Die Kerkbode*, the newspaper of the Dutch Reformed Church, complaining about his hostile attitude towards WCC officials who had condemned apartheid as unjust. The letter never appeared and Viljoen suspected that the editor of *Die Kerkbode*, Andries Treurnicht, had consigned it to the wastepaper bin. But Viljoen was soon to learn that the Afrikaner establishment never forgets the non-conformists among them. Returning to Pretoria to complete his thesis and examinations, Viljoen was informed that the qualifications he had already obtained were no longer valid and that all his examinations would have to be taken again. He was also told that his letter to *Die Kerkbode* had not endeared him to the church leaders. Quite obviously his letter had not landed up in the editor's wastepaper basket as he had suspected, but on the desk of the dean of his faculty.

At Pretoria, Viljoen read the works of Professor A. B. du Preez, a theological champion of apartheid, who held that certain people were to be saved and others to be condemned. Viljoen attended a question evening with du Preez and concluded that his philosophy represented 'an appalling view of God', one which allowed for separate development and separate churches and which assigned certain peoples to certain roles. Its implication was that God had elected the Afrikaner as a trustee over other race groups. Viljoen recalls:

'Riding home from that question evening through the streets of Pretoria on my motor bike I said to myself "If this is God I want nothing to do with it". I concluded that I could not remain within the theological camp of the Dutch Reformed Church and, at the same time, fight apartheid. The problem is not a philosophical one of what constitutes right and wrong. Rather, the problem goes right to the heart of the concept of God. You must have a specific view of God to justify apartheid.'

By 1961 Viljoen had concluded that he could not become a minister in the church. Instead he decided to teach at the University of South Africa, although this plan was thwarted for a while pending an investigation into his political views. Then in the late 1960s came his final break with the Dutch Reformed Church. At the instigation of du Preez, the regional synod of the church launched an enquiry into the Christian Institute, concluding that it was an 'organisation causing dissent and revolution in worldly and churchly affairs'. A deacon knocked on Viljoen's door one night to deliver a copy of a pastoral letter explaining the synod's decision – a decision which effectively threatened Viljoen with excommunication. 'Since that day I have never taken holy communion in a Dutch Reformed Church. Indeed I no longer attend church services.'

Even now, a quarter of a century later, Braam Viljoen still tries to grasp the implications of what he did in dissenting from his church and his people. 'I have been through an earthquake. It leaves one drifting. It leaves me searching for foundations.' Does he still consider himself an Afrikaner?

'I will never give them the joy of denying me something bestowed upon me at birth. It is the Nationalists who have adulterated Afrikanerdom. What has happened in this country since 1948 has been a deviation in the history of my people. I recall a letter written to the *Pretoria News* in 1961 on the eve of South Africa becoming a republic. It was written by the chief justice, N. J. de Wet, and was one of the most moving letters I have ever read. It recalled what had inspired those negotiators – victors and vanquished in the Boer War – who sat down together at the National Convention in 1908 to draw up a constitution for South Africa. He wrote of their sense of unity, their determination to build one nation; they had a vision for the common good. Those were exactly my sentiments.'

While working for the South African Council of Churches, Viljoen embarked on a report to explain why the World Council of Churches granted financial assistance to guerrilla movements – not a fashionable topic for investigation in South Africa under apartheid. His conclusion was that the aid represented an 'act of alignment' with people fighting for their freedom. Slowly Viljoen's religious transition was being sharpened politically through his contacts with black people and through his enquiries into the justification of liberation movements. In 1973 Viljoen attended a conference in Cardiff in Wales on 'Violence and non-violence in the struggle for social justice', a conference which drew up a non-violent strategy of opposition but which accepted the good faith of those who resorted to violence as their only course of action.

But it was close to home, rather than in the conference halls of international symposia, that Viljoen was to discover a cause through which he could express the years of pent-up religious turmoil and political estrangement. That was the moment when Braam Viljoen became a peaceful activist directly involved on behalf of South Africa's disenfranchised black masses.

In the early 1980s Viljoen was chairman of the farmers' union in the area bordering the black homeland of kwaNdebele. The territory was designated to become the fifth 'independent national state' after Transkei, Bophuthatswana, Ciskei and Venda. But it would have been hard to find an area less like a sovereign state. It consisted of a few shanty settlements whose occupants met the labour requirements of the nearest white city, Pretoria, commuting by bus three hours each morning and evening. The government's plans to turn kwaNdebele into an 'independent' homeland met the inevitable response: widespread protests by blacks who did not relish being hived off from the South Africa of their birth and subjected to the rule of black lackeys of Pretoria in what was to all intents and purposes a human dumping ground.

One day in 1986, while South Africa was being swept by black violence, Viljoen received a telephone call from one of the farmers in his association reporting that his lorry had not returned. The farmer drove into kwaNdebele in search of his lorry and ran straight into a mass meeting of 20,000 blacks protesting over their impending 'independence'. The meeting signalled the start of kwaNdebele's revolt against the South African and homeland governments. To defuse any confrontation he agreed that the protest organisers could use the lorry to transport some of the demonstrators. In the days that followed Viljoen observed at first hand the intensifying protests against the government's plans for the homeland. The true story of that period is never likely to be told but the reports which circumvented the authorities' attempts to seal off the territory suggest that the security forces simply went on the rampage, wiping out anti-apartheid opposition. Not surprisingly, the response was equally violent. Says Viljoen: 'I saw the wrecks of seventy per cent of the homeland's businesses – burned to the ground in two days. I witnessed repression at the hands of the South African police and of the homeland government. I saw Pretoria's policy of "co-opting" black leaders at its worst.' Viljoen reported on what was happening to his fellow farmers, most of whom are members of the right-wing Conservative Party. 'These farmers believe in apartheid', says Viljoen. 'But once they heard about the kind of things which were happening inside kwaNdebele in the name of apartheid they were horrified and wanted action. For them it was a religious duty to respond. Actions like that are the saving grace of such Afrikaners.'

A delegation of farmers met the Pretoria-appointed head of police, who denied that anything untoward was taking place. The farmers were told there was no cause for undue concern. But Viljoen had been told of an incident in which six blacks had allegedly been killed by the police. He challenged the police chief about the report but the officer did not wish to discuss the matter; in any case, the policemen involved had been transferred, a tacit admission that the killings had indeed occurred. Viljoen had been in contact with the PFP member of parliament Peter Soal who asked questions in parliament about the situation inside the homeland. A general election was approaching in May 1987 and Viljoen accepted an invitation to stand as a PFP candidate, 'having seen with my own eyes what apartheid really means today, having understood what this so-called reforming government is really up to'. Viljoen consulted Slabbert because he was concerned about standing for a legislature which the former PFP leader had quit as 'an irrelevance'. Viljoen was also disillusioned with conventional politics. 'But it was a process I had to go through,' he says, 'and Slabbert gracefully acknowledged that.' Viljoen stood in the predominantly Afrikaner constituency of Waterkloof in Pretoria and was roundly defeated by the National Party candidate.

Viljoen attributed his defeat to the Afrikaners' fear of the future. His hopes for influencing his people through parliament thus dashed, it was not surprising perhaps that Viljoen was one of the liberal Afrikaners who joined the delegation to Dakar. 'Through my contacts with black people I was perhaps able to expound black thinking more than many other white South Africans. Dakar was the culmination of my hopes that I would be able to meet some of the people who derive their ideas from those of Albert Luthuli which I had experienced in the fifties.'

Like many who went to Dakar, Viljoen faced difficulties over the ANC's commitment to an armed struggle to help overthrow the Pretoria government. Viljoen's view was that the use of violence was a flawed policy because it could make only a superficial impact on the overwhelming might of the South African security forces and because it undermined what he describes as the 'very strong moral ground on which the ANC stands'.

'I'd seen the horror of kwaNdebele but I had also heard about the terrible injuries to the victims of bombings in South African city centres or of landmine explosions. I went to Dakar knowing the ANC were planning bombings. But I had to accept them as human beings, people who were relevant to the future of South Africa.' Viljoen spent many hours in west Africa discussing the situation with Thabo Mbeki among others:

'I understood but was not happy about their opting for the armed struggle. But that did not seduce me into accepting it, although it is not for me to judge them. Perhaps it was the only decision they could have made. Perhaps like Hoekendijk's Dutch Resistance in the Second World War, the ANC's campaign of violence was an example of the "emergency case" which allowed individuals to stray from accepted Christian standards when the force they were confronting was, in the view of many, morally and politically illegitimate, yet wielding such superior power to uphold that immorality.'

The talks with the ANC were of course only one dimension of the visit to west Africa. The experience of Afrikaners getting to know their own continent was equally important. Viljoen contrasted their reception to his own in the United States, where he had had to excuse himself for being a South African and go to great lengths to explain that not all whites in his country were racists. The group's reception in west Africa overwhelmed him:

'I experienced disbelief at the jubilation and unreserved acceptance of this group of white South Africans. It showed that Africans want South Africans to be part of the continent. More than ever before I had a sense of belonging to Africa and that South Africa could only gain from solidarity with the whole of the continent if only it were not for the lunacy of apartheid.

'I was not blind to some of the shortcomings of west Africa. The hotel where we stayed in Ghana was dreadful, as were many of the conditions we saw. But we have the hearts of Africa. We could have the markets. Above all, I now know what it's like to share in the dancing of Africa.'

CHAPTER TWELVE
Young Men Shall See Visions

In early 1988 a group of young Afrikaners undertook what was for them the journey of a lifetime. Yet this was not an expedition to some far-flung corner of the globe. They were airborne for barely an hour. Their destination was Maputo, the capital of Mozambique – an immediate neighbour of South Africa, yet to all intents and purposes another planet for most white South Africans since the country had been taken over by the Marxist FRELIMO government after the collapse of the Portuguese empire in 1975. Shortly after their return three of the young Afrikaners were invited to the South African Institute of International Affairs in Johannesburg to address members on their experiences. Their impressions of the trip betrayed the isolation of South Africa's young people from the continent that surrounds them; it also showed the extent to which they are prepared to consider change in their own country.

The group comprised members of the national executive committee of Jeugkrag (Youth Force), a student body committed to a multiracial solution as South Africa's future. Jeugkrag leaders say their organisation represents a moderate point of view; it favours universal franchise, with one parliament, one cabinet, and black people included in both. Group rights would still be protected. In other words its position is a little ahead of the ruling National Party's. The student presidents of several Afrikaans universities were also part of the group which represented a new generation of Afrikaners – particularly those from the Afrikaans universities – looking for solutions to their country's problems and seeking to break out from the mind-set that has paralysed generations before them.

Marthinus van Schalkwyk, a graduate of the Randse Afrikaanse Universiteit (RAU) in Johannesburg, who led the Maputo visit, described his university as 'young and dynamic'. He went on: 'Students at RAU, living in Johannesburg and close to millions of black people, are becoming politically more aware, in the same way that students at Stellenbosch University in the Cape are now more concerned about the problems of coloured people.' It was to discover more about the lives of their black neighbours that he and his colleagues undertook the visit to Mozambique.

Another of the student leaders, Cedric de Coning, said they had not realised how short was the flight from Johannesburg to Maputo – 'quicker than flying to Durban'. When the plane arrived at Maputo airport, he recounted, the group were asked to remain in their seats. They were anxious about what was happening, not knowing what to expect in this foreign land that was so hostile to their own country. Eventually they realised that the delay was so that a reception committee could be organised on the tarmac. As they disembarked, they were greeted as VIPs. Mozambican television crews thrust microphones at them, asking questions about South Africa's alleged support for the RENAMO rebels and about their views on the African National Congress.

The invitation to Maputo had come from the state-controlled Mozambican Youth Movement in the hope of establishing contacts with their counterparts in South Africa – an attempt to circumvent the breakdown in relations between the two countries after the bilateral 1984 Nkomati peace accord had gone sour. The Mozambican youth body also saw itself as a mediator between the Afrikaner students and the African National Congress, although such indirect contacts were not in the minds of the South African delegation. As Marthinus van Schalkwyk told his audience: 'We didn't want a second Dakar.' Indeed the Jeugkrag delegation was alert to any embarrassments that might have arisen from their visit. They were worried about placing a wreath at Heroes' Acre where the dead of the FRELIMO war are buried, but concluded that this gesture would be counterbalanced by their laying a wreath – on the Day of the Vow, which coincided with their visit – at the memorial to Louis Trichardt, one of the Boer *voortrekkers* who led his followers all the way to Mozambique's Indian Ocean coast. As van Schalkwyk put it: 'This must have been the first time that a wreath was laid at the memorial stone of a white South African in a black-ruled state.' The group was impressed with how well the memorial had been cared for. Cedric de Coning said it was the only well-kept building in the city.

The young Afrikaners were shocked at Maputo's dilapidated state after a long civil war which had wrought devastation throughout the country. There was little food. On their first morning they were offered a 'full English breakfast' but there was only a small sausage and some toast. 'There are no eggs today,' they were told by their Mozambican hosts. The city's infrastructure was in ruins. 'You couldn't buy a Coke in a café.' Said van Schalkwyk: 'The one strong view we came away with was that we will do our utmost to ensure we never have a similar situation in South Africa. It was depressing to see the roads which had not been tarred for ten years, the lack of food, the buildings which had not been painted, the people without proper clothes.'

Their discussions convinced the group that the Mozambicans did not want to move away from socialism. They viewed the Maputo government's recent overtures to the West merely as attempts to obtain aid. With little experience of countries where the American dollar is the only usable currency, the Afrikaner students were amazed that Mozambican currency was not accepted in shops and hotels. But de Coning thought that the capital was less militarised than he had expected – 'there were fewer soldiers on the streets than in Pretoria'.

The group was shown around Maputo, inspecting a rehabilitation centre for children abducted by RENAMO rebels and freed by government forces. They saw one child who had had an ear cut off. Such visits were clearly aimed at driving home to the students the effects of South Africa's alleged destabilisation in the region. These encounters raised the temperature of the final round-table discussion between the two sides. Debbie Machard recalled that 'the jugular veins were really pumping' by the time of the final meeting, which turned into a 'full-frontal confrontation'. Despite the disagreements, the mood relaxed during the evening when the Afrikaners were hosted at dinner. As Debbie Machard put it: 'We had made friends, made enemies and made friends again.' She was presented with a red rose by a Mozambican student who told her: 'Together we will strive for peace and better relationships between our two countries.'

Looking back on the trip, the Afrikaner students reported widespread hostility towards South Africa and its 'racist regime'. The Mozambicans were convinced the South African state would have to fall. As one of the student leaders put it: 'I'm sure they expected a bunch of white racists to get off the plane when we arrived.' The Mozambicans had found it difficult to comprehend that the Afrikaners were in South Africa to stay; they had equated the whites with the Portuguese colonial occupation in their own country. Also, when the Mozambicans had talked about 'apartheid' they had been referring to the free market economic system as well as racially discriminatory laws. For the Mozambicans, said the students, abolishing apartheid meant abolishing capitalism as well.

So the trip had mixed results. Contacts had been established and the Afrikaner students expressed the hope that their Mozambican counterparts would accept an invitation to visit South Africa. On the other hand, the trip had reinforced some of the students' views, particularly, as one put it, that 'other people don't really care what happens in South Africa. They have their own agenda.' Van Schalkwyk was not emotional either about the symbolism of the trip; he felt the notion of 'reaching out to Africa' was just a cliché. Nevertheless he was convinced the trip had demonstrated that it was still possible for whites to start dialogue with black Africa.

Their most informal moments with their Mozambican hosts were at one of the few night clubs still open in Maputo. Of course the situation in South Africa was at the top of the list of subjects the Mozambican youngsters wanted to talk about. Says de Coning: 'They could not understand the difference between our opposing apartheid yet our not supporting the ANC.'

The schism which split the political, cultural, social and religious sanctuaries of Afrikanerdom did not leave its young people untouched. In the rural areas and the towns it split young farmers and up-and-coming businessmen, apprentices and young policemen. In the major cities the battle was at its most intense on the Afrikaans campuses where progressive ideas competed with more traditional views. The long-established student body for Afrikaner students, the Afrikaner Studentebond (Afrikaner Student League), took fright at the prospect of becoming embroiled in politics and withered under the pressure, leaving other groups to fight it out. The Jeugkrag was formed to promote reformist ideas. Its leaders insisted the organisation was not a vehicle of the National Party, saying that student thinking in the Jeugkrag was ahead of the government. For a start it was multiracial, with thirty people of colour attending its opening meeting. Also, the organisation campaigned for one central parliament for all South Africans instead of Botha's exclusive parliament; and the Jeugkrag was re-appraising principal apartheid laws like the Group Areas Act, the Separate Amenities Act and the Population Registration Act. Like the government, though, it refused to talk to the African National Congress unless it renounced violence. The body was in touch with the youth brigade of the Zulu-dominated Inkatha movement, a moderate anti-apartheid body, and it wished to establish contacts with other groups.

Right-wing students supporting the Conservative Party, the HNP and AWB formed a rival body, the Afrikaner Studentefront (the Afrikaner Student Front) whose leader condemned the multiracial Jeugkrag organisation and vowed to campaign to keep Afrikaans universities white.

At the other end of the political spectrum, Afrikaner students at Stellenbosch became caught up in the political whirlwind of the academics' revolt and Denis Worrall's campaign. They were looking for solutions outside the parameters of National Party policy.

Thwarted in their attempts to visit the ANC in Lusaka by the government's threat to withdraw their passports, a group of ten Maties (as Stellenbosch students are called) embarked on a fact-finding tour of South Africa, meeting various sections of the political establishment outside the National Party, among them the United Democratic Front, Inkatha, white and black civic leaders and businessmen.

Their report, leaked to a Cape Town newspaper, directly contradicted the government's position on holding talks with the ANC. The Maties concluded that contact with the black nationalist organisation was essential for effective political decision-making. A full understanding of the ANC's policy was necess-ary before making a proper evaluation of the programmes of other organisations. The report concluded that the intensity and momentum of the blacks' freedom struggle was too strong and deep-rooted to be quelled by force. Whites had to realise that they could only channel such currents of feeling, not stop them.

Whereas in the 1940s and early 1950s most young Afrikaners came from the *platteland*, the majority now have city backgrounds and a different set of values. The technological revolution has overtaken the symbolism of the Boer War. Today's youngsters know about the Great Trek but it is no longer an important issue. Mike de Vries, rector of Stellenbosch University, says Afrikaner students are far more critical than their parents' generation; while the latter would automatically follow what a political leader or church minister told them, today's young Afrikaner will ask questions and expect answers. Says de Vries: 'A significant change happened in the general election of 1987 when many students supported the Independent candidates like Denis Worrall. The reason was the authoritarian manner of the government in saying: "We know what is good for you." The students' response was: "Give us the evidence".'

That said, there is still a strong Afrikaner value system among students. They still attend church, says de Vries, who notes that 800 of his students spent a vacation doing missionary work among Mozambican refugees in camps close to the border. Unlike some of their English counterparts, they believe in order and discipline on campus. Within the residences, house committees are prepared to take disciplinary action against students infringing regulations. Anti-government feelings have never overflowed into violent demonstrations as on some English-speaking campuses. De Vries acknowledges that the student bodies at RAU and Pretoria University are a good deal more conservative than at Stellenbosch.

Stellenbosch was an exclusively white university until 1977. The following year it opened its doors to black students for courses not on offer at other universities. Three years afterwards black students were admitted solely on the grounds of merit. The university authorities engaged the support of the Students' Representative Council in selling the idea to the previously all-white student body. Later, at the university's satellite campus at Tygerberg medical and dental hospital near Cape Town, the student residences were desegregated. Mike de Vries says: 'Doctors are on call round the clock. It was impractical for coloured students to have to travel to the hospital from mixed-race townships miles away. The student residences are right next door to the hospital.' But why has he not desegregated the residences on the main Stellenbosch campus? 'The move will have the consent of the university council if we get the green light from the government. You have to do it in stages. Some students are enlightened; several of the residences accommodate students who are very conservative. When we are fully desegregated it will be a matter of placing black and coloured students in liberal residences.'

When de Vries was a student at Stellenbosch, political debate was so narrow that a meeting addressed by an opponent of the National Party was broken up. 'Now everyone gets a hearing. We've had addresses from Tutu, Boesak, the Independents, the National Party, Buthelezi, COSATU, Eugene Terre Blanche – you name them.' Indeed the political affiliations of the student body go right across the spectrum, from the United Democratic Front to the AWB. But in the main, says de Vries, a large middle group (about 90 per cent of the student body) is close to the Independents or the extreme left of the National Party. 'Although there's been reform, the lack of long-term vision worries these young people. They want the future spelled out. Will we get away from sanctions? Will unrest recur? Are we going to accommodate blacks? They become impatient if they don't get answers.'

Today's students at Stellenbosch University will be part of tomorrow's Afrikaner elite. Their generation will produce future political leaders. Already, it seems, they are moulding new ideas about Afrikaner nationalism. If the Afrikaner *volk* is eventually led forward by these young people then the exclusive nationalism of the past is destined to wither. Under discussion instead is the concept of a South African nationalism, a common identity to ensure a stable future for the country, in which Afrikaner nationalism will be just one component. It would no longer imply superiority. These students want to see a more open society with far fewer restrictions. They are looking to the government to issue a declaration of intent committing itself to a system in which the country's population can enjoy freedom of association or non-association. This means that if Afrikaners want to belong to their own exclusive Afrikaner group they are free to do so. But this should not preclude the right of others to ignore group identification or to associate with those of different ethnicity.

Says de Vries:

'Most students here would back some kind of federal system which accommodated blacks but not one man, one vote in a unitary state. A very large percentage would accept a black man as the country's leader if he were the best man for the job. On talking to the ANC, views differ. A lot would say: "We must talk to all the actors concerning the country's future". Others would insist on the ANC first renouncing violence.'

Students agree that these questions should be debated without government interference. Relations between the university and the government reached a low point when staff and students deserted the National Party en masse for its liberal opponents when P. W. Botha was chancellor. Before 1948 the chancellors of Stellenbosch had all come from outside the political arena. D. F. Malan, though a party leader, was appointed chancellor in honour of his contribution to Afrikaner cultural life and his senior position in the church. Thereafter prime ministers and leaders of the National Party assumed it was their right to be chancellor. Apart for the brief chancellorship of a non-political figure in the 1980s, this has been the pattern since. After the experiences under P. W. Botha many have vowed that never again will a political leader become head of the university. The academic community is determined that the university should be a vehicle for completely open debate and for allowing young people exposure to a wide range of views. Says de Vries: 'A university should lead a community. It should be critical and therefore differ from politicians when necessary. The government should not view an open debate as their being criticised.'

De Vries says he was personally opposed to the group of Maties talking to the ANC in Lusaka, fearing they were too naïve and too unschooled in debate to enter a discussion with the ANC's senior leadership. 'We had a discussion at my house one Sunday over a glass of wine. I think I was swinging them round to my view. We agreed to sleep on it.' Next day there was a lunchtime meeting at one of the residences. The vote was 418 against going to Lusaka and two in favour. On the Wednesday, after the government had threatened to seize the group's passports, there was another meeting and there was a fifty/fifty split.

Says de Vries: 'The students had made clear they were not prepared to be prescribed to.'

Vossie Vorster's student days are past. But as a young businessman with firm right-wing political views, he would no doubt be an important opinion-former should the Conservative Party ever come to power. If the views expressed at Stellenbosch are at one end of young Afrikanerdom's axis, those of Vorster, who lives in the hardline Transvaal, are at the other.

His family is of Austrian extraction. He comes from the northern Transvaal where he was a hotel owner before selling up and turning to financial broking. He says he was a staunch National Party supporter until 1978 when the party 'started deviating'. 'I looked hard at what was happening and, honestly and truly, I could not see how sharing power will solve our problems.'

'In 1978 the National Party was really making progress. The blacks were very happy in their homelands. There were no riots in the Transkei. The riots have been here in white South Africa where we have tried to share power.'

Mr Vorster is obviously doing well as a broker, but his prosperity does not make him any more liberal. 'The black,' he says, 'is not capable of ruling the country.'

Why not? 'You try to uplift him and educate him. You leave a black with responsibility and authority but in the end he lets you down. He's not ready yet. He's not ripe. Not like the European. The European has more perspective than your black. I've had my fingers burned as a result.'

How?

'In my hotel I appointed a black in the bottle store [off-sales counter]. He was a very responsible man, well educated. He could read and write like a European. He was well dressed. He had everything going for him. Then I started noticing liquor was going missing. I found out he was selling it to his friends at give-away prices. I gave him a chance and he let me down. I then employed a white man and it worked.'

Vossie Vorster is not interested in the broader South African nationalism being explored by young Afrikaners at Stellenbosch. To him the Afrikaner will play the most important role in the future of South Africa. He remembers his Afrikaner roots, his people's history, the Great Trek. 'Out of all that a great nation was born. Our forefathers tamed and civilised part of Africa.' Neither is Vorster studying plans for a non-racial federation, let alone under what conditions talks should be opened with the ANC. He is prepared, though, to welcome English-speakers on board the Afrikaner trek; that's as far as his South African nationalism will extend. Vorster is typical of those Afrikaners who once bitterly mistrusted English-speakers but who now ally themselves with the more rightist among them against a government supported by a coalition of liberal Afrikaner and English interests. 'The Conservative Party is not there for the Afrikaner alone but for the white man and a white homeland.'

Under his scheme of things, apartheid laws like the Mixed Marriages Act would be reimposed 'until such time as there are only whites living in white South Africa'. In as many areas of employment as possible, whites would replace blacks, who would then be repatriated to their respective homelands. Vorster feels certain that whites would be prepared to take on the menial tasks now performed by blacks, like road sweeping and rubbish collection.

'I've seen countries where not a single black is employed and they're doing very well. Near here, there are three brothers who've started a farm and they've been very successful. They don't have a single black working for them.'

'I have no emotional bond with what happened in 1948 when the Nationalists came to power. I am one of the new generation of Afrikaners. The distance between what is happening now and the events of those times make it easier for me to make up my own mind about things. I do not accept the National Party. But I can never forget or reject Afrikaner nationalism.'

Corné Mulder, younger brother of Conservative Party MP Pieter Mulder and son of the late Connie (Muldergate) Mulder, was himself elected to parliament as a Conservative MP. In Britain or America Corné Mulder would be a 'yuppie', earning hundreds of thousands on the stock market. He is a very modern young man. But the survival of the Afrikaner people is still his priority. In so far as history tells him anything, it says to Corné Mulder 'never entrust your future to anybody but yourself.' History also tells Mulder that throughout their three centuries in South Africa the Afrikaners have always been split between those wishing to go it alone and those willing to do a deal with others.

'The settlers who came here from Europe were a special breed of people,' says Mulder.

'Leaving everything behind to make the journey here was an extraordinary feat. At the Cape they were colonised by the British. They wanted to be free and so they trekked. Their guiding principle was "Let's get away from the sea where the English are" – whether they meant Cape Town or Natal. Others moved at the time of the Boer War but there were always Afrikaners who stayed behind, who accepted the rule of others, saying that to take on the might of imperial Britain was impossible – *Dit is nie haalbaar nie* [It is not realistic].'

Today's 'idealistic' Afrikaners are in the National Party. As Mulder sees it, they are now calling upon fellow Afrikaners to be reasonable, to be realistic, arguing that you cannot fight against black majority rule. 'Our response to that,' says Mulder, 'is "No, no. We want to remain a free nation in terms of the principle of self-determination recognised internationally and by the United Nations."'

'For thirty years the National Party told the people that their future would be based upon separate development. Now we're being told the complete opposite. The National Party has been unable to deliver the goods. Professional people like myself are now joining the Conservative Party because we have had enough of this government. People in all walks of life are appalled at the way the government is running the country with its control over the media and the stifling of the free flow of information. The Afrikaners are still a democratic free nation and we resent that.'

Mulder knows many young policemen among whom there is believed to be strong support for the right wing and whose loyalty to the government is

211

questionable. These are young Afrikaners often plucked out of rural areas and thrust into towns and cities where they feel as foreign as their predecessors who made the same journey half a century ago. They are not well educated; many of them can barely speak English. Whereas back home on the farm they deal with blacks who are unsophisticated, in the cities they confront black people who are often a good deal brighter than they are. Their view of blacks has been fashioned almost entirely by the fears of the *swart gevaar* which they absorbed with their mother's milk. How the police and the army would react if the right wing formed or came close to forming a government is a moot point. Mulder says that over the past few years the South African police have been right in the firing line maintaining law and order in black townships. 'The problem is that maintaining law and order has become the same as maintaining the National Party government and that's another thing people, especially young people, don't like.' Mulder claims substantial support for the Conservative Party among the rank and file of the police and security forces, even among the top brass. 'The young policemen have been into the black townships. They have seen at first hand the activities of the revolutionary groups. They understand reality. They understand that the direction the government is taking us in will lead to more of that.'

As an intelligent, well-educated man, does Corné Mulder really believe that the CP's call for a return to Verwoerdian apartheid can work, even economically let alone politically?

'There is no doubt in the minds of CP voters that the Nationalists' alternative will bring something more terrible. Trying to bring more groups into the system while retaining white political power is cheating the blacks. It won't lead to moderate blacks in government but eventually to a communist takeover. What kind of economic prosperity will we have then?'

Most people can remember one event in their youth clearly – an event which stands out and encapsulates the age in which they grew up. For older people in Europe it might be the outbreak of the Second World War. For their children it is probably President Kennedy's assassination. For young people in South Africa two events punctuated their younger years.

The first was the assassination of Verwoerd. The perpetrator – a deranged parliamentary messenger – was immediately linked with communism by the government propaganda machine, thereby luring an entire generation into unquestioning acceptance of the 'Moscow-inspired total onslaught' against South Africa. The second event, which left a devastating impression, was 'Muldergate' – the information scandal of the late 1970s when secret propaganda offensives were launched in South Africa and abroad to improve the country's image. The responsibility for the scandal reached the highest echelons of government and eventually led to the downfall of the man at the top, Vorster. Even though heads rolled, the scandal sent an unmistakable signal to the younger generation: the country's leaders were no longer in the mould of the great Afrikaner heroes of the past, who were men of integrity with a strong moral sense. It was the moment when the *volk* lost its innocence. Nationalist politicians had contravened the moral codes expected of them. Many young Afrikaners could no longer look up to their leaders or offer them unquestioning loyalty. It was a landmark in young Afrikaners' rebellion against the old order. For generations the *volk* had rallied around their leaders and followed them everywhere. With 'Muldergate' the myths were exploded. Coming on top of the Soweto riots and the collapse of Portugal's empire, young Afrikaners assessed that the country could not carry on as before. New ideas had to be explored.

It should have happened much earlier of course. But the process of urbanisation had at first set the Afrikaner back, not emancipated him. Only afterwards could he climb back on the ladder and strive for the top and only recently has the Afrikaner had time to start questioning the values of his society. Better education has opened new horizons. There is now a modern 'youth culture' among Afrikaners which didn't exist before.

The patriarchal system within Afrikanerdom loosened. Young people asked whether their fathers were members of the Broederbond (and, if so, why?) and mothers were challenged about their subservience. The arrival of television with its diet of American programmes liberalised codes of behaviour; commercial radio stations attracted young listeners away from the staid SABC. There was more contact between Afrikaners and blacks, despite apartheid. Young Afrikaners now want to put some distance between themselves and the *laager*.

The result is a stark generation gap within Afrikanerdom. At any National Party rally these days there will be few young people. The audience is generally made up of the over-fifties, with a few in their forties, people who are praying that apartheid will survive until they are dead. Younger people, however, know they have a lifetime ahead of them to live with the results of the policies being enacted now. And it bothers them. Across the spectrum of young Afrikanerdom there is a sense of disillusion with middle parties like the Nationalists. Young people feel that the party's policy of old-style apartheid mixed with new-style reform is getting the country nowhere. It is a time for risk-taking and for decisive action, they feel, a time to choose once and for all whether the country should return to hardline Verwoerdian apartheid or go all-out for a non-racial society.

Many young people, including a small group of intellectuals, are therefore moving to the right – to the Conservative Party, mainly, but also to the AWB. Others are looking seriously at parties on the left for a way out of the impasse. These parties, they feel, offer alternative, more clear-cut visions of the future; they are more attractive than what is perceived as the wishy-washy uncertainty of the Nationalists.

Young Afrikaners are currently caught up in major changes. Some liberals swing to the right and then swing back again, and vice versa, as they respond erratically to the hastening pace of events. In that fluidity lies one of the best hopes for South Africa's future. For the views and outlooks which will be shaped as today's young people mature can reinvigorate Afrikanerdom and revolutionise its thinking.

Young people – on the left and, to an extent, on the right – no longer feel held down by history. Stories about the Great Trek, the Boer War and the heyday of Nationalism no longer hold a fascination. The events of today and tomorrow are what concern them. Young Afrikaners want to know how they can survive into the next century when blacks will outnumber whites by up to seventeen to one (compared to the present six to one), when international hostility will grow unless there is a settlement and when their children could face a political and economic wasteland if their worst fears are realised.

These young people will shake out the system. They will refuse to be put down by the tired old men who have until now shaped their destiny.

CHAPTER THIRTEEN

'I also am a flower in God's garden'

On the morning of 2 February 1988 a small sailing ship put ashore at Mossel Bay on the southern coastline of South Africa. It was a replica of the caravel in which exactly 500 years before the Portuguese explorer Bartholomeu Dias became the first white man to land at the foot of the dark continent after rounding the Cape of Good Hope. Dias' boat was a small, lateen-rigged vessel based on Arab boats which plied the Mediterranean; it had been developed by the Portuguese during the fifteenth century for coastal exploration and African trade. The two-masted caravel, no more than twenty-five metres long and of shallow draught, could sail close to the wind.

Bartholomeu Dias de Novaes, a gentleman at the royal court, had been appointed commander of the expedition by King Joao II after earlier discoverers had edged further south along the west African shores, reaching the Gold Coast, the Equator, Angola and South West Africa. After a stormy voyage south when land was not sighted for thirty days, the vessels eventually made landfall at what is now Mossel Bay. No sooner had he landed than Dias and his compatriots became embroiled in what can perhaps be classified as South Africa's first 'unrest situation' involving the indigenous population and Europeans. The journal *Lantern*, in a special edition on the Dias anniversary, recounted those events thus:

> The fatal chain of distrust that led to [South Africa's racial] confrontation may have had its beginnings in that very first encounter between Europeans and Hottentots when Dias landed at Mossel Bay. The natives were astonished at the Portuguese ships and clothes; the Portuguese, on the other hand, by the scant items of Hottentot clothing. A tragic incident abruptly put an end to Dias's visit to Sao Bras [now Mossel Bay]. The Hottentots crowded round to receive trinkets offered by the Portuguese in exchange for sheep and cattle which would after many months provide the mariners with fresh meat. While they were filling their casks with water from the stream, the Hottentots suddenly started throwing stones down the hill. Dias became annoyed, snatched up a cross-bow and killed one of them. Dias withdrew to their ships and set sail.

Given the country's later history it was a wonder that Dias did not immediately declare South Africa's first state of emergency. Five hundred years later the blacks are still crowding round for trinkets and the riot squads fire more than crossbows to hold them at bay.

The vessel retracing Dias' voyage had embarked from Portugal several weeks previously. It was an emotional occasion for the Afrikaners, and President Botha was there to welcome the crew. Led by the 'captain' of the vessel and watched by the National Party establishment in best bib and tucker, the crew came ashore and in a spectacular piece of ham acting restaged Dias' landfall. As the organisers could not persuade any coloureds (descended from the Khoi people, slaves from the east and white settlers) to play the parts of the original locals, they used whites with 'Afro' wigs and their faces darkened by boot polish. Still, it was an historic anniversary.

But what was being celebrated? An epic voyage which paved the way for the discovery of the east? The courage of the explorers during the age of discovery? Or maybe neither of these. Was it perhaps a salute to the white man for discovering Africa, a dubious piece of National Party public relations to laud Europeans' contribution to the development of South Africa? This was how it appeared to many whose feelings were captured in a letter to the *Citizen* newspaper by a black man – Francis Tsheledi – who wrote:

> While there can be no question that Dias was indeed an intrepid sailor, the only reason some people in our country feel like celebrating is because Dias was basically a trailblazer for fellow Europeans to this part of Africa. That he did not himself participate in the colonisation of what is now called South Africa is totally irrelevant. The fact is that, when he sailed around what he ironically named the Cape of Good Hope, he unwittingly heralded a new era – the coming of the Afrikaner and the various white tribes and, of course, apartheid to this country. . . . Therefore blacks are highly justified in seeing the [Dias] festival as a celebration of apartheid.

Notable by their absence at the commemoration were the thousands of coloured people living in the Mossel Bay area, particularly the school pupils who had been expected to arrive on day outings. After all, it was as a result of miscegenation between the first European arrivals and the local Khoi that the coloured race had in part come about. Why weren't they there?

The boycott was due to apartheid: the beach where Dias landed 500 years before was now marked out for 'whites only'. To make matters worse, the city fathers had decided that, as a special favour to the coloureds on this historic occasion, they would open the beach to all races for the week of the festivities. It is a startling insight into the insensitivity of the administrators of apartheid that it did not even occur to the Mossel Bay authorities that to desegregate the beach for one week would only compound the insult to the mixed-race people. Said one coloured leader: 'The action by the authorities regarding the beach was as though apartheid were being put to sleep for a week.' Some compared the decision to Hitler's removal of the 'Aryan' and 'non-Aryan' signs on park benches in Berlin during the 1936 Olympics. At no point did anyone in government anticipate that the Mossel Bay beach issue was potentially explosive, guaranteed to arouse fury among coloured people.

The anger of the coloureds was heightened because a week previously a mixed-race member of the advisory President's Council was apprehended by the police after he and his family – sunbathing on Mossel Bay's whites-only beach – were reported by a white bather. There was a certain irony in a coloured man being thrown off a beach where whites were drenching themselves in expensive suntan lotion in an attempt to get brown.

The mayor of Mossel Bay, Mr Rudi Barnard, could not understand what all the fuss was about. He described the beach apartheid issue as an 'irrelevance'. 'We're a happy little town,' he told me. The coloureds had a very nice beach of their own, of equal standard to that of the whites. 'Why have a few protesters got to upset the celebrations?' Certainly there was evidence of some intimidation by radicals: the headmaster of a mixed-race school admitted privately that he'd received phone calls urging his school not to participate. But most of the schools had decided not to attend anyway, such was the depth of feeling that the opening of the beaches for one week was an affront to the coloured people. On the day of the boat's arrival, thousands of white children and their parents converged on the 'Dias beach', while coloured children took part in their normal school assemblies. At one school in Mossel Bay, they began the day with their school song, *'Ons kan'* ('We are able'), which urges pride in oneself and in one's race.

Until P. W. Botha brought the coloureds into parliament under his 1983 constitution, they had been something of a forgotten people as far as the whites were concerned. The 'coloured problem' was a social malady like drunkenness and bad driving that had to be endured. But the coloureds could not be dismissed quite so easily. Unlike the blacks they had no ethnic homeland of their own, so their political representation could not be conveniently compartmentalised. They were dispersed all over the country. The vast majority lived in the western Cape, a mixture of urban dwellers in the huge coloured township of Mitchells Plain near Cape Town and smaller rural communities dotted further afield. There was a large coloured community in the eastern Cape and in pockets in the Orange Free State and Natal. Johannesburg had its own coloured settlement area called Eldorado Park, located on the doorstep of Soweto some miles outside Johannesburg. Moreover there was the unspoken awareness that many of today's Afrikaners have a fair measure of mixed-race blood flowing through their own supposedly Aryan veins. Within a few months of van Riebeeck landing at the Cape there were unions between the Dutch settlers and local Khoi and slaves, some of which were solemnised in church. All these factors complicated the Afrikaners' relationship with their coloured relatives.

The Theron Commission (on which Stellenbosch dissident Sampie Terreblanche served) was appointed by Prime Minister John Vorster in 1973 to enquire into the coloured population. Quite clearly, though, Vorster did not foresee the commission's role as devising a plan for the political future of the coloureds. Addressing parliament in April 1976 just two months before the Theron report was tabled, Vorster told MPs that he wanted the commission simply to identify objectively 'all points of friction' (between the coloureds and other race groups) and to bring these to his attention in order that they might be dealt with. He did not want to hear any recommendations concerning the enhancement of the coloureds' political representation.

But that is exactly what the Theron Commission told him, expressing the view that 'provision should be made for satisfactory forms of direct coloured representation and decision-making at the various levels of authority and of government.' Aside from its political recommendations, many of the commission's findings were a graphic illustration of how far the coloureds had slipped back economically and socially during the long years of neglect. The Theron enquiry called for certain areas of towns to be opened to all races; salary gaps between whites and coloureds to be removed as a top priority, with promotion of coloured people into the higher echelons of employment to be speeded up; training centres and crash courses in skilled work to be set up for coloureds, with multiracial trade unions allowed to register; industry to be decentralised closer to coloured communities; coloured farmers to be allowed to buy land anywhere in the country; all universities to be allowed to admit coloured students; highest priority to be given to wiping out the coloured housing backlog; gaps between white and coloured pensions and medical services to be eliminated; the cultural development of the coloured people to be within the same framework as that of whites; barriers to interracial sport at several levels to be removed; and a gradual opening up of recreation areas, beaches, sports facilities, etc., on an interracial basis. The commission also called for the repeal of the Mixed Marriages Act and the clause in the Immorality Act banning sex between whites and people of colour.

The government's response was a grave disappointment to those hoping that the Theron Commission could be the vehicle for the coloureds' return to the mainstream of South African life. On Theron's recommendations for equalising conditions of whites and coloureds, a White Paper of 1976 decreed:

> The government is convinced that . . . recommendations that would amount to the recognition and development of the identity of the various population groups in the Republic being broken down are not conducive to the orderly and evolutionary advancement of the various population groups. . . . For this reason the government . . . is not prepared to change its standpoint . . . in regard to [retaining] the Immorality Act and the Prohibition of Mixed Marriages Act.

As for the political recommendations of the Theron enquiry, urging a voice for the coloureds in central decision-making, the White Paper was equally dismissive: 'Any recommendations to the effect that direct representation be granted to coloureds in the existing parliamentary, provincial and local institutions is . . . not acceptable to the government.' This was because the government had its own plans for the coloureds (and the Indians) up its sleeve, plans which eventually came to fruition when Botha unveiled his new constitution providing for a tricameral parliament.

When Botha allowed the coloureds seats in parliament it was within the framework of separate racial representation. Still the stigma of being an ethnic group separate from the whites plagued the mixed-race people, for whom the plethora of apartheid laws had caused humiliation and sometimes tragedy. The Population Registration Act (1950), classifying every citizen according to race, had had a devastating effect on many families, with some members classified as white and others as coloured, often on the basis of spurious scientific and biological analysis. There were numerous borderline cases: individuals accepted by their community as white were suddenly labelled as of mixed blood. It became fashionable among coloured people to 'try for white' before the population registration boards whose job it is to classify every South African by race. The coloureds did enjoy one privilege however, a legacy from the British administration at the Cape – the right to vote alongside whites for the South African parliament. But even this concession, which dated from 1853, was removed in Verwoerd's punishing drive for the perfect order.

Some 38,000 coloureds in the Cape were on the common voters' roll. They constituted only 3.1 per cent of the total number of voters in the country. Yet the government still regarded the coloureds as a threat. The Nationalists were alarmed by figures showing that there were more coloured than white children attending Cape schools. The coloured birth rate was considerably higher than that for whites. When they voted, the coloureds tended to support the Nationalists' opponents in the United Party. There was a very real danger, the government believed, of the coloureds one day wresting power from whites.

The government decided to place the coloureds on a separate voting register which would allow them to elect four white MPs to represent their interests. But the Nationalists faced a major hurdle. The voting rights of the coloured people were enshrined in the 1910 Act of Union and could be changed only by a two-thirds majority in parliament. The government could muster a simple majority only; nevertheless, the Supreme Court ruled that the bill could become law. But the Appeal Court then declared the coloureds' disenfranchisement to be illegal. The Nationalists responded by almost doubling the size of both the Senate and the Appeal Court, packing the former with government supporters and the latter with sympathetic judges. The subsequent Separate Representation of Voters Act (1956) opened the way for coloureds to be deprived of a direct vote. This cynical manipulation of the constitution added insult to injury as far as the coloured population was concerned. In 1969 the coloureds lost their right even to be represented by white MPs.

The removal of their limited parliamentary rights drove many coloureds into the black nationalist movements of the day; they were finally convinced that there was no place for them in the white man's order, that they shared a common destiny with the disenfranchised and oppressed black masses. The Labour Party, representing mixed-race people and led by the Reverend Allan Hendrickse, became a rallying point as throughout the 1960s coloured leaders were jailed, banned or forced into exile.

Hendrickse is a graduate of Fort Hare University in the eastern Cape, a nursery for many of Africa's black leaders including Robert Mugabe of Zimbabwe, Orton Chirwa, the Malawian opposition figure, the late Robert Sobukwe of the Pan-Africanist Congress and Chief Buthelezi, political chief of the Zulus – men who refined their political philosophies within a broad Africanist school. In the wake of the 1960 crackdown, hopes of furthering the cause of African nationalism within South Africa appeared slim indeed. 'For me,' says Hendrickse, 'the nine years after 1960 were the political doldrums.' In 1969, however, coloured leaders reviewed their strategy. 'We had no effective platform of protest. We had the security police breathing down our necks.' Participation, they concluded, was the only realistic way of reorganising themselves. Hendrickse's Labour Party decided to put up candidates for elections to the Coloured Representative Council (CRC), a body created by Pretoria. Promising to fight apartheid from within, the party won twenty-six of the forty seats. The government's response both then and in subsequent elections in 1975 was to inflate the number of pro-government members by appointment, thereby cancelling out the Labour Party's electoral success. Nevertheless coloured leaders continued to support the policy of participation.

'We were not the good guys the government expected us to be,' says Hendrickse, who was elected to the CRC executive while serving a jail term. As the executive member responsible for coloured schooling, all education papers had to be brought to him in his prison cell. Eventually Hendrickse's Labour Party forced the dissolution of the CRC, because it was nothing more than a puppet apartheid institution.

Nevertheless, the argument over participation or non-participation continued. Hendrickse himself was convinced that an armed struggle against Pretoria could never succeed. 'You take the town of Uitenhage where I live. Because of the Group Areas Act the coloured and black areas are clearly demarcated. There are only two roads in and out. The South African Defence Force can ring it within twenty minutes.' Moreover, says Hendrickse, the premise of black unity is false. Because of their strong religious commitment, millions of blacks oppose violence, he says, while many would never support the socialist state envisaged by some black nationalists. Hendrickse's problem, though, was to demonstrate that participation could achieve results; the government had to provide an effective vehicle to give the coloureds a meaningful share in the running of their affairs – not just a rubber-stamping body. Early proposals for the power-sharing parliament did not satisfy Hendrickse, but the Labour Party continued with discussions. Says Hendrickse: 'We had the choice of remaining on the road of conflict or trying to find a solution. It was a long period of anguish.'

It was nevertheless a devastating blow to many coloured people when the Labour Party – meeting in the Natal town of Eshowe in 1983 – decided to join Botha's parliament even though their share of power would be strictly circumscribed and with the blacks, their fellows in the anti-apartheid struggle, excluded altogether. Labour Party members justified their stand by pointing to the preamble of the party's constitution which stated that the party was 'dedicated to promoting and advancing the dignity, rights, socio-economic and cultural wellbeing of all South Africans, through responsible negotiations with the government of the day'. One of the party officials said the decision to participate was a 'question of upliftment of our own community in preparation for reconciliation'. Hendrickse said the decision did not mean abandoning the black struggle; it was designed to fight apartheid from within. Leading coloured churchman Allan Boesak described the move as 'reeking of opportunism' and wanted nothing to do with it. Zulu leader Chief Buthelezi, head of the Black Alliance against apartheid which had included the Labour Party, warned delegates at the Eshowe conference that acceptance of Botha's deal would render the coloureds 'enemies in the eyes of black South Africans'. The Eshowe decision came as even more of a shock because Hendrickse and his family had themselves suffered from racial injustice.

In Dale Street, in a white suburb of the eastern Cape town of Uitenhage, there is a piece of vacant land which is a monument to apartheid. It is now covered with grass, but once there was a church as well as a manse and a church school. It was, though, a church for coloured worshippers and the apostles of apartheid could not allow that to continue. One Sunday morning in 1978, while a service was in progress, they came with their bulldozers and demolished the minister's house. As the bulldozers went about their work, the worshippers in the adjacent church continued singing their hymns. Realising that their days as a church community in Dale Street were drawing to a close, they sang 'By the Rivers of Babylon' with its pertinent refrain: 'Shall we sing the Lord's song in a strange land?'

In fact the coloured worshippers defied the eviction orders for a short while after the house was destroyed. They continued to hold their regular Sunday morning services, but eventually they could hold out no longer and the church itself was bulldozed. But on that day the Lord moved in a mysterious way. The last section of the church to be destroyed was the belfry but, try as they might, the workers simply could not uproot its foundations. The white foreman took charge, lassoing a chain around the base of the bell tower and attaching it to the rear of his truck. As the truck accelerated in an effort to heave the stone out of the ground, it ricocheted and broke the foreman's neck. He died immediately. The possibility of divine retribution did not occur to the God-fearing men in Pretoria and forced removals continued in the years afterwards. Today the bottom of the bell tower remains protruding above the grass, a solemn reminder of those sad times.

Allan Hendrickse was among the coloured worshippers who witnessed the destruction of his church. His father was the minister when the eviction orders were served. Allan Hendrickse himself performed the service of deconsecration.

He was born in 1927, the fifth of seven children. He traces his ancestors on his mother's side to slaves and artisans who arrived in the Cape in the eighteenth century from the Batavian republic, the Dutch East India Company's far-eastern outpost. On his father's side he is descended from a Dutch family called Hendrikz. Three Hendrikz brothers came to South Africa as *siekentroosters* (sick comforters), fulfilling a dual role as pastors and teachers. The missionary

221

tradition is strong in Hendrickse's family history. His father, the Reverend Charles Hendrickse, taught at a college established by the London Missionary Society to train Khoi ministers and teachers. Later he married into a Uitenhage family and became minister of Dale Street Congregational Church and principal of the local school. His son Allan, after graduating from Fort Hare, returned to Uitenhage to serve as a minister with his father, who was elected the first black head of the Congregational Union of South Africa which later became the United Church of Southern Africa.

His father had spent fifty years in Uitenhage establishing the church and the school – his life's work – when the eviction orders were served. Under the Group Areas Act, the church was in a designated white area. After the removal notice was served, Reverend Hendrickse senior said to his son: 'Now I might as well die.' He passed away eighteen months later. Allan Hendrickse continued with his father's work, building a new church in the segregated coloured township of Rosedale. The church has a memorial wall with bricks from the desecrated church in Uitenhage, as well as an inscription on a marble tablet which reads: 'In memory of the Rev C. W. Hendrickse and Mrs M. L. Hendrickse and the founders of Dale Street Congregational Church – and all victims of the Group Areas Act.'

Allan Hendrickse knows all about the hardship the Group Areas Act can cause, which is why he increasingly dug his heels in whenever the government tried to force through measures to tighten it.

A debate in parliament on 28 September 1988 on reinforcing group areas legislation witnessed Hendrickse's finest hour. The debate was historic for another reason; it was the first time that white, coloured and Indian MPs had taken part in a joint sitting, convening in a new, multi-million pound chamber built specifically for such occasions. Hendrickse delivered a bitter and devastating attack on race segregation. His address left white MPs in stunned silence; their faces were ashen. It was a landmark in South Africa's parliamentary history – the first time that white MPs had received a dressing-down at the hands of a non-white representative. As one newspaper put it: 'Never before have the hallowed halls of apartheid seen such raw confrontation. . . . For the first time the lawmakers were confronted by the victims of their apartheid policies.' Rounding on white members, Hendrickse recounted his family's own suffering at the hands of apartheid laws:

'I was visited in the home where I was born by the police because I was living there in contravention of the Group Areas Act. That was the house in which I was born. Do honourable members know what I mean? Do they share my experience? Yet they sit here in judgement on the whole of South Africa and they want to make a law. Every neighbour living in the area where I grew up – Afrikaners, Jews, Afrikaans-speaking, English-speaking, Indians and Chinese – signed a document saying they were happy to have us there and that we had grown up there. Then the permit was refused!'

The atmosphere in parliament was *tjoepstil* – as quiet as a mouse – with everyone present focused on the coloured leader. Hendrickse held up photographs taken before and after his father's house was demolished.

'I should like some members as part of their education to have a look at these photographs to show them how it was broken down brick by brick. My brother (who was working abroad at the time) was refused a re-entry visa because he had married an English girl. . . . When my father was ill he applied for a visa to visit and it was granted. . . . The condition was, for the purposes of the Group Areas Act, that his wife would be regarded as "coloured" while in the country. What a strange land!'

Allan Hendrickse's son Peter also sits in the coloured chamber, having agreed to join the government's power-sharing plans despite similar harassment at the hands of the security forces.

As long as he can remember, he says, his family has been political. His grandfather demonstrated over educational grievances in the 1920s. Peter Hendrickse recalls a raid on the house in the 1960s when the security police seized a copy of the novel *Black Beauty*, believing it to be subversive. In the unrest of 1976 Peter Hendrickse organised the first demonstration at a high school in the eastern Cape, thereby challenging the Afrikaners' age-old assumption that when it came to the crunch the coloureds would identify with the whites against the blacks.

On the Thursday of the week when the violence blew up his father was arrested. Peter had returned home after collecting his first driving licence to find his father missing. 'Where's Daddy?' he asked. 'He's been taken,' replied his mother. By 6 p.m. the house was crowded with supporters. A meeting at a nearby church hall attracted 800 protesters who wanted to march on the police station. By the Saturday Allan Hendrickse still had not been freed. An inter-faith, open-air church service was attended by 3000. During the following two weeks prayer meetings were held every night.

Peter Hendrickse made placards and put up posters; then the security police came for him as well. He was taken to Port Elizabeth to be interviewed by Colonel Goosen, who later carved a dubious place in history for himself as the investigating officer in the notorious case of Steve Biko, the Black Consciousness leader who died in police detention in 1977. At the police station Hendrickse surrendered his shoelaces, trouser belt, watch and spectacles and was locked up in the same solitary confinement cell in which Biko was to spend the last few days of his life. A plank attached to the wall served as a bed. The lavatory was a hole in the ground. There was no lavatory paper so he had to rip up a magazine. Says Hendrickse: 'It suddenly dawned on me that these guys can keep me here for as long as they like. Detention without trial was something new to me. And this was back in the days when there were no detainees' support groups. You were on your own, totally defenceless. I could hear other prisoners crying.' His food was three dirty pieces of bread per day and two helpings of coffee served in a filthy jam jar. 'For two days I didn't eat. But then I became so hungry I broke off the outside of the chunks of bread hoping the inside was clean.' His blanket stank of sweat and urine and he had no water to wash. The window was left open and he froze at night.

'You are waiting all the time to be beaten up by the security police. You hear them approaching with the keys. The keys come closer. Your stomach knots. The keys pass and the tension goes away until the next time.' After spending two weeks in the police cell Hendrickse was suddenly released. 'They charged me with attending an illegal gathering and made me pay a thirty rand admission-of-guilt fine.' For that he had been held incommunicado for two weeks.

In 1977, with his political consciousness focused by his brief imprisonment, Peter Hendrickse went to the mixed-race University of the Western Cape (UWC). Police action against squatters in the Crossroads shanty town was at its height. A protest march was broken up by the riot squad, who chased Hendrickse and others across an open field. 'I could smell the tear gas and hear the shooting. My throat was burning but we managed to escape.' Hendrickse helped squatters build some of the first shanty huts which sprang up at Crossroads in defiance of police action. 'I can remember seeing a black mother holding her baby while the bulldozers destroyed her hut. Cops with guns were standing by and watching. It was the middle of winter. I had tears streaming from my eyes because I realised it was useless. There was nothing I could do.'

Hendrickse left UWC after seven months to go to the United States to take up a four-year scholarship in San Francisco. He lived with a white family. 'I was homesick every night. I craved for news from home. South Africa wasn't news in America at that time. You searched the newspapers for reports about what was happening.' With other exiled South Africans, Hendrickse formed a group which met once a month, exchanging information, reading out letters from home and cooking South African meals. His fellow-exiles were from the whole spectrum of black nationalist organisations – the African National Congress, the Pan-Africanist Congress and the Zulu-dominated Inkatha movement.

Returning home in 1981 Hendrickse spent a year without work. 'As Allan Hendrickse's son, I was regarded as a troublemaker and no one wanted to give me work.' Eventually he was taken on by the Volkswagen car manufacturer in Uitenhage in the education and training department, a job he held for eighteen months until he and his father took the momentous decision to enter parliament.

When P. W. Botha introduced new constitutional plans in 1983 offering the coloureds and Indians a limited share in power with each to have their own elected legislature, the boycott strategy which the Labour Party had pursued since quitting the Coloured Representative Council came up for review. The debate was bitter. One side believed that the coloureds should never participate in the government's plans until all South Africans were included. The majority black population had been left out of the new constitution – their political role was consigned to the black homelands. On the other hand, what had years of boycott achieved? Had black people moved any further forward by shunning the crumbs of political representation that fell from Pretoria's table? All these arguments were vigorously debated at the Eshowe conference. The final decision to join the new parliament was a decisive victory for Botha and a serious setback for the extra-parliamentary opposition, which was quick to label the mixed-race politicians as 'sell-outs'. The movement organised a widespread boycott of the first elections, thereby depriving the new coloured MPs of any substantial electoral support.

Peter Hendrickse was elected to the Addo constituency in the eastern Cape. Why did he decide to participate after his experiences in jail and his victimisation under apartheid? 'At the Eshowe conference there were certainly feelings that we should reject the whole deal. But this was tinged with a measure of pragmatism – that instead of rejecting the three-chamber parliament we should exploit it for our own purpose.' His father set the party the target of making a meaningful impact on the dismantling of apartheid within the next five years, suggesting that his MPs would pull out if they felt little or nothing had been achieved. His son says: 'The first two years in parliament were very frustrating. It was a learning process. We had never been involved in a full parliament before. We had to learn how to compete in a game where the Nationalists had drawn up all the rules.' There was a lot of hostility from friends back home in Uitenhage. 'An old school friend, who had previously been totally apolitical, walked straight past me in the street.'

Peter Hendrickse's verdict on the years in parliament since 1983? A mixed bag, he says. The Labour Party claims credit for dozens of amendments to apartheid laws and for the scrapping of others. They began to understand how to make the parliamentary system work for them. When the Labour Party delayed the passage of three bills strengthening the Group Areas Act, the government resorted to dubious parliamentary procedures to try to force through the legislation. The Labour Party's successful parliamentary manipulation and filibustering revived the near-dormant debate on whether participation might not after all be a sensible strategy.

But not among some staunch opponents of apartheid, those holding out for a full, non-racial democracy rather than ethnically based power-sharing. One of these is Franklin Sonn, rector of the (coloured) Peninsula Technikon (technical college) and president of the Cape Teachers' Professional Association.

Sonn sees apartheid as the transposition to the towns and cities of the racial arrangements that prevailed on the farms: the white man in his house using his coloured headman to marshal the natives. From time to time the white man and his headman would sit down together to sort out squabbles on the farm. To Sonn, that is how the tricameral parliament works:

'The coloured leader in parliament is cast in the role of headman with the head of government as farm owner. The former is fighting against government policies, but as the government's headman he's also implementing them. If the headman [Allan Hendrickse] hadn't been around, the farmer [P. W. Botha] would have had to speak to us directly.

'To the credit of the Labour Party and its leader is that they more than

225

anyone else broke down the Coloured Representative Council. The party leader is unfortunately not doing the same thing now with regard to the tricameral parliament. Despite strong opposition to the three-chamber parliament, the indisputable advantage of Hendrickse's position is that he could bring down the tricameral system.'

Sonn believes that Botha's bitter attack on Hendrickse when he and his supporters dared to swim on a whites-only beach made the coloured leader realise just how circumscribed he was. Hendrickse had staged the protest to make clear to the government his refusal to be identified as an upholder of race laws. The affair ended with Hendrickse having to resign from the government. Says Sonn:

'Botha's anger over Hendrickse's swim from the white beach showed the Labour Party that no one will be allowed to act outside an Afrikaner apartheid paradigm. Reform means obedience to new rules of apartheid. Efforts to change the rules or the parameters of apartheid are frustrated. The Labour Party must therefore either knuckle down or quit. Hendrickse should have walked out of parliament over the swim. That was a chance missed, a big disappointment.'

Says Franklin Sonn: 'We are talking about transforming society, not reforming it.'

'Because of the injunctions of Christ, I am very aware that I have no right to hate the Afrikaner. But I am compelled to hate his sin.' Franklin Sonn is bitter at his people's treatment by successive Afrikaner governments.

He was born in the Karoo, the huge, barren south-western plains of South Africa. His great-grandfather, of German/Jewish extraction, married a black Sotho woman, hence Franklin Sonn's 'mixed-race' status. His parents owned their home in the town of Carnarvon, in an area of 'poor whites'. Afrikaners lived in outside quarters in their back yard. Franklin Sonn's grandfather used to get up in the middle of the night to tell the whites to keep quiet whenever they were noisy – an ironic reversal of today's black/white relationship.

But with the imposition of the Group Areas Act, the Sonn family were forced out of their homes to make way for whites. They moved to Queenstown in the eastern Cape; but because there was no home ownership in the coloured locations, they moved on again, this time to Cape Town. Sonn says that the same journey was undertaken by thousands of other coloureds: from the *platteland* to the city and even overseas to escape apartheid.

In his childhood in Cape Town, Sonn often spent Saturday afternoons with his great-uncle. *Oom* (Uncle) Titus had bought a small house and built up a thriving carpentry business in the back yard. 'He was not a well-schooled man. But he was upright and decent, and very industrious.' The coloureds in the area had been told they would have to move to a segregated location to make way for whites. The

Saturday afternoon conversations became more and more concerned with the impending removal.

'He knew he wouldn't get much money for his house – which white couple would want his humble home? That meant he would not have enough money to buy a property in the coloured area. He feared that the furniture he had made would not fit into a rented house. He became obsessed about the move. I kept saying to him "Don't talk about it, uncle. It will kill you". Before the time came for his removal, he died.'

Such experiences were repeated in other coloured families. If the influx control laws regulating the movement of blacks were the most devastating intrusion into the lives of Africans, the Group Areas Act was what crippled the coloureds. Says Sonn: 'The Group Areas Act killed my people – economically and morally. The Afrikaners lifted themselves out of their misery and in so doing left the coloured people in poverty. Many, like Oom Titus, died of a broken heart.'

The most notorious of the forced removals of coloureds occurred in District Six on the outskirts of Cape Town, a bubbling, cosmopolitan area which housed descendants of slaves freed in 1834, many of whom were Muslims, as well as coloureds and blacks and 'poor whites'. The area was overcrowded but little was done to improve conditions. When the Group Areas Act was visited upon District Six in 1966 about 40,000 people of all races were evicted from their homes, which were subsequently bulldozed. The area was declared a white suburb but few construction companies, property developers or major firms wished to incur the wrath of the coloureds by building or investing there. It became a wasteland, like the open ground where Allan Hendrickse's church used to be – another monument to apartheid. The government has since proposed turning District Six into a multiracial area again, a lunatic instance of history coming full circle.

Even during that grim time when the apartheid bulldozers were moving against them, the coloureds of District Six and elsewhere continued to demonstrate the wit, humour, self-mockery and exuberance which has enabled them to survive; qualities that distinguish them from their white Afrikaner brothers with their dour Calvinist traits. The dark side of their bohemian existence was the violence and the alcoholism which was also a part of life in District Six. But there is a richness of character and culture among the coloured people of South Africa. The river of their history is fed from so many sources – European, Asian and African – it is no wonder they are resilient.

On account of the hardships caused by the Group Areas Act, Sonn describes his people as 'possibly the angriest community among the South African population'. The Africans, he argues, were hardly permitted to enter the current of South African life. Despite their efforts, they were always on the outside. But not the coloureds. In the 1920s and 1930s they were on the same social and economic level as the Afrikaner. Both were impoverished but in some cases the coloureds were better off. They became urbanised while the Afrikaners were still on the farms. 'In reviving their own fortunes, the Afrikaners simply pushed the coloureds out of the system. The coloureds are the only community who were ejected from the mainstream of South African society – that's what makes them angry.'

Nevertheless the coloured people of South Africa still yearn to be re-acquainted with their Afrikaner compatriots, but not at any price. Politically many may identify with the black struggle but deep down the desire is strong to forge a common nationalism and a cultural re-association between white and brown Afrikaners. The two have so much in common: their language, religion, often their looks. Allan Hendrickse remembers having his car fixed at a garage while on a visit to a coloured school in the town of Peddie near Grahamstown. 'The garage owner, classified as white, looked like a coloured. The school principal, classified coloured, was as white as the garage owner.'

Says Allan Hendrickse:

'The very language of the Afrikaner people had its birth in the kitchens of white Afrikaners. That's because it began as a slave language. There are lots of slave words from the east in Afrikaans. Malay words like *koeksister* for a doughnut, or *bredie* for a Malay dish of tomato and meat hash are just two examples. Our binding element is our shared language. My dad – at the time of his death – was still dedicated to High Dutch!'

The early Afrikaner, true to his patriarchal tradition, was proud of his coloured offspring from Khoi women; the coloured children belonged to him, he looked after them and many kept their Afrikaner names. Allan Hendrickse traces much of the Afrikaners' racism to the sexual tensions in mixed communities. 'White men saw the coloured men as a threat. The white women regarded the coloured women as a threat as well.'

As a child Hendrickse remembers playing with Afrikaner children. 'It was never a problem. We shared each other's tears and joys.' The problems started, he says, when the government began segregating the schools in pursuit of 'the inculcation of a racist ideology'. Until then Afrikaner and coloured children had shared a common syllabus, with teaching in the coloured schools principally in English. After 1948 Afrikaans became the teaching medium and English was hardly spoken. Churches, too, were compelled to hold separate services. In Uitenhage, says Hendrickse, there had always been one Congregational church (visited incidentally by the Scottish explorer David Livingstone on his way north). Suddenly there had to be separate churches and separate services.

The race laws which tumbled out of parliament placed grotesque strains on the coloured community. Says Hendrickse:

'In Cape Town employers used to advertise jobs for people who were "five-eighths coloured" or "slightly coloured". As long as you were not completely coloured you stood a chance of getting the job. These "whiter" coloureds became more racist than some Afrikaners. Even today, in the big supermarkets, you can find coloured check-out girls who will deal with the whites first and disdainfully keep darker coloured customers waiting.'

'I also am a flower in God's garden'

For many years the coloureds saw themselves as mere appendages of the white man. In the Cape peninsula, where more privileged coloureds live, their only experience of blacks might be the milkman. But with the growth of black nationalism and increased contact across the colour line, the coloureds' fight for justice became an integral part of the wider black struggle. In the Cape there emerged a strong Trotskyist trend, with schoolteachers giving a political lead among the coloured community. The boycott (of school classes in particular) as a political weapon became a strong ingredient in the coloureds' tradition of protest. Whenever nationwide demonstrations took place, coloured students were invariably in the vanguard. Steve Biko's Black Consciousness movement, stressing the Africanism of the black man, appealed to politically aware coloureds and had a profound influence on coloured students. The BC philosophy gave the coloureds a new sense of dignity. Hendrickse recalls meeting a coloured man in 1972, when Biko's influence was growing, who said: 'Today I can see that I also am a flower in God's garden.'

Franklin Sonn agrees that Black Consciousness was an important catharsis for the coloured people:

'To us, Black Consciousness was a real and emotional experience. We discovered ourselves. It gave us a sense of pride after the years of alienation. It opened our eyes to whom we were dealing with. We could at last tell ourselves that we were free of them – free of the Afrikaners and all that hardship and rejection, and callous, unfeeling racism.'

But having found their own identity, the coloureds, like the blacks, returned to the search for a common, non-racial South Africanism as reflected in the Freedom Charter drawn up in 1955. Says Sonn: 'BC got stuck. We grew out of it. But we believe that to be non-racialist, you first had to go through Black Consciousness to discover yourself.'

Despite all the hurt suffered under apartheid, the coloureds would dearly love to be the vehicle to guide the Afrikaner towards a new future, to help him fulfil a creative role as a true South African. Coloureds do not believe there can be a perpetuation of Afrikaner nationalism if that implies exclusivity. Franklin Sonn is convinced that, because they are steeped in non-racialism, the coloured people's distinct role is to free the Afrikaners from their confusion:

'The coloured churches, the sports and cultural bodies are all telling the Afrikaners they are quite willing to take them in and set them free from their fears. We have a mission to take them into *Ubuntu* [African humanism]. We have a mission to shake them loose from their racism and their inward-looking nationalism. Still, though, they want their bloody exclusivity! We can have rapprochement only on the basis of a non-racial South Africa. I don't think the coloureds will want to resume a relationship with the Afrikaners under the old Afrikaner leadership role.'

What happens, asks Sonn, if the National Party expands its power base to include non-Afrikaners? What happens then to Afrikaner identity? There are already many Afrikaners who are far removed from their brethren in the rural areas – they are now closer to the urban blacks. Says Sonn: 'This is what I think Wynand Malan [the National Party defector] is trying to get through to them. He is grappling with how to free the Afrikaner. Wynand and I, on so many occasions, have agonised through the night over these issues.'

Allan Hendrickse believes there is now a great sorrow among many Afrikaners about the way they have treated the coloured people. Even the Afrikaans newspaper *Beeld*, staunchly pro-Nationalist, has spoken in such terms, says Hendrickse. He adds:

'There are now six hundred coloured students at Stellenbosch. Similarly, if you had said to me ten years ago that Allan Hendrickse would attract an audience of eight hundred students at Pretoria University at the height of examination time, as happened recently, I would have said you needed your head examined. In 1972 I flew to London with my wife and, as coloureds, we were allotted two seats at the back of the plane. We bumped into two white South Africans at the theatre in London and I can remember being staggered when the white man helped my wife on with her coat. Today it would not surprise me. The Afrikaner has come a long way in a short while.'

Cinema-goers of all races turned out in large numbers to see a film called *Fiela Se Kind* (Fiela's Child) based on a book about a young white boy, deserted by his parents, who is taken in by a coloured family. He lives with them happily until his early teens when a government census takes place. As apartheid has no place for coloureds raising white children, the little boy is wrenched from his adopted parents and placed with whites. The book and the film recount his journey of self-discovery, torn between his coloured and white identities. White audiences emerged from the cinemas totally drained, devastated by what they had seen of the suffering apartheid had wrought on the coloured people.

If the central dilemma of the Afrikaner is a moral one, then his treatment of the coloureds is a major factor in his bad conscience. The mixed-race people could not be parcelled up and despatched to an ethnic homeland as were the blacks under apartheid. The coloureds could not continue to live within 'white South Africa' without enjoying political rights. Can the Afrikaner satisfy himself that he has done right by the coloureds in granting them a second-rung parliament? Why are the coloureds so different that they require separate political representation? Is their culture so far from that of the Afrikaner? If the answer to these questions is 'no' then the only conclusion is that the Afrikaners have discriminated against the mixed-race people solely on the grounds of colour. There can be no confusion about that. There can be no complexities of 'different ethnic traditions' as some argue with regard to the blacks. And if the conclusion is that white and brown Afrikaners are of the same people, then the Afrikaner is left profoundly uneasy. He will have to search for ways of righting the wrong.

In its present form the ruling National Party cannot survive as an exclusive Afrikaner club. It has already needed English-speaking support and increasingly it will have to look for allies beyond the white community. The coloureds provide a potential reservoir, but the price will be high. The abolition of the Group Areas Act and other race laws is the minimum the Afrikaner will have to pay to re-enter the heart of the coloured community – and not simply abolition of these laws but also compensation for the hardships they have caused. The Afrikaners will also have to restore the constitutional privilege whose repeal hurt the coloureds most: their removal in 1956 from the common voters' roll, after which their franchise was limited to four white MPs selected 'because of their knowledge of the coloured people'. It was at this point that the Afrikaner denied his history and shrugged off responsibility for his mixed-race relations. The Afrikaner will not have signalled his earnest desire to make amends with the coloureds until the latter's voting rights – a symbolic issue – are fully restored. That said, it is questionable whether the coloureds would return to the political mainstream in any numbers until a place is found for the blacks also.

Most Afrikaners remain locked into the *laager*. Says Allan Hendrickse: 'What is Afrikaner culture? Their mode of dress is European. Their concertinas are like those in America. Their folk-dancing is from Europe.' Perhaps more than any of South Africa's peoples, the coloureds can observe at closest range how the Afrikaner's search for ethnic supremacy has been the agent of his own decay, and that only his extraction from the self-created racial morass will guarantee a worthwhile future.

Allan Hendrickse describes the 1988 Great Trek celebrations as a laughing stock 'even among whites'. 'The festivities showed they still want to be so white. They still don't want to confer any importance or reliance upon blacks. Even the ox-wagons they used in the commemoration were driven by whites. But in 1838 they were driven by Hottentots!'

Franklin Sonn believes the Afrikaners are experiencing the same traumas on their new great trek as on the original journey. 'The Afrikaner is moving away from himself towards something new. They are fighting among themselves – they're not united. They are aware that they are no longer a chosen people and they don't know where they're going.'

They wrote a musical about the coloureds. *District Six – The Musical* must be the only instance in show-business history where a stage production has been based on a story about mass deportations. The show captured the joys and the anguish of the coloured people, especially the anguish. One of its songs is called 'Seven Steps of Stone' – a reference to a popular meeting place on the streets of District Six. Two verses reflect the torment of the coloured people and the sorrow and the hurt they feel over what the Afrikaners have done to them:

> It was here you must remember
> Our children played their games
> And the skollie [teddy-boy] gangs smoked dagga [marijuana]
> Young lovers scratched their names.

The Afrikaners

These seven stones bear witness
Can these stone steps forgive
The people who destroyed our homes
And told us where to live.

The children will revenge us
For better or for worse
'Cos they can clearly hear the steps
And understand its curse.
For they too have been broken
And scattered like the bricks
The stones, cement and concrete
That once was District Six.

CHAPTER FOURTEEN

'A Holding of the Angry Breath'

In the shadow of the mountains,
shielded by bush on all sides,
stands alone the mud and daub house,
on the border of Kaffir land.

Softly Amakeia comforts,
on the bank of River Kei,
till he sleeps,
the tender offspring of the white pioneer.

Silence, hush, hush, hush, Babani,
See how shines the evening star.
Nobody will beat this tender child –
even if Mummy is far.

Amakeia made the promise
at the time her Madam died,
to tend the helpless child
until he had fully grown.

Lovingly she cares for the white child,
until for him the light of life
began to shine from Nanny Amakeia's
friendly, faithful black face.

With presage of danger
did she see the signs,
that war was coming over the lands.
Rapid the attack, house and cattle butchered and burned down.

Selflessly and defying death,
with the white child on her back,
did she to the Amatola mountains
flee in panic.

'Hush, hush, small Picannin,
over the mountains the moon is rising.

Nobody will see us here.
Tomorrow we shall go home.'

Oh! that the eyes of spies
should also her hiding place have seen.
'Spare him, he's still so small,' she begs
with her hands stretched out far.

Furiously the wild gang rages:
'Die or give us the white child.'
'Over my dead body,'
answers Amakeia with fire.

'My promise to my madam –
best there ever was –
where he goes must Amakeia
go too to care for him.'

'If you are not to be parted in life
be then united in death.
Let there be short process with her brother Xhosas,
let the shiny assegais rain.'

In the Amatola gorges
sings just the winter wind
through the reeds in the moonlight:
'Quiet, quiet, hush my child.'

The poem *Amakeia* was written by the Afrikaner poet A. G. Visser (1878–1929). Prompted by the guardians of Christian-National education, it became a set work for school pupils studying Afrikaans literature. It is an epic Afrikaner tale, the Boer *Beowulf*. The verses encapsulate the crisis facing the Afrikaner.

The poem tells of a black nanny, Amakeia, entrusted with a white baby when its mother dies. The nanny and her charge find themselves in the border country close to 'Kaffirland'. They seek a hiding place from the wars raging around them but are discovered. Amakeia is slaughtered by the Xhosa warriors wielding their *assegais* (native spears). The poem does not recount the fate of the child. Did the Xhosa warriors care for him and bring him up as one of their own? Or did they butcher him too? That unanswered question is the central agony still facing the Afrikaner. If he entrusts his future to the blacks what will be his fate? Liberals believe the blacks will take the white man under their wing and care for him. Hardliners are convinced the blacks will annihilate the Afrikaner race. Not knowing is the worst thing. Until they do know, the Afrikaners do not want to take the chance.

More than forty years of Afrikaner nationalist rule edged the question of the black man's future to the fringes of South Africa's political debate. Apartheid delayed the crucial choice the Afrikaner will one day have to face: whether and on what terms he will overcome the uncertainties so dramatically embodied in the story of Amakeia. Only recently has the Afrikaner – tentatively and warily – begun to contemplate what the poem warned him about: entrusting his future to the 'wild gang'. In the meantime, the Afrikaner's black compatriots have grown tired of waiting for him to make up his mind.

Black liberation movements elsewhere in Africa mounted successful campaigns against European settlers to seize power for themselves, a process which was often rapid. Yet, while supported by thousands inside the country, South Africa's main black movements – the African National Congress, the Pan-Africanist Congress and the Zulu-dominated Inkatha movement – have failed to dislodge successive governments in Pretoria or to divert them from the path of racial politics.

The first black political organisations emerged towards the end of the nineteenth century. The Natal Indian Congress, led by Mahatma Gandhi who was then a lawyer in Natal, was followed in 1902 by the African People's Organisation, a precursor of the ANC. Its founders had grown up at the end of the last century in mission schools, a common denominator among many of today's ANC leaders. Their Christian education has deterred moderate black nationalists from unleashing an uninhibited terrorist war on South Africa; they have restricted themselves to strategic and economic targets, but have conceded in recent years that civilians might be killed 'in the crossfire'. The ANC resorted only reluctantly to the armed struggle.

African organisations grew in the wake of the Boer War when black nationalists feared that the blacks' already limited franchise in the British-controlled Cape might be jettisoned because of their complete exclusion from the vote in the two Boer republics of Transvaal and Orange Free State which were about to join the Union. The South African Native Convention was formed in Bloemfontein in 1909, the first national body to campaign for black political rights. It fought for an extension of the Cape franchise to the rest of the country, undertaking a mission to London to lobby for their cause. The South African Native National Congress was established two years later, and was subsequently renamed the African National Congress. By this time an even greater threat than the loss of the franchise was looming, in the shape of the 1913 Natives Land Act which entrenched the concept of the racial separation of territory in South Africa's political system. The ANC adopted a Bill of Rights in 1923 stating that 'the Bantu inhabitants of the Union have, as human beings, the indisputable right to a place of abode in this land of their fathers.'

The ANC's campaign was to no avail. Under Prime Minister Hertzog, the Cape franchise was abolished in 1936. Africans would be represented by white members of parliament in the House of Assembly and the Senate. A largely impotent Natives' Representative Council became the blacks' only voice in any official political structure. In response to the relentless drive towards the political subjugation of the blacks, increasingly militant African organisations with Marxist leanings sprang up and eclipsed the ANC during the years before the Second World War. But the organisation was reinvigorated under the leadership

235

of Dr A. B. Xuma. In the 1940s the ANC campaigned aggressively for full citizenship and franchise rights for all South Africans regardless of race, as well as for equal rights to land, education, labour and welfare. The call for 'one man, one vote' was made for the first time. At first the demand was simply within the confines of racially separate voters' rolls, although this was modified in 1946 to 'one man, one vote' on a common roll, the principle which remains ANC policy to this day.

Prime Minister Smuts rejected these demands, and when the National Party came to power in 1948 the gap between the white authorities and African nationalism widened. The Congress Youth League of the ANC produced talented, politically acute young men like Nelson Mandela, Oliver Tambo, Walter Sisulu and Robert Sobukwe. The ANC hardened its strategies, embracing strikes, boycotts of government institutions and non-violent civil disobedience: a policy of non-cooperation with the authorities. The programme culminated in the Defiance Campaign of 1952 when thousands of black people were arrested for taking part in the largest non-violent demonstration of black protest that the country had seen. The campaign was at a time of harsh apartheid laws and tough security measures, but it failed to deflect the government from its course. The Defiance Campaign was probably a sobering experience for black leaders, since it showed the limits of effective black resistance, but it raised the ANC's international profile and alerted the world to South Africa's growing racial legislation. The ANC emerged more determined and disciplined, with a new leader Albert Luthuli (a Zulu chief and Africa's first winner of the Nobel peace prize) who steered the organisation towards the Freedom Charter, adopted in 1955 at a conference near Kliptown attended by hundreds of delegates. The Freedom Charter, which has remained the pillar of the ANC's ideology ever since, declared:

> We, the People of South Africa, declare for all our country and the world to know: that South Africa belongs to all who live in it, black and white, and that no government can justly claim authority unless it is based on the will of all the people; that our people have been robbed of their birthright to land, liberty and peace by a form of government founded on injustice and inequality, that our country will never be prosperous or free until all our people live in brotherhood, enjoying equal rights and opportunities; that only a democratic state, based on the will of all the people, can secure to all their birthright without distinction of colour, race, sex or belief; and therefore we, the People of South Africa, black and white together – equals, countrymen and brothers – adopt this Freedom Charter. And we pledge ourselves to strive together, sparing neither strength nor courage, until the democratic changes here set out have been won.

The charter declared that the 'people shall govern'; that 'all national groups shall have equal rights' (a reference which worried some black nationalists because its reference to 'national groups' appeared to endorse Pretoria's definition of separate ethnicity); that 'the people shall share the country's wealth'. The following year

156 activists were arrested and appeared in the famous Treason Trial, which started in 1956 and lasted five years before all the accused were acquitted.

The adoption of the Freedom Charter caused a major split in black nationalist ranks. Divisions had become apparent some years previously between those favouring a common front with whites to achieve equal rights for all, and those organisations believing that the black man, in an exclusively African struggle, should challenge the existing order. This discord broke out into the open in 1959 when members of the ANC's Youth League contended that the charter's commitment to 'share the land with all who live in it' implied that the land was not a birthright of the African people in the first place. Africanists within the organisation resolved that the liberation struggle should be founded upon the solidarity of the African masses, their cause uncorrupted by collaboration with whites. The Pan-Africanist Congress that emerged from the rupture had strong ideological roots in movements elsewhere in Africa; it was also influenced by African exile circles in London and other European capitals and by the Black Power movement in the United States. The PAC was popular among black intellectuals, especially in political cauldrons like Soweto.

The confrontation between the ANC and PAC came to a head in 1960. Led by Robert Sobukwe, the PAC took the battle for influence to the ANC's own door by calling for a campaign against the controversial pass laws. Sobukwe called for a non-violent campaign in which participants should, if necessary, allow themselves to be arrested. The response to the call was patchy, reflecting the difficulties of mobilising the black masses. The largest protest, involving 30,000 people, was in Cape Town. But outside the police station in Sharpeville township near Vereeniging the police lost their nerve and shot dead sixty-seven demonstrators, injuring almost 200 others. As a sign of solidarity the ANC called for a general strike and the burning of pass books. The government declared a state of emergency and outlawed both the ANC and the PAC; Mandela and others then began to reconsider the strategy of non-violent protest. The government had ignored the peaceful demands of black nationalists and had silenced their organisations.

Out of the strategy review was born Umkhonto we Sizwe which became the armed wing of the ANC, instructed to carry out limited attacks on selected targets to put economic pressure on the government and white population. In 1961 Umkhonto carried out its first acts of sabotage. An altogether more violent campaign was mounted by a group called Poqo, linked to the PAC, which was held responsible for the killings of several people until it was infiltrated and neutralised by the security police in 1963.

Those who did not stay to fight, fled into exile to build the ANC's political structure in the capitals of Africa and Europe and establish training camps for its guerrillas in Angola and Tanzania. It engaged the backing of the South African Communist Party, a decision which fuelled Pretoria's paranoia about a Moscow-inspired 'total onslaught' against South Africa and gave the authorities considerable ammunition in their propaganda campaign against the ANC. By the time of the 1976 Soweto riots the organisation had firmly established itself in the political consciousness of thousands of black people as the vanguard force in the struggle to overturn apartheid and white domination.

The PAC too found itself in exile, but the organisation proved ineffective both politically and militarily. Robert Sobukwe died in 1978 but the organisation's Africanist philosophy received a boost with the emergence of the Black Consciousness movement led by Steve Biko. This movement emerged in the early 1960s in the wake of the ANC and PAC bannings. Strongly influenced by Black Power – and especially by writers like George Jackson, Malcolm X and Stokely Carmichael – Black Consciousness drew also on the writings of Kwame Nkrumah, Julius Nyerere, Kenneth Kaunda and Franz Fanon, influential figures in the anti-colonial struggle. The upheavals on the campuses of Europe in the late 1960s further spurred the movement's young thinkers such as Biko. Through the South African Students' Organisation, Biko's message to the black man was that he was on his own, that he had to create his own identity and analyse carefully the racial and economic order which was the source of his oppression. Biko was banned before dying in police custody in September 1977, and most of the major BC organisations were outlawed at the same time.

The Black Consciousness philosophy was sharpened when the notion of a class struggle was introduced by the organisation that picked up Biko's mantle – AZAPO, the Azanian People's Organisation. (Azania, the ancient Greeks' word for the land mass south of Egypt, is the Pan-Africanist name for South Africa.) The cause of oppression was the 'racist/capitalist order', said AZAPO. A National Forum of BC organisations met in 1983; its inaugural manifesto stated: 'Our struggle for national liberation is directed against the system of racial capitalism, which holds the people of Azania in bondage for the benefit of the small minority of white capitalists and their allies, the white workers and the reactionary sections of the black middle class.' The manifesto called for the creation of a 'democratic, anti-racist worker republic in Azania, where the interests of the workers shall be paramount through worker control of the means of production, distribution and exchange.'

But the BC tradition was eclipsed in the wave of violence which gripped the townships in the mid-1980s. The political protests against the government were coordinated by the United Democratic Front, an alliance of hundreds of anti-apartheid organisations supporting the Freedom Charter. Many former BC supporters switched to the Charterist cause. Thus the division between the United Democratic Front and AZAPO mirrored that between the ANC and the PAC a quarter of a century earlier.

Inkatha ka Zulu was founded in 1928 by King Solomon kaDinuzulu to defend the Zulu ethnic group, its history and its heritage, from outside influences, particularly western encroachments. The organisation was revived in 1975 as Inkatha Yenkululeko Yesizwe by Mangosuthu Buthelezi, as a national cultural movement for the Zulu people as well as a vanguard body in the struggle for black freedom and an end to apartheid. Claiming 6 million members, Inkatha is supported by those pledging devoted allegiance to the Zulu royal family, of which Buthelezi is a member, and those who place a high price on Zulu unity.

Buthelezi's own position betrays the dilemma facing the Inkatha movement. Buthelezi is chief minister of the Pretoria-created kwaZulu homeland. He claims he occupies this position not by the grace of Pretoria but because the Zulu territory in Natal predates the Nationalist government by decades; his authority derives from his Zulu heritage, he argues, adding that he has continually fought the government's plans to create *bantustan* homelands. Nevertheless his black opponents consider that Buthelezi and his tribal-based Inkatha movement lend credence to Pretoria's assertion that 'separate black groups' are a founding principle of the country's politics. Inkatha has in recent years opened its ranks to non-Zulus, although its membership remains overwhelmingly Zulu.

Inkatha is committed to the search for a one-nation South Africa. It urges black people to rediscover the history and traditions of the African people before the age of colonialism. Human dignity, the importance of family life and civic duty, and the maintenance of cultural identity are strong undercurrents in the Inkatha philosophy. The liberation struggle in South Africa is as important to Inkatha as it is to other nationalist organisations, but not at the cost of the principles of African humanism to which Inkatha aspires. Thus Buthelezi is opposed to the use of violence, not simply because of religious abhorrence but because he perhaps takes a more measured view than other black nationalists of what it is possible to achieve through armed campaigns. No less committed to an apartheid-free South Africa, he feels the blacks are deluding themselves if they believe that the government is about to crumble. At the height of the township revolt in the mid-1980s, some liberal newspapers were referring to a time 'when apartheid goes' as though the Pretoria government were about to collapse within days. Interviewed in *Leadership* magazine in 1985, Buthelezi said:

'Some people think this government is on the run. In spite of our problems, it isn't. In my assessment after more than thirty years of political life, I would say that they are not on the run. I would say that P.W. and his colleagues have not lost the will to rule. There is an illusion about the violence that we are facing, that in fact liberation is just around the corner. I want it to be around the corner. But I know it is not. There is an illusion that because of the violence the state president might be frightened into doing something he doesn't want to do. And I say to people, especially abroad, that this government has not even used a fraction of the awesome powers it commands.'

Buthelezi's opposition to economic sanctions against South Africa is rooted in similar doubts about their effectiveness in moving the Pretoria government. Sanctions jeopardise Inkatha's appeal for the black man to uplift himself instead of relying on outside help.

Buthelezi's moderate stance on such issues has inevitably led to a bitter struggle with the African National Congress and the United Democratic Front. Battles between Inkatha and UDF supporters left hundreds dead. Inkatha claims to be the true heir of the ANC before it went into exile and began its armed struggle, when its policy was one of disciplined, non-violent opposition. Attempts to bridge the gap between Inkatha and the exiled leaders of the ANC have failed, although Buthelezi always distinguishes between what he disparagingly refers to as the ANC's 'external mission' and the ANC leader in South Africa, Nelson Mandela. The two men were friends in the ANC Youth League. Buthelezi has always shown great respect for Mandela and often recalls with affection visits to his home before he was arrested.

The Zulu chief has defied government attempts to woo him to the negotiating table. Buthelezi is unlikely to make the same mistake as the moderate black leader in Rhodesia, Bishop Muzorewa, who allowed himself to be compromised by the white minority government under Ian Smith and consequently wrote himself out of the equation when the country became independent in 1980. Buthelezi knows he has some trump cards. A solution without the Zulus is almost inconceivable. Thus Buthelezi may be calculating that one day South Africa's largest white tribe may have to come in search of an historic compromise with the largest black tribe, a meeting which would be a formidable alliance. After all, the two sides have some old enmities to resolve dating back to those bloody events at Dingane's *kraal* and on the banks of the Ncome River.

Africans, unlike Europeans, have little sense of urgency or of time running out. The Zulus, politically and temperamentally, can afford to wait.

It is perhaps extraordinary that despite four decades of apartheid black nationalists in the ANC still have a place for whites in their plans for a future South Africa. It is a recognition that the Afrikaners are not colonial settlers but, like the blacks, migrants from distant lands with nowhere else to go.

How do blacks explain their willingness to forge a common future with the very people who have oppressed them? Is apartheid an aberration in the history of Afrikanerdom, a freak storm in the Afrikaners' voyage to self-fulfilment? Or is it an inevitable consequence of three centuries of hardship which have taught the Afrikaner that control over his own life is paramount for survival? There was always a yearning for separation, from the moment van Riebeeck and his settlers landed at the Cape. Black activist Dr Nthatho Motlana, a supporter of the African National Congress, says the Afrikaner pysche is obsessed with division. 'They have been besotted with the notion that there should be no mixing of racial blood' – an obsession which is, in itself, fraudulent given the miscegenation which in part produced the mixed-race people of South Africa.

Does Motlana have any sympathy with the Afrikaners, given the subjugation they suffered at the hands of the colonial British prior to the Great Trek? 'If the Afrikaners' history started with the Great Trek, then there might be some sympathy for them. But we have to go back to the early settlements when the Afrikaners were under no pressure from the local Hottentot tribesmen. Yet they still put up boundary fences to keep them away.' Motlana compares the Afrikaners' treatment of blacks to the way the Jews deal with the Palestinians. The Afrikaners, like the Jews, have suffered discrimination and yet, says

Motlana, they are practising the same thing against the blacks and the Palestinians respectively.

'Afrikaners,' says Motlana, 'fail to identify with blacks at a human level. When the Afrikaner, through his religion, denied the theory of evolution, it was not because of the missing link, but because he found it difficult to believe that all mankind could be members of the same family. Mankind had to have a sub-species to explain the "superior" species.'

'After all,' says Motlana, 'why does the Afrikaner need the panoply of apartheid to protect himself? The Jews survived hundreds of years in the diaspora with their language, their religion, their culture intact. I once asked Professor Carel Boshoff [the right-wing Afrikaner] why his people needed all these state laws. He couldn't answer. I tried to explain to him that we don't want to go to bed with white women, if that's the fear, because we happen to like our own black women.'

For three centuries the blacks cooperated in their own oppression by putting up minimal resistance. That day is past and the struggle for political power is now well and truly on. But a seizure of power in a classic revolutionary sense is unlikely under present circumstances. Black nationalists foresee a long-drawn-out process in which political and economic pressures accompanied by frequent outbursts of violence, despite tough government measures, will force the Afrikaners to the negotiating table. The black protests and the rejection of all government structures for black political representation have compelled many Afrikaners to look at solutions within the concept of a single South African nation state. The Conservative Party's plan for a partitioned white heartland is met with derision by National Party loyalists, a fundamental shift in the latter's outlook from the days of Verwoerd and Vorster. Verwoerd's plan for a 'commonwealth of states' comprising 'white South Africa' and the homelands is dead. The vast majority of whites know that some form of integrated democracy will have to come. The preparation for that day is slowly beginning on an individual basis.

On the shop floor, in offices or in occasional social gatherings the barriers between blacks and Afrikaners are slowly coming down. Dr Motlana says that 'on a personal level, the two are starting to find each other.' He helped an Afrikaner-owned firm of coal suppliers, who wanted to supply coal to Soweto, to make contact with black coal merchants. 'OK, they weren't doing it out of philanthropy, but it's something and one welcomes this.'

Increasingly, says Motlana, blacks will have to take responsibility for their own self-improvement and for breaking out of the cycle of poverty and ignorance, but without becoming pawns of the Afrikaner economy. 'Any effort by blacks to strengthen the economy is bad,' says Motlana. In the years ahead blacks will have to prepare themselves for the eventual government of a non-racial South Africa. Motlana, a frequent visitor to Israel, sees a model in the way the early Zionist settlers prepared the ground in Palestine prior to the declaration of the Jewish state in 1948. By the time Israel came into being, he argues, the infrastructure – farming, textiles, furnishing and other light industries – was already in place. The trade union movement Histadrut became a mass employer. In other words, the structures were already in place at the time of independence so that the kind of disasters which befell countries like Mozambique after decolonisation could be avoided. But, says Motlana, this did not mean strengthening the economy of the British-mandated Palestine prior to the formation of the Jewish state.

The difference is, however, that whereas Israel's economy in 1948 was largely agricultural with a few cottage industries, South Africa today has the essential dynamics of a large western-style economy. For blacks, virtually starting from scratch, to establish a rival economic structure to compete with the existing one would be a monumental task.

The sobering realisation that black freedom, along with black economic independence, may be some way off has caused sections of the Black Consciousness movement too to look at ways in which blacks can prepare themselves for their hoped-for role in government.

The PAC and Black Consciousness have in any case been enjoying something of a revival among black intellectuals, especially in highly politicised black townships like Soweto. The black newspaper the *Sowetan*, several of whose editorial staff are Pan-Africanists, published the results of a mock general election in May 1987 at the same time as whites were voting in their own polls. Black leaders identified with the Pan-Africanist school attracted 1,430 nominations, compared with 350 for those in the ANC/UDF/Freedom Charter camp, a result which might have reflected the pro-PAC stance of many readers of the *Sowetan* but which could not on that account be dismissed. The multiracial approach of the Charterists had borne little fruit; it had failed to deliver any tangible gains in the struggle for liberation in 1960, 1976 or in the violence of the 1980s.

But BC philosophy had not stood still since Biko's days and was about to be significantly extended.

BC proponents observed the relation between the Afrikaner and black nationalist power blocs: the former militarily superior, the latter numerically. Many leaders believed that after the 1976 unrest in Soweto the time was approaching when blacks would take over the central power base. It did not happen then and it did not happen in the widespread rebellion in the black townships a decade later. Black leaders concluded that there were no effective political structures through which blacks could hope to exercise power. Says Aggrey Klaaste, editor of the *Sowetan*: 'It has become our responsibility as a black nation to sort out this mess.' For many black leaders that means returning to the roots of the black community. Essentially it is a 'do it yourself' strategy, encouraging black families whose lives have been destroyed by apartheid to come together, urging black youngsters to regain a sense of belonging to a family. Says Klaaste: 'When I became editor of the *Sowetan* [a leading position in black journalism] my kids were not at all impressed. They had no role model with whom they could associate me.' Black communities are being called upon to unite parents and pupils in a drive to improve education. Out of this, it's hoped, the next generation will emerge better prepared than their predecessors to counter

Afrikaner hegemony – to be cleverer than the Afrikaner.

Several black leaders concede that because of sweeping security measures against blacks the political debate in the townships has been toned down. Previously some political organisations were arrogant in their control of the lives of township residents. What Aggrey Klaaste calls 'a period of silent reflection' has replaced those heady days. The aim is now a true African consciousness which will one day confront its Afrikaner equivalent on more equal terms.

Aggrey Klaaste emerged as one of the most influential black journalists of his generation. A graduate of Witwatersrand University, he rose through the ranks of black journalism to become news editor of the *World*. When it was banned in 1977, Klaaste was detained without trial for six months. Later, after a year as a Niemann fellow at Harvard, he was appointed assistant editor of the *Sowetan*. Opponents complained of a lack of political commitment in his writing. But he refused to slip into easy, 'agit-prop' rhetoric. Instead, after assuming the editorship of the paper, he quietly set about defining a new strategy for blacks, to accommodate their hunger for political rights while acknowledging their continued subjection to the overwhelming might of the Afrikaner state.

Klaaste unveiled his ideas at a dinner attended by blacks and whites at the Shareworld leisure complex near Soweto. Shareworld is Johannesburg's answer to Disneyland and, although multiracial, tends to attract mostly blacks because of its proximity to the black township. Rock music in an adjacent discotheque (filled mostly by young whites on this particular evening) was a distraction from the speeches but somehow added to the spirit of the occasion. The chairwoman, Mrs Sibongile Khumalo, apologised to the white guests for the intrusion: 'We, who live in Soweto, are used to ghetto blasters next door!'

In any case Aggrey Klaaste's address gripped the audience. It was the most important contribution to black political thinking for some time, an oasis in an intellectual desert. He called his programme of action 'Nation Building'. It said to black people: 'Violence has got us nowhere – let's think of smarter ways of confronting white rule.'

Klaaste began with these grim words: 'I am forty-eight years old and have lived through forty years of National Party rule. It has been a daunting experience, full of despair, small triumphs, of helplessness, tempestuous bouts of anger, grief and very little hope.' He recalled the cyclical violence of 1960, 1976 and 1984; each time journalists like himself had 'declaimed the evils of the government'. But the angry words only fuelled the next pointless round of violence. 'Blacks lost many things. Worst of all we lost the innocence of our children. We also lost their respect for us.' After the explosion of violence in September 1984 Klaaste had concluded that 'something desperate, something unusually creative would have to be initiated' because there was 'a holding of the angry breath in the black community'.

Klaaste poured scorn on the words of the former Ghanaian leader Dr Kwame Nkrumah who in those first euphoric days of African decolonisation coined the words 'Seek ye first the political kingdom and all else will follow' – an exultation which had inspired the liberation struggles in most African countries from the late

1940s onwards and which had left most of those countries, once independent, in economic ruin. Urging his fellow blacks to turn their backs on such indulgent slogans, Klaaste declared:

'Political kingdoms do not stand up on their own, pristine, exultant as a galvanising abstraction. They are also not the result only of politicising or rhetoric. Political kingdoms to be effective, lasting and particularly democratic, need all sorts of power structures to underpin them.'

The Afrikaners had learned that lesson when they had lifted themselves from the depths of despair and formed their own network of economic and social support groups enabling them to seize control of the state. But the Afrikaners had made grave errors: they had forgotten the majority of the country's population. Now their 'total contempt for the humanity of others is reaping the whirlwind,' said Klaaste. The monolith of Afrikaner unity was cracking amid the anger of the dispossessed; it was the responsibility of blacks to save the country from certain ruin. 'It stirs in the very depths of my soul, the certainty that blacks have a unique and remarkable humanity called *Ubuntu* that others do not have. We have this indescribable ethic, to forgive and to forget.'

'Nation building' was the vehicle for saving the country, argued Klaaste. The blacks' political vocabulary – the language of the revolution – had become jaded. Klaaste's message was that blacks had to develop their talents to the full – as 'a strong people of thinkers and doers'. The focus had to be shifted from a political struggle whose fruits were not around the corner. Blacks had to exploit the period until liberation by elevating themselves above their present status of 'a vast number of angry and plainly dangerous people'. Courageously challenging many of the scriptures of the black nationalist struggle, Klaaste announced: 'We need to have the type of black leadership that will decrease the fear in the hearts of the young Afrikaners.' In other words, blacks had to fulfil themselves other than through regular bouts of carnage. They had to demonstrate that they were worthy of citizenship and equipped to inherit the political kingdom when it came.

Said Klaaste: 'The ultimate ideal is that we, who are in the majority, will build ourselves . . . to build South Africa for all its people.'

Where did international economic sanctions, supported by many black groups, fit into the scenario? How could blacks hope to improve themselves if they were denied employment by the withdrawal of foreign companies? The 'Nation Builders' concluded that sanctions were counterproductive if they destroyed the economy which the blacks were hoping to wrest from white control. Better that foreign countries direct their anger over apartheid into 'positive investment' in those areas which would assist black advancement. Figures in the pro-sanctions lobby, like Archbishop Tutu, had told the world that blacks did not mind if the economy was destroyed in the cause of toppling apartheid. 'We are prepared to suffer for a generation,' he once declared. But were they? As international companies withdrew and overseas investment dried up, blacks became the first to lose their jobs. Some black leaders began asking themselves: 'Do we really want to inherit an economic wasteland?' A rational debate was hindered, though, because support for sanctions had become a kind of political virility test in the anti-apartheid struggle – and no man likes to see his manhood called into question.

How much impact would the 'Nation Building' concept have on the ranks of the young 'comrades', the township activists, or on the proponents of sanctions? Klaaste's arguments appealed mainly to black intellectuals and middle-class entrepreneurs; would they strike a chord with the black masses, nursed on years of radical slogans urging the destruction of white power? Whatever its immediate impact, 'Nation Building' was a fundamental reassessment of where the black struggle was heading. The old methods had got nowhere so blacks were being called upon to use their heads instead of their hearts, to emulate what the Afrikaners did sixty years before, when with cunning and resourcefulness they claimed the political kingdom.

The 'Nation Building' programme dovetailed neatly with a trend already evident: blacks were forcing changes through sheer economic leverage. A 'silent revolution', as it was termed, resulted in blacks making themselves indispensable in crucial economic sectors. John Kane-Berman, executive director of the South African Institute of Race Relations, observed that: 'experience since 1970 shows that minority rule has a soft underbelly. The South African economy cannot run for very long without black collaboration – collaboration that is becoming increasingly conditional.'

The government has had to bow to the blacks' indispensability by granting certain apartheid reforms like black trade union rights and the desegregation of central business areas. Alternatively, blacks discovered they could make reforms inevitable through sheer weight of numbers. The flood of blacks into white areas resulted in some relaxation to the Group Areas Act; urbanisation compelled the repeal of the pass laws. These concessions are likely to grow in the economic sector and must eventually place greater strains on continued white control of the political sector. Certain aspects of apartheid are dying because they are incompatible with a thriving economy and can no longer withstand economic forces generated by millions of blacks. Black urbanisation is speeding up. Future privatisation of state industries may shake loose many of the protectionist practices which have excluded blacks from certain work opportunities. Business leaders, Afrikaners among them, recognise these dynamics. They have also noted the explosion that can occur if blacks' economic uplift is not matched by political advancement.

Can there ever be an accommodation between Afrikaner nationalism and black nationalism? The fundamental question must be answered before constitutional formulae can be discussed. The Indaba power-sharing plan for kwaZulus and Natal began to tackle the issue; it was a first cautious step by Afrikaners towards entrusting their political future to an overwhelmingly superior number of Africans. The outlawing of black nationalist organisations has stifled any kind of significant debate between rival nationalisms, so there is little indication as to whether common ground is possible. The occasions on which Afrikaners and

Africans have come together to discuss their futures have been rare.

But as the meeting in Dakar between the liberal Afrikaners and the ANC demonstrated, the issue is of crucial importance to the future of the country. The Dakar debate was at its most controversial when Hermann Giliomee of Cape Town University and Pallo Jordan of the ANC's national executive clashed over the question of Afrikaner and African nationalism finding a meeting point. Jordan defended the ANC's vision of a non-racial South Africa, and could not accept Giliomee's 'sad compromise' of a bi-communal system in which both nationalisms were recognised and accommodated side by side. The debate did not finish with the end of the Dakar meeting. Six months later, in February 1988, after the dust had settled and the two sides had had time for reflection, the liberal Afrikaans publication *Die Suid-Afrikaan* (The South African) published an exchange of open letters between Giliomee and Jordan – arguably one of the most substantive expositions of views on South African nationalism to have been placed before the country. There was also a contribution by the exiled Afrikaner poet Breyten Breytenbach, who had also been at Dakar.

Giliomee's letter sought to explain the irrevocable force behind Afrikaner nationalism which had to be taken into account in any political settlement. He could not excuse the abuses perpetrated in the name of Afrikaner nationalism but he believed that the Afrikaner's fears of black nationalism could not be dismissed. Addressing Pallo Jordan, Giliomee said:

> You come from the background of black nationalism in South Africa. Although the African National Congress represents itself as a non-racial movement seeking to include people of all ethnic backgrounds, the driving force of that movement is an African nationalism that wants to take over control from Afrikaner nationalism. You and I have often talked past each other in our conversations because we could not agree on the essence of the conflict. You say: 'It is a struggle between good and evil.' I say: 'No, it is a tragic conflict between two warring nationalisms, each of which thinks it has right on its side'.

Giliomee had touched a raw nerve in South Africa's race relations; the idea of a non-racial society, while appealing to many liberal Afrikaners, is seen by many others as a code word for black majority rule and with this the threat of Afrikaner subjugation. Such fears have, after all, inspired the growth of the right wing. Breytenbach described Giliomee's argument as 'totally objectionable and even dangerous'. He went on:

> As an historian you should know it is simply not true to allege the ANC 'represents itself' as non-racial while the actual driving force is supposed to be black nationalism. . . . We have no right to suspect them of . . . false appearances, no matter how attractive it may be to want to see them as black nationalists, and therefore, as a counterpart of white nationalism.

Giliomee took up the challenge:

Understand me well. I don't say Afrikaner and black nationalisms are, in objective terms, equally good or equally bad. Afrikaner nationalism with its instruments of apartheid is responsible for massive inroads into individual rights and freedoms; its record provides evidence of ethnic intolerance and racism. Against that, your African nationalism is far more inclusive and tolerant. . . . But – and this is an important point – your 'non-racial democracy' is after all only an ideology which is to help your black nationalism come into power, and – if you succeed in that – to justify your regime. When I seem sceptical about ideology it is not because I doubt the good intentions of you and your people. It is only that I know how good the intentions were of the SABRA intellectuals of Stellenbosch in the 1950s when they presented apartheid as a justifiable solution. History is not exactly full of examples of nationalist movements that can transcend themselves. You will certainly concede there is a chance that your nationalist movement, as a result of circumstances, can become just as oppressive as my Afrikaner nationalism has become.

In response, Breytenbach asked Giliomee: 'Who wants to replace Afrikaner nationalism with black nationalism? Why does nationalism automatically exclude democracy?'

Pallo Jordan's response was published by *Die Suid-Afrikaan* under the title 'Why won't Afrikaners rely on democracy?' He argued that whereas African nationalism stood for non-racialism, Afrikaner nationalism had been identified with exclusivity or superiority. As he put it:

The tradition which the Afrikaner nationalist has associated himself with is one of opposition to the ideals of equality before the law and democracy. There is a consistent thread that runs through his history, claiming differential treatment for persons on the grounds of race and ethnic origin. Whether this is the voortrekker principle of 'no equality between master and servant, white and black' or the latter-day claims of group rights, it seeks to undermine the notion of the juridical equality of citizens. In this respect the cores underlying the two nationalisms are irreconcilable.

In the same way that one could not support tyranny or slavery, argued Jordan, so there could be no two views about apartheid: hence Afrikaner nationalism, which fathered apartheid, could not be equated with black nationalism which had struggled against it. Jordan referred to the position of the Jews in Europe who were subjected to mass extermination in Hitler's camps but who now continued to live in Europe, many as minorities without separate ethnic protection under the laws of those states. As Jordan wrote:

. . . it is democratic institutions and practices that protect Jews and other minorities from fascist and racist movements. I cannot understand why you as an Afrikaner cannot rely on precisely these same democratic practices to protect you from possible persecution.

In other words, for Jordan, a future South Africa would have to shed the notion of group protection, as this implied maintenance of rights and privileges for a select few. In a non-racial society there would be no place for Afrikaner nationalism if it remained a vehicle for Afrikaner superiority and the suppression of the majority. The philosophy of non-racialism, of a society in which whites would be accommodated as equals, had underpinned ANC thinking since its inception, despite frequent attacks from the black exclusivist school – the Black Consciousness movement and the Pan-Africanist Congress. Jordan explained:

> Non-racialism in ANC political practice is something we have had to fight to maintain on a daily basis, against every sort of temptation. You may well imagine how difficult it must have been to sustain such a perspective among a people who are daily assailed by institutions of white racism, acting on behalf of a government that is exclusively white, which has repeatedly been returned to office by the majority of white electors. . . . The very fact that we have had to struggle to maintain it has drilled non-racialism into the average ANC member so that it is almost second nature.

And that perhaps explains why, throughout the turmoil of the mid-1980s, only a handful of whites were attacked by black radicals on account of their colour; the targets were the security forces and related agencies associated with the white government, as well as black moderates who 'sold out' to the white authorities by serving as policemen or local councillors. Whether the young 'comrades' in the townships – hardened by years of confrontation with the state – will be quite so controlled in the future is debatable. Nevertheless, the underlying philosophy of the ANC remains one of black and white meeting as equals. As Jordan concluded:

> It was in that spirit that Thabo Mbeki [a fellow-ANC executive member] declared in Dakar 'I am an Afrikaner'. It was to demonstrate that we have no animus against the Afrikaners and embrace them as fellow-countrymen. Is it not high time many more Afrikaners began to declare 'I am an African'. . . . The door as always is open to the Afrikaner to come on home – but as an equal, as a countryman, as an African.

At which point one returns to the dilemma of the Afrikaner: whether he is in fact an African or a latent European. European history may have passed him by for the past three centuries but there is little doubt that his points of reference, the civilisation to which he aspires, the life style he adopts, the way he thinks, are still essentially European. Claims that Afrikaners are just another African tribe are not convincing. The Afrikaners want to continue living in South Africa: the country has been good to them. But an Afrikaner is an African only up to the point where he has to meet Africa on equal terms, at which point his European instincts reassert themselves. Only when the Afrikaner gives himself to Africa in its fullest sense can that meeting of Afrikaner and African nationalism take place. Until that time the Afrikaner will continue to seek separate dispensations and demand the right to determine his own future.

248

Some Afrikaners – like those who went to Dakar, some young people, sections of the universities and the church – have taken the plunge by concluding that the future of the Afrikaner cannot be guaranteed so long as he demands special privileges for himself on account of his ethnicity. They believe his survival will be assured only when he has surrendered to a common South African nationalism. The anxieties Giliomee referred to may never be overcome so long as Afrikaners see themselves as not quite part of the African continent. Perhaps South Africa's eventual brand of African nationalism will be unlike that of countries elsewhere on the continent; one that is not overwhelmingly black, but accommodating a concept of 'African-ness' as understood by whites, coloureds and Indians as well. If he explores this new nationalism, the Afrikaner may increasingly tend to place less emphasis on 'race' and more on 'standards'.

For its part the ANC may discover that blurring the nationalist boundaries in South Africa might not be as easy as it appears, and that means the divisions between rival black schools as well as between blacks and whites. That half the deaths in the violence of the mid-1980s were due to 'black on black violence' cannot glibly be attributed to the pressures of apartheid. There are real divisions among blacks which many prefer to ignore.

Throughout his history the Afrikaner has lived under the fatal delusion that vast numbers of black people have little concern about their political inferiority so long as they are happy and contented in day-to-day life. Without question many black people have little knowledge of or interest in South Africa's political issues. But even in the democracies of the west large numbers of people have scant interest in politics; that does not mean they would sit idly by and watch their political rights being taken away. Since 1948 the National Party has been convinced it can expect acquiescence from the blacks of South Africa, hence the policy of co-opting unrepresentative black figures who are prepared to sit at the white man's table.

There are historical precedents. In the wake of the Battle of Blood River, the Afrikaner *voortrekkers* forged an alliance with a rebel Zulu leader Mpande, half-brother of the Zulu ruler Dingane. The *voortrekkers* agreed that Mpande's army of 10,000 should be despatched into Zululand to crush Dingane's empire. Dingane sent envoys to the Boer headquarters to sue for peace; the envoys were promptly arrested and court-martialled. Mpande – the *voortrekkers'* compliant tool – was judge and jury, and when he pronounced them guilty the *voortrekkers* accepted the verdict and shot dead the two envoys. What remarkable similarities there are between this and today's relationships between the white government and the assorted black groups. If Dingane was the equivalent of today's communist-inspired black revolutionary, then Mpande can be seen as a compliant homeland chief or the head of the black township police forces, who serves the white government in holding back the advance of the rebellious black masses.

In the shared experience of suffering lies perhaps the best hope for peace between Afrikaners and Africans. Despite the liberal-sounding noises of some English-speakers, blacks arguably feel closer to Afrikaners. They both belong to strong peoples; they have both known poverty and dispossession. It is acknowledged that the skills of whites will still be needed under a majoritarian democracy. The whites are South African, after all, and very loyal South Africans at that. Says Motlana: 'Although the Afrikaners have perpetrated unspeakable errors, their children are as much entitled to have a place in the country as black people.' The attitude of most blacks towards the Afrikaner remains one of 'more in sorrow than in anger', sorrow in that apartheid has caused the Afrikaner to commit outrageous deeds in the zealous pursuit of ideology, brutalising him in the process. Motlana believes that the Afrikaners are essentially a pragmatic people. 'People can change. Humanity has the ability to adapt. When the Afrikaner is eventually faced with reality, the world will be surprised at his ability to change.'

In his letter to Pallo Jordan, Hermann Giliomee said:

I am dumbfounded that in spite of the persecution endured by your leaders you [and your people] are still remarkably free from hatred.

As an ultimate testament to the potential for understanding between blacks and Afrikaners, Dr Motlana recalls Nelson Mandela's prostate operation in 1986. Motlana, a medical adviser to the Mandela family, was present as were leading doctors flown in from overseas, the government being terrified of something going wrong and of being accused of 'murdering' the ANC leader. Says Motlana: 'The state brought in top urologists from the United Kingdom and France as well as South Africa's leading urologist and the top black nephrologists. Who do you think Nelson chose as his surgeon? An Afrikaner doctor in government service – that speaks volumes.'

And yet, and yet, the Afrikaner still remembers the story of Amakeia. . . . Can they really trust the blacks' assurances or should they, like Amakeia, continue to be on the look-out in case 'the shiny *assegais* rain'?

CHAPTER FIFTEEN
The Old Enemy

On a bare, sun-baked hilltop in the province of Natal, not far from South Africa's border with Lesotho, there is an enduring memory of the bitter conflict which pitted the small Boer nation against the might of the British empire in what was one of the most pointless wars ever fought. Spion Kop (Spy Peak), on 24 January 1900, saw one of the bloodiest and most intense battles of the Boer War, for control of the vital summit. Today there are individual and mass graves where the British dead are buried and a stone cenotaph in honour of the fallen Boers. The graves are fenced off to keep animals at bay. The long scrub grass rustles in the wind. A few black shepherd boys are the only living souls around.

The calm is in contrast to what it must have been like on that scorching January morning when the British seized the summit, only to be repulsed by a determined Boer counterattack. Amid the shell fire, the Boers from the summit and the British from their trenches fought it out from sunrise to sunset. The British forces, running low on water and frantically calling for reinforcements, were at times on the point of surrender. Winston Churchill was among a group of correspondents who reached the summit and later reported back to British headquarters that the British position was untenable unless help was sent up urgently. The Boers suffered terrible casualties too. By nightfall each side believed it would face extinction if the battle went into a second day. The British disengaged; so did the Boers. Neither side knew how crippled was the other, until the Boer general Louis Botha realised that the British had deserted the summit. He rallied some of his men, who promptly retook the *kop*.

The British lost 1200 men, the Boers 300. British stretcher-bearers fetched the wounded, many of whom had been lying three deep among dead bodies for several hours. Mass graves were dug immediately. One headstone reads: 'In loving memory of the officers, NCOs and men of the 2nd Lancashire Fusiliers who fell in action January 24, 1900.' Another, where dozens of men whose names went unrecorded are buried, bears the simple inscription: 'Here lie several brave soldiers.' The Boers took most of their dead away and buried them in their home towns. In a corner of the battle field the Afrikaners erected their memorial some years later. It bears the words: *As Huldeblyk aan die Republikeinse offisiere en burgers wat gesneuwel het in die slag van Spionkop* ('In tribute to the republican officers and citizens killed in action at the Battle of Spion Kop').

251

At Spion Kop, the Boers and the British fought each other to a standstill but the Boers had the final say, a harbinger of how their intertwining history would unfold in the years ahead.

The British seizure of the Cape in 1795, consolidated in 1815 by the treaty that concluded the Napoleonic Wars, spelled the end of 150 years of inefficient rule by the declining VOC – the Dutch East India Company. Through the VOC's neglect, the settlement had become a backwater. Competent government had now arrived for the first time with a new class of professional administrators, many of whom had served in India. Most were from the British upper classes, in contrast to the uncultivated Boers leading austere lives in remote settlements.

In the main, the new British overlords continued the VOC's policy on race relations by upholding separate areas for whites and indigenous peoples. But these soldier-administrators were children of the expanding British empire and they had brought with them a strong commitment to free trade. A century and a half before the National Party leaders, the British colonial rulers came face to face with the crucial question of whether racial segregation could coexist with an expanding capitalist economy. They concluded that it could not, and relaxed some race laws to allow for the free exchange of goods. The British occupation therefore introduced a strain of enlightened administration which, though not reversing the trend towards white supremacy over blacks and Khoi, succeeded in softening some of its harsher edges. Here lay the beginnings of the 'Cape liberal' tradition which throughout decades of creeping racial repression kept alive western democratic values.

The arrival in the eastern Cape in 1820 of the first main group of British settlers brought South Africa a very British way of life. The new arrivals were recruited from all parts of the British Isles. Like their Dutch predecessors, they were leaving behind a Europe in the depths of a depression following a major conflict, in this case the Napoleonic wars. They were attracted by a government scheme under which each able-bodied man would be granted 100 acres of land in the eastern Cape, to be occupied free of rent for the first ten years. As the British government saw it, the settlers would help shore up the eastern frontier against the Xhosas.

As with the earlier Huguenot arrivals, the 1820 settlers were a broad cross-section of the society they had left behind: middle and lower-class people mainly – artisans, including carpenters, weavers and coach-builders, as well as churchmen and veterans of the war. For the most part they were decent, religious people who respected freedom of thought and education. They were also imbued with the spirit of political freedom that Britain had enjoyed since the middle of the seventeenth century. Among them were some highly articulate and gifted individuals who helped nurture a strong tradition of liberal democracy in South Africa. Their arrival led to the establishment of democratic organisations, leading to fully responsible government in 1872. They brought with them the jury system and law and order administered by local magistrates. Grass-roots democracy was established through municipal councils. Respected authors, artists and poets – men of conscience – fostered a humanitarian tradition.

Among them was Thomas Pringle, born in Scotland and educated in Edinburgh, who led a small party of Scottish settlers among the 1820 emigrants from Britain. He and a Scottish friend, John Fairbairn, edited the first independent newspaper, the *South African Commercial Advertiser* started in 1824 by another champion of press freedom in the colony, Robert Greig. Pringle chose to cease publication rather than bow to attempts by the governor Lord Somerset to stifle reports critical of his administration.

Outside of Cape Town the *Grahamstown Journal* appeared in 1831, and the *Natal Witness* in 1846, followed six years later by the *Natal Mercury*. The newspapers generally started from humble beginnings. Thomas Grocott, a printer by trade, emigrated to South Africa from Liverpool. On his arrival he worked in a print shop in Grahamstown. A few months later the printing works went into liquidation, so in 1869 Grocott established his own printing company. The following year he published *Grocott's Free Paper* later renamed *Grocott's Penny Mail*. Today, as *Grocott's Mail* it is still published in Grahamstown by the Grocott family's printing and stationery company.

The arts and sporting life flourished. Cricket and rugby appeared, the latter adopted as his national game by the Afrikaner. On the whole the settler society reflected a broad span of views and outlook, from those who became as hostile to the natives as some of their Dutch counterparts, to others who were regarded as dangerous radicals and black sympathisers by their fellow-British.

Among the latter were the missionaries sent out by the Glasgow and London missionary societies, who became a thorn in the side of more conservative British settlers through the publicity they gave to the plight of the Khoi and Xhosas. These men – John Philip, Bishop Colenso and John Mackenzie among others – took up the cause of the blacks with determination, thereby establishing another tradition continued to this day by some English-speakers. Guy Butler, Honorary Research Fellow at Rhodes University in Grahamstown, says: 'Out of this blending of frontiersmen and missionaries emerged some of the very best South Africans.' Typical was Dr James Rose-Innes, a Scottish educationalist, who despite lack of funds laid the foundations of African education in the Cape.

A third pocket of British settlement in Natal in the 1850s was the result of an emigration scheme organised in the north of England. Whereas in the Cape the British protected the limited voting franchise of the blacks, in Natal there was an altogether more stringent view of race relations. This was perhaps because in Natal the settlers were surrounded by far larger numbers of black people than in the Cape. The Zulu heartland was right on their doorstep. Until a few years ago some old-timers in Natal could still remember 'pulling the spear out of great-grandad's back'. In the Cape, by contrast, the presence of a large coloured population made the black/white divide less stark. Moreover the Cape blacks were wooed as allies by the English, who were outnumbered by the Afrikaners. At the National Convention in 1908 the prime minister of Natal urged a complete electoral colour bar throughout the country, declaring: 'The history of the world proved that the black man was incapable of civilisation.'

Already then the twin strands of English thinking in South Africa had been established: those who broadly shared the Afrikaners' fears about black encroachment and black power; others who tried to thwart the ascendancy of racial politics by struggling for liberal democratic values. The latter were a civilising influence and their voices echo today in the many civil rights organisations struggling against apartheid.

Many British were among the foreigners – the *uitlanders* – who descended on the northern Cape in the diamond rush of the 1870s, and on the Transvaal after 1886 in search of gold. These included engineers, miners, lawyers and financiers, all those required to service the booming mining industry. They were responsible for introducing capitalism on the grand scale to South Africa. The new British immigrants had little in common with the previous arrivals. These were acquisitive, urban spirits worlds apart from the earlier agricultural pioneers. There was little evidence of any missionary commitment. Indeed British officials and mining companies helped impose laws on black migrant workers which later formed the basis of the Nationalists' legislation severely restricting the movements of black urban dwellers. Cecil Rhodes pioneered the system of mining compounds (in which black mineworkers are housed), while the idea of the industrial colour bar was hatched when whites insisted that blacks should not be allowed to stake out claims at the mine diggings.

The liberal tradition was reasserted by another wave of immigrants from Europe – the Jews. Fleeing pogroms in Russia, eastern Europe and the Baltic states, they began arriving in South Africa towards the end of the nineteenth century, an exodus which was reinforced during Hitler's time. Many joined the aggressive financial and mining worlds of Johannesburg. Some Jewish entrepreneurs steadfastly opposed racial discrimination. A large number of Jews were disturbed at having left behind one system of persecution only to find themselves witnessing another. Samuel and Frieda Gavronsky, the parents of Helen Suzman, were among early Jewish immigrants from Lithuania. The Jews, through their own experiences in Europe, felt deeply about the inhumanity visited upon the blacks of South Africa. Many were already enlightened when they arrived; the more they got to know South Africa, the more articulate they became in representing the blacks' case. The Jews became a radical force out of all proportion to their numbers. The most radical among them – men like Joe Slovo, the former ANC military chief – joined the South African Communist Party, once described as an 'east European old-boys club'.

The English-speaking South Africans never lost touch with Britain or the rest of Europe because their community was continually regenerated by new waves of immigrants. According to Guy Butler: 'In almost every family there is a grandparent born in England or Europe. The life of Europe is present in every English-speaking family. That is not the case with most Afrikaners.' Until the 1940s most of the senior clergy, newspaper editors and university professors were English-speaking. In *English-Speaking South Africa Today* David Welsh,

Professor of Political Science at Cape Town University, has written:

> The tie with Britain also meant a continuing restraint and revitalisation of values. Fresh waves of immigrants, 'home' news carried in the local press, English books and magazines . . . ensured that the South African English did not fall out of the cultural orbit. . . . The importance of this tie is that it forced the South African English to remain part of the international cultural community.

Unlike the Afrikaners with their Great Trek, there was no central myth binding English-speakers together. The Afrikaners came to consider themselves a 'nation'; not so the English, who were divided by the schisms characteristic of their mother country – birth, class, geography and religion. Emotions ran high on only a few occasions: during the two world wars when South African support for Britain was challenged by some Afrikaners; in the 'flag crisis' of 1926–7 when Afrikaner Nationalists outraged English-speakers by demanding a national flag without the Union Jack, the two sides eventually agreeing on a compromise emblem; and when South Africa withdrew from the Commonwealth in 1961. But the survival of the English was never under particular threat, so there was no issue around which they needed to rally as a people.

But there was one common denominator. Says Guy Butler: 'What held the English together was the expansive consciousness of Victorian England – its mystique and its overriding confidence, symbolised by Cecil Rhodes' pledge to expand the British empire throughout Africa "from the Cape to Cairo".' The English united around the Victorian principles of mercantilism and self-improvement. For the English, the glamour of empire-building took the place of a Great Trek.

But imperialism came to be discredited, first by the abortive Jameson Raid and then by the Boer War which followed. Colonial expansion lost its glitter. Many English-speakers had opposed the war, among them J. X. Merriman, a Cape liberal who in 1910 narrowly failed to become the first prime minister after Union. The Afrikaners used the war as a powerful weapon to attack the English. Many of the poorer English-speakers took sides with their Afrikaner counterparts against the giant mining companies financed by Anglo-Jewish capital. In the Rand Rebellion of 1922, English-speakers and Afrikaners fought side by side. White trade unions were dominated by communists and labour leaders who had emigrated from Britain or from the Jewish *stetels* (settlements) of eastern Europe.

Many English-speakers were overwhelmed by the tide of Afrikaner nationalism that gathered momentum from the 1920s onwards. By 1934, when the National Party (committed to Afrikaner domination) fused with the South Africa Party (favouring Afrikaner/English rapprochement), many English had thrown in their lot with the Afrikaners. In 1936 a majority of English-speaking MPs went along with the decision to deprive blacks of their qualified franchise on the common voters' roll, a right which had been steadfastly defended by British interests in the previous century and the repeal of which marked a sad defeat for the Cape liberal tradition.

The lean times in Britain after the Second World War brought another influx of immigrants to South Africa. These were mostly tradesmen, skilled workers, small businessmen and the like, who felt they had no future in class-ridden Britain. They were followed, throughout the 1960s and 1970s, by others who saw prospects for the 'good life' in South Africa.

They were indeed good times for the newly-arrived British. The economy was booming and there was good money to be earned; the climate was a definite improvement; many had swimming pools in their gardens. Husband and wife would both go out to work so as to afford a black maid. Most were good, honest working folk seeking to better themselves. Most had little concern about human rights; some were downright racist. After all, they were escaping a Britain experiencing its own 'black problem' with the arrival of large numbers of West Indians and others from the new Commonwealth. There were race riots in Notting Hill and other inner city areas. The right-wing Conservative MP Enoch Powell warned of 'rivers of blood' if immigration were not checked. South Africa was depicted as a country where the white man knew how to keep the black man in his place.

Thousands were so enamoured of the new life that they took up 'permanent residence' in South Africa, under which they were taxed but not granted the right to vote. Most did not surrender their British nationality for South African citizenship. After all, South Africa did have a potentially explosive race problem; they needed a bolthole. The crises accompanying the Sharpeville massacre in 1960 and the black unrest of 1976 saw British consulates in South Africa jammed with expatriates checking that their passports were still valid. But they weathered the storms and the passports were put back in the drawer. The South African economy had survived the political turmoil; the good life continued.

By 1980, when the price of gold (South Africa's major foreign-exchange earner) hit $850 an ounce, the country was riding high. International confidence in South Africa had returned. The black townships were quiet. Few people paid attention to the pattern of cyclical black violence which was becoming apparent – that in boom times black unrest diminished only to explode when the subsequent slow-down came along. The tide of liquidity after 1980 was squandered. Recession took over, in part stimulating the unrest which broke out in 1984. Financial disinvestment and economic sanctions further weakened the economy. Some British immigrants packed their bags and returned home but found that the world had passed them by in the two or three decades since they had left. The old country was changing. Mrs Thatcher's Britain was thriving, at least for some. Britain had become a harder, more competitive society; it was the survival of the fittest. British exiles in South Africa suddenly realised that their capital would be near worthless in Britain, such had been the depreciation in the value of the rand.

The post-war British exodus to South Africa coincided with a flood of white refugees from Rhodesia, later independent Zimbabwe. If the views of the British immigrants on racial matters were in part formed by the West Indian problem, those of the Rhodesian exiles came from their experience of blacks slowly taking over their own country, despite a long bush war in which they had fought tooth and nail to maintain white minority rule. Relocated in South Africa, they were determined that their new home should not go the same way. They belonged to the 'give them an inch and they'll take a mile' school of thought regarding blacks. These were people who had left one insular white society for another. If anything, their views were narrower than those of many white South Africans. They became known as the 'when we's', because their every other sentence began with: 'When we were in Rhodesia . . .'. There was a standard joke: 'What's the difference between a jumbo jet and white Rhodesian? Answer: the jumbo jet stops whining at Johannesburg airport.' Along with fugitives from Britain's other former African colonies (Kenya and Northern Rhodesia), the 'Rhodies' formed influential pockets wherever they settled. Says David Welsh: 'Many of them were unreconstructed racists, spreading a racist poison.'

The Rhodesians were not the only refugees from African decolonisation. South Africa's Portuguese community of 6–700,000 includes large numbers who fled Mozambique in the mid-1970s as the Marxist FRELIMO government took over. Like the smaller groups of Hungarian and Polish exiles, they were determined to withstand perceived communist encroachment. Other European circles, especially German and Italian businessmen, were equally conservative. Nearly all these various groups of exiles became staunch supporters of the National Party.

After 1948 the National Party hit on a winning formula for retaining power. The party leaders realised that by appealing to both Afrikaner loyalties and the fears of all whites about *swart gevaar*, they could keep any English-speaking liberal party at bay. Quite simply, many English came to regard an alliance with the Afrikaners as preferable to one with the blacks. Consequently, increasing numbers have thrown in their lot with the National Party, the very symbol of the Afrikaner force which sidelined them.

The tight control of television has also helped attract English-speakers to the Nationalists. They do not see the police opening fire on blacks, they do not see the appalling consequences of forced removals, they have little inkling as to why their country is unacceptable on the world stage. The 'good news bearers', who day in and day out convey the view that South Africa's problems are largely due to foreign meddling, have been hugely successful in winning some English-speaking support for the National Party. All that thousands of English-speakers want from South Africa is prosperity, good weather and security. They support reform, cautious reform, if that means stability. Concern to liberalise apartheid is prompted largely by self-interest. Many English-speakers have little interest in the political future of blacks, beyond paying lip-service to their cause.

How many whites in the plush English suburbs of northern Johannesburg have been into Alexandra township, on their very doorstep, or into Soweto where most of the city's black population live? How many have sought to break through the walls of apartheid by inviting blacks to their homes? How many really know what life is like for millions of black South Africans? For many affluent, apolitical English-speakers, the tennis match, the boutiques, jogging and the beauty parlour are their points of reference. South Africa's political turmoil is pushed to the back of their minds. They return from trips to Europe or America damning the foreign media for painting a 'false picture' of South Africa. At the height of the township revolt, the complaint was often heard that in 'most of the country life carries on normally and we don't see that on the world's television screens'. Of course they didn't, because the vast majority of the population do not live in the secluded, segregated white suburbs which are the frontiers of English-speaking South Africa, but in the teeming, violent black townships where life was far from normal.

But there are exceptions in the English camp, the heirs of those early missionaries and philanthropists who had planted the seed of liberalism in South Africa. The English-speaking community produced many outstanding individuals who placed at risk their careers, often their freedom and on occasions their lives in defending human rights against the tide of repression. Others worked away quietly at bringing the races together: the multiracial private schools where black and white pupils learn and live together; the groups of white volunteers who undertake the exhausting journeys into the depths of the homelands to help suffering blacks or who assist township blacks; the campaigners who risk arrest in demonstrating against harsh race laws. These are an important minority who have made a significant contribution towards upholding liberal values in an increasingly illiberal society.

Many others gave up in the face of the Nationalist takeover. Outnumbered by Afrikaners, the English-speakers concluded that their room to influence government policy was extremely limited. Consequently the Nationalists remained unchallenged in any substantial sense for forty years. But as the party marked its four decades in office, there emerged, for the first time, an alignment of political forces with the potential to inflict serious damage on a demoralised National Party. The Conservative Party was strident on the right; to the left was the PFP, Denis Worrall's Independents and Wynand Malan's National Democratic Movement. The Nationalists stood to be pulled in both directions. Could the centre hold? The English-speakers ensured it did. When the 1987 general election came round the National Party had succeeded in replacing those Afrikaners who had defected to the right with English-speakers supposedly from the left. One of the new English-speaking lights of the National Party is Sheila Camerer, a lawyer who became MP for Rosettenville, south of Johannesburg, in 1985. Writing in the *Financial Mail*, Ms Camerer explained that English-speakers were heading for the National Party because they wanted to encourage the government in its reform programme. They recognised and supported Botha's efforts to South Africanise the party and create a broadly-based South Africanism. English-speakers, she said, wanted to be part of the political decision-making process again. By 'South Africanism', Ms Camerer was not referring to a broad, non-racialism but rather to 'white nationalism', which is slowly replacing Afrikaner nationalism.

English-speakers who go along with this do so even though the National Party has rarely bestowed senior government positions on non-Afrikaners. English cabinet ministers have been few. There is no reason to believe that the National Party will not continue to be Afrikaner-dominated in its highest decision-making councils. Moreover, some English-speakers have allowed themselves to be persuaded that the National Party is now like the old United Party (UP) of Smuts which once represented their interests. David Graaff, son of the former UP leader Sir de Villiers Graaff, is now a Nationalist MP, evidence enough for some English-speakers that the National Party has moved leftwards. The rise of the right wing has helped make the Nationalists look a good deal more liberal than they really are.

In the 1987 election English-speakers were faced with a clear choice. Were South Africa's problems a result of apartheid? Or were they to do with the security threat posed by those struggling to overthrow it? It was the latter, they concluded; English-speakers rallied behind the National Party and helped return it to power, confident that it would crack down on black radicals while granting apartheid reforms at a very restrained pace. The vote for the Progressive Federal Party, the traditional haven of English support, collapsed. Until then 20 to 30 per cent of English South Africans had supported the Nationalists, prompted by world hostility towards South Africa, sanctions, the collapse of white Rhodesia and the frequent bouts of internal black protest. By 1987 political analysts estimated that the figure had risen to 40 to 45 per cent.

English support for the Nationalists began growing at the time of a referendum in 1983 on the power-sharing constitution, when large numbers of English-speakers deserted the PFP because it was opposed to the new deal. They opted instead for the National Party, convinced that granting limited power to mixed-race and Indian people was a 'step in the right direction'. Reform with security was what was on offer from the National Party. David Welsh of Cape Town University says: 'The referendum was an important milestone. For many English-speakers the political ice was broken. For them, the Nationalists were no longer the party you never voted for.'

A measure of how well the National Party has succeeded in co-opting the English is the silence of many of them during the government's intensifying assault on civil liberties. Again there have been exceptions: liberal politicians, activists, lawyers and journalists, who battled against the creeping eradication of basic freedoms that accompanied Botha's policies. Regulations under the state of emergency were repeatedly challenged in the courts and sometimes overturned by English-speaking lawyers who also represented several leading anti-apartheid figures accused of treason for their opposition activities. Detainees' support groups campaigned against formidable odds on behalf of those held without trial, not allowing them to be forgotten behind the wall of silence imposed by the emergency. Newspapers fought to sustain a liberal debate even though some were closed down for weeks for doing so.

But other English-speakers seemed unaware or unconcerned that human rights once shed are very difficult to replace; that the civil liberties discarded under a white government might not be resurrected by a black administration.

Despite his very English name, Clive Derby-Lewis has thrown in his lot with the Afrikaner to such an extent that his liberal opponents regard him as more right wing than the most extreme Afrikaners. Derby-Lewis is a member of parliament for the Conservative Party and represents a breed of English-speaker who became convinced that rigid apartheid was the country's only answer and who became terrified that under Botha black majority rule would become inevitable. Increasingly the right wing targeted English-speakers for support.

Derby-Lewis admits to being a dyed-in-the-wool nationalist. In about 1978, he says, he 'began getting edgy about what was going on'. He was concerned about creeping integration in some of the nation's schools. 'Non-white children were starting to attend private white schools and this appeared to be condoned by the government.' He stayed on in the National Party, believing it could be reformed from within, but now admits that he underestimated P. W. Botha.

'The Afrikaner is respectful towards and fearful of his leaders,' says Derby-Lewis, 'and P. W. Botha knew it. He intimidated them and since then the whole history of the National Party has been to intimidate whites into voting for it.'

The CP's concentration on capturing the English vote could be crucial for the future shape of white politics in South Africa if Afrikanerdom remains split between the Nationalists and the CP. Derby-Lewis is convinced that the Conservative Party will be the first political movement in South Africa to succeed in bridging the 'small differences' between the English and the Afrikaners. Derby-Lewis, whose family has been in South Africa since 1792, resists the labels 'Afrikaans-speaking South Africans' and 'English-speaking South Africans'. 'Let no one question my Afrikanerness,' he says.

Derby-Lewis sees the whites of South Africa – English and Afrikaners – as one nation divided into two groups by language, although such a distinction, he says, fails to take account of where family allegiances have become blurred. For example, he says, there is a South African clan of MacDonalds who cannot speak a word of English and who are Afrikaners through and through. Similarly, he argues, there are quite a few van der Merwes (a common Afrikaner name) who cannot speak Afrikaans.

If labels have to be used, he prefers the distinction of 'Boer Afrikaners' (descendants of the original Dutch and French immigrants) and 'Settler Afrikaners', those whose families arrived with the 1820 settlers from Britain. Such a distinction, of course, raises some interesting questions. How can Derby-Lewis speak of a common South Africanism among whites given the history of the Great Trek when the Boers escaped British rule, the bitter struggle between the British and the Afrikaners during the Boer war, and the near-eclipse of the English-speaker this century when his political interests were overwhelmed by Afrikaner nationalism?

The right-wing MP has little problem in explaining these apparent anomalies. Under British administration of the Cape, relations between the British and the Afrikaners were generally good, he says. Indeed the Boer *trekkers* were presented with a Bible by English settlers before they departed. It was rule from Britain they were escaping, says Derby-Lewis, adding that over a dozen settlers fought alongside the Boers against the Zulus at the Battle of Blood River. As for the Boer War, he is convinced that the struggle has been wrongly portrayed. He sees international financiers as the root of the conflict. He accuses them of forcing Britain into the conflict and ensuring that other European nations afforded little or no financial help to the embattled Boer nation. Why? To secure South Africa's vast mineral resources for themselves. A sense of common purpose was forged between English and Afrikaners during the Second World War, says Derby-Lewis, with many Afrikaners volunteering to fight for the British Empire. But wasn't the subsequent National Party election victory in 1948 a thundering rallying-call on the part of Afrikanerdom, with the English taking a back seat? Derby-Lewis says it was not quite as simple as that. English-speaking soldiers arriving home from the war turned against the United Party under Smuts because of the poor treatment they received upon their return. 'So it was not exclusively Afrikaner nationalism that defeated Smuts,' he says.

As for the English-speakers who have emigrated to South Africa in the post-war years, and the refugees from white Rhodesia and Portugal's colonies, do they have a place in a common white nation? Do they have a home in a country whose political life has been dominated by the pursuit of Afrikaner nationalism? Can they be considered 'Settler Afrikaners'? Derby-Lewis believes so. Many Rhodesians who came to South Africa upon the independence of their country were not of British origin, he says, but of Afrikaner stock – a somewhat dubious contention:

'The British Rhodesians either returned to the home country or went to Australia. For them, coming to South Africa was like jumping out of the frying pan into the fire. Whether you are talking about the Rhodesians or the Portuguese or the post-war British immigrants, they are all part of the nation-building which is taking place in white South Africa. They have the same western origins in the same way that the African peoples are culturally similar.'

But surely there must be doubts about such people's commitment to South Africa, given that many of them have European passports tucked inside their jackets ready for a white exodus. Derby-Lewis contends that such lack of commitment might be the case for today's generation of parents but not for their children. 'Their parents may be reluctant citizens of South Africa, but not their children.'

On that he is correct. Young whites – Afrikaners and English – who fight side by side in the army are now mixing more freely socially. John Hammond, in his twenties, son of an English immigrant and living in a nominally liberal northern suburb, married an Afrikaner girl from 'the other side of the track', from one of the almost exclusively Afrikaner districts. Her four-year-old daughter from a previous marriage could not speak a word of English. At the wedding half the speeches were in English and half in Afrikaans.

It is estimated that 25 per cent of all white marriages are now between Afrikaners and English. Among Afrikaners *ondertrouery* (intermarriage) no longer carries the stigma it did in the 1930s and 1940s.

Because English-speakers generally chose to pursue business interests over politics, the Afrikaners won by default. Helen Suzman says: 'The English-speakers failed to realise that government was the biggest business of all and they stood by as the civil service was taken over by the Afrikaner establishment.' As a body English-speakers exerted little or no influence on power politics in South Africa after 1948. Lacking their own effective political base and comprising only 40 per cent of the white population, the English-speakers faced an impossible task in trying to halt the advance of Afrikaner supremacy. Furthermore, under electoral law, the government was permitted to weight the distribution of parliamentary seats in favour of the predominantly Afrikaner rural areas to the detriment of the mainly English-speaking towns and cities.

Although the National Party attracted thousands of English voters, the most politically aware among them continued to give the party a wide berth. Says Guy Butler of Rhodes University:

'The Afrikaners have said to the people of South Africa "The most important thing about you is your race." They have elevated a biological accident to the main plank of their policy. The Nationalists will never really win the support of the most articulate English-speakers because it is abundantly clear to such people that the blacks will not settle for it. For my part, I am quite prepared to accept a federal structure to accommodate differences. But you can have a successful federation only providing that there is a constitution which looks after basic questions like the sharing of economic resources, finance, transport, foreign policy, etc.'

Throughout the first forty years of National Party rule, enlightened English-speakers sought their political home in a succession of liberal parties. The United Party under Smuts failed because it did not address the racial question before the latter became too big to grapple with. Immediately after the Second World War – a struggle for democracy against tyranny – the feeling prevailed in South Africa that the victory of liberal democracy was inevitable, that the post-war period would see blacks being granted a political voice. When that failed to happen under the Nationalists, liberals created their own parties.

The Liberal Party made an important attempt at breaking through racial barriers in the 1950s and 1960s. The party's early membership was largely white but the number of blacks increased, particularly in Natal and the Transvaal. The Cape liberal tradition strengthened the party, which favoured a return to the pre-1910 Cape franchise, under which the vote would be granted to blacks who had reached Standard Six education (aged thirteen) with an economic qualification as well. By 1960 the party came out unequivocally in favour of universal franchise.

The Liberal Party, led for a time by the late Alan Paton, author of the novel *Cry, the Beloved Country*, fought a brave but forlorn struggle against the resettlement and forced removals of black people. In 1962 and 1963, most of its members involved in work across the colour line were banned, including its leader Peter Brown. One of those affected, John Harris, a Johannesburg teacher, carried a bomb into Johannesburg railway station. His plans to issue a warning never materialised, and one person was killed and several injured. Harris was hanged. The bombing was a damaging blow to the Liberal Party, whose members had not been party to Harris's action. In 1968 the government passed the Prohibition of Political Interference Act which banned multiracial parties. The Liberal Party dissolved itself. Says Peter Brown: 'To have abided by that law, would have meant abandoning the whole principle of a non-racial party.' The Liberal Party never won or looked like winning a parliamentary seat.

Within parliament, the Progressive Federal Party picked up some of the remnants of the old United Party, though many former UP supporters backed the Nationalists while a few ended up in the Conservative Party. The PFP's importance has been twofold. Its call for universal franchise in a federal system has offered a blueprint for a non-racial South Africa which has the potential to attract whites and blacks to a compromise formula. The attraction of the federal option is that it fudges the racial dividing lines. Secondly, the PFP became the main vehicle for challenging the government's record on civil liberties. In tabling parliamentary questions to ministers, PFP members placed on record alleged transgressions of human rights and civil liberties arising from the treatment of detainees, forced removals, the death penalty, conditions in the homelands, the freedom of the press and information, etc. The roots of the PFP could be found in the tradition of liberal opposition that goes all the way back to those early missionaries and Cape liberals who, though opposed by far greater numbers, left for society a legacy of decent values.

The cause of the Progressive Federal Party suffered because of the lack of interest in politics of large numbers of English-speakers. Potential supporters among young people started dwindling as more of them left the country, either because they could no longer uphold liberal values in today's South Africa or, at the other end of the spectrum, because they did not want to live under the black government which they feared was coming. To the left of the PFP there were radical white youngsters who eschewed everything the party stood for, aligning themselves instead with the socialist cause, to such an extent that even veteran liberal Helen Suzman was prevented by student pressure from speaking on the campus of Witwatersrand University during the 1987 general election for whites.

Outside the parliamentary mainstream, liberalism has survived at many levels.

If the missionaries were an important voice of dissent in the early settlements, as they championed blacks against the government, so today the clerics of the English churches are in the vanguard of the struggle against apartheid. Just as the early missionaries were branded dangerous radicals, so today's churchmen are accused by the government of furthering the aims of violent organisations. Under the umbrella of the South African Council of Churches, the English churches firmly believe that following Christ's calling requires them to be vociferous in demanding justice for all the people of South Africa. There has been a long history of church/state confrontation over how far the legitimate role of the priest extends.

An early challenge was mounted by Father Trevor Huddleston after the Group Areas Act led to the mass expulsion of blacks from long-established settlement areas. One such was Johannesburg's black suburb of Sophiatown, renamed Triomf (Triumph) by the Afrikaners after the blacks had been expelled to make way for a white area. Father Huddleston, who later led the Anti-Apartheid Movement in London, was asked by a magistrate: 'Is it the function of a priest to defy the government?' Huddleston's immediate reply was: 'Is it the function of a priest to remain silent in the face of injustice?'

Ambrose Reeves, appointed Anglican Bishop of Johannesburg in the year the Nationalists came to power, closed all church schools under his jurisdiction rather than allow them to be taken over by the state and subjected to the racially weighted 'bantu education' system of the Native Affairs Minister, Hendrik Verwoerd. In the wake of the Sharpeville massacre, Reeves was in the forefront of anti-government demonstrations. Fearing his imminent arrest, he slipped out of South Africa and surfaced in Swaziland, before making his way to England. He later returned to his country but was promptly deported.

Roman Catholic priest Father Cosmas Desmond was banned and placed under house arrest following the publication of his book *The Discarded People*, about settled black communities which were being uprooted from their ancestral lands and dumped in resettlement camps. Colin Winter, Anglican Bishop of Damaraland, was expelled from Namibia after frequent clashes with the government. The Anglican Dean of Johannesburg, Aubie Gonville ffrench-Beytagh, was subjected to security police surveillance leading to charges of terrorism. A five-year jail sentence was overturned on appeal.

More recently the head of the Anglican church, Archbishop Desmond Tutu of Cape Town, has emerged as the most forthright exponent of the priest as champion of the oppressed. His calls for economic sanctions against South Africa have angered many white members of his church, who consider that he is venturing beyond his calling by taking 'political stands'. Tutu's reply is that his appeals for justice are firmly rooted in the Bible.

The running confrontation between church and government reached one of its frequent crescendos during early 1988 when the government imposed sweeping restrictions on anti-apartheid movements. Tutu and other churchmen marched on parliament and were arrested after some were hosed down with water cannon. Anglican bishops from throughout southern Africa converged on Johannesburg to express their solidarity with Tutu, a gathering which prompted near-hysteria in government circles, as reflected in a commentary on state-controlled radio which spoke of the 'politicisation of the Anglican church'. Echoing the attacks on the early missionaries, the commentary declared that: 'The confrontation . . . is not between the state and the church but between the state and certain individual church leaders whose intent it is to make South Africa ungovernable.' The radio referred to 'certain political clergymen' adopting a 'high political profile'.

One Sunday morning – when the anti-church campaign was at its height – the South African Broadcasting Corporation transmitted a service from St Columba's Presbyterian church in Parkview, Johannesburg. They clearly had not vetted the minister's sermon.

The Reverend Alan Maker told his congregation and the nation at large: 'Anyone who says that politics and religion don't mix has something wrong with their politics.'

The English universities (Witwatersrand, Cape Town, Rhodes and Natal) have proved another oasis of liberal thinking in post-1948 South Africa. Inspired by the fine tradition of Scottish universities passed on by Scottish missionaries, the English-medium campuses have fought vigorously to defend their freedom from government interference. Prior to the Nationalist government, the universities had established themselves as centres of free thought and expression, independent of government. They are now fighting to preserve that independence.

Their long struggle has been directed against the government's attempt to restrict both the racial mix of their students and the views that they are allowed to express. Since their inception the English universities pursued a non-racial policy on student admissions, even though few blacks met the entry requirements or had sufficient funds to finance their courses. In 1959 the government banned the universities from admitting black students, who were consigned to inferior and racially-segregated campuses elsewhere. Notwithstanding the new rules, the government continued to invite applications from blacks. Successful applicants then had to apply for a special government permit to take up the places. These were granted sparingly and only if the applicant could not find a place at one of the 'bush colleges' as the black universities were called. The law was changed in 1983 to abolish the permit system. Instead, the government could limit black student entry, although in practice it has rarely invoked this right. The number of black students on English-speaking campuses is still comparatively small, though growing; up from 7.2 per cent in 1986 to 9 per cent in 1987. Over the same year the number of coloured and Indian students at English universities also increased.

At the height of the unrest in the mid-1980s, political feelings were running as high on the English campuses as they were in the townships. The government moved quickly to curtail student opposition; heavily armed police frequently broke up protest meetings. New regulations required English-speaking universities to prevent unlawful gatherings and rein in the kind of spirited undergraduate protest common to most universities in the West. At Witwatersrand University, Professor Phillip Tobias declared before a gathering of hundreds of staff and students on 28 October 1987 that the

'conditions constitute the most serious assault on university autonomy, as well as on freedom of speech, freedom of assembly, freedom of thought and freedom of the academy. These principles, so dear to our university, are being butchered to make a Roman holiday for the apostles of intolerance and tyranny.'

Elsewhere the liberal English have inspired independent thinking and set out alternative agendas for the future. English-speakers were among those behind the kwaZulu/Natal Indaba power-sharing plan. There are a range of informal think-tanks. In 1987 Clem Sunter of the Anglo American Corporation produced an influential study in 'futurology' entitled 'The World and South Africa in the 1990s' which forecast 'high road' and 'low road' scenarios for the country: the former a transition into a stable democracy, the latter a descent into a political and economic wasteland. In 1986 Afrikaner author Leon Louw and an English-speaker Frances Kendall published a book entitled *The Solution*, an imaginative constitutional plan for South Africa foreseeing the country's division into a multitude of cantons accommodating dozens of individual groups. Year in and year out the respected South African Institute of Race Relations monitors the swings and roundabouts of apartheid as it affects the lives of the country's citizens. Such contributions by English-speakers help sustain a flourishing intellectual climate outside the National Party.

Increasingly, the debate among liberals is becoming more rigorous. Some believe it is no longer enough to say 'apartheid is evil' and engage in protest politics. Similarly, given the unlikelihood of imminent revolution or a sudden switch to a non-racial society, certain liberals have concluded that they cannot spend time postulating visions of a 'post-apartheid South Africa'. Instead they are concentrating on a strategy for moving South Africa forward. The question of parliamentary or extra-parliamentary opposition to the government is central to this debate.

In the law courts, English-speakers have been an important watchdog in the drive to uphold the rule of law amid the panoply of apartheid and security legislation. South Africa's modified Roman Dutch law was brought to the country from Britain. It was not until the 1930s that the first Supreme Court judgement was handed down in Afrikaans. Under the Nationalists, Afrikaner judges, presiding over a non-jury system, have generally taken the government's view on the limits of protest and the measures required to defend the state. In a long-running treason trial, the judge was revealed as a member of the Broederbond but continued to hear the case; his assessor had to remove himself from the trial when it became known that he had signed a petition in support of the anti-apartheid United Democratic Front. Some of the judgements handed down in political trials set wide interpretations on what comprises treason or terrorism.

On the whole, the most talented legal figures in South Africa do not sit on the bench. English-speaking advocates, generally more liberal, have been overlooked in appointments to the highest courts. Aside from the fact that they can earn more at the bar, English lawyers have little desire to sit on the bench enforcing security laws which many find abhorrent; neither do they want to be responsible for sending men and women to the gallows. The result is that leading English-speaking lawyers have made their names defending anti-apartheid activists in some of the major political trials of the past thirty years – men like Arthur Chaskalson, George Bizos and, most prominently, Sydney Kentridge, who represented the Biko family at the inquest into the death of the Black Consciousness leader Steve Biko.

An important exception to Afrikaner domination of the bench is Chief Justice Michael Corbett, who by universal consent is an unrivalled jurist. He is the first non-Afrikaner to fill the position for many years and his appointment in 1988 could not have been withheld other than on political grounds. His appointment was delayed by two years, however, as the government in an unprecedented move extended the term of his Afrikaner predecessor beyond normal retirement age. Given the sweeping security laws, it is uncertain whether Corbett can redress the balance away from the state in favour of the individual. However, in one of his first judgements, he ruled that residents of Soweto taking part in an anti-apartheid rent boycott had been charged rent illegally in the first place.

For those without the protection of the courts, a network of civil rights movements has sprung up, led in the main by the English. Among the longest established is the Black Sash women's movement, its name derived from the black ribbons worn by protesters in 1956 when they mourned what they saw as the death of the constitution when coloureds' voting rights were abolished. From its offices around the country Black Sash has assisted hundreds of thousands of people whose lives have been made a misery by apartheid: those without the right papers, those forcibly removed from their homes, squatters, parents whose children are missing. At the height of the violence in the eastern Cape, PFP provincial councillor and Black Sash worker Molly Blackburn (later killed in a car accident) became a Florence Nightingale figure, the only civilian white who could gain entry to the townships as she tried to help the wounded and the families of people arrested or missing.

As political protest has grown, so a new generation of civil rights groups has emerged to monitor the fate of the thousands detained without trial under the state of emergency. The most prominent of these organisations is the Detainees' Parents' Support Committee (DPSC) headed by an English-speaking couple, Audrey and Max Coleman. Courting tough action by the security authorities, the Colemans and the DPSC have challenged government figures on the numbers detained, particularly those for young people, and have catalogued allegations of detainees mistreated or tortured. The government accuses them of blackening the name of the South African police and the country's law and order authorities. The DPSC was placed under severe restriction orders by the government.

The spirit of opposition has been reflected in a long history of protest writing by English authors.

Olive Schreiner, a missionary's daughter, published *The Story of an African Farm* and *Thoughts on South Africa* towards the end of the last century, starting a line of books on South Africa's racial problems by English-speaking authors. William Plomer published *Turbot Wolfe* in 1923, one of the first South African novels to deal with the issue of miscegenation. The literary career of Nadine Gordimer began almost at the same time that the Nationalists came to power, and her writings have tracked the imposition of apartheid through the lives of ordinary South Africans of all races. Several of her works, including *The Late Bourgeois World* and *Burger's Daughter*, were banned. But it was *Cry, the Beloved Country* by Alan Paton, published in 1948, that first alerted the world in literary form to South Africa's growing racial tensions. Dissident Afrikaner authors too have chosen the English language as their medium. Laurens van der Post's *Venture to the Interior* and *The Lost World of the Kalahari* tell of the author's journey in search of man's origins. Other works tackle racial issues. In similar vein, several of André Brink's novels are in both English and Afrikaans.

The English-language press has faced the toughest battle to maintain its freedom. The Nationalists have always regarded the English press with suspicion, and the plethora of laws circumscribing the media keeps newspaper lawyers busy round the clock. Despite these constraints, the main anti-government newspapers remain highly critical of government policy.

Ken Owen, controversial editor of *Business Day*, has refused to be swept along by easy rhetoric and political slogans. His columns have lambasted those who betray liberal democratic values. He has waged a strong campaign against Witwatersrand University over alleged Marxist leanings in some of its teaching. He has taxed churchmen who support the concept of the 'just war', writing that: 'It is easy to see where this argument leads. When . . . anybody judged by a kangaroo court to be a sell-out is killed, it is not violence but liberation. Killing ceases to be an absolute sin; its legitimacy depends on one's perception of the struggle, and life itself becomes conditional.' Owen firmly believes the Progressive Federal Party should stick to its liberal fundamentals and not flirt with those in the left-wing, extraparliamentary opposition espousing revolutionary or socialist doctrines. Owen is a maverick in South African journalism. Whether one agrees with his views or not, his is a refreshing voice at a time when conformity is being demanded increasingly from both sides of the political and racial divide.

Newspapers like *Weekly Mail* and *New Nation* – the 'alternative media' – have at times been banned for straying outside officially sanctioned parameters of debate. Government ministers claim that South Africa still has the freest press in Africa. But is that any yardstick?

Has there been a common strand embracing all these disparate groups? In the same way that Victorian England fashioned earlier settlers, so Britain and its role in the world after the Second World War have strongly influenced English ideas in South Africa. The message which has come through loud and clear is that in an age of liberation struggles and decolonisation there is no place for racism. As David Welsh of Cape Town University writes:

The South African English faced peculiar dilemmas. They were impotent in the face of a government that was steadily cutting the ties with Britain. Many did not like what Britain was doing in Africa, especially in Kenya and Southern Rhodesia. The world-wide, English-speaking community, as represented by the Commonwealth, was becoming an effectively multi-racial association in which racial discrimination was anathema. The gulf between the values for which the world-wide community stood and the values expressed in apartheid grew wide. It was not a gulf that could be ignored: crucial segments of the English could not escape, even had they wished to, membership of the international community. . . . All of these factors profoundly affect the English view of the racial problem: they exacerbate the schizophrenia and further divide the community, for not all are confronted so starkly with the dilemma.

That their country has been so out of step with the international community, has been the source of the English-speakers' anguish. Those believing that the rest of the world, not South Africa, has got it wrong have generally thrown in their lot with the National Party. The liberal English, though seeing some international hostility as petty and misguided, have resolved that the blame for South Africa's troubles can be placed at one door and one door only – that of apartheid and the Afrikaner government that enforced it.

The English are unlikely to play a principal role in the resolution of South Africa's problems. The political dynamics of South Africa suggest instead a meeting of Afrikaner and African nationalism in which the interests of the English will not be near the top of the negotiating agenda.

But can the liberal values so steadfastly defended for almost two centuries be preserved amid the bruising clash of two strong, unbending nationalisms? Will either side take cognisance of the democratic standards which liberals have sought to uphold? Peter Brown, once leader of the Liberal Party, will only go so far as to say 'I don't despair.' Liberals look for signs of encouragement that their views can be reflected.

On one side, there is some evidence that liberal values have influenced black politics. English is the *lingua franca* of most black nationalist organisations and their policies are often couched in radical liberal terminology. The 1955 Freedom Charter which remains the credo of the ANC is unclear about how a post-apartheid society would be organised. Would it be heavily centralised with state control of political and economic life? Or would the model be more social democratic? The ANC has repeatedly been challenged to clarify its position. During 1988 the organisation drew up a new set of constitutional guidelines, described in one report as 'astonishingly liberal'. Its provisions included: a multi-party democracy in a unitary state; a bill of rights enforced by an independent judiciary; protection of cultural and linguistic rights, freedom of association, the press and religion; independent trade unions; land redistribution coupled with recognition of private property rights; a ban on all forms of racism and tribalism; and a mixed economy. It was pointed out that the guidelines could simply have been window-dressing to appease western audiences. Hermann Giliomee, who has helped elevate the debate about the ANC above the level of the 'total onslaught', concluded that the ANC's commitment to a pluralist system had certain limits. Moreover, its plans would be unlikely to appeal to more than a small minority of whites. So, in that direction, liberals' hopes remained cautious.

They are encouraged by the fraying of the Afrikaner monolith. The defections at Stellenbosch, the ANC initiative of Slabbert, and the resignation of Wynand Malan continued the liberal Afrikaner tradition of among others Jan Hofmeyer, the United Party's deputy prime minister under Smuts, who had fought the removal of black voting rights in 1936 and subsequent segregationist moves, incurring the anger of his own people in the process.

The ruling National Party now embraces policies once the preserve of the PFP. Some Nationalist policies may be dressed up in different clothes, but they owe a lot to those expounded by the liberal opposition over many years. The fact that Nationalists are now flirting with federal options (albeit still within the confines of 'group rights') is evidence of how the PFP has prepared the debate in advance.

All these various signposts give cause for hope that liberalism will not be overwhelmed amid the scramble for power by rival nationalisms. As Professor David Welsh put it:

> There is some truth in the common stereotype of the English genius for compromise and for hard-headed common sense. These are qualities which will be needed as South Africa moves into new and demanding times. Let them be imbued with that tolerance and respect for the rights of people that have always been a part of the English tradition, however much circumstances may have dimmed its light.

CHAPTER SIXTEEN

Race – The Final Frontier

'The Grammar of Racism' was the title of an article by South African journalist Max du Preez which appeared on 11 November 1988 in a liberal Afrikaans-language newspaper *Vrye Weekblad* (Free Weekly) which tries to encourage Afrikaners towards an apartheid-free society.

The article began:

For many decades, the Afrikaner has been telling himself and everybody else who wanted to hear it, that his policy of apartheid is just, and not based on racism. Everybody knows the 'separate but equal' argument: 'We are not better, merely different'. Today, even extremists like the Afrikaner Weerstandsbeweging and the Conservative Party still claim regularly that they are not racists and that their policy of partition is merely aimed at preventing racial friction. Black South Africans have never believed these arguments. It is generally accepted that a language reflects the soul of its people. Judged by the official 'Dictionary of the Afrikaans Language', which is printed by the government printer, Afrikaans has a heavily racist substructure. In Part Five of the dictionary, which covers J to K, there are *twelve pages* about the word 'kaffir'. No less than *three hundred and three* words starting with 'kaffir' are dealt with. And the golden thread running through all these words is that 'kaffir' is equal to inferior, useless and lazy.

The official dictionary defines the word broadly as 'the general denomination for a member of the Bantu race in South Africa' but because of 'the negative value that if often has' it is replaced nowadays by 'native or preferably Bantu'.

The dictionary goes on to define different usages; they indicate that there are different sorts of 'kaffir'. For example, a 'white kaffir' or a 'Boerkaffir' is defined as a 'kaffir of good character'. But that is about the only favourable reference. The other meanings have strong racial and political innuendoes. One definition of a 'kaffir' is: an 'uncivilised, uneducated, ill-mannered, rough person'. It can also be a 'fictional person used to frighten children' or a 'subservient person – one of low standing'.

Several variations of the word were cited by the newspaper, including the following gems:

Kaffirlike – like an uncivilised, ill-bred kaffir.

Kaffirbrother – an abusive nickname given to a white who demonstrates a preference for kaffirs or particularly favours them; a negrophile.

Kaffirgoat – a goat of inferior quality, as those often found in the possession of kaffirs.

Kaffirdog – inferior, impurely bred dog, as found with kaffirs.

Kaffirmanners – bad, uncivilised manners.

Kaffirplace – bad, miserable, unpleasant place.

Kaffircourtship/lovemaking – lovemaking in the kaffir way, in which the lover hurts/bullies the girlfriend in a playful manner, for example by pinching her or beating her with a light cane, etc.

Kaffirwork – work regarded as beneath the dignity of whites.

Kaffirbad/useless – intensification of bad/useless, very bad/useless, as bad/ useless as one can find.

Kaffirslow – particularly, irritatingly slow.

To illustrate 'kaffirslow' the dictionary cites an article in the Afrikaans newspaper *Die Burger* which states: 'One finds many types among students – the good, the bad and the kaffirbad.'

A *kaffircaboodle* is a 'caboodle consisting of kaffirs' or a 'lot of useless, unemployable workpeople'.

Kaffirdom has two meanings: either 'all the kaffirs together, the whole Bantu race' or 'very stupid or dumb', the Afrikaans word *dom* meaning 'dumb'.

As *Vrye Weekblad* noted: 'The dictionary was published in 1968 but it is still the valid, official Dictionary of the Afrikaans Language.'

In 1962 Nico Smith, then a stalwart of the Dutch Reformed Church, attended a youth congress in the Kenyan capital Nairobi. Some 500 young people from all over Africa came together, only forty of whom, from South Africa and Rhodesia, were white. Confronting black counterparts was something of a culture shock for Nico Smith. Constricted by the ideology of apartheid, he had had no idea that beyond South Africa's borders was a vibrant continent filled with young people who were his equals and shared his feelings.

Such was his lack of exposure to black Africa that when meeting the Sierra Leone foreign minister in his hotel room he was shocked when the black man answered the door wearing a dressing gown and slippers. Smith said to himself: 'Why is he trying to be like a white?'

The two men discussed the position of whites in South Africa. The foreign minister thought the future was bleak, telling Smith: 'You are a young man, you can make your choice: either become a white African or remain a European. If you choose to be a white African, stay in Africa because we need you. If you want to remain a European, get out of Africa as quickly as possible.'

Nico Smith made his choice. Most Afrikaners have yet to do so; they have yet to allow Africa to embrace them. They will remain in Africa – it is their home. To 'get out as quickly as possible', as some English-speakers have done, is not an option for the Afrikaners. Yet until they cross the racial frontier – until they begin to lose their obsession with ethnicity – their future in South Africa will continue to be a troubled one.

The Afrikaner has always seen life at the southern tip of the dark continent as one of challenge, survival and hardship. He has never adjusted to the easy rhythms of Africa. He has never learned humility. He can rarely contemplate conceding ground. In the same way that the Dutch Reformed Church, in its crucial document 'Church and Society', could not repent its support for apartheid, so the Afrikaner nation cannot bring itself to confess openly in a spirit of making amends that decades of racial discrimination were a tragic error. The changes now being made are seen by blacks as too little, too late and grudging. Whether others in similar circumstances would have done things differently than the Afrikaners is hard to judge. Maybe the time for judging the Afrikaners' past is over; perhaps, instead, they should be judged by how they face the future.

How can the Afrikaner begin to make the journey into the soul of the country that is his home? The Afrikaners have always quarrelled among themselves, but once they have resolved their differences they follow their leaders obediently. Afrikaner leadership is therefore bestowed with an extraordinary degree of responsibility and authority. Towering figures have helped direct Afrikaners' fortunes at crucial times: the *voortrekker* leaders led their people to a new life; the Boer generals took on the British Empire and then made peace with the enemy to help forge a new South Africa; General Smuts gave his country a respected place in the world. But Afrikaner leaders since 1948 have generally lacked a world view. They were the products of a resourceful yet isolated community; through the narrow self-interest of apartheid they eventually corrupted and impoverished their own people.

Even when they realised their mistake and started rolling back some aspects of apartheid, most Afrikaners remained fixed by the notion of race. The exclusion of blacks from the 1983 power-sharing constitution would have been understandable if the government had subsequently moved to accommodate them at a significant level, after whites had got used to having coloureds and Indians in parliament. That did not happen. The blacks were to be allocated alternative governmental structures at a lower level. When the government insisted it genuinely wanted to negotiate power-sharing with blacks there was little disguising the poverty of thinking on how this might be achieved. The government remained firmly locked into the concept of 'group rights', the fundamental concept underpinning the new constitution which set the parameters for all subsequent political debate. The ensuing stalemate was a reflection of the intellectual limits of those deciding constitutional policy.

If South Africa is to explore an accommodation for the majority black population a new debate must begin soon. It will happen when the country's political leadership resigns itself to the limited scope of constitutional models which rest on 'group rights'. Thus, barring a right-wing surge, a new concept is likely to edge closer to the centre stage of the debate; that of 'voluntary association'. It will be an important sea-change for South Africa. The notion of separate groups would remain but their distinctions would fade. A coloured person, for example, could associate politically and socially with Afrikaners, if he so wished. On the other hand an Afrikaner, say, wishing to remain within his own

273

group would enjoy the right to do so. 'Voluntary association' would be an important first step towards blurring some of South Africa's racial borderlines and towards the creation of a common society.

In other words the obsession – often an absurd obsession – with race has to be massaged out of the South African political system before any kind of significant agreement can be negotiated. But the Afrikaner mentality still focuses on the compartmentalising of people. When the Orange Free State decided in 1985 to lift its decades-long ban on Indians living and working within its borders, a handful of Indian people moved into the provincial capital Bloemfontein but there was no 'group area' for them. Such an infringement of the strict racial order of things could not be encompassed by the Afrikaner mind. So what was the authorities' reaction? The Indians – no more than twenty of them – were put up in a hotel. They were not allowed to find housing in a group area which was not their own.

Botha and his generation of leaders had little interest in moving beyond undiluted group identification: hence their policies ran into a cul-de-sac. They knew that more fundamental change was required but lacked the vision to pursue it. By contrast, Mikhail Gorbachev in the Soviet Union, facing equally demanding challenges, did have the vision to act despite opposition. But then the Soviet leader was a younger man than Botha, with no emotional tie to the events which had formed his nation. Botha was a child of the Boer War and a disciple of Malan and Verwoerd in the same way that Yuri Andropov, the Soviet leader after Leonid Brezhnev, was shaped by the Russian Revolution and the rule of Stalin. Botha was the party bouncer who made it to state president, as Andropov was the KGB chief who reached the top of the Soviet Communist Party.

The next leaders of South Africa will have to address more imaginative reform, because a solution acceptable to the majority of the country's people is unlikely to emerge while their political, economic and social aspirations are funnelled according to the racial tag they carry. A negotiating forum attended by South Africans as South Africans – not as white, black or brown South Africans – is a concept still foreign to the government. Their opponents believe that once people have shed their apartheid labels, once they can consider themselves as equals, then meaningful negotiation is possible about various political systems.

The Afrikaners' position is a good deal more fluid than at any time since 1948. After the 1976 Soweto riots, whites told themselves they had five to ten years before black majority rule would overtake them. In the wake of events since then, no one is even guessing now how long exclusive white rule can last.

Afrikanerdom, indeed the white population as a whole, is in a process of redefining its divisions. Afrikaner/English schisms are now less important. Increasingly the debate will focus on an argument, cutting across language groups, over whether South Africa is to be an integrated or a non-integrated society. At one end of the spectrum are those determined to hold out for old-style apartheid, possibly by retreating into some kind of white homeland and defying economic realities. At the other extreme, some are so uncertain about the future that they say: 'Whatever happens, there's going to be a degree of chaos. Let's get it over and done with quickly.' In between, the majority are prepared to trust their future to the government's cautious and seemingly prolonged reform programme.

It seems unlikely at present that the country's black nationalist organisations could mount a realistic challenge to Pretoria's military might. For their part, the whites are not about to surrender their survival to promises from black organisations. The reforms introduced by the government do not suggest that the ruling National Party will shed 'non-negotiables' like separate housing, schooling and political representation. The reforms so far could not have been envisaged when Botha succeeded Vorster, but they have barely touched the pillars of racial segregation. Race laws already being defied were abolished as well as those threatening stability and economic incentive. There was no moral crusade against apartheid. In general, the National Party has overturned apartheid laws not because they are unjust but because they don't work. There were no measures, for example, to halt the vilification of couples of different races, married or living together legally, since the 'sex across the colour line' laws were repealed. In some cases such couples became political footballs between the parties in election campaigns. The government's approach seemed to be: 'We can allow you to marry but we cannot protect you from the consequences.' No thought has been given to a body like Britain's Race Relations Board through which racial abuse can be checked – this in the country where, according to government ministers, 'apartheid is dead'.

When the Conservative Party seized town councils in the Transvaal and resegregated facilities in Boksburg, the government's reaction was equivocal. The CP action provided a glimpse of a future South Africa still dominated by undiluted racial discrimination. The black consumer boycott which followed pointed to stepped-up black protests over race laws. But it was by no means certain whether the 'reforming' National Party would simply ignore the racist measures or choose to exploit Boksburg in order to accelerate change. For political expediency it seemed content to leave the Conservative Party stewing in its own juice. There was little sign of the government immediately seizing the moral initiative to harness support for more fundamental reform.

But the very fact that reforms have taken place means the dam wall has been broken and other changes must inevitably follow. With each reform the debating forum shifts on to what comes next. But how far can the debate progress when its confines are still ordained by principles of racial separateness? Writing in the journal *South Africa International* in January 1988, Steve Friedman, policy research manager of the independent South African Institute of Race Relations, identified certain non-negotiable 'core issues' and 'marginal issues' where changes were possible:

. . . in the Verwoerdian era, rigid social segregation was a core government goal, but by the mid-1970s pressures such as the international sports boycott had turned it into a marginal one which the government was willing to concede because doing so would not force it to concede over more fundamental core issues.

275

Friedman argued that as marginal issues were conceded, so 'core issues' would come up for a rethink or would themselves become 'marginal'.

The National Party sees itself as a modernising force – the only party that can be entrusted to promote reform while maintaining stability. But in which direction is the party modernising the country?

Under the National Party, an attempt is under way to disguise or redefine the fundamental conflict in South Africa. Its object is to turn the focus of attention away from the question of 'race' to that of 'class'. The aim is to create a constitutional panoply allowing blacks an entrée to political and economic privilege in limited power-sharing with whites. They will be carefully selected blacks – those who will accept the whites' retention of control over many areas of their own affairs. Under such reforms blacks will find more and more doors open to them, but only on certain corridors.

There are two ways of regarding such changes. Are the reforms simply aimed at co-opting 'tame' black representatives to lend credibility to an essentially white-dominated system? Or are they of deeper significance, a learning curve for whites and blacks to get used to exercising power together, in preparation for the day when, as Foreign Minister Pik Botha has acknowledged, there could be a black person leading the government? If the latter were the government's object, current reforms would be a precursor to a future negotiating process in which more representative black leaders would be involved. But there is little sign of the political socialisation getting under way to prepare whites, or indeed blacks, for such a process. Legalised apartheid may slowly wither. But the problem of who has power will remain. In this regard, what is emerging is a government attempt to modernise the status quo. An extraordinarily complex system of devolved administration is taking shape, granting blacks increased representation at township, regional and homeland level. Increasingly, blacks will become more and more responsible for running their own affairs.

Pretoria appears to think that once blacks have been accommodated at local and regional level, consideration of their place in national government will be academic. By that time, goes the theory, power will have become so fragmented that the crucial question of who retains central control will be of less importance; almost by default, therefore, it might remain in white hands. This fallacy simply puts off the day when the essentials will have to be tackled. To believe that a measure of devolved power will deter blacks from claiming their fair share at the centre is rather like saying that bank clerks can never aspire to be bank managers. Such a model, not based on free and competitive elections, is unlikely to satisfy blacks or to gain the recognition of the international community.

Pretoria's plans for the black population rest on a breakdown of the black community under which, according to government-commissioned polls, it is believed, that 30 per cent of blacks are middle-class and want law and order; 20 per cent are radicalised, demanding black majority rule; and the remaining 50 per cent are 'don't knows'. Pretoria's policy therefore is to convince the undecided 50 per cent that they should support government power-sharing proposals. Government planners have concluded that one way of winning over the black majority and isolating 'radicals' is to improve the standard of living of blacks in the townships. Following the imposition of the second state of emergency in June 1986, considerable efforts went into 'upgrading' black areas by vast injections of capital. There was nothing particularly new in this policy; Vorster's government did the same thing in Soweto after the 1976 riots. But although the upgrading work of the late 1980s was far more extensive, again there was a serious flaw in thinking. Government supporters argued that improvements in black living conditions, and the gradual creation of a black middle class, would assuage blacks' political demands – they would be less likely to press for far-reaching political reforms if they felt contented economically and socially. It was an extraordinary expectation. Among the intelligentsia of the black community – the opinion-formers – the acquisition of life's 'goodies', far from blunting their political aspirations, is likely to sharpen them. After all, if a black man graduates to work alongside a white as, say, a senior manager, the black man is unlikely to decide that his improved economic status should preclude him from living in the same area as his white colleague, from sending his children to the same school or from voting for the same parliament.

Experiences in other parts of the world show that socio-economic privilege which is not matched by political power seriously unbalances the political system and can generate conflict. It is an illusion that the middle classes do not make revolutions. The leaders of the African National Congress do not come from the unemployed masses on the streets, but from the ranks of lawyers, doctors and academics who see no reason why they should not be equal to a white person with similar or even fewer qualifications. To them it is unthinkable for political and economic realities to be separated.

In South Korea and Taiwan the extension of economic power was an important precondition for the furthering of political democracy, although this was not achieved without conflict. The lesson of other countries is that if an authoritarian government meets only the socio-economic needs of the people while dispensing political power at its own pace, the seeds of further conflict are sown. The government cannot earn legitimacy from the majority by buying off blacks or by uncompetitive elections in which accommodating black spokesmen are co-opted at the expense of more representative leaders, who are either imprisoned or silenced. The government may find some tame blacks willing to serve on political bodies, but they will be unacceptable to the majority of black people and the stalemate will continue.

The process of change will continue to be defined by the interests of the ruling party. But these too are in a process of redefinition. Previously the thrust of National Party policy was the pursuit of Afrikaner nationalism and the ideological imperatives of apartheid. As part of its attempt to regenerate itself, the National Party is now preoccupied with less grand concerns – matters less to do with ideology and more with preserving stability; they include the economy, labour relations, international trade links and political reform. But the government's traditional power base has shrunk so dramatically that it cannot achieve its aims on its own.

The government under P. W. Botha split Afrikanerdom and fell back on the support of English-speakers to fill the gap. But that may not be sufficient to sustain the National Party, if only because the English vote is so ephemeral and because the Conservative Party is itself reaching out to the English electorate. White politics is fraying and the National Party, in order to hold on to power, may have to look seriously at forging alliances beyond white politics – among the coloureds and the blacks. The government will therefore seek to enhance the status of its black recruits on the various devolved bodies, to be its allies in the struggle against black 'radicals'. Blacks will be appointed junior ministers in the cabinet. It is not inconceivable that there could be black members of the National Party, albeit as part of a segregated black wing and still remote from the bastions of white power. In the search for allies, the National Party might bring the coloureds and the Indians back on to the common voters' roll where they would still be a minority compared to whites.

To oversee this process of widening representation within racial boundaries, the Afrikaners have slowly begun to inveigle their own version of 'democracy' into the South African body politic. The Afrikaner technocrats who surrounded the Botha government concluded that the Westminster style of democracy in which individual rights supersede those of the state was not suited to South Africa. Anglo-Saxon notions of rights and accountability could not guarantee the survival of the Afrikaner. Amid the turbulent events in South Africa, went the theory, the state could not afford to take a back seat but had to be heavily involved in day-to-day control. This amounted to a form of 'state democracy' based on the premise that the majority of the people, though entitled to exercise political power, could not be trusted with it. The fear was that if the democratic process continued unbridled the majority would take all, and the temptation would be great for it to abuse the minority.

Is this acquisition of state power any different to the one-party states elsewhere in Africa? Barring an extreme right or left wing régime, black or white, South Africa's multiplicity of interest groups, competing political forces and economic diversity may ensure that the country does not descend to the restrictive, crippling societies of black Africa. But in terms of how the political process is being controlled, the comparisons are coming closer.

Whether they have decided to fight it out to the finish, or have accepted that they are now in the pre-negotiation stage with their black opponents, the Afrikaner 'securocrats' appear to feel hampered by the trappings of western democracy and are increasingly prepared to jettison them. The departure from the old constitution in 1983 in favour of the tricameral system was the first substantial sign of this. The massive accumulation of power around the office of the state president was a further indication, as was the demise of the National Party caucus as an engine-room of policy-making. The powerful state security management system, embodying the State Security Council and the president's office, emerged as the forum for defining the political and strategic aims of the country. The introduction of the state of emergency and the steady suspension of civil liberties, press freedom and freedom of speech all combined to enhance the power of the state. Nationalist leaders have resolved that if their final confrontation is to be with black nationalists backed by strong black tribes, they had better become strongly centrist, authoritarian and less democratic themselves.

Many Afrikaners are not comfortable with this departure from the style of politics they have known until now. The increasingly coercive powers would be more acceptable if the government had something to show by way of significant progress towards a political solution. But the government has failed to convince black leaders that their participation in the negotiations could lead to real change. The country's leaders had to tell the Afrikaners that slowly they would have to accept more blacks in government; instead hints of such a development were obfuscated so as not to upset the right wing. When Botha told whites that change was necessary, they inferred that this was because they had to bow to black pressure and international hostility. The government failed to inspire Afrikaners with a vision of how a society freed from apartheid could open up new horizons and opportunities. It fed their fears not their hopes. Instead Botha harped on about there never being black majority rule. What did it all mean? Instead of easing white fears, the government seemed intent on fuelling them. P. W. Botha had the opportunity to prepare the country for imaginative change. The state of emergency gave him sweeping powers to clamp down on the townships revolt; his security forces gave him a breathing space. But instead of exploiting the calm to force through more far-reaching reforms, he squandered the opportunity by striking out at black and liberal white opponents in a fruitless exercise in pandering to the right wing. A golden opportunity was tragically missed.

As the government's legitimacy was challenged, it resorted to increased coercion. The suppression of anti-apartheid groups alleged to be part of the 'total onslaught', the banning of opposition newspapers, the fiasco when the government overruled the official censor in banning the anti-apartheid film *Cry Freedom* were the actions of a government which knows its policies cannot be implemented without confining public debate.

If the restrictions on information were to prevent a communist-inspired revolution, then heads would have rolled for allowing the security situation to deteriorate so far. Of course the restrictions had little to do with security. Instead they were aimed at preventing the 'wrong ideas' being planted in the heads of blacks while at the same time shielding the whites from political realities. The whites were told that the unrest was instigated by radical blacks assisted by international trouble-makers. Through its powerful instruments of propaganda, like the SABC, the National Party convinced most white South Africans it was the only bulwark against such forces.

It is probably misguided to think in terms of 'a solution' to South Africa's problems, an all-embracing settlement which will suddenly transform 'apartheid South Africa' into 'non-racial South Africa'. It is very doubtful that this is going to happen. P. W. Botha once referred to South Africa 'governing [itself] into a new constitution', the suggestion being that the country would gradually edge forward, two steps forward and one step back, always exploring new avenues. Unquestionably, the passage to a more egalitarian society is going to be a messy business. It will not satisfy the radicals at either end of the political spectrum. The current model for power-sharing will eventually be ditched in favour of less exclusive proposals. They in turn will be overtaken by other initiatives. International pressure and the sheer cost of holding on to power will force further change from the government. Black economic advancement will release forces which no government can control.

There is a substantial middle ground of blacks and whites who do not want to see their country go up in smoke if it can be avoided. There are leaders within Afrikanerdom who have the talent to capitalise on this. Equally there are hundreds of thousands of blacks – a patient and caring people – willing to respond to the Afrikaner if only he would come a little way towards them.

Can the Afrikaner compromise? The Afrikaners and the African National Congress have been compared to two drunks holding each other up. The former wants continued racially defined politics; the latter is demanding unadulterated universal franchise. The two are likely to flounder around for some time before they sober up. In the medium-term, common ground might be found in a political process similar to the kwaNatal Indaba which, in marked contrast to Pretoria's constitutional plans, won some support among people of all races.

The Indaba proposed a two-house legislature: a non-racial upper house of 100 seats to which members would be elected by proportional representation; and a lower house comprising fifty seats made up of five ten-member groups – African, Afrikaners, English-speaking, Asian and 'South African', the latter for those who did not wish to vote according to their race classification. The plan incorporated a bill of rights to guarantee individual freedom. The linguistic, cultural and religious rights of individual groups would be protected, but not their political interests. It was on the latter score that the government objected. The Indaba did not enshrine sufficient 'group protection' so it was not acceptable. The National Party's leader in Natal, Stoffel Botha – in a grave political blunder – immediately dismissed what was the only imaginative piece of constitution-making to have emerged. Fortunately wiser heads prevailed to rescue the plan from the dustbin. There was wide feeling that, if not the model itself, then at least the negotiating process involved in the Indaba had been a success worth preserving.

The government's initial opposition to the Indaba was shared by the ANC – for opposite reasons. They refused to support the proposals because the Indaba still enshrined the principle of ethnicity. But is it realistic to expect the Afrikaner to join a power-sharing arrangement without protection? According to at least one source, even the Soviet Union under Gorbachev is beginning to reassess whether undiluted one man, one vote in South Africa is attainable or indeed desirable. Writing in 1988 in the journal *Africa Notes*, published by the Centre for Strategic

Studies in Washington, Winrich Kühne, head of the Africa department at the Research Institute for International Politics and Security of the Stiftung Wissenschaft und Politik near Munich, quoted Soviet officials as speaking of:

> . . . the need to solve ethnic problems not through isolation and one-sided domination but by getting all groups involved. The participation of Inkatha, AZAPO and possibly even one or other homeland leader [besides Inkatha's Chief Buthelezi] at the negotiating table is advocated more or less openly. Starushenko's [an Africa specialist's] statement on white minority rights contains an implication concerning the nature of the political system in post-apartheid South Africa warranting closer examination than it has been accorded. He advocates a parliamentary system with two chambers, one formed on the basis of proportional representation and the other possessing the right of veto on the basis of equal representation of 'the four communities'.

Hermann Giliomee, who subsequently met Soviet officials himself, urged caution over such statements, noting that another prominent official had distanced himself from them.

The Indaba pointed towards what will almost certainly be the focus of government policy in the immediate future – the search for a federal solution. It is a search which offers possibilities of compromise between blacks and whites – providing federalism is not so weighted as to leave exclusive power in the hands of whites. A majority of blacks in government is inevitable; any jerrymandering of the federal option to obscure this eventuality will be dismissed by blacks. A federal solution appears to be the most attractive vehicle – at least in the medium term – for all races to learn to govern together. For forty years the Afrikaners were told they would rule exclusively. They are not suddenly going to switch to the opposite extreme.

The moves will be slow in coming. Progress towards more majoritarian government will be punctuated by frequent bursts of violence and will be determined to some extent by the quality of black and white leadership. The political forces will be overwhelming. But even they may be eclipsed by the economic pressures building up against the apartheid wall. The South African economy cannot meet the demands of the rising black population. All the might of the country's armed forces cannot feed hungry mouths or give employment to the millions of blacks flooding the jobs market. These are the pressures forcing real change in South Africa. In many ways the government is a bystander as these forces unleash themselves. Faced with such daunting demands, the government has two choices. It can either lead white South Africa into a siege society; or conclude that the country cannot survive without international capital and investment and therefore bow to calls for faster change.

Can the Afrikaners survive the traumatic adjustments which undoubtedly lie ahead?

The Afrikaners may easily fail to respond to the challenge, sliding instead into self-pity and self-destruction, egged on by leaders of diminishing stature, to become an irrelevant minority – a kind of ethnic black hole collapsing in on itself.

There is another possibility. At the end of the Boer War, when the Boer generals surrendered to the British at the Peace of Vereeniging, few would have placed bets on the Afrikaners emerging from the conflict as anything other than an estranged minority. But they pulled themselves up by their own bootstraps and made themselves indispensable to the new South African state. They might easily do the same again if and when apartheid is abandoned and a new order emerges. The Afrikaner would no longer enjoy exclusive political power but his talents might ensure him a place in the future of the country. An Afrikaans expression says *Die Boere is soos 'n kakiebos* (The Boers are like a kakie bush) – a reference to a South African weed which is impossible to kill off.

The Afrikaner will no longer belong to a *volk* in the sense of a select, chosen race. Afrikaner nationalism – old-style – is on its way out. The institutions of Afrikanerdom have been shaken too profoundly for unquestioning tribal loyalty to survive. But a strong ethnic consciousness may remain. The Afrikaner will continue to be aware of what it means to be an Afrikaner; but he will give expression to his Afrikaner-ness in ways other than aggressive nationalism or Afrikaner supremacy. Perhaps the Afrikaners will become like the Zulu tribe whose members have allegiances right across the political spectrum but who never forget they are Zulus. Within such a framework there is vast scope for variety and argument, which can only enrich the Afrikaner people.

At a meeting at the University of Pretoria, student leaders brought together on a platform the AWB leader Eugene Terre Blanche and Frederik Van Zyl Slabbert, the liberal Afrikaner who has held several discussions with the African National Congress. The two debated the future of their country from two totally opposing viewpoints. At the end of it Terre Blanche turned to Slabbert and declared: 'Although I think you are naïve, I accept you as an Afrikaner. I accept you want the best for your country.'

For Afrikaners, that was a very special moment, a sign that they can retain ethnic cohesion yet also diversity, as they embark on their final, uncertain journey.

When the creaking ox-wagons were hauled up the Drakensberg mountains on the Great Trek – sheer exhaustion, every yard, for the Boer families – the Afrikaners' spirits must have been at their lowest ebb. There was the ever-present danger of the wagons running out of control and tumbling into one of the many ravines, taking the Boers' possessions with them. One of the *trekkers* later recounted those deeds to his children:

The hardest part may well have been the trek across the Drakensberg. . . . Many took off the rear wheels of their wagons. We, children, fetched branches of shrubs to place in front of the wheels to keep the wagon back for a time.

When everything was in order, down they went with the hind part of the wagon dragging along. Some also used wheel-drags to keep the wheels from turning and some took the whole wagon apart. Some emptied their wagons and then all the possessions had to be hauled over the Drakensberg by our own efforts. No, my child, it was by no means a simple business, it was a big affair.

The Afrikaners' first Great Trek began a century and a half ago when they fled British rule. The second was in the early twentieth century when poverty on the farms drove the Afrikaners into the towns and cities. Their third and final trek is the search for an accommodation with the blacks. It too will be 'by no means a simple business'.

The Afrikaners' journey to date has been long and arduous and they have taken many false paths. But they have the inventiveness to forge a new future for themselves. Their fate is in their own hands. After more than three centuries at the southern tip of Africa they have yet to find peace and security. Their journey is not yet over.

Their last great trek is now under way.

LIST OF ABBREVIATIONS

ANC	African National Congress
APK	Afrikaans Protestantse Kerk (African Protestant Church)
ARMSCOR	Armaments Development and Production Corporation
AWB	Afrikaner Weerstandsbeweging (Afrikaner Resistance Movement)
AZAPO	Azanian People's Organisation
BC	Black Consciousness
COSATU	Congress of South African Trade Unions
CP	Conservative Party
CRC	Coloured Representative Council
DPSC	Detainees' Parents Support Committee
EPG	(Commonwealth) Eminent Persons' Group
FAK	Federasie van Afrikaanse Kultuurvereniginge (Federation of Afrikaans Cultural Associations)
HNP	Herstigte Nasionale Party (Reconstructed National Party)
IDASA	Institute for a Democratic Alternative for South Africa
MWU	Mineworkers' Union
NGK	Nederduitse Gereformeerde Kerk: Dutch Reformed Church
NUSAS	National Union of South African Students
OB	Ossewabrandwag (Ox-Wagon Fire Guard)
PAC	Pan-Africanist Congress
PFP	Progressive Federal Party
RAU	Randse Afrikaanse Universiteit (Rand Afrikaans University)
SABC	South African Broadcasting Corporation
SABRA	South African Bureau for Racial Affairs
SADF	South African Defence Force

List of Abbreviations

SWAPO	South West Africa People's Organisation
UDF	United Democratic Front
UP	United Party
UWC	University of the Western Cape
VOC	Generale Vereenigde Nederlantsche Geoctroyeerde Oostindische Compagnie (United Netherlands Chartered East Indian Company: Dutch East India Company)

SELECT BIBLIOGRAPHY

Adam, H. and Giliomee, H., *The Rise and Crisis of Afrikaner Power*, Cape Town, David Philip, 1979

Berger, P. L. and Godsell, B., *A Future South Africa*, Tafelberg, Human and Rousseau, 1988

Breytenbach, B., *The True Confessions of an Albino Terrorist*, Taurus, South Africa, 1984

De Klerk, W. A., *The Puritans in Africa – A Story of Afrikanerdom*, London, Penguin Books, 1975

Dunbar Moodie, T., *The Rise of Afrikanerdom*, Berkeley and Los Angeles, University of California Press, 1975

Du Toit, A. and Giliomee, H., *Afrikaner Political Thought*, Cape Town and Johannesburg, David Philip, 1983

Gastrow, S., *Who's Who in South African Politics*, Johannesburg, Ravan Press, 1987

Harrison, D., *The White Tribe of Africa*, London, British Broadcasting Corporation, 1981

Leach, G., *South Africa – No Easy Path to Peace*, London, Methuen, 1987

Leatt, J., Kneifel, T. and Nürnberger, K., *Contending Ideologies in South Africa*, Cape Town and Johannesburg, David Philip, 1986

Liebenberg, B. J., 'Myths surrounding Blood River and the Vow', paper to the South African Historical Association, 1988

Lipton, M., *Capitalism and Apartheid*, London, Wildwood House, 1986

Lodge, T., *Black Politics in South Africa since 1945*, Johannesburg, Ravan Press, 1983

Muller, C. F. J., *500 Years – A History of South Africa*, H. and R. Academica, Pretoria, 1986

O'Meara, D., *Volkskapitalisme*, Johannesburg, Ravan Press, 1983

Pakenham, T., *The Boer War*, London, Weidenfeld & Nicolson, 1982

South African Institute of Race Relations, *Race Relations Survey 1987*, Johannesburg, 1988

Turnley, D. and Cowell, A., *Why Are They Weeping?* New York, Stewart, Tabori & Chang, 1988

Van Jaarsveld, F. A., *Honderd basiese dokument by die studie van die Suid-Afrikaanse geskiedenis 1648–1961*, Cape Town, 1971

Select Bibliography

Van Zyl Slabbert, F., *The Last White Parliament*, Johannesburg, Jonathan Ball and Hans Strydom, 1985

Villa-Vicencio, C. and De Gruchy, J. W., *Resistance and Hope*, Cape Town and Johannesburg, David Philip, 1985

Welsh, D., 'English-speaking Whites and the Racial Problem', in *English-Speaking South Africa Today*, ed. André de Villiers, Cape Town, Oxford University Press, 1976

Wilkins I. and Strydom, H., *The Super Afrikaners*, Johannesburg, Jonathan Ball, 1978

Wilson, M. and Thompson, L., *The Oxford History of South Africa*, Oxford, Oxford University Press, 1975

Index

apartheid – *cont*.
  laws, 79, 172, 227; and fascism,
  105–6; Dutch Reformed Church
  attitudes to 113–32; Stellenbosch
  revolt, 169, 172–6, 180–6; Theron
  Commission, 170–1; Tomlinson
  Commission, 169–70; and racism,
  271–6
Appeal Court, 219
Argentina, 102
Argus, 18–19
ARMSCOR (Armaments
  Development and Production
  Corporation), 71, 187
army *see* South African Defence
  Force
Australia, 145
authors, English-speakers, 267–8
AZAPO (Azanian People's
  Organisation), 238, 281

Baden-Powell, Robert, 27, 103
Banda, Hastings, 151
Bantjes, Jan, 12
Bantu, 169–70, 271–2
Bantu Education Act (1953), 44
bantustans *see* homelands
Barnard, Rudi, 217
Barth, Karl, 111, 117
Batavian republic, 17, 221
BBC, 63, 81–2, 102, 174
Bechuanaland, 26
Beeld, 81–2, 187, 230
Belgium, 159
Belhar Confession (1982), 118, 119,
  127
Benoni, 106
Bezuidenhoud, Timo, 193–7
Bezuidenhout, Frederik, 22
Bible, 31, 113, 114, 115, 117, 120,
  121, 130, 261, 264
Biebault, Hendrik, 19
Biko, Steve, 152, 223, 229, 238, 267
Bill of Rights (1923), 235

Bizos, George, 267
Black Alliance, 221
Black Consciousness movement, 152,
  229, 238, 242, 248
Black Power movement, 237, 238
Black Sash women's movement, 64,
  267
Blackburn, Molly, 267
blacks: introduction and
  consolidation of apartheid, 32–40,
  168–9; education, 44; Cape Town
  squatters, 46; Afrikaner isolation
  from, 49; and the Afrikaans
  language, 51; and reform of
  apartheid, 54–7, 63; township
  revolts, 239, 242, 243, 258;
  attitude to Conservative Party, 90;
  Terre Blanche's aims and, 104;
  apprentices, 108; social mobility,
  108; vigilantes, 111, 196; pass laws
  scrapped, 148; influx control
  system, 79, 172, 227; squatter
  camps, 193–7; black movements,
  235–40; Defiance Campaign, 236;
  'Nation Building', 243–5;
  disenfranchised, 255–6; National
  Party changes attitudes towards
  275–8; *see also* African National
  Congress
Bloemfontein, 27, 115, 274
Bloemfontein Convention (1854), 25,
  103
Blood River, Battle of (1838), 1, 2,
  3, 4, 8–16, 29, 249, 261
Boer War, 5, 8, 11, 12, 13, 15, 26–8,
  214, 235, 251–2, 255, 261, 282
Boers: Great Trek, 1–15, 23–5, 28–9,
  103, 207, 210, 214, 240, 282–3;
  struggles against British, 23–8; in
  history teaching, 45–6
Boesak, Dr Allan, 57, 99, 118, 208,
  221
Boksburg, 92, 275
Bophuthatswana, 36, 86
Boraine, Alex, 148

Corbett, Chief Justice Michael, 267
COSATU (Congress of South
    African Trade Unions), 67, 99,
    208
Cottesloe Conference (1960), 115–16,
    199
Council of Seventeen, 17, 19
Craven, Danie, 90
Craven Week, 90
Criminal Law Amendment Act
    (1953), 38
Criminal Procedure Amendment Act
    (1965), 38
Cronje, Piet, 103
Cronkite, Walter, 65
Crossroads, 36, 145, 165, 193–7, 224
Cry Freedom, 279
Cuba, 52

Dakar meeting (1986), 149–64, 185,
    186, 202–3, 246, 248, 249
Dale Street Congregational Church,
    Uitenhage, 221–2
Day of the Vow, 1, 11–15, 205
de Coning, Cedric, 204–6
de Gaulle, General, 69–70
de Klerk, F. W., 60, 71, 82–3, 98,
    179
de Klerk, Professor J. J., 122–3
de Klerk, Theunis Christiaan, 23
de Klerk, W. A., 35
de Klerk, Dr Willem 'Wimpie', 54,
    55, 57, 90–1, 178–9
de Klerk family, 19, 23
de la Rey, Koos, 103
de Lange, Professor J. P., 133, 136,
    137–8, 140–1, 149
de Ville, Rosier, 80–1, 84
de Villiers, Dawid, 179, 181
de Vries, Mike, 207–9
de Wet, Christiaan, 103
de Wet, N. J., 200–1
de Wet Nel, M. C., 169
democracy, 277–8
Democratic Party, 58, 186

Derby-Lewis, Clive, 260–1
Descartes, René, 167
Desmond, Father Cosmas, 264
Detainees' Parents' Support
    Committee (DPSC), 267
diamonds, 26, 254
Dias, Bartholomeu, 17, 215–17
Dictionary of the Afrikaans
    Language, 271–2
Dingane, Chief, 2–3, 10, 25, 101,
    103, 240, 249
'Dingane's Day', *see* Day of the Vow
Diouf, Abdou, 154
'Discussion Group of Eighty Five',
    183
District Six, Cape Town, 227, 231–2
District Six – The Musical, 231–2
Donkerhoek, 3
Doyle, Sir Arthur Conan, 20
Drakensberg Mountains, 2, 25,
    282–3
Drakenstein, 19
Drommedaris, 17
du Pisani, André, 151–2, 154, 159,
    160–1, 162
du Plessis, Barend, 100
du Plessis, Deon, 18–19, 47, 70–1
du Plessis, J. J., 47
du Plessis, Jean Prieur, 19
du Plessis, Pietie, 97
du Plessis, Wennie, 77
du Preez, Professor A. B., 200
du Preez, Max, 271
du Toit, André, 58, 155, 156–7,
    164, 192
du Toit, Professor J. D., 115
du Toit, S. J., 29
du Toit, Wynand, 144
Duncan, Sheena, 64
Durand, Anna, 20
Durand, Marie, 20
Durban, 79
D'Urban, Sir Benjamin, 22
Dutch East India Company, 17–18,
    19, 21, 112, 167, 221, 252

Springs, 171
squatter camps, 46, 116, 145, 165, 193–7, 224
Stalin, Joseph, 105, 274
Stallard Commission, 39
Stander, Adriaan Hendrik, 77
Standerton, 76–83, 98
Star, 65
Starushenko, 281
State Security Council, 68, 148, 279
Stellenbosch, 19, 166–8, 175, 179–80
Stellenbosch Farmers' Winery, 160
Stellenbosch revolt, 167, 169–70, 172–7, 180–6
Stellenbosch University, 46, 112, 132, 143, 150, 151–2, 166, 168, 172, 176, 181–2, 195, 204, 207–10, 230, 270
Steyn, President, 27
Stock Exchange, 47
Stormjaers, 106
Strijdom, J. G., 33, 34
Strydom, Hans, 133
Strydom, Hendrik, 109–10
suicides, 41
Die Suid-Afrikaan, 246–8
Sun City, 107, 165
Sunday Star, 3
Sunday Times of Johannesburg, 65
Sunter, Clem, 266
Suppression of Communism Act (1950), 38, 188
Supreme Court, 106, 187, 219, 266
Suzman, Helen, 65, 254, 262; early years in parliament, 34; on Verwoerd, 36–7; on Vorster, 37, 38; on P. W. Botha, 69; attacks government's double standards, 100–1; and the 'Sharpeville Six', 106; on Slabbert's resignation, 147–8; prevented from speaking at Witwatersrand University, 263
Swaziland, 25
Switzerland, 159

Table Bay, 17
Taiwan, 277
Tambo, Oliver, 142, 153–4, 236
Tanzania, 237
Tas, Adam, 166, 193
television, 257–8
Terre Blanche, Etienne, 104
Terre Blanche, Eugene, 76, 208; attacks Professor van Jaarsveld, 16; image, 96–7, 109; disrupts Pik Botha's meeting, 97; mass rally in Pretoria, 98–102; love-hate relationship with Britain, 102; aims, 103–4, 106; background, 104, 107; forms AWB, 107–8; debate with Slabbert, 282
Terreblanche, Sampie, 35, 37, 67, 170–3, 176, 180–2, 186, 217
Terrorism Act (1967), 38
Thaba Nchu, 24
Thatcher, Margaret, 64, 67, 76, 87, 102, 256
Theron, Erika, 170
Theron Commission, 170–1, 217–18
The Times, 102
Tobias, Professor Phillip, 265
Tomlinson, Professor, F. R., 169
Tomlinson Commission, 35–6, 169–70
Toms, Ivan, 196
townships, 212; revolts, 66, 69, 172–3, 239, 242, 258; black vigilantes, 111; Theron Commission, 171; riots, 196; 'upgrading' of, 276–7
Transkei, 36, 165, 191, 197
Transvaal, 31; Boer trekkers, 25; Britain annexes, 26; Vaal River Treaty, 25; Boer War, 26–7; First World War, 30; education, 43; Conservative Party power base, 92, 94, 275; Terre Blanche's claim to, 103; 1987 election, 180; Liberal Party in, 262
Die Transvaler, 37, 105

302

Treason Trial (1956–61), 188, 237
Treurnicht, Andries, 4, 70, 135, 200; and the Day of the Vow, 7; formation of the Conservative Party, 88; background, 89–90; campaigning, 94; and the 1983 constitution, 136; Standerton by-election, 81, 82–3; Voortrekker Monument meeting, 98; and the split in the Dutch Reformed Church, 129–30
Trichardt, Louis, 8, 23, 205
Triomf, 264
Trotskyism, 229
Tsheledi, Francis, 216
Tshwete, Steve, 155
Tutu, Desmond, Archbishop of Cape Town, 24, 57, 64, 99, 100, 126, 208, 244, 264
Tygerberg medical and dental hospital, 208

Uganda, 64
Uitenhage, 62, 220–2, 225, 228
uitlanders, 26–7, 43, 254
Umhlanga, 79
Umkhonto we Sizwe, 161, 188, 237
unemployment, 108
Union of South Africa, 29, 30, 31
UNITA, 47
United Church of Southern Africa, 222
United Democratic Front, 149, 155, 186, 208, 266; formation of, 118; and the township revolts, 64, 238; banned, 67; AWB attacks, 99; struggle with ANC, 148, 239; Maties' fact-finding tour, 207
United Nations, 103, 151, 211
United Party, 32, 34, 38, 74, 219, 237, 259, 261, 262, 270
United States of America, 148, 199, 203; dedication to causes, 50; broadcasting, 64–5; sanctions against South Africa, 71; Edward

Kennedy visits Crossroads, 196–7; Black Power movement, 237, 238
universities, English, 265–6
University of the Western Cape (UWC), 152, 224
Unlawful Organisations Act (1960), 38
Uys, Dirkie, 4

Vaal River, 25, 26, 27
Vaal River Treaty (1857), 25
Vaalkrans, 27
Vaderland, 178
Van Arkel, Jan, 43
Van Blerk, Hendrik, 106
Van der Lind, Marie and Tol, 79–80
Van der Merwe, Stoffel, 71–2, 73
Van der Merwe family, 260
Van der Post, Laurens, 268
Van der Stel, Simon, 167
Van der Stel, Wilhem Adriaan, 19, 166, 193
Van der Westhuizen, Adriana, 45–8
Van Eck Commission on Industrial and Agricultural Requirements, 39
Van Jaarsveld, F. A., 23
Van Lingen, Rina, 41
Van Rensburg, Manie, 152
Van Riebeeck, Jan Athoniszoon, 17–18, 32, 112, 166, 217, 240
Van Rooy, Professor J. C., 133
Van Rooyen family, 48–9
Van Schalkwyk, Marthinus, 204–6
Van Zyl, Johan, 152–3
'Vaz diaries', 146
Venda, 36, 111
Vereeniging, Peace of (1902), 28, 31, 84, 282
Die Vereniging Bybel en Volk, 128
verkramptes (narrow-minded ones), 53, 54, 55, 107, 135, 136
verligtes (enlightened ones), 53, 54, 55, 58, 107, 123, 135, 136, 137
Verwoerd, Hendrik, 118, 274; 'grand apartheid', 5, 34–7, 63, 91–2, 168;

Picture Acknowledgements

The Argus: pages 1 below right, 2 below, 7 above, 8 below. *Die Burger*: pages 1 top left and top right, 3 above right, 5 top right, 6 above right, 7 below right and 8 above. Herman Potgieter, courtesy of *Leadership*: page 4 above left. *Rapport*: page 4 above right. *The Star*: pages 2 above, 3 above right and below right, 5 below, 6 above left and right, below. Rashid Lombard, courtesy of *Die Suid-Afrikaan*: page 4 below left.